Fishing with Lee Wulff

Fishing with

LEE WULFF

Edited by EDWARD C. JANES

ALFRED A. KNOPF

New York

1972

Library of Congress Cataloging in Publication Data

Wulff, Lee.
Fishing with Lee Wulff.

1. Fishing. I. Janes, Edward C., ed. II. Title.
SH441.W79   799.1'2   78-171117
ISBN 0-394-46920-8

Grateful acknowledgment is made to the following for permission to reprint articles by Lee Wulff:

The Ridge Press, Inc.: "Marlin on a Fly Rod" from Volume 1, Number 2 of *The American Sportsman*, published by The Ridge Press, Inc. Copyright © 1968 The Ridge Press and American Broadcasting Company.

Popular Science Publishing Co., Inc.—*Outdoor Life* Magazine: "Where There's a Will," November 1944. Copyright © 1944 Popular Science Publishing Co., Inc. "The Riffling Hitch," August 1952. Copyright © 1952 Popular Science Publishing Co., Inc. "Why Salmon Strike," March 1955. Copyright © 1955 Popular Science Publishing Co., Inc. "Fly Casting Made Easy," August 1957. Copyright © 1957 Popular Science Publishing Co., Inc.

The Hearst Corporation—*Sports Afield* Magazine: "The Toughest of Them All," June 1944. Copyright © 1944 The Hearst Corporation. "How to Use Dry Flies for Atlantic Salmon," Sports Afield Fishing Annual 1951. Copyright © 1951 The Hearst Corporation. "Where Salmon Lie and Why," Sports Afield Fishing Annual 1954. Copyright © 1954 The Hearst Corporation.

Holt, Rinehart & Winston, Inc.—*Field & Stream* Magazine: "Killers in the Rain," April 1942. Copyright © 1942 Holt, Rinehart & Winston, Inc. "The Silver Fontinalis," May 1942. Copyright © 1942 Holt, Rinehart & Winston, Inc. "September on the Serpentine," September 1942. Copyright © 1942 Holt, Rinehart & Winston, Inc. "Spare the Rod and Prove a Point," January 1946. Copyright © 1946 Field & Stream Publishing Co.

Esquire Magazine: "Angling's Charmed Circle," first published in *Esquire* May 1964. Copyright © 1964 by *Esquire* Magazine. "A Fly Rod over the Deep Blue," first published in *Esquire* December 1966. Copyright © 1966 by *Esquire* Magazine.

To Joan,
*with whom both
fishing and living
are delightful*

CONTENTS

Foreword by *Edward C. Janes*   *xi*

Introduction by *Arnold Gingrich*   *xiii*

PART ONE *Salmon and Trout Fishing*

1. Salar Beware   *3*
2. Advice for Salmon Anglers   *10*
3. Where Salmon Lie and Why   *18*
4. Why Salmon Strike   *27*
5. How to Use Dry Flies for Atlantic Salmon   *35*
6. The Riffling Hitch   *44*
7. Where There's a Will   *51*
8. The Toughest of Them All   *54*
9. Address at the Atlantic Salmon Emergency Dinner, January 20, 1971   *62*
10. Between the Lakes at Ugashik   *64*
11. Trout Fishing Notes   *68*
12. Fish Deep and Slow for Early Trout   *73*
13. The Lost Art of Worm Fishing   *79*
14. Streamers for Trout   *84*
15. How to Use Wet Flies   *90*
16. Early Summer Trout   *93*
17. Catching Big Trout   *100*
18. Where Are the Trout?   *106*
19. The Silver Fontinalis   *112*

CONTENTS

20. September on the Serpentine   *120*

21. Nestucca Steelheads   *127*

PART TWO *General Fishing*

22. Bass on Live Bait   *135*

23. Choose Your Lake   *142*

24. Taking 'Em on Plugs   *147*

25. Bass on the Long Rod   *156*

26. Black of Night   *164*

27. Fishing the Lakes   *172*

28. Angling Surprises   *185*

PART THREE *Saltwater Fishing*

29. Fly-Rod Bonanza   *193*

30. A Fly Rod over the Deep Blue   *199*

31. Marlin on a Fly Rod   *210*

32. Angling's Charmed Circle   *219*

33. Casting Techniques Go to Sea   *228*

34. Killers in the Rain   *238*

PART FOUR *Rods, Tackle, and Technique*

35. Fishing Temperaments   *249*

36. Tips on Spinning   *258*

37. Fly Casting Made Easy   *265*

38. Spare the Rod and Prove a Point   *273*

39. Tips on Bait Casting   *279*

40. How to Play a Fish on a Fly Rod   *288*

41. Using Featherweight Rods   *293*

Contents

42. How to Wade a Stream   299

43. What Frightens Fish?   306

44. Your Guide Is a Friend   312

45. Talk about Tackle   319

46. Line–Rod Balance   325

47. Leaders Make a Difference   331

48. Choosing the Dry Fly   337

PART FIVE *Armstrong Creek*

49. Armstrong Creek   343

Photographs by Lee Wulff
follow page 196

FOREWORD

A NUMBER OF YEARS AGO, when the world and I were somewhat younger, I functioned for a time as Associate Editor of the former *Outdoors* magazine. One of my duties in this capacity was to edit the copy of its Angling Editor, Lee Wulff, and the experience was a valuable one for me, if not for Lee.

Editing, in the case of Lee's material, consisted of catching the occasional typographical error, writing subtitles, captioning photographs and, in the process, absorbing massive doses of fishing lore from one of the country's foremost anglers. For this pleasant and educational labor, the company paid me money. The money has long since been spent, but the fishing lore remains. Over the years it has stood me in good stead so many times that, gradually, I have come to consider it my own sometimes.

On several occasions when I have lured a king-size fish to strike and have played it successfully to the net, I have congratulated myself upon my knowledge and skill, only to recall upon reflection that I had learned the stratagem that rose the fish and the proper method of playing it from Lee Wulff. And I'm sure there have been countless other occasions when I have owed a subconscious debt for my success to Lee, for memory does not always categorically assert: "In the September issue, Lee said that 'Time is an important factor in the playing of a fish. The longer an angler takes to tire a fish on a given leader, the less he has to be proud of!' Or, in April, Lee pointed out that "It is motion that gives the fish his first warning of danger and it is motion which you must avoid."

No, this knowledge was absorbed gradually and subconsciously over a period of time as a result of poring over Lee's manuscripts as they appeared month by month. It has been deepened and broadened by reading Lee's books and his articles in other publications and, of course, by experimenting and expanding the basic tenets of angling, many of which I learned from him. For experience goes far to make an angler.

And now this long association has come full circle. In preparing this anthology of Lee's fishing articles, gleaned from *Outdoors, Sports Afield, Outdoor Life, Field & Stream, Collier's, Esquire,* and other publications, I have once again had the oppor-

tunity to edit Lee Wulff's copy. And again I have been struck by
the clear, concise, and at the same time chatty, manner in which
this master craftsman describes the habits of various species of fish,
the proper tackle to choose in pursuing them, and the correct way
to use it in order to derive the utmost in skill and satisfaction from
one's fishing.

Editing Lee's writings has brought new horizons to my angling
career. And so I am happy to have had the opportunity to help in
the preparation of this new book—*Fishing with Lee Wulff*. Reading it, I feel certain, will not only increase your own skill but will
also heighten your enjoyment of the great sport of angling.

EDWARD C. JANES

Westfield, Massachusetts

INTRODUCTION

As FAR BACK as 1939 Lee Wulff was the answer man if you wanted some new dodge or wrinkle that would make your fishing easier, simpler, handier, and more efficient. In that year, the *Handbook of Freshwater Fishing* came out, and our indebtedness to Lee Wulff began. It has grown by leaps and bounds, through his articles and films as well as books, until today it is mountainously awesome.

Probably no other single figure in the world of participant sports is as widely known to the public at large. And as for the angling public, certainly no one else has had as much influence on methods and tackle, nor acted as effectively both as pacesetter and peacemaker, among its several divergent and sometimes nearly embattled groups. His has been that greatest form of teaching: instruction by example.

The crux of Wulff's creed has been stated succinctly in this book, so it's better to give it to you in his own words than to try to put words in his mouth: "The essence of the *sport* in fishing is to take the available fish and, by the use of very sporting tackle, demonstrate an uncommon skill. If the skill required is not uncommon, neither is the angler."

That's the simple common denominator of all his exploits of the last thirty years, and especially of the last eight or nine, when by example he has broadened the range of the fly rod's utility and given it a new versatility—setting a few new records in the process —and at the same time brought fly fishermen of both fresh and salt water persuasion closer together than they had ever been before.

"Closer" probably isn't the right word. "Close" is more like it. Because their closeness, before Lee Wulff began showing them some identity of interests, was that of strange bulldogs. Actually, of all the high deeds of the last three decades, this last is by far the most remarkable thing Lee Wulff has ever done, but it is like all the rest in that, up to the time he did it, nobody would have believed it could be done.

But to go back a bit, Lee Wulff's name, like Theodore Gordon's, was first known to the angling world in connection with flies: the Gray Wulff, and the White, and subsequently the Brown, the Grizzly, the Blonde, and the Royal, were known for a decade before the appearance of his first book, in 1939. And since the *Handbook* came out when he was thirty-four, you can readily see that he must have been a very young man when he first began to be famous as an angler.

My awareness of his name, and my indebtedness to him as an angler, began back in the days before this country's involvement in the Second World War, when a trick that I had picked up from the *Handbook* began enabling me, all of a sudden, to catch a lot more fish than ever before. Those were the days, if you can remember back that far, when we had to carry something to keep our leaders moist, because gut was brittle until soaked, and putting on a dry-gut tippet was a guarantee to lose immediately any fish you were lucky enough to hook. Those were also the days, pre-nylon, when we had to have something—a chairback if nothing else was handy—to dry our silk lines on overnight, because a rotted spot in either line or backing was another sure way to instant loss of any fish sufficient to give you play, even if you had been foresighted enough to soak the leader.

At Lee's suggestion, via the *Handbook*, dental floss was substituted for the terminal tippet at the all-important last length of the knotted leader, right next to the fly itself, and the difference it made was not to be believed until you tried it. Gut is relatively stiff, even when saturated, so it was always hard to avoid drag, even on 4X, which was as fine as most of us could either get or in fact had ever heard of in those primitive times; also it came in relatively short lengths, so you had to have a lot of knots at the place where you least could tolerate them, near as well as next to the fly.

The next improvement, equally simple but again something that no one but Lee seemed to have thought of, was to cut the fly line off at the reel, after making the longest cast that a test on the lawn showed you could make with it, and to replace with backing the space that the useless bulk of the rest of the running line preempted on the core of the reel. Suddenly a line on a reel that you'd thought was limited to stream and pond fishing was "enlarged" to become perfectly adequate for the biggest fish in the broadest rivers, and your trout outfits were overnight postgraduated to use for steelheads and salmon.

But of even more universal application, since not everyone gets to go for the big fish—which are for most people in remote places—was a stunt so obvious that you kicked yourself for never having thought of it before. Most fly fishermen in this country use a rod and reel exactly the way they use a knife and fork: they switch them back and forth. They cast the rod with the right, or knife, hand, and then change over to hold it in the left, or fork, hand while they use the right hand to reel in the line. When eating, Europeans, much more sensibly, avoid all this useless motion by keeping both knife and fork in hand until they've finished with them, instead of switching back and forth throughout the main course of the meal.

And thanks to Lee again, a lot of us who may still be stupid at the table are at least much smarter on the stream, because we leave to our stronger right arm the job of controlling the rod at the one time it might make any difference—that is, while actually playing a fish—and let the weaker left hand do the less strategic job of turning the reel handle. Nothing could be simpler. All you do is mount the reel in what to the less enlightened seems the back to front position on the rod's reel seat, so that when you reel in with your left hand, the line and the backing accumulate on the reel spool in a counterclockwise direction.

As frequent as the slips 'twixt cup and lip have been the freedom-achieving jumps by fish that have got away between hands, so to speak, during the needless and purely habitual shifting of the rod back and forth between casting and reeling. If a time-and-motion study of the average angler's day were to be made, it would show the hundreds, even thousands, of waste motions that are made between actual hookings of fish. Such a study would of course dissuade all but the least sensible from further pursuit of an activity in which effort is so minimally rewarded. But it would also convince all but the most adamantine of those who were left that anything that can reduce those wasted movements by as much as two thirds—back and forth and back again, where forth is all that's needed—is the obvious thing to do. I know I changed the mounting of my reel the day I read Lee's advice to do so—this was years before I ever laid eyes on him—and I have never since even thought of going back to the old way.

It's ironic, though, that I cite these tricks learned from Lee, which all seem calculated to make things easier, when the man's influence—his achievements and his records—has always been in the direction of doing things the hardest way possible. As far back as 1938, Lee was attracting attention by doing things the hard way, as when he landed the first tuna ever taken on rod and reel in Newfoundland, in a makeshift boat and with a crew recruited for the occasion. That was on 130-pound tackle. Almost thirty years later he was back doing the same thing, but this time on fifty-pound tackle. In the latter instance the weight ratio of fish to tackle had risen to an impressive level of very nearly 11 to 1, as the tuna in question, played through daylight and darkness, weighed 597 pounds.

In other words, Lee Wulff in his sixties was doing what he couldn't have dreamed of doing—and in fact what none of us then would have believed could be done—when he was in his thirties.

But even that feat, which in writing and on film seems a terrific test of endurance, is less significant than some of his other angling exploits, for they have involved the kind of tackle and lure the average person would think of as suited only to trout and bass. As such, they actually go even farther out, as demonstrations.

Lee has been doing these innovative things at an age when other skilled performers, concert musicians for example, are thinking of retirement, and many businessmen, whether thinking about it or not, have been retired compulsorily. Lee was born, in case you're wondering about it, at the beginning of 1905—in Alaska, as it happens, and his schooling was in civil engineering at Stanford, followed by art at Julien's in Paris. (Nothing is usual about this man.) As he says in this book, it's lucky that the sort of thing he's been doing "requires swift movements combined with excellent judgment more than youth or strength or dazzling speed." Just how speedy speed has to be before it's dazzling is a question you might feel like raising when you get to the page where Lee's timed speed with a cast from one of those "toothpick" rods he uses on salmon turns out to be ninety-six miles an hour—but let's leave that, or we'll never get you there.

As he says, "It's a glorious thing that a man whose hair has gone gray and whose muscular power is not what it once was can continue to improve his abilities to take on the top challenges of angling. Few sports or games offer such a lifetime of enduring activity and challenge."

Well, the part about the gray hair is true enough. His looks like pewter, and his features are as scraggy as if carved on granite by someone like Gutzon Borglum. And as for the longevity angle, all of us, if we were honest enough, would admit that we fish as a cheap form of life insurance, placing our bets on such long-lived favorites as Izaak Walton, who made ninety in a day when the actuarial statistics averaged about a third as much, and such latter-day distance runners as Hewitt and La Branche, who were stream cronies for longer than the allotted threescore and ten years.

But still the key word in that statement of Lee's is none of these, but the word "challenges." The odds against success in angling must be longer than in almost anything else you can think of. Speaking of the study of anglers' motions, as we were a while back, I remember that a study made years ago about warfare said that only one out of every thousand shots fired ever found not just its mark but any mark at all. I'm sure the score of anglers' casts, if there were any way to keep it, would make even such a random thing as gunfire equate with total efficacy.

Yet here is Lee, now and for the last thirty years, constantly trying to lengthen those odds, as if they weren't long enough, and what's more, getting us to like it. Somewhere in this book he likens his kind of angling to golf, and such candor is becoming, because what he has been doing to and for the fly rod over all these years reminds me of that old definition of golf that, sparing you the dialect, is supposed to be of Scottish origin: The art of getting a small ball into a wee hole, with instruments ill adapted to the purpose.

Certainly no more appropriate comparison could have come to mind to describe the time he and Stu Apte went after tarpon—armed with a bass rod and a Beaudex reel, not even a Landex, which at least has a free-stripping release to let the fish take line without making the reel handles turn (I say handles because the Landex has two), but a simple Beaudex single-action, single-handle, no drag, no adjustable brake, no nothing but the angler's thumb on the practically smoking line—if he has the temerity to put it there. Lee has the temerity, all right, but actually the word is out of place in reference to the tarpon exploit, because this was really act one of Lee's three-act drama of demonstration of the fly rod's range, and the beginning of his successful attempt to bridge the gap that formerly estranged the fly rodders of fresh and salt water.

As has often been remarked on in the past, each of fishing's many forms has its devotees, so passionately addicted to their particular form of the pastime as to be anywhere from surlily non-

committal to downright contemptuous of its other forms. It often
seems that the contempt of the trout purist for the spin or bait
fisherman is exceeded only by the dedicated salmon angler's contempt for the trouter, which in turn is exceeded only by the
tarpon man's contempt for both of them. As for the tarpon man,
he in turn is looked down upon by the billfish anglers. And overlooked in this vicious circle is the contention of the great but now
almost forgotten Dr. James Alexander Henshall that the black
bass is inch for inch and pound for pound the greatest fish that
swims.

Be that as it may, Lee Wulff set out to attempt to turn this
vicious circle of contempt into a charmed circle of content by
positing this simple angling equation: It is equally hard, and
equally a matter of pride, to take on a fly rod and with a fly a
tarpon of over a hundred pounds on a leader of twelve-pound
test, or a salmon of over sixteen pounds on a size 16 fly, or a
trout over twenty inches on a No. 20 fly.

Having set up the charmed circle concept, it was of course like
putting a chip on his shoulder, and having set up the tarpon claim,
along with the new 16/16 goal for Atlantic salmon, against the already established 20/20 par for trouting skill, he simply had to go
do it.

Back in the fifties, he had already well established his ability
to take salmon of substantial size on featherweight tackle, and in
his 1958 book, *The Atlantic Salmon*, he had shown by many records and pictures that these fish could be taken on small flies—although he had not actually taken heavier than sixteen-pound salmon at that point on anything smaller than a size 14 spider. To
his recollection, the best he'd done on a size 16 fly was a fourteen-
pounder. But that was such a small difference that it could always
wait, whereas the tarpon goal was something else.

He took the tarpon, comfortably clearing by twenty-odd
pounds the hundred-pound mark that he had posed at Islamorada
in April, 1963, and then twice in the summer of 1964 cleared his
own salmon mark by taking fish of $22\frac{3}{4}$ and 24 pounds on a size 16
of a new skating fly of his own devising. That was on the Moise,
one of his favorite rivers, and he named the fly the Prefontaine in
honor of his host there. The fly looks like a cross between his own
stone fly and the one known as Whiskers. It has a surface-riding
action, like a small hydroplane, as opposed to the semi-submerged
swath of the Whiskers fly. The forepart is of white bucktail with

white hackle aft and a ring of badger hackle slightly abaft of midship.

There remained, to close the circle of contempt completely even though the charmed circle of equal skills had been rounded, only the ticklish question of the billfish and Lee set out to see if this gap too could be bridged.

He set the second record with a ninety-five-pound Pacific sailfish at Piñas Bay in Panama in April of 1965, making the breakthrough by establishing that sailfish could be taken with fly on an ordinary fly rod, without extension butt, fighting chair, or harness, and with a dragless reel; though the fish was only of average size for the Pacific, where the sailfish run larger than on the Atlantic side, it set a pattern, no matter how long or short a time the record itself might stand. In other words, much more important than the size of that particular sailfish was the fact that sailfish could be fought on this tackle and under these conditions—a feat which amounted to taking the freshwater fisherman's technique and limitations to sea.

It was this last factor that made the taking of the sailfish more significant than taking the even larger tarpon the year before. Tarpon had been fished for from skiffs, and in fact the playing of tarpon was almost exactly analogous to the playing of Atlantic salmon, which also, everywhere except New Brunswick and Iceland, were much more often fished for from canoes than by wading. It could be argued, and often has been, that one of these two fish is much rougher and tougher than the other, but leaving that aside, the fact is they both had been fished for in much the same way before.

But the billfish had always been fished for quite another way, and it was a way that gave the starring role to the handler of the boat rather than to the angler. The latter, up to the point of the actual playing of the fish, had a passive and really secondary role, sitting in a fighting chair, lolling at his ease with perhaps a cold drink in one hand and his rod in the other—if indeed the rod were not stashed away in a socket on the stern—with plenty of time to begin playing the fish after the snapping of the "clothespin" on the outrigger signaled the taking of the trolled bait. The captain was really doing all the work, finding the fish and, in effect, even getting the fish to strike by his strategic manipulation of the bait via the actions of the boat. And even after the point of getting the fish on, the captain's role in maneuvering the boat was always a crucial determinant of the angler's subsequent success or failure. In any case, it was the captain who, if not always credited when things went right, at least invariably was blamed if anything went wrong.

The one way to remove this variable element that flawed all arguments about the relative skills involved in deep-sea fishing for sailfish and tidal or coastal small-boat fishing for tarpon (and, indeed, river fishing for salmon) was to take everything out of the captain's hands and return it to those of the angler. Stop the boat. Cast to the fish. And let the angler, rather than the action of the boat, bring the fish to the fly and set the hook, and play it to the capitulation point where it could be either boated or released.

This leaves only one argument. Which is toughest to play on a fly rod, a tarpon or a sailfish or a salmon? True, the argument could start right up again, like the band resuming play after the intermission between sets, because the tarpon man and the sailfish man can be strident in their claims, nor is the salmon man famous for taciturnity.

But there is one word alone that could shut them all up, and indeed make them scurry like Indian natives at the shout of "Tiger!" And that is marlin.

Wow! Striped marlin? Not on a fly rod?

Yes. So that was Lee's next move and that was the third record, at Salinas in Ecuador in April, 1967. The fish weighed 148 pounds, but again, more important than the record, in and of itself, was the proving of the point that it could be done. Once the way was shown, others would be sure to go and do it too. And this, rather than any need to demonstrate further his exceptional skill as an angler, was the underlying motivation for this series of exploits.

Lee had one really basic point to make, and he made it—by example. He wanted to show what the fly rod could do, making all kinds of fly fishermen realize how identical their basic interests are and how much more sense it would make for them all to come together rather than to remain standoffishly apart.

There is, after all, only one fish, the Atlantic salmon, that must by law—at least on our side of the water—be fished for only with the fly rod. Lee has fished for them every year since the early thirties—daily when he ran a camp on the River of Ponds in Newfoundland—and he could have stuck to fishing for them the rest of his life. There's nobody who does it better or enjoys it more. As far back as 1962, in his celebrated match with Jock Scott on the Dee in Aberdeenshire, he settled to everyone's satisfaction that consummate mastery of this regal quarry can be effected with a six-foot rod weighing less than two ounces. And in July of 1968 he upped his own salmon mark on a size 16 fly to 27 pounds. But he was also aware long ago that the Sport of Kings was steadily pricing itself out of the reach of all but economic royalists, and that the kind of sport fishing which it exemplifies would soon be unavailable to all but a very few.

Lee used to talk about this on the Wednesday-noon angling lunches at the Midtown in New York, and his one constant theme, to which he returned again and again with many variations, was that it's not the fish but the fishing that counts, the kind of fishing you do rather than the kind of fish you fish for—that's the essence of the sport in fishing. We could see then that there was method in his madness, not just a mania for ever bigger fish on ever smaller rods, but the spreading of this attitude toward angling skill—call it the Atlantic Salmon attitude if you like—into other forms of fishing, with a consequent broadened range and wider use of the fly rod.

The founding of the Federation of Fly Fishermen came more or less directly out of Lee's talks, these aims and ambitions which he had so long and so often expounded. And in the wake of his own exploits with the fly rod in saltwater came the adherence of saltwater fly fishermen to that one big organization. I don't mean to suggest that he did it alone, but certainly he struck the spark from which others caught fire, as for example when Gene Anderegg went around from coast to coast to fishing clubs, carrying what was essentially Lee's message; and others like Stu Apte and Lefty Kreh aided and abetted what Lee began, to bring in the representation of the saltwater side.

Thus Lee moved a mighty step nearer to the attainment of his avowed hope that a considerable body of anglers would start being "prouder of the quality of their fishing abilities than of the abundance of their catches" and that fly fishing might "spread out from the streams, lakes, and saltwater shorelines onto the deep blue sea."

In this light it can be seen that his approach to the sport of fly fishing is statesmanlike, for as he says, "Freshwater fishing is limited and most of our fresh waters are heavily fished. Where fishing is private it's expensive. The best Atlantic salmon fishing, for example, can cost the angler as much as $5,000 per week. But the seas are free and open."

That certainly makes long-range sense, in a world that's three-fifths wet. And it is consistent with that tenet of Lee's sport fishing creed that puts the stress on "the available fish" as well as on "the uncommon skill."

But this is still only a part of the total score of Lee Wulff's contributions "to and for the fly rod." For one thing, he took the ultra-light rod out of the toy class and showed the way it could be used on all but the very biggest fish and waters, that it offered an actual advantage over the heavyweight rods which had traditionally been employed and considered necessary. To do this, he had to revolutionize the whole conception of the featherweight rod's nature and the manner of its use. Leonard made the first one and put it at the foot of their Baby Catskill class, as a super-delicate trout rod, actually featuring it as a lady's rod, and when Paul Young took the same idea and beefed it up into a stronger-backboned creation, he called it the Midge, to indicate the tiny flies and gossamer tippets to which he thought its utility was limited.

But what Lee Wulff did with the light rod can only be likened to what Paganini first did with the Guarnerius violin—he brought things out of it that the maker could never have believed were there. Lee did a lot of experimenting with the possibilities of ultra-light rods between 1940, when he wrote *Leaping Silver*, and 1958, when he published his findings on their capabilities in *The Atlantic Salmon*. First of all, he determined that a salmon could be played with no rod at all, establishing a *ne plus ultra* in the argument on behalf of ultra-light tackle. Then he applied the principles that he had found most successful as a pilot, as a seat-of-the-pants bush flier, in outwitting the wind. He showed that if you cast fast enough, you can often take advantage of the vagaries of even strong winds by getting a quick cast in between puffs. Timing himself with a stopwatch, and giving his best effort in turn to two of his own rods, both made by Orvis, he found that there was a distinct advantage in speed in his little 6½-foot, 2-ounce rod over his 9-foot 5-ouncer. The time he needed on the former to straighten out his back casts and forward casts averaged only 18.4 seconds (for ten consecutive false casts), whereas on the latter, the larger rod, the operation took 23.1 seconds. But in the course of such experiments he found he could get the maximum performance out of the little rod only by quite literally "throwing the book away," not by using it as fly rods were used in the past, with the easy and graceful rocking-chair motion of the forearm alone, with an imaginary book held between ribs and elbow, but by lifting it up and treating it as if it were an extension of his forefinger, with his whole arm as upthrust as that of the Statue of Liberty.

Watch Lee on a TV sports program as he uses the little rod, and you'll see that on his back cast his arm is fully extended a good eighteen to twenty inches behind his head—and on the forward cast his whole body goes forward in a follow-through like that of a baseball pitcher.

The style is heretical, but the results couldn't be more orthodox, as Lee gets off eighty-foot casts from a rod that Paul Young, its foremost maker, thought limited by its size and weight to casts of about thirty-five feet, or at most—and tempting fate every time —around forty.

But the same is true, to a degree, of everything else he has done, thought up, devised, or improved. We used to fear drag on a floating fly as a fate worse than death to fish-taking, until Lee introduced the Portland Creek hitch as a means of imparting a sort of bias motion to a wet fly, with the unexpected result that a lot of us found that a riffled hitch on a dry fly, creating a wake like a toy motorboat as it was pulled back just beneath the surface on the retrieve, provoked more strikes and took more fish than it had in the course of its natural float.

And we used to wear cumbersome fishing jackets until Lee Wulff had the inspiration for the first tackle pack vest, with its blessed provision for all needed gear above the waterline when wearing chest waders. For that matter, we all used to believe those horror stories about guys in waders found drowned, feet up and heads down, after wading accidents, until Lee deflated that myth. Again you might say he did it the hard way, by diving off a high bridge into a deep pool of the Battenkill, wearing chest waders, to prove that the air in them will not up-end a man who has taken a spill.

But the innovation that best expresses Lee Wulff's fishing philosophy—"In this sport of catching fish I like to do the entire job myself"—is beyond a doubt his invention of the tailer, that spring-steel device which, when looped over the tail of a large fish, obviates the need of either the clumsy and fish-scaringly awkward net or the cruelly disfiguring and often lethal gaff. It also reflects another tenet of his angling creed, expressed in his words "These fish are too valuable to be caught only once," for a tailed fish, momentarily paralyzed and completely subdued and thus spared the injurious thrashings induced by either net or gaff or even sometimes by beaching, can be returned to the water completely unharmed.

And, though of course he didn't originate it, that's another practice which Lee pioneered long before the establishment of the first stretches of public waters restricted to fly fishing only and long before the first designation of areas limited to the fishing-for-fun concept, which confines all angling to catch-and-release and which is now practiced in a number of states.

It's a disservice to any man to make him sound too much like Goody Two-shoes, and I realize that any attempt to characterize Lee Wulff as a fisherman must seem like a strained effort to achieve the personification of the Complete Angler, but the best and worst I can do, to counterbalance any such tendency, is to say that to see Lee fishing is to shatter the theory, as formulated by Walton or anybody since, that angling is the contemplative man's recreation.

Lee on a stream is as constantly in motion as a pacing wild animal in a cage. As he says of himself, somewhere in this book, he's a mover. He appears to be of a restless, seemingly impatient disposition. Of course you know that no man can really be impatient who will try a hundred casts to tease a single fish into taking one of a succession of flies, and he has done this often on salmon rivers. But watching him on a trout stream I could never think of a word more suited to him than Fish Hawk. I didn't say Hog, because he puts them back as fast as he brings them in. But while you, the contemplative type, are working on three fish, say, he'll have darted around enough to swoop down on fourteen. (That was an actual and honest scorecard, the last time I counted.)

But the very fact that he can still get excited in the pursuit of twelve-inch trout, after he's caught individual fish weighing over a quarter of a ton, is to me one of the strongest character counts in his favor. Expert as he has become, he still has to be considered the farthest possible remove from a purist, and if my harping on the fly rod has had the effect of making him seem so, then I hasten to apologize. Why, there's even a chapter on worm fishing in this book, and if you look carefully you'll find more than one reference to spinning that is anything but derogatory.

Introduction

Atlantic salmon still come first in Lee's book, as you'll see when you go through it, and undoubtedly they always will, though he confesses an occasional sneaky yen to go bonefishing. But for all his insistence on quality fishing, his appetite for the sport would still have to be categorized as more gourmand than gourmet. It isn't that he has to yield to anybody in the ability to appreciate and enjoy the best fishing, but rather that his attitude remains the wholesome one that while some fishing is obviously much better than others, still any fishing is better than no fishing.

So those whose fishing haunts and habits will never take them within leagues of either trout or salmon country need not feel shut out of Lee Wulff's pages. They have only to leaf past the portions devoted to the salmonids and they'll find that when they come to their fish, be they bass or pike or even walleyes, Lee will be right there beside them, acting as if he'd never had more fun in his life and as if a chance to go fishing, any kind of fishing, were the rarest of treats.

That he should have a wife who shares his feeling for the sport would seem to be too much for any man's portion, combining into one incredible parlay such a triple feature as vocation, hobby, and mate. But in Joan Salvato, as no angler needs to be told, the all-American angler has found his counterpart. They are Mr. and Mrs. America, wherever a fly rod can be told from a buggy whip. Yes, you really would say that this exceeds all likelihood.

But then, as I've earnestly tried to suggest, and every page of this book attests, nothing that has to do with fishing is too much for Lee Wulff.

ARNOLD GINGRICH

PART ONE

Salmon and Trout Fishing

CHAPTER 1

Salar Beware

THE ATLANTIC SALMON is an aristocrat. From the beginnings of modern angling in England it has stood for the best the sport could offer. Only a few other game fish—the tarpon, the steelhead, the broadbill, the marlin—can challenge it. For the salmon has the attributes of greatness. It is tremendously powerful and leaps freely when hooked. It fights in running water. It is caught by casting. And it demands a very small lure and very delicate tackle.

Come, stand beside me on a salmon pool. It is late June and evening. The wind is still. The long, warm days have filled the surroundings with a feeling of life and growth that is more felt than seen. The spruces and firs have covered their deep, eternal green with countless new shoots that look like light green blossoms. Feathery new leaves spring upward from the birches' snow-white stems. The river, the wild fury of its snow-run spent, rustles contentedly as it fills its banks in perfect flow. Late sunlight dances riotously on the swift water spilling into the pool, sparkles gaily in the smoothing flow, and highlights the bits of foam that fleck the slick, shimmering water where the salmon lie.

We stand on a long gravel bar on the inner side of the pool's sweeping arc, facing the gradually deepening water toward its far-side depth. Behind us in the small log cabin all but hidden in the woods, the guides are making tidy after the evening meal. The canoes are drawn well out of water just downstream, their amber caverns showing briefly above the weathered canvas coats. This is a small river and, although we have used the canoes for travel, we will wade for our fishing. The water itself is not absolutely clear. It bears a faint brownish stain traceable to the peat bogs on the high slopes of its origin, adding to the pool's depth and mystery.

As we watch, the dark waters open to let a great silvery fish arc high, then disappear in a surge of spray. We are ready to fish the evening out, you and I, and these are the things I would like to have you know about the Atlantic salmon.

The salmon that just leapt and toward which you will soon direct your fly was a hen spawned five falls before. She spent the first three years of her life feeding in the river beside which we stand and at the end of that time she weighed less than two ounces and was about 5½ inches long. During those first freshwater years as a "parr" her food increased gradually from the smallest of sub-aquatic insect life until it included anything living that came within her reach and was small enough to swallow, and many things that had to be taken in several bites. For her size she was one of the swiftest and most voracious of fishes.

Then, two springs ago, her mottled protective stream colora-tion was coated with a layer of silver that left only a dark streak along her back. She moved down the river and disappeared in the great expanse of the sea. In saltwater her feeding became more ravenous, if possible, than it had been before. With the bounty of the sea within her reach she grew amazingly. At the end of the year she was two feet long and weighed five pounds; now, after slightly more than two years of steady saltwater feeding, her weight has reached fifteen pounds.

Under an urge that nature creates and men try feebly to ex-plain she moved inshore and found her native river. Steadfastly she swam the current, feeling a nature-created nausea that made all food distasteful. Already her teeth had begun to be absorbed, for she no longer needed them. The stream which fed her as a parr and which she hoped would feed her spawn could not supply even a meager diet for a full-grown salmon. Nature, wisely, had let her store up strength so that she would need no nourishment at all, leaving the full food productivity of the stream for growing parr.

She lies behind a large stone embedded in the gravelly bed of the pool. Water eddying behind the rock has lost the force of its flow and it requires little of her strength to hold her place there, yet the gentle movement of the water against her body soothes her restlessness. She is a strong fish, bursting with energy, but since she will take no food in the long months ahead, and will gradually lose weight and power, she must not waste her strength in useless swimming. Only when the boredom is too great does she make a sudden surge or leap to reassure herself of that magnificent power that is hers.

You have marked down in your mind the location of her jump and move waist-deep into the water to reach the proper spot from which to cast. What fly will you present and why? From your fly box you select a well-worn Jock Scott on a No. 4 hook and fasten it to the .012 diameter gut that tips your twelve-foot leader. You chose a Jock Scott not because it looks like food to the salmon or because it represents any nymph or fish or insect that has ever lived in that stream; you picked it out because for centuries its counterparts have lured salmon to rise from the depths and take them in their mouths.

The fly lands lightly above and beyond the salmon, and follows your barely submerged line and leader in a smooth, sweeping arc toward the beach below you. The fly swims smoothly with none of the jerks or twitches a trout fisherman habitually gives his fly to simulate life. It rides upright, varied tones etched sharply by the setting sun.

When its first swing is finished, you lift it with your rod and send it out to settle quietly into the water again at a spot quite near the first cast. Again it swings across the place where the salmon leaped. And again and again. Then, when the fly swings 'round, there is an almost imperceptible flash of silver and a slow swirl patterns the water behind the fly as it maintains the even tenor of its swing. The fish that we saw leap or another lying close to her has risen behind your fly but has failed to take it.

With an interested fish before you there are now several procedures open. You may rest the fish awhile and then tempt it again with the same fly. You may switch to another fly, preferably a Jock Scott of a smaller size, and repeat the cast. Or you may cast again with the same fly without a pause in your fishing. The latter procedure is my choice because it is by far the simplest way and because I've found it very effective.

Let us say that you, too, are eager and the light is fading. You send the same fly out in the regular, continued rhythm of your casting. The retrieve begins and puts an easy pressure on your rod. Just when the fly should pass the fish your rod tip dips a little and the pressure builds up. Your eyes, glued to that spot, have seen nothing beneath the water, but now your rod is bending in a hard arc and you are playing a salmon. Let us say that it was the one that leaped.

Line moves out slowly under a steady pressure. You hold her lightly, for you know that she can move with sudden speed. Then the reel sings and she somersaults out of the water and speeds upstream. Your line, quivering slightly under the heavy pressure of the flow, aims well downstream as she moves across the current and upward toward the head of the pool. The initiative is hers and she will have her way as long as she retains that dazzling speed and has the current and a long, long line between you.

She moves at will about the pool, shaking her head, leaping, sometimes rolling over and over in a series of wild gyrations. She cannot stand the torment of any curb upon her freedom, however slight. Fear drives her into a number of wild rushes that slowly drain her splendid strength. It is not through hiding from them under obstructions or swimming into water where they could not follow that, till now, she has escaped all her enemies; she has clung to the open water and outswam and outleaped them. She holds to the deep, open water of the pool now, and when the line is caught and held for a breathless second on a submerged rock around which she swam it was not because of any plan of hers but, rather, simply that while coursing open water she happened to pass beyond it.

With her peak strength gone, you can hold her a little tighter with the assurance that her runs will have lost the suddenness that breaks a leader almost before the power of the salmon's movement can be felt. Now you will have a brief interval of time to release the pressure on your line when you sense the starting of a run. Under greater tackle pressure she resists stubbornly, weakening herself further when otherwise she might sulk and feel new strength come to her tired body from her stored-up energy.

She flashes silver as she twists, then drifts with the current for a few feet before she heads into the flow again. She leaps but barely clears the surface as your rod drops quickly to avoid a tackle-breaking shock. You swing her close in that moment of weakness, but when she sees the set-up tailer moving toward her she whisks away once more to the deep, steady flow. The minutes move slowly by before you can draw her close again and hold her there with the rod arched high in one hand and the pressure of your fingers braking the line while the other arm moves the tailer up over her slowly fanning tail.

An easy pull of the steel spring against her body slips the noose down to tighten in its secure grip while you wade her gently to the beach. The guides, until now quiet statues behind us, come forward to inspect the fish, kill it quickly, and bear it proudly to a little cavern in the rocks where cool water drips on moss and where the fish will keep.

You have caught your salmon but you will not have understood salmon fishing if you feel that a Jock Scott fly so fished will always produce a salmon or that salmon will continue to lie in that same pool when the river has dropped to its sun-baked summer low or when the high flood's current overlays the bushes on the banks. The wisest salmon anglers are much more prone to say "I think" or "Chances are" in humble tones than those who, knowing less, try to lay out an iron-clad course of action for salmon fishing.

Even though the salmon frequently makes a bold head-and-tail rise to the barely sunken wet fly, showing most of his body as he takes the feathered steel with slow deliberation, it is not until you have explored the dry-fly field of salmon fishing that you will have reached the angling peak or found the need for the greatest amount of self-control.

When, as your small fly follows its buoyant course, a great salmon appears, head and back above the water, beside your fly or just below it, and you can watch calmly and wait with perfect control until those massive jaws engulf the fly and take it down into the water, then and only then do you touch the sport's high pinnacle.

Salmon fishing is much like trout fishing and most of its recruits come up to salmon fishing through experience on the trout streams. The type of water in which they're found and the general fishing conditions for both fish are so similar that the angler with trout fishing experience is apt to fish for salmon as he would for trout. This is a mistake.

Trout lie with an eye to the food supply. Salmon lie where they find comfort and feel secure. Trout in a given stream might be caught in a thousand places where, if the river held salmon instead of trout, Salar would be caught at only four or five. To catch salmon you must fish where they lie. Fishing the water is to waste at least ninety percent of your fishing time.

No man who hasn't seen a river in wild flood, in sun-baked drought, and in all the stages in between, studying well where the salmon rested under each condition, can pick out with complete accuracy the proper spots to fish. And that, in all simplicity, explains why a salmon guide is at least a good investment and in most cases a necessity.

A good guide will know his river thoroughly. He will know which flies can be depended upon to take at least an occasional salmon under any set of conditions, although he cannot know what untried flies may be used on "his" river with success. He will have a sense of the river and the woods around it. He will be a companion who will watch your fly as it swims through the water on each cast as intently as if he, instead of you, were handling the rod. And above all, he will have a true respect for the magnificence and courage that mark the salmon and lift him above the run of ordinary fish.

Salmon fishing is a little like big-game hunting. If you miss a chance it may be your only one for the trip. To catch one salmon a day is to have a good and interesting trip. To take one in a week may still be a satisfying achievement. No fishing is less predictable. The salmon need not rise to your fly nor to anyone else's, nor need it search out or take one solitary morsel of food from the time it comes into the river from the sea until, many months later, spawned-out and spent, it turns back toward the salty source of all life once more. (Unlike the Pacific salmon, fish of an entirely different species, the Atlantic salmon may live to spawn several times.)

To most of us who fish for Atlantic salmon, a "salmon" is a fish of at least two years' sea feeding, a fish that ranges in weight from about seven pounds on up to more than forty. A fish that has spent only one year in sea feeding we call a "grilse." This term applies to a special run of salmon that are smaller ($2\frac{1}{2}$ to 7 pounds), slimmer, and have slightly forked tails. They are incredibly swift fish and remarkable leapers. They take a fly more eagerly and demand less skill to hook and play than the heavier, sturdier salmon.

The movement of salmon up their rivers to the spawning grounds may vary from river to river and from season to season. On many streams the fish must travel up the rivers on the high water of spring in order to clear certain barriers that block the way in lesser flow. In other rivers where a good depth of water holds throughout the season, they may come in late or early as they choose.

In moving up the rivers, salmon will select certain spots in which to lie, usually spots that give them favorable resting without much exertion, where they enjoy the soothing effect of flowing water along their sleek, nervous bodies. They will seek a position from which they have access to deep, open water upon which they depend for their safety. Salmon running the river in high water may be spread out along its entire length. When the rivers are low, salmon will be found in only a few pools.

The Atlantic salmon rivers are not many in number when you compare them to this continent's many other streams and rivers.

Compared to the other sporting fish of the continent salmon are pitifully few. Atlantic salmon will never be plentiful or common, for there will always be more anglers anxious to fish for them than there are rivers and pools to fish. Where salmon fishing has not been limited by much stricter restrictions than those enforced for other freshwater fishing it has already been dissipated or is on the downgrade. Salmon fishing is not for all anglers. If you are fortunate enough to become one of the select few you will find that successful salmon fishing is neither easy nor certain, but that it is distinctly worthwhile.

CHAPTER 2

Advice for Salmon Anglers

FISHING FOR BRIGHT Atlantic salmon is not like fishing for any other fish, for the salmon rarely, if ever, feeds on anything in the rivers. Therefore, he cannot be tempted by hunger, which is the downfall of most fish taken by angling.

The only legal way of angling for Atlantic salmon is by fly fishing, and the small fly is thought by many to be a torment rather than a tidbit. It is small and inconspicuous, almost always fished near the surface and in moving water. There is a great deal of water to cover and the fly must usually be placed close to the salmon to be effective. The first mistake beginners usually make is to fish for most of their time over water that is barren of fish, where salmon neither see nor react to their flies.

An experienced angler who knows a pool well will realize just where salmon tend to lie and rest. He will fish those spots and his fly will be passing just in front of the resting salmon in cast after cast, hour after hour. The novice who hasn't the knowledge of where salmon are lying in the pool usually covers all the seemingly good water and will have his fly passing near salmon only ten percent or so of the time. Obviously, the angler who knows the pool in this case has ten times as much chance of catching a salmon as one who does not.

A suggested remedy for the novice is to fish for at least fifty percent of the time over spots where he has seen salmon jump or where, for any other reason, he is sure salmon are lying. The surest remedy is to hire a guide who knows the waters thoroughly and follow his advice. Salmon move from one resting spot in a pool to another when the water level rises or falls, and only experience can teach where salmon will lie under a particular water condition in a given river.

A second major fault of the novice is his failure to watch his fly intently and continuously. Whether fishing wet fly or dry, the angler should always watch his fly and the water under and around it. The angler who does and who notices the slightest flash of silver or other sign of a salmon moving beneath it, and then stops to fish cast after cast to that spot, will usually hook or catch that fish. This may happen several times in a fishing day and result in his taking several salmon, while the angler who has not been watching his fly intently and so has failed to concentrate on catching these interested fish takes none at all.

Salmon often take a little coaxing before they will rise. The first cast does not always bring them up to the full effort of taking the fly. Changing the fly may be the answer, but more often than not it is something else, a certain path the fly follows or a certain speed and direction of the fly at a certain point. Of a hundred casts over a salmon, only one or two follow the particular path and speed that will cause him to take the fly. How to achieve the right path and speed of travel for a wet fly over a salmon is not very easy to explain, but to understand that such a need exists and that the hundredth unsuccessful cast to the same spot may be followed by one that hooks a salmon is a long step forward in becoming an accomplished salmon angler.

Once a salmon takes a fly, most novices hold him too hard, and the greatest percentage of salmon hooked and lost are lost in the first few seconds or first minute of play and for that reason. The salmon should be allowed free rein for a period of several minutes before the angler tries to put any serious tackle pressure upon him. Tackle pull should be used only after some of the wildness is out of the salmon and his runs are more readily predictable and more easily cushioned by the rod.

In playing a salmon the habit of some trout fishermen of playing their fish by stripping line instead of working the line directly from the reel usually ends in disaster. A salmon is too fast and strong a fish to be handled readily with coils of loose line in danger of tangling between the reel and the first guide. And an automatic reel is not suitable equipment for salmon fishing. Automatics do not have the necessary line and rewind capacities in proportion to their weight. When a fish runs fast and far against an automatic reel the playing pressure at the reel builds up instead of being relaxed as a good fisherman with a standard reel prefers it.

At the end of the fight the tired salmon should not be forced. He is too big to "hold" with normal tackle and must be led into landing position by skill rather than force, no matter how weary he seems to be. Salmon are famous for that last bit of reserve strength, and a final unexpected rush or leap that wins freedom for them.

If a fish is hurried in the final moment and is missed by the net, tailer, or gaff, he will be doubly hard to bring into good landing position again. Advice for the novice is to be particularly sure your fish is ready for landing before attempting it and to exercise extreme caution once you have tried and failed.

It takes long experience to know precisely where salmon will lie in any given river under a specific water condition. However, there are general rules to follow and every salmon angler should know them. The Atlantic salmon is a restless fish, torn between a desire to use and enjoy his remarkable stored-up energy, which may give rise to his periodic leaping, and the need to conserve that energy, for he will gain no more through feeding or in any other way. The long ordeal of river travel and spawning lie just ahead.

So he will choose a slow current or an eddy to lie in where a slow flow soothes his restlessness. These positions or "lies" normally stretch from the point in the pools where the inrushing current slows down enough to lose the extreme turbulence of its entry on down through the length of the pool to the tail. Salmon do not scatter themselves casually but select only certain spots that please them. And, as the flow slows down from spring to summer, some salmon will move closer to the heads of the pools. Others, resting in a pool, will change their lies or move on with a raising or lowering of as little as an inch of water level.

Salmon often lie at the edges of the current, near or upon the shallow bars, and close to shore. Those greener pastures well out in the middle of the river or near the far shores may not hold half as many salmon as the shallow waters of the shore from which you fish. Salmon tend to take a fly more readily in shallow water than in deep, another factor to keep in mind. Wading through the good salmon lies near the shore without fishing them first is a very common fault among beginning salmon anglers.

The perfect wet-fly cast for most conditions is one in which the line straightens out completely as it falls to the water at a downstream angle of approximately 45°. If the line does not straighten out all the way, the fisherman not only loses the farthest and often the best part of the fly's retrieve while waiting for the fly to come under proper tension and follow the line as the current swings it down and across the stream, but also a little fishing time is lost with this wait in each slack cast.

Such a minor loss of time before the poorly cast fly is fishing correctly may not seem important at first glance, but time during which a wet fly just sits still in the water, like time spent in false casting, is wasted as far as catching fish goes, and many extra wasted moments added together may make up just the extra time needed to turn a blank day into a successful one.

As the wet fly swings with the current it may be necessary to mend the line by a partly completed roll-cast to one side or the other. It may be wise to lift the rod tip to speed up the fly's pace or to lower the tip to slow it down as it crosses a particularly fast bit of current. These are the niceties of fishing the wet fly to be worked out *after* the perfect, straight-out cast has become a habit.

When the Portland Creek hitch is used and the wet fly is skimmed across the surface on the retrieve, the necessity of a good, straight cast is increased since, if the fly sinks far (on slack) after it lands, extra time is required for it to plane up to the surface to reach the right fishing position.

Bad casts are made occasionally by all anglers. If they land in the water you're fishing and there are or may be fish beneath them, the smart thing to do is to tighten up the line quickly and fish the bad cast through for whatever distance it affords. The worst thing to do is to snatch the cast back into the air, disturbing the surface with a fish-frightening commotion. No other angling fault so clearly denotes the bumbler as that he compounds his error in this manner because he is too lazy to use his left hand, take in the slack, and fish through to a normal pickup point. Although one always aims for perfection in every cast of the day, the bad cast, made occasionally and fished through, instead of putting a salmon off may make just the swing that causes him to rise.

As long as there is a possibility in the angler's mind that his fly is still in good salmon water, he should fish the cast through till the line straightens out below him. Extending the time on each cast during which the fly travels properly through good fishing water increases the percentage of real fishing time in proportion to "dead time" (casting, changing flies, motionless fly, etc.).

The angle of the cast to the current has a bearing, too, on the time a fly fishes in each cast. The nearer the cast is to straight downstream the less time and shorter distance per cast the fly will swim. As the angle with the downstream flow is increased, the time of the sweep is increased, but the angle grows bad beyond 45° and the fly may become (1) less attractive to the salmon and (2) so fast in its travel that it will be missed if a fish does rise.

The wet-fly rise depends upon many things—the speed of the water, the mood of the fish, and his accuracy are among them. Salmon miss flies through error. They also miss them on purpose, passing close as if to frighten them or just to practice. Regardless of the reason for the rise, a fish that has risen and failed to connect is more likely to rise again than is another fish, beside him, which has not yet been stirred to make a move toward the fly.

The common fault involved when a rise is missed is a failure to fix immediately in mind the exact length of line out at the moment of that rise in order that future casts and retrieves can duplicate the one that moved the fish. More often than not the angler has an illusion that the distance is greater than it actually is and he tends to strip more line from the reel. As a result, the following casts are longer, and on the retrieves the fly passes downstream of the path it took which first drew interest from the fish. Indications are strong that the identical cast is the best one to bring a fish back to the fly again.

Some anglers rest a fish after a missed rise. Others, who do not want to lose their ability to duplicate that cast exactly by moving away or wasting time in inaction, cast back immediately, a system which is often successful. There can be no hard-and-fast rule here, for not all salmon react the same way. Sometimes, apparently, it is wise to wait and sometimes it is not. If a decision is made to cast back immediately, experience dictates that if a few good casts do not produce the desired rise a resting of the fish is indicated before working the spot over with a variety of flies.

Strike or do not strike when a salmon rises to a wet fly? *Do not strike! Do set the hook!* Any movement of the fly before the salmon gets it into his mouth is more likely to cause him to miss it than to help in hooking him. So, until he takes the fly into his mouth and causes a distinct pressure upon the line, the angler should not cause the fly to deviate from its appointed path. Setting the hook is something that may be accomplished automatically by the drag of water on the line or the movement of the fish.

However, unless the hook is very small and sharp and the rise is deliberate and accurate, some pressure may be needed, not to start the point of the hook into the flesh, but to drive the hook in beyond the barb. Such a lifting of the rod to sink the hook is advisable with large hooks or with doubles—or when the rise is awkward and the points may embed in tough gristle or bone.

No long-fishing angler will come out with a perfect record on hooked rises, but most will admit it is better to deliver too little pressure too late than too much too soon. A wet fly is normally under enough tension and moving at a sufficient speed to embed its point into the flesh. The salmon's movement and the current's tension on the line will usually do the rest. Hooking the dry-fly rise is quite another story.

I recall one new angler who joined in the luncheon conversation at camp, sounding as if he were experienced at salmon fishing, but when he came in after his first afternoon on the river I was surprised to hear his guide report, "Sir, that man won't live long enough to catch a salmon."

"He was doing a pretty good job of casting," I remarked, having watched him from a distance.

"Oh, he casts well enough at times, sir. But he doesn't fish."

Then the guide went on to elaborate.

"When he casts a dry fly it plops down and just about as quick as it lands he hauls off again and whips it through the air half a dozen times before he lets a salmon get a peek at it again. He casts so long a line the wind won't let him put it in the same place twice. And the wind blows so much slack into his line that by the time the current brings it tight he's hauling it out for another cast. He won't listen to me, sir."

The sum of the faults of that angler caused him to fish his fly properly for only a very small fraction of his fishing time. A good angler, able to keep his fly in actual fishing position for eighty percent of his time on the river, would have had that much more chance of hooking salmon.

The same guide had often taken out men who had never before held a fly rod in their hands and, with a brief period of instruction, using a short but consistent cast and the proper dry-fly float or wet-fly swing, had them fast to a salmon in no time.

Too short a float of the dry fly is poor fishing practice. Unless you want to concentrate on one certain spot where a fish is known to lie it is wise to cast a fairly slack line and get a good long float on each cast. Only while the fly is in the water can it catch a fish. The rapid pickup of a dry fly scars the water's surface roughly and will keep fish down.

When working good water if a bad cast is made with the dry fly let the cast lie where it falls. Let it drift over the fish or the area you're working on till it's well downstream before making the pickup. A pickup right over a salmon's head is much more likely to deter him than encourage him to rise. And, strangely enough, many a seemingly hopeless cast, when fished out, will bring a salmon to the barbed steel. I've seen salmon come up to take a dry fly floating in a tangled mess of line and leader which, after all, may be no more unnatural than a grasshopper riding the water atop a tangle of straws.

Wind is a common casting problem on many salmon rivers. It makes precise casting difficult, often impossible. The wise angler will not cast a longer line than he can control well. Fishing all over the pool, wherever the wind blows a long line, is a poor way to fish. An angler's casts should be consistent, especially when he's trying to duplicate a cast which has caused a fish to show interest.

The wet-fly cast should straighten out at its completion. If it doesn't, the slack should be taken up immediately to bring tension on the fly and cause it to swim through the water. The time that elapses while a wet fly is drifting free and before it starts the intended cross-current retrieve is wasted.

To ignore a guide's knowledge is a luxury only affordable to those blessed by unusual intuition and exceptional judgment. Trying the guide's way takes only a little time. If his suggestions fail then he'll usually second the idea of trying your own. If you catch fish his way he'll be pleased and won't mind if you experiment. By and large, anglers who ignore their guides catch far fewer fish than those who listen carefully.

Aimless fishing is a frequent cause for blank days with the wet-fly angler. It is important to have a fishing pattern, a certain consistent rate of travel of the fly through the water which serves as a basis for your fishing. The erratic fisherman whose fly is retrieved at a dozen different speeds in a dozen different casts may occasionally be a lucky angler but is rarely a good one.

In fast water the retrieve can be slowed down and in slow water speeded up in order to achieve a uniform speed of fly-through-water retrieve. What speed is it? A speed that consistently catches salmon. If you're a novice, study a good angler closely. Copy his speed of fishing a fly as closely as you can and stick to it.

Later, when you've caught a lot of salmon you'll be able to tell by watching a wet-fly retrieve whether or not it is "right." If you use the Portland Creek hitch on your wet fly the speed is right when the fly skims the surface but doesn't throw spray. If it sinks, you're too slow. If it throws spray, you're too fast. The same speed of retrieve is valid for both the hitched or normally fished wet fly. Tying on the hitch around the shank just behind the eye is a good way to check your speed and pick up an occasional fish that wouldn't have responded to any other method.

More salmon, I believe, are lost by too hard a strike than for any other cause. Strikes should be fast but no harder than necessary to set the hook. When salmon get away it is almost always because they were "held" by the angler. A fish doesn't break a man's tackle, the man himself breaks it. It is designed to allow a fish to run, and an angler's failure to give slack when needed is not half so much a sign of the fish's strength as of his own inadequacy. A good rule is to free the handle of the reel whenever the pull of the fish puts a good arc in the rod. Pressure is felt much more readily in the rod than at the reel handle. The rod and not the reel handle is the sensible measure of the pressure on line and leader.

The size of a salmon often misleads anglers into thinking a big fish requires more pressure from the tackle than a small one. Nothing could be further from the truth. The leader will snap just as readily when its breaking point is reached against a five-pound salmon as against a thirty-pounder. A big fish may require a little more time but no other change in the playing method.

Yet big fish are often lost when they're almost exhausted because the angler tries to handle them in the manner of lesser fish. He thinks in terms of turning a fish in a certain arc or stopping it at a certain distance rather than of putting just so much bend in his rod and no more, just so much tension on his line with reel drag or fingers and no more.

When a fly loses its grip on a fish's jaw, that is unfortunate, but in most cases unavoidable. If the leader is a reasonable one, matched to the fly, it should break before the hook pulls out. When an angler breaks his tackle that's an angling error and should be so marked on his scoreboard. In that case the angler's skill wasn't up to the combination of tackle or circumstances. Perhaps he didn't look for knots in his leader or otherwise check his tackle. Perhaps his tackle was too fine for his reflexes. Perhaps the water and the fish were too rough for him.

Mistakes are common in salmon fishing, but perhaps the greatest mistake of all is to lose heart. There is no salmon, anywhere in a stream, but he may take a fly if it is suitable and properly presented. Wherever there are salmon there is opportunity . . . and wonderful sport.

CHAPTER 3

Where Salmon Lie and Why

THE MIND OF THE FISH rather than his stomach must be your target when fishing for Atlantic salmon. Salmon return from the sea with a great store of energy which usually carries them through about half a year of starvation. Then they turn oceanward again, for the Atlantic salmon do not die after spawning as the Pacific salmon do.

Mature salmon, averaging about ten pounds, return to the rivers they left as fingerlings. These rivers must serve not as restaurants for the mature fish but only as nurseries for their young. The food supply required to nourish a million young would be not even a drop in the bucket for the returning silvery horde. So in nature's complex scheme of things the returning salmon's hunger dies. He wants little to eat, yet still will rise to something resembling the food of his fingerling days.

It is a conditioned reflex, a strange whim, or a deep-seated annoyance that pulls the salmon to the fly. A hungry fish makes a distinct effort to seek out food, but the salmon, content with his stored-up energy, will not go a-searching. He simply lies and waits.

The fly that takes him must come in such a way that it stirs him inwardly, forcing action on his part. The proper positioning of the fly therefore takes on a special importance which the average fisherman finds hard to accept. Feeding fish cruise the waters looking for their food or seek out locations where the food will come to them. Salmon neither cruise nor hunt for food and, except when running the river, choose their positions purely on the basis of comfort and safety.

Strange by nature, salmon are never stranger than when seen from the eyes of a dyed-in-the-wool trout fisherman. Yet the angler who has concentrated on trout finds himself very much at home when he first turns to a salmon river. Some of these rivers are no larger than the waters he normally fishes, and even the largest is little more than overgrown trout water.

Also, the general methods of fishing for both species are quite similar (practically all Atlantic salmon waters on this continent are limited to fly fishing only), and modern salmon tackle, which varies little from trout tackle, even in flies, is often identical. One of the most important differences is where the fish choose to lie.

There is a classic story of the old-time salmon fisherman who came along and rested on a high bank to watch a novice casting diligently over a salmon pool. Time after time the beginner worked the pool from one end to the other without a rise from a salmon. After his fifth trip down through the pool, he gave it up and puffed his way up the sandy bank to sit down on its crest of sod beside the watcher.

"You try it now," he said. "I'll be darned if I can catch them."

"Of course you can't," the old-timer replied, "for there aren't any there."

From that vantage point every rock, every patch of sand on the bottom of the entire pool lay exposed before their eyes. The veteran angler quietly pointed out that not a single salmon rested in it anywhere and continued, "You were enjoying it so much I didn't want to spoil your sport."

Unfortunately there aren't high banks beside every pool or run where salmon lie and you must make your casts by what you can see of the water from eye level. To know where the salmon are, you must know why they lie where they do, and under what conditions they will change their lies. The answers are important.

Salmon settle into certain places and may stay there, day after day, week after week. Although they may leave the spot momentarily to leap or make a sudden restless surge, they will return to it consistently. Only a change in the level of the river or the urgency of renewed travel upstream makes them change their lie or move on to another pool.

While trout fishing is a game of fairly fast action, salmon fishing is more like a stalk for big game. Many a salmon angler is content to average a single rise a day from a salmon; few trout fishermen would consider so little activity even passable sport. By its very nature salmon fishing must produce far fewer fish for a given stretch of river than trout fishing could. Five miles of river may contain only one salmon pool and its entire quota of salmon may range from zero to a maximum of thirty, while the number of legal-size trout in a similar stretch of trout water may run into the thousands. Although salmon will pause at only a few special points, the nonmigratory trout would be scattered throughout the entire stretch.

Salmon fishing is concentrated fishing. It normally takes a lot of casts to bring a salmon to the fly, and as an old watcher-from-bridges, I believe that some salmon will rise to a fly only if it passes a given spot at a given speed in a given direction. From a good lookout it is possible to watch salmon carefully as another man's fly is being presented to them. Usually the casts vary no matter how much an angler tries to make them identical. At a certain variation the salmon will show an interest in the fly and rise toward it.

The particular positioning of the fly that draws his interest may come on the first cast, again on the twentieth and then on the fiftieth. It may take a dozen such properly positioned casts to actually get him to take the fly into his mouth. Only concentrated fishing and consistent casting can accomplish such a salmon's capture.

This is a far cry from the trout fisherman's usual viewpoint that if the fly is right and well presented within reasonable reach of the fish, he will come and get it. The extra thickness of the leader or its approach ahead of the fly may cause a trout (or a salmon) to refuse it, but the matter of an inch or two one way or another simply doesn't bother trout as it does the nonfeeding salmon.

Because the surroundings, tackle, and general methods are so similar, the trout fisherman starting with salmon often falls into the error of thinking he should fish the water as if for trout, which is just about the poorest way to do it. The frustration that may follow can drive these normally competent anglers to the wildest extremes. I have seen rods broken in anger, trips canceled midway in a sudden fury, and long-time friendships rent asunder because a beginner at fly fishing catches more salmon than one of these fly-rod veterans.

I was once caught in the trout-thinking-for-salmon trap myself. The river was lower than it had been in many years. My fishing companion, who had been lagging behind my catches in his usual manner, for he fished nowhere near as diligently as I, suddenly began catching two salmon to my one. A few days of this really put a crimp in my ego and drove me to fishing harder and longer than ever. At the end of the week I was still stymied and puzzled.

The water was hard-fished and each pool was worked at least once daily and sometimes in both the morning and afternoon. The secret of his catches was that he'd discovered salmon lying at the very lip of several pools where the water at the point of spilling over was less than a foot deep. Sizable trout would never have lain in such a spot and it was ridiculous to the trout-fishing mind that these large salmon would choose to lie in the very shallowest water of the pool. One of the axioms of salmon fishing applied there: The shallower the water in which salmon lie, the more likely they are to rise; the deeper it is, the more difficult to bring them up to the fly.

My companion had made a practice of starting his casting from a long way back from the water, just barely reaching the narrow outlet of the pools without frightening the fish which had only settled into these spots after a long period of rest. When a salmon took the fly he'd rush up to the water's edge to play him. The rest of us were getting too close to the pools before starting to fish, thus scaring the salmon back into the depths where they were much harder to catch.

Salmon are a fish of the open water, accustomed to the sea and its infinite space, where only their speed and agility will save them from predators. Having learned to rely on speed and elusiveness in the sea they bring this quality back to the rivers with them. A trout may dart in under an overhanging bank or seek out the labyrinth of stems a sunken brush pile offers in an effort to hide from sight. But no salmon wants to get into such a position where he can be cornered without a chance to use his superior speed. Though it is often possible to approach a resting salmon from the shallow side of his lie and even touch him with the tip of a rod, to approach him from the deeper water, closing off his avenue of retreat, is next to impossible.

Salmon like to rest just about where the swift flow into a pool first moderates. Having found such a berth they will stay there. How long they remain depends upon how much the rising or falling of the river affects their chosen spot, a spot generally used by one salmon or another, year after year.

The very situation that creates a good salmon lie is subject to change. These fish seek out eddies where they can rest and yet have the slight flow or turbulence to soothe their restlessness while they wait. Where the normal pool level provides such a spot, an additional inch or two of water may increase the flow enough to make holding that position too serious a drain on their unrenewable supply of strength—or it may even reverse the flow completely in a certain eddy.

As the water rises and the flow entering a pool grows stronger, the fish usually drop back toward the center of the pool, following a certain preferred water speed. As the stream level falls again, they will shift back toward their original positions. And if it drops even lower than before, they will keep on edging up closer to the point where the diminishing flow pours into the pool.

Another preferred lie is near the tails of the pools where the still-smooth water readies for the rapids, frequently in shallow water and very close to the bank or near prominent boulders. There, with their tails waving slowly at the quickening pulse of the run behind them, they are headed upstream into the safety of wide and open waters. As the river rises, the salmon tend to move farther up into the pool, but if the water drops to an even lower level, they move back closer and closer to the lip over which the pool empties.

Where a river flows through a lake there are usually two pools for salmon, one at the inlet and another at the outlet. Salmon will nose into the flow as it comes in and tail back into the flow going out of such a lake. When the waters warm up and the rivers run low during midsummer, these "running in" and "running out" pools lure many salmon at the expense of the normal pools scattered throughout the river's flow. From these pools the fish can move out into the lake for safety or cooler water when hard-pressed, but they'll still have the tendency to return to their accustomed lies from sunset to sunrise. The added safety that salmon find in lakes during low-water periods, when they are most vulnerable to their enemies, is reflected in the better fishing usually offered by rivers having lakes in their watersheds.

When the rivers rise well above normal, there is a satisfactory depth and space for salmon through a greater part of their length and the fish become much more difficult to locate. With such a wide choice of resting places to cover, it takes a lot more fishing to reach a given number of salmon with a fly, and because there is little certainty about which of the hundreds of available places they will rest in, the element of luck is at its peak.

In real floods the usual pools are filled with rushing water through which salmon might travel if the urge were upon them to run the river, but which no longer affords them any places to rest. In seeking a good place to lie they may follow a river right out of its banks. I recall once hooking a salmon while I was sitting on a pole fence and fishing a flooded pasture completely out of the regular riverbed upon which I had turned my back.

That taught me as did no other single incident that a salmon pool is a little patch of water of certain qualifications which, though it is usually well established during normal flow, may be found in any spot in the river if conditions vary widely enough. My salmon from the field had enough water to cover him amply in a gentle flow situated in a broad reach of water where he felt assured of safety.

Each salmon lie is usually dependent upon a rock, a sunken log, a slight depression or drop-off which creates a break in the steady flow. In normal water the pattern of these spots is so consistent that a good guide can take a look at the water level of a familiar pool and know exactly the spots that should hold salmon.

The guide is the key to the average angler's salmon-fishing success. He lives on his river, seeing it season after season in both high water and low. He has searched it not only with flies but with his sharp vision which picks up the fish where the average fisherman would fail to see them. Chances are he has climbed trees that overlook the pools to view them under the bright sunlight so that he may mark down in his memory every fish that he sees.

Another difficulty plaguing the accustomed-to-trout fisherman who starts fishing for salmon may be a poor guide–sportsman relationship. The beginner who relies completely on his guide normally has moderate success. The experienced trout angler may start with enough humility, but as soon as he begins to feel at home he may also get the notion that he is learning salmon fishing much more rapidly than he really is.

He does not have to be taught how to cast or to work his wet fly or to let his fly drift free or to raise his rod when a fish takes the dry fly down. Because he is so far ahead on these things, all stemming from his trout-fishing background, he erroneously assumes he's equally far ahead on choosing the water to fish. If he begins to show that he's learned the right spots to fish and needs no help from his guide, that worthy man will withdraw a little, letting him place his casts without advice, while saying to himself, "All right, mister! If you are so sure of yourself go right ahead on your own. I'll watch."

One of the maddest men I have ever seen came to our salmon camp with a coast-to-coast background of trout fishing. He conversed authoritatively and frequently on the subject without delay. His wife, who occasionally accompanied him on his fishing trips, but usually spent little time at fishing, was with him. She was a quiet woman but with a twinkle in her eyes. Her simple comment that first night was that she didn't know much about any kind of fishing but liked to be out on the water, and hoped someday she'd learn how to catch fish.

She drew one of the camp's best guides, a quiet man named Tom who had grown up on the river. Tom was polite but firm about salmon fishing. He would tell his charges how and where to cast and how to make the retrieve. If the cast was good and the retrieve well fished, he'd say so or nod in approval.

If not, he might say, "I believe the wind took your fly a little too far upstream that cast, ma'am, and the fly never tightened up and fished right."

Like most guides, Tom was a little touchy. If he felt his advice was being ignored, he would soon stop giving it and resort simply to answering questions from his fisherman. As it turned out, he and this lady got on famously. Whenever Tom told her she had made a poor cast, she only laughed and made a face and tried again. Tom had it all worked out and when she hooked a salmon, he talked her into playing it just as if it were a half-pound trout. She played it lightly and longer than usual, but she landed her first one and killed three of the five fish she hooked in her first three days.

Her husband's guide, Ned, was much like Tom, but a little younger and with more temper in his makeup. When they came in after the first morning's fishing, I could see that Ned was nettled. At the guides' lunch table he muttered into his soup a little and passed a remark or two about "fellas that know all about fishing before they start."

One of the other guides said, "Well, anyway, your man seems to be able to cast well."

"Casting don't catch salmon unless the fly comes in right," was Ned's rejoinder. "Two salmon followed his fly and he never even saw them and wouldn't believe me. Said he could see if a fish followed his fly. He wouldn't stay in one spot long enough to work a fish up to the point where it would take."

At the end of the third day he'd hooked one fish and lost it, so his score was zero to his wife's three. He insisted that they exchange guides, which is almost always a mistake. So next morning he and Tom went off down the river, and his wife went out with Ned.

About midmorning I stopped by to see how Tom was getting on with his new charge. While I watched, a salmon rose to his fly but failed to touch it. He stripped off a few feet of line and cast again. I don't know why, but that's a common fault with fishermen new to salmon. They think the fish must be farther away than he is, or that he's going to retreat a little. It's obvious that if there are three extra feet of line out through the guides, the fly won't make the same swing, and the chances of catching a fish that has risen to a shorter cast are mighty slim.

Tom sang out to him, "I think your cast is a little too long for that fish, sir." And when the angler failed to change his length of cast, Tom looked at me and shrugged.

I sat there and watched him cast for half an hour. He could cast beautifully but he never did shorten his line enough. Finally I gave up and moved on. At lunchtime Tom told Ned where that salmon was. That afternoon Ned took the woman to the same spot and, sure enough, when they came back that evening, they had the salmon and it was a good one.

I caught snatches of the couple's fishing progress over the lunch table during the next few days. He wasn't having much luck. He kept fishing too far beyond the fish he rose or crowded out onto the fish himself. Salmon don't always lie in the deepest water as big trout tend to. They are likely to hug the fairly shallow bars where the current is gentle.

Instead of staying close to the shore and fishing the nearby water, this man was always wading out and fishing far out into the stream where there was lots of swift and deep water but darn few salmon, if any. First thing you know, he'd be standing in water over his knees right where the salmon had been lying and, of course, the fish had taken fright and moved away. Even if he did put a fly on them in whatever spot they settled, it would have been a miracle if one took it, according to Tom.

The thing was getting under this fellow's skin so much, and he was so ill-tempered, that his wife just quit fishing altogether and went picking berries, or had Ned take her out to the old Indian campsite near the sea where they could search for arrowheads, lest she catch more fish and make the situation worse.

Miracle or not, a very big salmon finally took the disgruntled angler's fly and held it long enough to be captured on their seventh and final day of fishing. If it hadn't been for that, there might have been one more divorce on the books. The point is that a poor fisherman can catch salmon if he fishes only where the salmon are, and the best darn caster in the world can't catch them where they aren't.

CHAPTER 4

Why Salmon Strike

THREE ATLANTIC-SALMON fishermen were on their way back to camp after a fruitless morning. Their path led them across a bridge over the river, and they paused to look for fish in the pool below. Several large salmon were resting at the customary spot, lazily fanning their fins and tails. The men watched the solid-gray shapes for a while, then one of them flipped his cigarette butt out over the railing. It made a high arc and hit the water just ahead of the cluster of fish. A salmon swirled up from the bottom and took the bit of paper and tobacco into its mouth.

"Here we've fished for hours with every fly in the book," the cigarette tosser mourned, "and what do they really want? Cigarettes. Nuts!"

The same thing might happen with trout, bass, or many other game fish, but the basis of the rise would be quite different. Another fish would think in terms of food and feeding, but the Atlantic salmon, returning to its river on a spawning run, needs no food and seeks none. This is a fact that many anglers, new to this fishing, find hard to accept.

These anglers think that because humans have to eat frequently, all animals and fish do, too. The salmon is an exception, and for a very good reason—the salmon rivers are nurseries for the young. All of the limited food of the northern rivers is needed for the fingerling salmon, or parr, which stay in fresh water an average of three to four years. They grow to about five inches before they're ready to go to sea.

Once they reach saltwater and the abundance of food in the northern seas, they feed ravenously and grow prodigiously. In one year they expand from five to twenty-five inches and from a few ounces to five pounds. If they stay at sea for two full years before returning to the river to spawn, salmon reach an average weight of more than ten pounds, and if they stay for three years they may

27

weigh as much as thirty pounds when they first return to their rivers.

Consider this returning horde of fish that have fed in the sea to such advantage. Is there anything in fresh water to approximate the vast shoals of shrimp or capelin or herring they're used to eating? The salmon rivers have little to offer except a few insects and a fair quantity of salmon parr or trout.

If the salmon tried to maintain their strength by feeding, they'd not only clean up almost all the immature salmon but would eat all the small living things on which the parr feed, and having cleaned the rocks bare of moss, would still be almost as hungry as when they started.

One of the most diligent fishermen I ever met was a novice at salmon. The water was high and the run just in from the sea. He hooked a number of parr on his first morning and as he brought one of them skittering in for releasing, a good-sized fish made a pass at it. It was probably a big sea-run trout that had swirled up out of hunger, but the angler was convinced it was a salmon, and his guide, a bit diffident about correcting him, let him think so. He thought these salmon wanted food and, though it was illegal to fish with bait, he bribed his guide with rum to let him do so.

He ran the gamut of all the baits he could lay hands on, including worms, salmon eggs, pork rind, bacon, beef, and lamb. These were usually in big chunks, on the theory of "big bait, big fish." He did hook a fish briefly, but it held to the deep water and never jumped at all. It showed a flash of silver just once before it got off. Sea-run trout are as silvery as salmon and one could well have been in the river that early, but I'm sure this man never wavered in his belief that he had hooked a salmon.

He fished with flies when other anglers were around, but as soon as he and his guide were alone, one or another of his assorted baits went splashing out to where he'd seen salmon leaping. Twenty-two good fish were caught during the ten days he was on the river, but not one of them fell to him. I've often wondered whether he gave up salmon fishing in disgust before he learned that hunger is not the key to a salmon's rise.

A salmon can store up enough energy to climb rivers and go through an arduous spawning period without feeding for an incredibly long time. Once an angler accepts that fact he can begin to understand salmon fishing. If he keeps thinking that food interests them he will remain bewildered by this swift and beautiful fish.

The great majority of Atlantic salmon enter their rivers soon after the snow water runs off. This is several months before the spawning period, which is usually in November, and during these months they will be starving instead of gorging themselves in the sea. The rivers are safest for them to travel in the late spring or early summer before the low water sets in. The spawn, which is just starting to ripen as they enter the streams, will grow while they rest in comparative safety.

Fish entering the river late will have developed their spawn to an equal extent, and some of the late-running fish will be almost ready for spawning when they enter. Such fish carry a heavy load of spawn and do not have the full-muscled energy, speed, and power of the fish that arrived earlier.

If all salmon entered the rivers just prior to spawning there would be a very brief fishing season for a less energetic fish. "Spring" salmon, or "slinks," are the fish which have spawned in the previous season and are returning to the sea again, gaunt and hungry, after spending the winter in the rivers. Their strength is at a minimum and their hunger at its peak. They are the easiest salmon to catch and the poorest of all for sport.

The argument about the relative merits of fresh-run salmon versus starved-out slinks often runs hot and heavy. I know of an angler who had several seasons of spring-salmon fishing behind him and who caught his first summer salmon during a drought in a short, deep pool which the salmon could not leave. Since it had nowhere to run, the fish was landed—after a longish time—without having taken any of the backing off the reel. At lunch the fisherman remarked that this fish had not been as difficult to take as the spawned-out fish returning to sea.

He might well have clung to that erroneous belief if it hadn't been for a three-day rain that raised the river to flood stage. On his last morning he hooked another bright salmon in the same pool, which by then had become a raging torrent. Not only did the fish get into his backing, but when he came to the end of it he snapped it neatly and departed with everything except the rod and reel. Then the angler realized that in flood water even a tired and hungry fish may put up a scrap, but that a bright salmon in such water will make a slink look like a piker.

The salmon spread out through the rivers, which spill over ledges in waterfalls, tumble about in their rocky beds, twist slowly through alder-fringed meadows, or gather into long, deep pools. To the unpracticed eye there may be no pattern to the resting places which the salmon choose. No one knows for sure why salmon rise to the feathered steel, but I believe there are two main reasons.

The first reason is that he has a conditioned reflex developed during his parr days of stream feeding. Throughout that time, he feeds voraciously on any small fish or insects that come within his reach. He reacts immediately to take any small and moving object. A flying insect, just touching the water nearby, is snapped into his mouth automatically. Later, when the mature fish, back from the sea to his familiar stream, sees an artificial fly, he rises instinctively.

There is considerable basis for this theory, because grilse, the salmon which have been to sea for only about a year, rise much more freely than those that have been there two or three years. This ratio of interest in flies is universal and found in all rivers and all sections of the salmon-fishing area. The parr that prepare fastest for their sea migration are most certain to remain at sea for a longer period and become large fish.

The parr that require the longest freshwater period before going to sea are almost certain to come back after a single year as grilse. The grilse have a much longer freshwater feeding period and a shorter sea period, and so they haven't forgotten their freshwater habits. That seems to explain their greater readiness to take a fly.

After having been convinced that a salmon does not feed in freshwater, the fisherman may discover one rising to an occasional Mayfly or flinging himself wildly into the air for a small white butterfly.

One angler came to me and said, "You say they don't feed, but the big one I've been trying to catch took three bugs off the water."

"You've been fishing for that salmon for a week all day and every day," I said. "Do you think he can live on those three little bugs?" He shook his head and I continued, "Of course he'll take a fly or two in his mouth but he probably spits them out. Even if he doesn't, it would be like a man's rationing himself to three blueberries a day."

Some anglers have said that salmon take these occasional insects and squeeze the juice from them, ejecting the crushed carcasses. The theory was that the bug juice contained vitamins which are essential to their survival and that this was a form of feeding. Nothing is ever found in a salmon's stomach after he gets into freshwater on his spawning run, so some such theory had to be developed if his feeding was to be made at all reasonable.

However, its plausibility fails. If Atlantic salmon needed vitamins, it's obvious that the larger ones would need more vitamins than smaller ones. Thus, a thirty-pounder would need six times as many bugs and be six times as ready to rise to a fly as a five-pound grilse. Anyone who has fished for salmon knows that the exact opposite is true.

Now we come to the second major reason for a salmon's rise to the fly. It is, I believe, his restlessness. He is a nervous fish, full of pent-up power, like a prizefighter on the eve of a championship match or a small boy waking from a nap, full of energy and deviltry. But because he has only so much strength, he must lie where little or no energy is required to hold his position. This inactivity bores him.

Occasionally he feels the need to reassure himself of his speed and strength. So he leaps or makes a sudden swift surge—or rises to a fly, a maneuver that calls for a nice turn of speed and timing. He takes a fly for much the same reason that a boy goes out of his way to kick a tin can.

Salmon fishing is not easy to learn because the average angler catches so few fish. The fishing varies with the river, and each river varies with its changes of water level and temperature. Two weeks of fishing at high water teach little about low-water fishing. Two weeks of normal late-spring fishing teach almost nothing about fishing in either very high or very low water. For each time, the salmon's choice of places to lie and their reactions to a certain fly will be different than at the other time.

Few anglers have had the good fortune to fish for one full season after another on a wide variety of rivers. Few guides, who are on their rivers all season long, year after year, are able to switch from river to river and thus learn the special preferences which change with the salmon areas. For some reason, perhaps the insects in them, different areas call for different sizes or types of flies. Newfoundland salmon, for example, are much more receptive to dry flies than are the fish on the mainland.

The first American sportsman to fish Portland Creek on Newfoundland's west coast arrived by boat many years ago with Johnny Lucas, a guide he'd brought with him from the southern part of the province. Johnny was completely lost on this strange river, and although the local guides remember that he kept a remarkably clean campsite and was an excellent cook, they still laugh about the places he took his sportsman for salmon.

After many days without even a rise, a local guide showed him how to fish these unusual waters. They are devoid of normal salmon pools; a hitched and skimming wet fly will take five fish for one against wet flies fished in the normal manner, and the salmon lie in front of rather than behind the rocks.

Dry flies are less effective on brownish, peat-stained streams than on very clear waters. Some brownish waters stay dark through all water levels, but others lighten up when the rivers are low. This may be the reason why dry-fly fishing is so much better in low water on these streams. It is generally true that dry flies are more effective when the water is low and the fish are concentrated in predictable locations.

The free-drifting dry fly covers only a small fraction of the water that a wet fly covers in its normal swing. When the water is high and the fish widely scattered, the dry-fly fisherman is at a serious disadvantage. But whenever individual fish can be located exactly, the dry fly should be fairly effective, regardless of the water level.

Salmon lying in pools at the foot of a falls are poor risers. My guess is that, with the falls just ahead of them, these fish are pre-occupied with the problem of getting up over them and are less likely to be restless and nervous than the fish in other pools. Salmon are whimsical fish, and there are no generally accepted rules of conduct that they don't break.

Before one of his salmon-fishing trips, my friend Okey Butcher had spent a lot of time sticking feathers and fur onto plastic-bodied hooks. One special creation was made up of a No. 4 hook and a big wad of natural polar-bear hair. When a considerable number of the preferred patterns had been cast without effect over some salmon that were visible in a clear pool, Okey pulled out this monstrosity and tied it to his leader.

"If you can catch a salmon on that feather duster," said my other companion, "I'll eat——"

At that precise instant a fifteen-pounder came up and sucked the thing down, was hooked, played, and landed.

There is, nevertheless, a very definite preference as to fly coloration, fly size, and the method of fishing them. Anglers who consistently fish the accepted method for any area and water condition make the best catches, season after season. But the uncertainty is always there. In a single day I have taken fish on flies as widely divergent as a No. 16 spider, a No. 6 Jock Scott, and a No. 1 White Wulff.

Almost any method of working a fly of approximately the right size can be made to take salmon. Some anglers, fishing conventional wet flies in the normal swing, make a practice of twitching their rods constantly in order to make the fly's progress through the water uneven. A greater number let the fly swing with the current without any action whatever. Both methods take fish in about equal proportions.

The greased-line method of drifting a wet fly with the least possible motion, especially effective in low water, was invented by an Englishman who took thousands of salmon that way. But there was another Englishman who believed in a swift retrieve, and the lower the water the more swiftly he retrieved. And he was equally successful.

One angler I knew took a great many salmon by dragging a dry fly across the surface in the same paths the normal wet fly takes. However, my own conviction is that I can take more fish on the dry fly when fished in the conventional manner without any drag. Occasionally I put drag on a dry fly after a fish has consistently refused the fly without it.

Sometimes I pull dry flies under and fish them wet with ultimate success. I caught a good many salmon on one river by retrieving a small spider wet in short jerks which made it travel through the water like a jellyfish, contracting as it moved forward and expanding to full diameter at each pause.

The riffling hitch, developed at Portland Creek, skims a wet fly along the surface like a miniature aquaplane. It is more effective on some waters than the conventionally fished wet fly; on others, both methods will take fish in about the same ratio.

The Newfoundland guides shun red in a fly and think a Durham Ranger, a good fly on the mainland, would poison any salmon waters they put it into. And the sight of a 3/0 Lady Amherst, which will take salmon well in Quebec, would nauseate these guides. They use nothing larger than a No. 4.

One of the oddest situations illustrating the same unpredictability of Atlantic salmon occurred at our camp some years ago. It centered around a gentleman from Texas whose entire fishing experience had been at Wedgeport, Nova Scotia, with big tuna.

He only half believed these tales about the salmon's poor appetite.

One lunchtime he and his guide boiled the kettle at a falls where salmon nosed up close under an overhanging ledge. Struck with a sudden notion to try "chumming" on them, as with tuna, he crept out with a supply of bread crumbs and gently dropped them over, one at a time. Eventually a salmon rolled up to have a look at one.

The Texan then got his rod and crept back to his vantage point, with twelve inches of leader extending from the tip and a bread crumb on his fly. Like an Indian stalking a deer, he eased the rod tip out over the water and lowered the crumbed fly to the water.

Darned if a salmon didn't take it. And then the fish dashed off with the bread, fly, and half the leader when the reel jammed. I know this happened, and it remains a favorite story of the guides. I can no more explain it than any other salmon rise. But, like all devoted salmon anglers, I'm glad the urge to rise is there, no matter how ridiculous it sometimes makes us look.

Men have fished for days to catch a single large salmon, sometimes successfully, more often not. Salmon, especially the big ones, rise rarely. Yet every true salmon angler knows that any salmon may rise at any cast. On this slim hope he is willing to spend day after day on a given fish. Many a salmon will rise up under a fly to inspect it closely time and time again without taking it. To capture such a fish becomes a challenge, a personal duel between the angler and that particular salmon. Barring a serious change of conditions, the fish will remain in his lie for days and the fisherman may cast to him till his arm aches and his head swims. There is no other fishing quite like it.

CHAPTER 5

How to Use Dry Flies
for Atlantic Salmon

NOT TOO MANY YEARS AGO I could go to almost any salmon river with the foreknowledge that no one else would be using a dry fly. The ability to fish either wet or dry gave me a distinct advantage over other anglers, for salmon that had resisted everything in a long list of wet flies often would rise to a floater on the first few casts. Confirmed wet-fly men, seeing the pioneer dry-fly anglers taking fish under conditions where all wet flies were scorned, soon took up the floating fly as a second method.

The results were not always as fruitful as they had hoped because dry-fly fishing for salmon also has its periods of failure. Not only are there limitations in the times when floaters are effective but certain types of water have special problems, and success varies both with the individual river and the inclinations of the fish. The generally accepted rule is that Atlantic salmon will not take dry flies when they first enter the rivers on their spawning migrations. This is largely true.

Salmon returning from their sea migrations have their memory of surface feeding dimmed by the saltwater period of their lives, a year or more during which they have taken no food from the surface. While they are in saltwater, all the food they take swims through the water in the manner of a wet fly and none of it floats on the surface like a dry. This may account for some of the salmon's preference for a sunken fly and his reluctance to take a floater when he first comes back to the streams.

Later on, when he's been in freshwater again for a while, the association of his stream location with his early habits as a parr feeding on floating insects reactivates his youthful urge for surface feeding. This is an intangible factor and one that cannot be calculated, but for anyone who knows the habits of salmon and their reactions to similar minor inner urges, it is a logical one.

When the water is rough and high and the fish are deep, a good presentation cannot be made with the dry fly, and these are the conditions normally prevailing at the outset of the season. But despite the general rule and the reasons for it, fresh-run fish can be taken on the floating fly. I have taken them as early as June 1 in Newfoundland with sea lice still clinging to their sides.

I have a simple rule about when to start dry-fly fishing. I fish wet in the early season until I see a fish "porpoise" or make a surface roll that brings the upper half of his body out into the air. This gives me his exact location in the pool and tells me that he's surface-minded. A porpoising fish in the early days of the salmon run is duck soup for a properly presented dry fly. Later on, when the salmon porpoise much more freely, these surface rolls will not have the same significance.

Also, in the early season if I can determine the exact position of a fish as indicated by a jump or a swirl at my fly, I may present a dry fly to him when the wet one fails. The biggest handicap to dry-fly fishing in the early high water is the difficulty of presenting the fly to enough fish.

Dry-fly fishing is most successful when the water is low and the fish are concentrated in groups in the pools. There are two factors involved in this fishing and they work out this way. A wet fly, when cast, covers, let us assume, the fishable width of a small river. The fly lands on the far side and swings all the way across the flow to the near side, covering at least forty feet.

During the same period of time a dry fly cast out on the same water would drift no more than ten feet downstream from the point at which it landed. The wet fly, as a consequence, reaches four times as many fish as the floating feathers. When the salmon are scattered over a wide area, the advantage is always with the wet fly. Later on in the summer when the water drops and the salmon tend to congregate in small groups in known locations, the dry fly in its short float will be presented to as many fish as a wet fly on its full swing because most of the wet fly's travel is through barren water.

The speed of the water is the second factor. A wet fly moves faster than a dry fly in order to cover more water, but it occupies an important place in the salmon's vision for a longer period of time. The wet fly moves in contrast with the objects the water carries instead of at their identical speed and is, therefore, more conspicuous. The wet fly is first glimpsed out of one eye as it approaches, then just ahead as it passes, and, finally, going away on the other side. The dry fly, difficult to distinguish amid the ripples, debris, and surface foam that convey it, approaches head on and disappears into the salmon's area of blindness behind him.

When the waters slow down and lose much of their surface motion, the dry fly becomes more conspicuous and increasingly effective. This speed of water is in direct ratio to the speed of the dry fly relative to the stream bed.

The speed of the current is only one of two factors with the wet fly. It is also affected by the pull of the angler through his tackle. The angler's pull is normally used to impart speed as well as direction, but the tackle can be used to slow down the movement of a wet fly in regard to the stream bed. Even if the tackle is not used to slow the wet fly, it still helps maintain it in a better position for the salmon to see and rise to it than the dry fly for which, in very swift water, a salmon must turn and make a downstream rush.

The clearer the water, the better for dry-fly fishing. It has been my observation that the rivers with peat-stained waters are not as good for dry-fly fishing as those that are clear. In the early season almost all the northern rivers run dark brown with peat stain coming from the runoff of bog water in their drainages. Some of them carry the brown stain all through the season, but the stain is less noticeable once the main flow comes from springs instead of runoff. It is at this point that most streams reach their peak for dry-fly effectiveness. Anglers who have had successful dry-fly fishing on a clear river may suffer a rude shock when they try the same flies on a dark one.

The salmon's interest in a wet fly seems to taper off as the season progresses. It may have sudden revivals after heavy rains, but wet-fly effectiveness generally shows a persistent downward trend as time passes. The interest in the dry fly, in contrast, seems to build up consistently until the end of the season; and for this I have no explanation beyond those already given.

It is pertinent to add here, however, that though the interest continues to build up, the chance of hooking a fish on a dry fly reaches a peak some weeks after the wet-fly peak and then drops off because of the particular penchant of the Atlantic salmon for making "false rises," a subject that will be discussed in detail later on.

Salmon, I believe, rise to a dry fly out of a restless impulse coupled with their memories of the thousands of floating insects they devoured while spending the greater part of their lifetime in the rivers as parr. They rise out of a memory of all surface flies and very rarely in the manner of a trout that is feeding on a particular hatch of insects and seeking an exact imitation.

The effective salmon dry fly should look like an insect, but it need not look like any special insect; it should have the quality of looking like *all* bugs instead of just one. Consequently, few dry flies are needed for fishing for Atlantic salmon. I like to have a variety of shapes and sizes, but I do not consider minor variations in silhouette and coloring important.

A good selection might include some bivisibles (Nos. 6 to 10), some surface stone flies No. 4 (my secret weapon), some White Wulffs and Gray Wulffs (Nos. 4 to 10), a few Black Gnats (Nos. 10 to 14) and some spiders (Nos. 14 to 16). To this basic groundwork may be added any patterns that lend confidence to the angler and distinction to his fly boxes. A high-floating durable fly has a big advantage in salmon fishing, as it requires less attention and can be fished cast after cast, an asset when the pressure is on and a time-out period to re-oil might upset a campaign of consistent casting to which a certain salmon should succumb.

When a trout fisherman refers to a "rise" he means that a trout came up and took, or tried to take, his fly. When a salmon angler uses the same term he means that a salmon moved up to *look* at his fly, perhaps taking it but more likely turning away short. A trout, moving up close to take a fly, rarely turns away short of taking it. With a salmon, a fish that may never have seen an artificial fly before and is much less schooled in the detection of insect "fakes" than the trout, the reverse is true.

More salmon are hooked after one or two false passes at the fly than are caught on their first pass at it. Time after time a salmon may rise to the dry fly falsely before taking it, and in many instances he will rise and rise without ever opening his jaws.

As a result of many hours of stalking, I've had a close-up view of hundreds of salmon rising to my own and my friends' dry flies. At a distance of six to ten feet I have watched them ease up gracefully from the bottom, with their mouths locked tight, to poke a dry fly up into the air on the tips of their noses. I have seen them put their chins up over the fly and sink it with the same maddening deliberation. They will sometimes swamp a floating fly with their tails; more often than not they will simply come up below it, materializing as if out of nowhere, put their noses up to within an inch of it, and then turn downward again, leaving the fly bouncing madly on the surface of the water.

The false rises made by salmon have thrown a good many dry-fly anglers off the track. Salmon rises are rare and on many rivers two or three a day is considered good. Consider the novice angler's situation. He has heard conflicting reports on the timing of his strike. One acquaintance has told him he must strike quickly, as soon as he sees the rise. Another has insisted that a strike is not necessary and that the fish will take the fly down with him and hook himself. Still another may insist that a salmon's rise is like that of a deliberate old brown trout and the strike should come as soon as the fish has the fly in his mouth and starts downward.

When the novice gets his first rise he strikes quickly . . . and misses. Next time he tries striking a little later . . . and still he misses. Finally, he lets the salmon take the fly down with him and feels a gentle tug but fails to hook the fish. In each case he has done the wrong thing and is still no closer to the solution of when to strike.

His first two rises were false and he should not have struck at all, but in the excitement of seeing so large a fish boil up under his fly, he was unprepared to make a thorough check on that little matter of making sure the fish actually took the fly. His third rise was a good one, and because he failed to strike, he also failed to set the hook.

The dry-fly angler should always strike his salmon when the fish closes his mouth on the fly. The dry fly, without drag, is always fished with some slack in the line. This slack must be tightened and enough pressure added to drive the hook into the flesh beyond the barb. The salmon tends to spit out the dry fly soon after taking it. In my own tests those fish that took the fly and were given slack were rarely hooked.

Salmon do rise to a dry fly much in the manner of an old brown trout. They like to come up under the fly, suck it in, and go down again. With the suckdown the fly is usually safely in the salmon's mouth before the angler can verify its disappearance. Salmon rise in many other ways, the most spectacular of them being the head-and-tail rise in which the fish opens his mouth an instant before his jaws break the surface. He takes the fly, closing his jaws on it, and rolls on over into a downward drive that brings the upper half of his body above the water and shows a large part of his tail as he submerges.

This is his most deliberate rise and—unlike the one where he sucks the fly down beneath—is the one that offers the greatest tendency to strike too soon. As a rule, salmon are deliberate risers and no matter how swiftly they must move to reach the fly they tend to take it gently. But this is not always the case and some salmon will take the fly with a savage swirl. I have had salmon take the dry fly on their way out of water on a clean, high leap, a rare spectacle which once seen can never be forgotten, and have even recorded this type of rise on movie film.

Some salmon have a habit of waiting until the dry fly has drifted over them and passed on down into their blind area. Then, turning with a rush and almost always making the turn away from the angler, of whom they are already aware, they come around downstream to take the fly. They rush at the fly open-mouthed, heading downstream and toward the angler, already turning back at the take to complete the circle to their former lie. I am ashamed to admit how many times I have lifted the fly right out of that cotton-white open mouth without giving it a chance to close.

I know of no more exciting moment than the false rise of a salmon, no moment in the sport that requires greater control and judgment. The angler must have keen enough vision and must watch his fly so closely that he can determine whether the salmon really takes the fly or just comes up alongside and opens his mouth, missing the floating feathers by a fraction of an inch. If the fly is taken he must strike . . . and if that great fish, suddenly appearing after hours of inactivity, does not close his jaws on the fly he must not twitch his rod arm even a little bit, but must hold steady and let the fly drift carelessly on its uninterrupted path.

Such control is far from easy, but it is essential to the taking of many of these curious fish. If the fly is yanked away at the false rise the fish will usually sulk and come no more. If the fly drifts on and the salmon keeps returning to look it over, sooner or later he can be brought to the steel.

The Atlantic salmon is essentially indifferent to food on his return to the rivers, and he needs none. He may take a dry fly on its first pass over him, he may rise a dozen times and then take it, he may rise twenty times and lose interest, or he may not rise at all. Salmon do not have the wary brown trout's aversion to the dragging dry fly. They do not find "drag" unnatural, and some anglers make a practice of fishing for them that way.

My experience leads me to believe that the dry fly is far more successful when fished in the conventional manner without drag, and I fish it just as I would for brown trout, with emphasis on timing of casts and consistently uniform delivery. However, before giving up on a sulky fish, I often drag the fly across just in front of him, sometimes pulling it under the surface just over his nose, and these tricks have been rewarded by some savage rises.

One of the advantages of dry-fly fishing is that more than half the time a sharp-eyed angler can see his fish before he hooks him. The easiest way is to fish the dry fly across the stream. Then the least effort is required and the stripping of line is held to a minimum. The fly floats in a path abreast of the angler and not decidely toward or away from him. From this position it is possible to see the flash of the big fish as he rises for a look at the fly. In this respect dry-fly fishing for salmon differs from fishing the floaters for trout.

The trout angler looks only for rises that actually show a fish breaking the surface; the salmon angler must look for flashes of the fish well down in the water. Failure to spot these interested fish, whose presence may be given away only by the slightest flash or shadowy movement, often means the difference between success and failure. For of a dozen salmon in a pool, many of which may be porpoising and leaping, the one most likely to take the fly is the one that shows restlessness when it passes over him.

A salmon may rise only a foot from the bottom and still be two or three feet under the fly on his first show of interest; but if the angler sees him, he has found a likely prospect and is on his way to some sport. This is an important phase of dry-fly fishing which few anglers have yet mastered. Remember—salmon do not always look like salmon. Sometimes all one sees is a bit of white under his chin, or the light spot on his tail, or the white slit of his open mouth, or a combination of mouth and tail, correctly spaced. It may be the shadow, often more conspicuous than the fish himself, that gives away a salmon's location by its movement.

The dry-fly angler from his position abreast of the fly has a better chance of locating these likely prospects than has the wet-fly fisherman. The wet fly is presented to the salmon well downstream from the angler, and the fish that move toward it are pointed toward the angler at the time, exposing not the silvery length of their bodies but the small, head-on view.

Under these conditions they can rarely be seen and usually remain unidentified unless they make a noticeable swirl as they turn away from the fly, and the angler, unaware of their presence and location, fails to concentrate on that spot and so fails to connect. My experience in locating fish under the dry fly has improved my ability to spot these slight movements and so has added to my wet-fly effectiveness.

The same tricks that will fool wary brown trout are worth-while when used for salmon. Long, fine leaders will bring more rises. Casting a downstream loop so that the fly reaches the fish before the filament does is important. The dry-fly fisherman should work upstream, so that his dragging fly, returning from each cast, passes over the heads of the fish he has given up as a bad job and not over those farther upstream which he still hopes to cast.

In dry-fly fishing for salmon there are no rules that cannot be broken. The floating fly can be fished upstream, across the current or downstream. Salmon may take it with drag or without, or they may finally succumb to it when pulled underwater on the retrieve.

A leader of twelve to fourteen feet is average for salmon on the dry fly, and it can taper down to a fine end ranging from .013 to .010 of an inch. When the fish won't cooperate on that basis, keep adding tippets and making the leader longer and finer, up to your ability to land the fish. There's no point in hooking fish that are certain to be lost, since to do so may eliminate a chance at them another way. My limit in fineness for grilse (five-pound average) is 4X and for the larger fish of ten pounds upward, 2X. Below that limit I believe my chances of bringing in the fish are not worth the risk of missing a possible rise that might come any-way if I continue with leaders of the same weight and strength. The novice should use a point or two coarser to give himself a chance.

Single-handed rods are preferable for dry-fly salmon fishing because they simplify the stripping of line so essential to that type of fishing. There is a lot more casting to be done with the dry fly than with the wet, and a rod that is light enough to permit long periods of fishing is to be preferred over one that tires the arm quickly.

A detachable butt is wise for the confirmed right-hand reeler, but being right-handed I use my right hand to hold the rod *all* the time, whether casting or playing a fish, and reel with my left, or weaker, hand. That is the best utilization of normally developed skills, I believe, and permits me to move about freely while play-ing the fish and to hold the rod higher, shift its angle more readily, and generally have better control of a hooked fish.

There is probably no sight in all fishing more exciting than the rise of a salmon to a dry fly. The playing of any species of fish tends to fit into a pattern and follow a certain routine if you catch enough of them. But the rise of an Atlantic salmon is so varied and unpredictable that there is never any routine about it. A salmon that will keep fooling around with my dry fly, showing a definite interest and giving me an occasional view of his silvery bulk without letting me tag him, presents a problem so intriguing that I would rather find one such fish to work on than several that will whip up and latch onto the fly the first time over.

The angler versus salmon duel with the dry fly is, to my way of thinking, the most exciting thing in all angling. It may go on for hours . . . or for days . . . and it can be a most exasperating as well as a most satisfying experience.

CHAPTER 6

The Riffling Hitch

THE RIFFLING HITCH was hidden away in the Newfoundland wilderness for over a quarter of a century, but now the idea is spreading to other salmon rivers—and to other fly-rod waters as well. It is time that the method, its origin, and something of its special effectiveness should be described at length.

For this particular technique, which borrows from both wet- and dry-fly procedures, promises to become a third distinct method of fly fishing—suited not only to Atlantic salmon but to trout, black bass, pickerel, tarpon, and perhaps other game fish where water conditions are right.

The riffling hitch began at Portland Creek, a short, broad river on Newfoundland's northwest coast which has consistently led all the other rivers of the province in the average weight of salmon since the establishment of fishing camps there. It empties on a rough stretch of coastline, forty miles from the nearest harbor.

Since Newfoundland's travel until recently has either been by sea or by rail (seventy miles distant), this lack of a harbor has meant almost complete isolation for the few settlers in the area. Before 1946 only a handful of anglers fished the river. One of them was Arthur Perry.

Arthur couldn't remember back beyond the time when he started to fish. And with Arthur, fishing always came first. I met him in 1943, when three of us landed at Portland Creek in one of Uncle Sam's seaplanes. We had scarcely carried the mooring lines ashore when Arthur arrived on the scene, though it was a full mile from his summer lobster-fishing shack. He was, he informed us, the aircraft spotter for the area. Convinced by the U.S. markings on the aircraft that we weren't Germans, and noting our fishing tackle, he offered to take us fishing—and did.

The district was settled long ago by West-of-England fisherfolk who drop their *h*'s and pronounce *f* like *v*. So it was that after eyeing my wet fly as I finished tying it to the leader, Arthur said, "Better let me put an itch in it, sir. To make it rivvle."

I must have looked very blank, for he continued, "If you don't put an itch on the fly it won't rivvle, and if it doesn't rivvle you won't get any salmon."

Still thoroughly puzzled, I said, "I don't get it. Show me what you mean."

Whereupon Arthur picked up the fly in his gnarled hands, put a loop in the leader just in advance of the fly, deftly threw it up and over the eye, then pulled it tight to form an overhand knot (*not* a hitch, strictly speaking) around the shank of the hook at the base of the head. Then he did a repeat, tightening the second knot just beyond the first. After inspecting the results he passed the fly back to me with a flourish.

"Now, sir, it will rivvle and I believe you'll catch a salmon," said Arthur.

I had fished more salmon rivers than Arthur had years. Many a guide had watched openmouthed as I hooked a salmon on a fly he thought fantastic or landed it on a slender split-bamboo stick he knew was ridiculous. In the past, guides had said, "They won't take a fly in saltwater," so I caught them there on flies, or "They won't take dry flies here," and I took them on dry flies. Carefully I loosened the monofilament and undid first one loop and then the other.

"Arthur," I said, "the Turtle knot has been working satisfactorily for a long time. We'll try it that way."

Arthur shook his head sadly, as if watching a small child at a picnic who, advised by his parents to be good, goes right on being naughty. He shook his head frequently that afternoon as we fished our way down through that marvelous mile of river toward the sea. Finally, at the Low Rock salmon lie, the last fishing spot above the tidal rise, Arthur could hold back no longer.

"We've fished all the best lies, sir," he explained. "I know it's a little hearly but there's got to be some fish in the river where we fished. But you won't catch any without an itch."

So I threw the loops over the eye myself, drew the leader tight, and passed the hitch to him for inspection before casting to where the deep water swirled high and slid on over the low rock. When the fly came in on the retrieve it rode the surface like a miniature surfboard, the black head and eye of the fly riding the crest of a tiny wave and a rippling V spreading out in its wake.

It swung in the familiar path a wet fly takes, passing just above the ridge of water pushed up by the rock. The rising water rose a little higher, then parted as a big salmon broke the surface and rushed at the fly. His strong jaws closed on it, and I had hooked my first fish on a riffling fly.

My conversion was neither immediate nor complete. Mine is a Missouri frame of mind, and when Arthur declared that the *only* way to catch a Portland Creek salmon is with a riffled fly I was sure he must be wrong—either because the men who had fished the wet fly conventionally weren't very good at it or had fished the wrong flies.

On the trips that followed I fished with both the normally tied and the hitched fly and found both effective. The hitched fly, however, although fished less frequently, took more fish, and I had to admit that it not only was much more fun but had several other advantages.

The turning point came on an afternoon when a cool wind was blowing up from the sea. I had fished the stretch above the low rock and reached a lie where another group of rocks curved upstream in a U. In Portland Creek the salmon make a habit of lying ahead of instead of just behind the rocks. I can think of no reason for this except that when the ice jams up against the larger rocks the churning current, working underneath it, digs out a deep hole on the upstream side. Much of the river is shallow and without pools, with the depressions in front of the larger rocks holding most of the fish.

Fishing had been slow and I had covered several good lies without a rise. I was ready then to stick at this one good spot and succeed or fail there in the half hour remaining. I fished the wet fly, attached normally, under the surface in the accustomed manner. I tried No. 4's, then 6's and finally 8's. I watched closely, for if I should miss the most insignificant gleam of silver as a restless salmon moved slightly under the passing fly I'd fail to make a dozen or more identical casts that would bring him to the hook. I was alert to what happened, though it was unexpected.

As the No. 8 Jock Scott swung its arc—with the fly just beneath the surface, where the salmon usually like a wet fly best—it happened that a leader knot several feet ahead of the fly was just creasing the smooth surface and sending out a small V wake as it did so. A salmon drove up from the depths and struck that leader knot, insignificant as it was in contrast to the fly. If the riffled knot would draw a rise from the fish, I decided, so would the riffled fly. My fingers threw the hitches on the Jock Scott, and on the second cast a salmon hit hard. Ever since that moment I have fished the hitched wet fly more than the conventionally sunken one on Portland Creek.

No one now at Portland Creek claims to have been the originator of the riffling fly, but here is the accepted story. Long ago warships of the British navy anchored off the stream and officers came ashore to fish. They left a few old-style salmon flies, which had a loop of twisted gut wrapped to the straight-shanked hook to make the eye.

Soft and pliable when in use, the loop enabled the fly to ride more smoothly on its course and avoided the stiffness and canting which accompanied any solid attachment of the stout leader to the fly. But the gut loop grew weak with age, and many a goodly salmon, when hooked on an old and cherished fly, broke away with the steel and feathers. So to play safe, anglers often gave away old flies. To most recipients they were Trojan horses. Only to the Portland Creekers were they a boon.

Quickly realizing that a salmon hooked on a gut-looped fly was likely to break free, they made sure the fly would stay on by throwing those "hitches" around the shank behind the wrapping. The fact that the fly skimmed instead of sinking bothered them not in the least, for they were practical fishers of the sea. They fished the flies on spruce poles with makeshift reels or none at all. They cast them out and drew them back. And because they had no proper flies with which to fish they developed a new technique.

Now, instead of lying in pools and deep water, most of the salmon in Portland Creek are in relatively shallow water and close to the surface. When they lie in the depressions ahead of the rocks they may actually be lying at a lower level than the stream bed all around them, which restricts their field of vision.

The river surface is usually ruffled, and this makes a sunken fly less conspicuous than it would be in smooth water. Perhaps the additional commotion made by a riffling fly is just the extra something required to make a salmon rise.

In 1946 I established a fishing camp at Portland Creek, and many famous fishermen have since come to marvel at the number of salmon in so short a river—and to learn the effectiveness of the hitched wet fly.

The making of the hitch is important. Arthur Perry, in common with most Portland Creek guides, made his so that the mono-filament pulls away from under the turned-up eye at the throat. This will make both the double- and single-hooked flies ride correctly (hook down) on the retrieve. Such a hitch is effective on standard salmon-fly hooks with turned up eyes but awkward if the eyes are turned down.

I use the same throat hitch for double-hooked flies, but with my favorite—the single-barbed iron—regardless of whether the eye turns up or down, I shift the hitch 45° to one side or the other, depending upon which side of the current I cast from, so that on a cross-current retrieve the fly will always ride with the point on the downstream side. This position seems to give it much better hooking and riding qualities.

Using this method, it's easy to learn how to fish *any* wet fly correctly, whereas it usually takes years before you can watch the water under which the fly is traveling and guess correctly just where it is and at what speed it is moving. Too much speed or too little will not draw salmon's interest. The perfect speed is the speed at which a hitched fly riffles best.

If the speed of the retrieve is wrong, the hitched fly will either throw spray or sink below the surface. If one of these things happens, a strike is most unlikely. Since the fly is visible at all times, the angler can slow down his retrieve if he sees the fly making spray, speed it up if it starts to sink. Almost without conscious effort he learns to maintain his fly at the right speed through fast water and slow, matching the speed of retrieve to the water the fly is in. Through cross-currents and eddies, on glassy glides, the lifting or lowering of the rod to speed up or slow down the retrieve soon becomes automatic.

And thereafter it's not difficult to match these tactics to a sunken fly which, though still invisible, can now be readily imagined as it travels through the likely water. I think it is largely because of this that the guides at Portland Creek have been able to teach novices to catch salmon almost as well as old-timers.

With the riffling hitch, fish are hooked just as readily and held just as securely as when the fly is tied on in the conventional manner. And they're so sold on it at Portland Creek that ninety-five percent of all the wet-fly fishing done there is done with a hitched fly.

It's worked out well on other salmon rivers, too, like the Humber and the River of Ponds. Having had sea-run brook trout at

Portland Creek hit the riffling fly savagely, I wasn't surprised when even the sophisticated brownies of the Battenkill River of New York and Vermont rose to the skittering feathers. Eastern brook trout have long been taken by dragging the dropper fly on the surface while the tail fly sinks underneath. With the hitch the solitary tail fly riffles by itself, an especially good method for fishing for the more wary brookies.

The first black bass to take a hitched fly of mine, a hefty Hudson River smallmouth, gave me a thrilling rise. He hit it just as hard as he'd have hit a spinner-and-streamer combination, and he did it on top of the water where I could see it. After all, our grandfathers used to skitter with a long cane pole and a strip of pork rind and there's not much real difference between the two methods. The hitched fly, of course, is designed for stream fishing, requiring a certain speed to keep it riffling. But with greased line and leader this can be managed even on a lake or very slow-moving stream.

I find myself using the hitch more and more instead of normal wet-fly fishing simply because it thrills me to see a fish break the surface in his strike. As compared with the dry fly the riffled fly moves faster, since it moves across the flow as well as with it. A trout or salmon can wait until the dry fly comes to him, then quietly rise up and suck it in. With the riffling fly the fish must not only rise to but *catch* the fly; and a big salmon, in doing so, rolls up a wave of water ahead of him one never forgets. The same goes for bass, pickerel, and tarpon—each must poke his nose up into the air and show himself with at least as much flourish as if he were after a dry fly.

Are skittered dry flies as good as the hitched wet fly? Experience at Portland Creek denies it. Granted that the hitched fly stays up only because of its motion, the fluffy dry fly rides at a different angle and height, and develops little wake.

Like any method of fishing, riffling the wet fly will be especially effective where the fish have seen a lot of flies presented in the old way. That is why the original dry flies, which were essentially only greased and floating wet flies, brought such remarkable results when first used over trout and salmon, and why long, thin, floating bass bugs—shaped almost like streamer flies—made such wonderful catches. It was not because the design or the shape of the lure was so different. That came later. It was the new approach.

Various sorts of insects skim across the water instead of flying over it or swimming through it. Water spiders, bugs, and striders or skaters, as well as stalled-out land bugs, slide their way over the ripples and eddies. Many an injured minnow flutters his way across a pool, nose breaking into the air and tail lagging downward until a game fish snaps him up. Hence, to imitate such action with a riffled fly is both natural and effective—and it doesn't cost a nickel. To make your wet flies more effective and to make the strikes more fun, simply follow Arthur Perry's advice and put an "itch" on them.

CHAPTER 7

Where There's a Will

A MAN-SIZE SALMON on a tiny rod suited to the catching of little brook trout—a wacky ambition, perhaps, but I had it and stuck to it. The rod picked for the thrill of the experiment was seven feet long and weighed only 2½ ounces. I was confident that a big Atlantic salmon could be licked to the last gill gasp on such a fragile thing, and craved to prove it. Right then, in 1940, on the Serpentine River on the west coast of Newfoundland, I had seen the flash of just the fish I wanted.

I'd argued plenty with fishing friends as to whether it could be done. They maintained that a big and stubborn fish, insisting on sulking, could never be moved on such a rod. I'd rebutted vigorously that when a fish is played properly, he can't sulk long because of the strain on him; that it's the fish's own struggling, not the size of the rod, that wears him down. Was I right? I'd let this trial prove the merits of the case.

I settled down for a long period of continual casting. It is my belief, based on experience, that prolonged casting of a dry fly over a salmon will result in a rise at least half of the time. I had on a big dry fly—a No. 4 White Wulff—a leader fifteen feet long, tapered down to .010, and a casting line balanced to the rod. The backing was a hundred yards of ten-pound test nylon. The breaking strain of the leader was about five pounds when tested on a straight pull without a knot, less when tied to a fly.

As I made cast after cast my eyes never left that salmon, which I could plainly see. For a full half hour I kept casting. Then, at last, as the fly drifted over him, he lifted.

He rose until nose and dorsal fin broke the surface together. His mouth opened slightly and closed again as the fly came to him. Then, as his head went under, his broad tail broke the surface. But the big white fly still floated. Fortunately, it was between me and the disappearing fish, so that I could see it all the time. Had it not been for that I'd have struck, missed, and put the salmon down for good. An hour passed before he made another false rise.

After two hours of patient and monotonous casting, the real rise came. As his mouth closed down on the high-riding bucktail, I lifted the rod sharply and felt his weight as he sank back to his resting place. But the pressure on his jaw soon moved him. With three or four vigorous shakes of his head he started upstream, slowly at first, then with accelerated speed until the reel fairly screeched. Out he came into the sunlight with a somersaulting leap.

Jack Young, my guide, came over to walk the shore, paralleling me as I waded upriver, trying to recover some line. He said nothing nor was there need for words. Watching from the bank he had followed every cast I made. Now the slugging match that was on had thrilled him into action, and he was all eyes.

The salmon didn't like that upper pool with its shallower water, and now shot downstream to his old lurking place, passed it, and drove on to slick water below, where great boulders broke the river's flow. He leaped again, rushed toward the far bank, returned to deep water, and there was my line, looped around one of the boulders. Possibly I should have used the canoe to free it, but I waded out into the current and crossed the river below the boulder. I got some water into my waders, but was able to free the line, using the utmost care not to startle the fish into another run. That done, I crossed the river again to my old stand by the pool.

The salmon leaped twice more, and made two great runs, but the struggle was tiring him. Then he resorted to the last device of most heavy fish by working across the current and using the power of its flow against his broad side, together with his ponderous weight, in an effort to break away. Thus he carried me down into the pockets of water below the main pool where there wasn't so much room for him to run, but where there were many rocks. The current pressed heavily against me and clawed at my felt-soled shoes as they touched the riverbed. But wherever the salmon went, I followed, whether the water was one or four feet deep. Now I unsnapped the tailer from its clip behind my left shoulder and set up the bow in readiness to slide it over the fish's tail when the time should come.

As I drew near the salmon, the whiteness of his mouth was easily seen, for he was opening and closing it rapidly, gasping for breath. The sunshine spotlighted him against the dark background of the river bottom. He came in close three separate times, then pulled away with great surges. But at last I felt that the moment was right to slip the tailer over that slowly fanning tail. The tailer moved upcurrent to the right position. I drew it tight with an easy motion and the loop closed down.

Just then, with victory in sight, there popped into my mind a long talk I'd had with a veteran salmon fisherman who is quite properly rated as an expert. His long and varied experience qualifies him for that. He'd said, "When you get a big salmon in close, it takes brute strength to put him where you want him. His sheer weight is enough to break your leader if you don't have a long rod for leverage." But now I held my short rod high and well over my head so it arched down from a horizontal grip, just as I'd done with the smaller salmon I'd caught before this one. It was all the leverage I needed, and the leader didn't break.

It was twenty-six minutes after the rise, and the fish was mine. I closed my hand around his powerful tail and carried him ashore. He was a heavyset, hook-billed male, and weighed exactly thirty pounds. When Jack carried him over to the canoe, the tail dug a wet furrow where it dragged along the beach.

A thirty-pound salmon is not a record. On some rivers, perhaps, it might not be considered an unusual fish. Yet few anglers have captured one as large. And I think for the tackle used, so frail, so easily broken, my fish probably was a record. I know that this was an event in my life, for I had proved "it can be done!"

CHAPTER 8

The Toughest of Them All

THIS IS A STORY I never expected to write . . . because as year after year went by with only one stray salmon ever taking more than half an hour to bring in, I grew confident and was bold enough to say that I never expected to hook a salmon that would take me over an hour to land, no matter what the tackle. And then along came this "bottle" fish.

But I'm getting a little ahead of myself since this isn't just the telling of a contest with a tough Atlantic salmon, but the story of a perfect fishing weekend as well. It begins in a caboose, jolting over the narrow-gauge tracks of the Newfoundland Railway in the wake of an itinerant freight.

That particular frieght's schedule put her through Corner Brook, on Newfoundland's west coast, at an unpredictable-in-advance time between 5 A.M. and 6 P.M. on Saturdays, depending upon the amount and type of freight she carried. The uncertainty of departure time was a drawback, but since it offered the only weekend transportation between Corner Brook and the fine salmon pools of Harry's River to the southwest, it usually carried some anglers in season, and on that Saturday afternoon, in addition to its freight and a few other passengers, it carried five anglers and their equipment.

Captain Geary and his wife, Peg, were headed for North Brook Pool in the upper section of the river a few miles below the point where it empties out of St. George's Lake. Ray Doucette, Ed Burry, and I were going on down to the Lower River where the flow bends away from the railroad track and there's a walk of a mile or two to the fishing.

We rocked and swayed our way along with numerous stops that gave us plenty of time to look over the scenery. The fresh green of the newly leaved white birches spoke eloquently of the soft, warm days ahead, and the light green tips of the evergreens made those dark-hued trees appear to be in blossom. But when we passed the high point on the tracks from which we could see the mountains that overhang the north shore of Serpentine Lake in its hidden valley, the broad patches of winter's snow still remaining there were as white and bright as the fleecy clouds above them. Then we picked up speed and rattled along the downgrade to St. George's Lake and its outlet, Harry's River.

There was a hushed moment as we caught our first glimpse of the river, running parallel to the tracks. The water was clear and the flow was a bit less than normal, quite low for the early season. That meant that the bigger fish would be lying only in the deeper pools instead of being scattered all over the stream as they would have been in the usual spring runoff. The conditions automatically limited the number of pools that would hold big salmon and would call for real skill in bringing the larger salmon to the steel.

It was Ray Doucette who conceived the idea of a "pool" for the largest salmon of the weekend. It met with immediate favor, for all of us had put in years of salmon fishing, and in such a contest any one of us might win. So it was agreed that the angler taking the heaviest fish before 5 P.M. the following day, which was Sunday, would be presented with a bottle of Scotch by the four less successful fishermen. Since we'd all be going back to Corner Brook on the Sunday night express it would be easy enough to get together and compare notes and salmon.

We waved the Gearys off at North Brook, secretly envious of the time they'd have for fishing before we reached our section of the river several stops farther along the line. However, the few hours of fishing we put in Saturday evening brought none of us anything that had a chance of winning the pool. We did take a few small salmon, and Ray raised one that looked to be twenty pounds or more. As we walked back from the river through the slowly gathering dusk, Ed said, "I wonder if Peg Geary brought in a big one this afternoon. She may not catch as many fish as the Captain does but, doggone, she sure does get the big ones."

Ray concluded, "There's no use worrying about that till tomorrow night. Believe me, there are some old soakers down in that pool we just left," and then, after a brief pause, he added, "Why not put on a little speed and get out of here? It's getting cool with the sun gone and the mosquitoes are going into action."

We awoke to one of those perfect days of late June and went down to the best pool in that section of the stream while the low-hanging sun was sending long shadows over the water. The clear flow slid around a wide curve of bubbly rapids and eased into the deep water through several channels separated from each other by huge boulders. Once in the pool proper, the stream slowed down gradually and loafed through a quarter mile of still water before spilling over into rapid flow again. The bigger salmon tended to lie just below the big boulders at the pool's head, and we concentrated our fishing in that section.

The sun burned down hour after hour, and in its brilliance we played and released eight fish ranging from four to six pounds and kept two that were between ten and twelve. The salmon we caught had all the life and leaping spirit of salmon fresh from the sea, but pleasant as the day was, and the fishing, each of us was working as best he knew to bring in the "bottle" fish. There were big fish under our flies. Occasionally one leaped or showed us his length in a flash of silver as he turned on his side in the current—the weight well over ten pounds.

When the sun was an hour along its way in the slant from noon to sunset we lunched and moved on down to another pool, a fifty-yard-long pocket of slick, boulder-studded, fast-sliding water that wormed in and out between rocks that ruffled but failed to break up the flow. The half mile that separated us from the pool we'd just left was made up entirely of rough water, and below us the river tumbled and twisted in continuous rough flow for over a mile. The long rough stretches may have been the secret of the popularity of those two pools with the salmon, which entered their comfortable waters after a hard bout with the current.

We spread out and fished the various good salmon lies, and Ray came through with a fourteen-pounder, a fish that might possibly win the pool but carried little certainty of it. The salmon seemed listless with the warmth of midday, although we tempted them with the best we could think of to offer, both dry and wet. After a while we gave up fishing to rest the water for a spell. That pool was somewhat shallower than the one we'd left, and I climbed partway up the high bank it hugged and sat looking over the wrinkled water below me.

I spotted salmon here and there, gray shadows above the vari-colored rocks of the stream bed, made indistinct by the overlapping water currents, but I saw no big ones until some slight movement drew my eyes to the far side of the stream where the water was comparatively shallow. Watching steadily while the water alternately cleared and blurred, I finally made out three good salmon lying close together. They weren't monsters, but it would take some good fishing or a lot more luck to beat any one of them out for top honors.

Telling the others that I'd located a couple of good fish on the far side of the stream beyond the coverage of our previous fishing, I dropped to the tail of the pool and waded across, coming close to the top of my waders to make it. I moved up the far bank slowly, clinging to the alders and their protective screen since the sun was now at my back. As carefully as I could, I waded out till I was forty feet from the white rock by which I had marked down the salmon. Then I stood quietly until my eyes became used to the light on the water and I could make out the three long, grayish shapes.

After a time I could see the salmon plainly and I knew that they could see me, too. But I knew as well that if I stayed put long enough and made no commotion with my casting, they'd get used to me and cease to be actively aware of my presence. I waited perhaps ten minutes before starting to cast. Then I dropped a big White Wulff No. 4 over their heads and let it drift down over their tails, giving it a float of about nine feet before I picked it up and dropped it down on their heads again.

The casting was steady and rhythmic. The fish showed no interest and made no movements, nor did I expect them to . . . at least not right away. The sun was too bright and the salmon in the pool weren't generally active. But these fish were all fresh-run, having come into the river within two weeks at the longest. They were lying in shallow water where the fly would pass close above them, and I was certain that the continued presence of the dry fly would prove so annoying that one of them would eventually rise.

Time went by and I could make them out more plainly, the largest fish in the center with the two flanking fish somewhat smaller, and I judged them to be from twenty to twenty-five pounds. I timed my casts at about ten to the minute. With the big bucktail-winged fly there was no need for false casting to dry it off. It was simply a matter of a pickup and single cast out again for the short float over the fish. I looked at my watch to find that twenty minutes had gone by. Still there was no sign that any of those salmon had even noticed the fly that kept passing over them so continually.

There were beautiful cloud formations to watch, whiskey-jacks that scolded from the trees. There was the river itself to look at and enjoy and the broad green slopes and endless patterns of sun and shadow. I was tempted to close my eyes and listen to the sounds of spring and feel its warmth. But such things were not for me. My eyes stayed glued to those salmon.

Finally one moved. Not much of a movement, just the slight push of his tail to carry him a little to one side of the fly as it drifted over him. Already there was some clamor from Ed and Ray to go back to the other pool. Without looking up, I answered that I had some unfinished business and couldn't leave but would join them later. They stayed on to watch. Ed curled up on a sun-warmed grassy spot, and Ray planted himself on one of the boulders in the pool.

I concentrated on the fish that had moved, the one nearest to me. He moved again a few casts later. Ten casts farther along he lifted up just beneath the fly, then sank again after it passed over him. The next cast he lifted again, let the fly pass, and drowned it with his tail as he went down. That was all. From then on, he stayed as motionless as a log.

At the end of an hour he still hadn't moved, but the center fish, the biggest one, left his position and leisurely poked his nose up at the fly, mouth closed, and lifted it above the water. Abruptly he surged down again without ever having opened his mouth. Ed and Ray saw the fish come up and immediately asked why I hadn't struck. If I hadn't been able to see the fish so well I certainly would have . . . and would have missed him. Many dry-fly rises are missed because the fish is just annoyed with the floating fly and wants to drown it or drive it away without wanting to take it.

The casting continued with all three fish stonily refusing to show any interest. But the fact that I'd made two of them make half a pass at my fly was something. I changed to one of my smaller gray flies for fifteen minutes. Nothing happened. I went back to the big white one again. The far fish edged out a trifle when the fly floated directly over him. I started dropping it right on his nose every time. He lifted a little, settled again. For twenty or more casts he showed no interest.

Ed and Ray were out on the other bank getting their gear ready to go on up to the pool above. I stopped to tell them I'd be along eventually and to look through my fly boxes for some fly that might startle that far fish into rising. On a whim I put on a cork-bodied creation of Preston Jennings that I'd tried before without success. It looked like nothing a self-respecting salmon would look at twice—but then, neither did my own unconventional bucktail patterns.

I sent the bass-buggish No. 4 out to plop down on the far salmon. At the third cast he lifted beneath it and stretched out, a long gray shadow, to let it pass inches over his head. He flashed silver for his full length as he turned out of vertical going down. The fly settled in precisely the same spot, hitting the water with a little slap since that lure has little fluff to break its fall. It seemed hardly to have started its float before the salmon nearest me crossed over the other two fish and took the fly. Already turning downstream on his swing, he made his first run in that direction when the steel went home.

I was using my favorite light rig, made up of a 7-foot, 2½-ounce rod, 3⅜-inch reel, and a line to balance. The water was heavy and deep and it was a mighty tough pool to wade. Dropping below the salmon I kept him moving and used my tackle to the safe limit of its strength. When he made the first of his jumps, Ed and Ray, who had already started upstream but had turned back for a last look just in time to see the fish rise, shouted in unison, "Twenty-pounder!"

Things happened quickly and the line went off and on the reel and off and on again. My big worry was keeping the line from fouling the rocks. Once the fish did curve around a boulder, but I managed to wade out and clear the line in time. The salmon reeled off a series of three cartwheel leaps and abruptly settled down to the bottom, and from my position below him I began inching him back toward me. Soon he was almost at my feet. I held the pressure of the tackle on him and he stayed motionless. I looked at my watch. Six minutes! Something was fishy.

Grinning at the others from my spot in midstream, I unhooked the tailer and set it up. The salmon held his position. With a shrug of my shoulders to indicate to the others a "Well, I shouldn't do this, but if the fish is crazy enough to let me I'm foolish enough to try" attitude, I stretched the tailer to my arm's full length and leaned down toward the salmon, expecting him to bolt at any second. He didn't move.

If I missed him I knew it would take a long time to bring him close again, but just how long I was yet to realize. I knew that he was still strong and capable of a wild, swift surge. But I rarely missed with my tailer, and when the landing device slipped up over his tail and reached a point even with his anal fin I drew it sharply toward me to pull the noose tight.

I was prepared for his plunge ahead, but it was so powerful that it almost took me in over my waders and started my arm from its socket. White spray flew back at me as his tail flapped and fluttered on the surface. For a brief instant he relaxed, then surged ahead, and by some miracle became the first salmon to slip through the tailer noose once I had him tailed. He swept off downstream because he happened to be headed in that direction.

I waited for him to turn. In a few seconds, surprised that he didn't either slacken or turn, I made for shallower water to follow him. Finally in desperation, I broke into as much of a run as a man can make with chest-height waders on in order to keep a little of my 175 yards of line on the reel as he swept over the lip of the pool and down into the ragged water below it.

Past experience told me that things were going to be tough, and in particular I remembered another smaller salmon that I'd tailed, brought to the bank, and had then slipped back to the stream to fight it out for another fifteen minutes. Once a salmon has felt a gaff or tailer he's wary of letting anyone come close to him. Usually such fish are already pretty well tired out when the first attempt is made. This fish was fresh and strong.

Ed and Ray followed down their side of the stream for a while, then went back to the pool, certain that I'd lose the fish in the rough water. I had the same feeling. Two or three times I had to wade out into swift, deep water near midflow to pass my line over rocks or a jammed piece of pulpwood. It was half an hour before the tail end of my casting line followed my backing onto the reel again.

I was as hot as I can ever remember being and dog-tired from running down the shallows in heavy waders, or running more slowly but just as vigorously through water that varied in depth from hip to knee. I still carried the tailer in my left hand, since I hadn't had a moment to refasten it to its clip, and badly as I needed the full and unencumbered use of that hand, I hoped I'd need the tailer again, and more emphatically.

Whenever I closed in on the salmon he knew only too well what I had in mind and he surged off again. At the end, with one short, shallow stretch lying between the fish and another long piece of real tough going, I took a wild gamble. The salmon had to cross a forty-foot stretch of water about a foot deep that rippled down over a gravelly bottom. He was twenty feet ahead of me and moving steadily. As he broke into that shallow water I lowered my rod, letting the line go slack, and galloped in slow motion after him. I overtook him just as he was about to scoot into the deeper swirls, and the ghost of old Izaak must have guided my hand because the tailer slipped up over his tail and came tight. That time there was no monkey business; he was mine.

Thousands of salmon ranging up to thirty pounds have come my way, a fair share of them on my "light rig," but that was the toughest of them all. Strangely enough, but for the fluke of his slipping out of the tailer, he would have been one of the easiest. No type of angling follows its generally prescribed pattern to the letter; Atlantic salmon fishing is perhaps the least predictable of all.

It had taken a few minutes over the hour to finally capture the salmon, and with the job done I sat for a while and rested. When I was reasonably cooled off and restored to normal breathing, I started back up three quarters of a mile of river, either wading along the edge or beating my way through the alders and evergreens on its banks until I burst out with the trophy, hot, tired, but triumphant, at the pool where Ed and Ray were waiting. It was too late then to try the upper pool so we took the trail back toward the railway.

Ed and Ray were right. He did weigh twenty pounds. And he was the "bottle" fish.

CHAPTER 9

Address at the Atlantic Salmon Emergency Dinner

Waldorf Astoria, New York, January 20, 1971

THANK YOU, Curt Gowdy [Toastmaster]. Friends, anglers, people, men and women who live with me today and look out on a wild world endangered. I speak as an angler. I began to fish with a deep and enduring love before I can remember. I hope to fish with a deep and continuing interest until I die.

I do not fish like those who say, "I don't care what fish it is, I just love fishing." Not quite in that sense. More like a connoisseur of wines or of gems. It has been my career, my endeavor, to know fishing, its types, its relationships with people, and to evaluate them. And so, just as topaz will scratch quartz, and ruby will scratch topaz, and diamond will scratch ruby, but nothing will scratch a diamond, so, as a long-studied and considered opinion one can say no fish offers more to an individual angler than the Atlantic salmon.

He comes, after a number of years in the river, as a five-inch fish that magically knows how to swim 2,000 miles to where he feeds off Greenland. He knows how to feed and grow and he knows how to find his way home across the ocean to his own river and his own pool. He returns with enough stored-up energy to carry him through as much as eleven months of absolute starvation on his spawning run with all its trouble and requirements of exercise and energy. He doesn't feed. For the angler, it isn't just a matter of finding him and working on his hunger. It's a matter of working on his mind . . . on his mind in relation to the river he's returned to.

People who might catch any other sort of fish if they were to fish where those fish had never been fished for before might well be baffled by the salmon, and they almost always are. The salmon are right there in the rivers; we know where they lie and rest, but only a few of us, sometimes, are able to catch them.

So this is a special fish. And to kill him off for his flesh is like killing the goose that laid the golden egg; we'd realize afterward what we'd lost when we couldn't do anything about replacing him.

Ours is a movement of people. We are determined, as people, to do something that has rarely been done before—save a resource. The one similar example that comes to mind is Ducks Unlimited, where ordinary people with a deep interest and with their own industry and money did what governments had been unable to do. I think it is up to us, from the depths of our hearts and with friendship for the Danes, to say, "We spend nine million dollars a year protecting this magnificent fish on these shores. Is it reasonable for you, for less than a million dollars a year in profit, to put this dream in jeopardy and perhaps deny salmon fishing to your children and mine forever?"

We stand people to people to act where international law has no power, and I trust all of us who feel deeply for the salmon, which is not just another fish but probably the most magnificent of all gamefish, will do our part.

Thank you.

CHAPTER 10

Between the Lakes
at Ugashik

WE WERE THERE for only six hours. We came in the late morning in a Dehavilland Beaver bush plane with a pilot, and left when the wide sky to the west was filled with a gaudy northern sunset.

Both of the two Ugashik lakes are many miles across and they lie in the flat tundra area of Alaska that drains into Bristol Bay. The thoroughfare between them is less than eighty yards wide and 250 yards long, a flow into which a man can wade deeply and cast out, but could not, when we were there, hope to wade across. The water was clear and it swirled and rippled as it flowed through the narrow channel but did not race and foam at any point.

Nate had told Tommy that this was the best place in Alaska for big grayling, the erstwhile home of a four-pounder he'd taken a few years before. So we rigged our tackle and made our first casts.

We were as alone as if we'd been out on the open sea. The sky stretched from near the horizon on one side to the pencil line of land that marked the far shore a score of miles away. There was no wind and our flies flew straight and dropped gently. We started well down the flow toward the lower lake and worked our way upstream, leap-frogging as each of us fished out his casting area and moved around the other to try a new section. Nothing happened until after the third position change. Then Tommy's rod bent beautifully and he sang out, "Fish on!"

It was a grayling that had sucked in his dry fly and then flashed in a splashing arc across the ripples. It was big for a grayling, well over three pounds, and it hung doggedly in the deeper water off-shore before it allowed the tackle's pull to wear it down. It came into the shallows half on its side with its big dorsal waving gently, all purple and pearl. It shimmered briefly in the sunlight as

Tommy drew it from the water. A minute later, on the bank, it was a dull, dark shadow, losing luster, colors fading, turning softly black.

We caught grayling after grayling, marveling each time at the soft pattern of iridescent colors of their fins, the soft and easy waving of the great, high dorsal, the swift, sharp speed with which they twisted and splashed as they finally came to shallow depth. They were quite uniform, being just under or just over three pounds, good, solid fish that struck readily once we'd found the water they liked to lie in. We fished until catching them ceased to be a challenge, and we paused to eat a chocolate bar and watch the reflections on the water and some sandpipers that skittered feverishly over the slatey pebbles of the beach.

"Let's try a streamer fly," I suggested, "and see what else is here."

And so we did, and Tommy caught a grayling a little larger than the others, and I had a strike and missed a bigger fish. . . . A few casts later, I had a solid tug and a fish of six or seven pounds flashed silver and gold under the swirl. He didn't leap but bored down hard and bulled his way out to a deep pocket just behind a bar that lay transverse to the flow.

He stayed there as long as he could, but pressure finally moved him in, a dolly varden that was long and slim and, since it turned out to be a female, small-headed. Beautiful fish they were, these charr, for Tommy caught its mate, a male with heavier head and narrower back, both beautifully colored in that clear, smooth flow.

Again we paused and admired our fish as they reflected sunlight beside the dry, dark shadow of the grayling. We tipped the thermos for hot coffee and, though the day was warm, we relished its warmth because the water swirled coolly around our legs and our waders were worn enough to let the damp seep through.

"Let's switch to deeper lures."

It was Tommy's idea, and he laid aside his fly rod for his spinning tackle and a wobbling spoon. I rummaged in my fly vest to find something I could still throw with a fly rod that would be heavy enough to sink a bit and bright enough to flash. I stuck my finger into the point of a double-hooked spinner-streamer combination when Tom nudged me and whispered, "We've got company."

We had, indeed. A big brown bear had wandered out of the low bush on the other shore and watched us from the water's edge.

We wondered if she'd try for one of the reddened salmon we'd seen hanging in the eddies as we flew over, but she merely sniffed the air and ambled off along the beach and out of sight. I tied the spinner-and-streamer combination on and waded out.

Tommy cast his wobbler out into the curling waves and let it sink. When he tightened up, he felt a fish and his rod bent down. I watched it go through some fancy bends and vibrations for several minutes and then, splashing in the shallow water at his feet, I could make out the high dorsal of a grayling. We were amazed that a grayling with its small mouth and preference for a dry-fly diet would tackle a Dardevle but that one did. He couldn't get it into his mouth. One of the hooks gripped him on the outside of the cheek. Tommy freed him and he swam away.

Awkwardly, I cast the fly-and-spinner combination, a long combination on a double No. 2 salmon hook, out into the flow and let it sink into the deep hole that fell away behind one of the shallow transverse bars. The bar had a depth of about four feet. It was beyond my wading range and the pocket below it must have held ten feet of water. The pocket water was slack, and I let the lure sink slowly for a long time.

I moved it slowly shoreward when I thought it was somewhere near the stream bed. A foot . . . two feet . . . a yard . . . and then no more. It took a good strong arch in the nine-foot rod to move the fish, and then he moved away instead of toward me. I thought it might be a late-running king, but as far as I knew, they'd all be well upstream by now. I thought it might be a silver, but if it were, he ought to come up to the top and splash or jump . . . and he didn't. When he did come up, I was surprised to find I'd hooked a lake trout of about nine pounds. He came in reluctantly but without fanfare, and we put him on the bank beside the others.

Tommy caught a lake trout, too, when he ran his wobbler down along the bottom. After that, he hooked a chum salmon that pulled free. Then, suddenly, we hit the silvers. Tommy began taking them consistently, once he'd found the far-off point to cast to, and adopted a low and slow retrieve.

I had a strike and lost the fish. Then hit a second and lost it, too. I had a feeling they were grayling. I had a hard time reaching the silvers with the fly, but finally I hooked one solidly and he came leaping out for a broad jump and then a skittering slosh that slid him back under the surface again.

The fly rod bent all the way down to my grip and I gave line

. . . but gained it back when he struck slack water on the current's far edge and turned back toward me. The struggle seesawed back and forth, but the double hooks were well set and in the end he slid up on the beach, fresh from the sea and shining silver. Ten pounds, I judged him. That one I kept to round out our strange, assorted bag. I caught two others and released them both, and Tommy with his periodic call, "Fish on!" took and released many more.

It was a day to remember, a lonely day in which we saw a bear and watched some shore birds on the beach and some gulls flying over, but a day in which we heard no human sound until the Beaver's roar again broke the silence.

There are gray days and stormy skies much of the time in the north, but that day was calm with only the slightest of occasional ripples to break the endless mirror of the lake. It was bright, with only the lightest screen of clouds to dim the sun slightly from time to time. We were much too busy fishing to move more than a hundred yards from where the plane's floats grounded when we landed or took off. It was big, wide, open country, and we felt its spell all day long as we fished.

When we finally lifted off for Naknek to the north, the sky was filled with silvers and reds to match the colors of the fish we'd caught. It held us silent with our thoughts till we were back to other humans and the edges of our busy world again.

CHAPTER 11

Trout Fishing Notes

ON THOSE FIRST early trout-fishing trips of the year anglers often run into a number of interesting problems. However, this "problem business" in trout fishing gets into the picture almost any time of the year because the trout family is a challenge in angling techniques and tackle.

The fly rod is the natural and usual weapon of the trout fisherman. Only by fly casting can the very light wet or dry fly be presented properly to the fish. Spinning, which permits the casting of trout lures of fairly light weight, has become increasingly popular in recent years. A smaller number of anglers successfully use bait-casting equipment and casting lures ranging from 1/4 ounce up to the standard 5/8-ounce weight or over. Bait fishermen will use any of the above casting methods or any other sort of tackle that will put a bait within reach of the fish.

Of all the fishing methods, fly casting requires the greatest skill. A combination of timing, power, and judgment is essential. That's why those who master the sport of fly fishing derive great satisfaction from it. The use of tiny insect imitations, which must on occasion be so close to perfection that even the angler has difficulty differentiating between the natural and the artificial, opens a field of interest as absorbing as any in the whole field of angling.

The number of different insects trout feed upon is myriad, and although some anglers feel that a few flies are all that are needed in their fly boxes, almost every trout fisherman who has made more than a few trips finds that there are times when only a perfect imitation of a flying ant or a Mayfly or a particular beetle will creel a fish.

Trout fishing in a small mountain or swampy brook is largely a matter of a stealthy approach and a natural presentation. Trout in the narrow waters do not have much room for running and leaping, and the overhanging branches usually preclude much casting or rod action by the angler. The brush fisherman sneaks up and presents his fly or bait on a short line. When a trout is hooked, he comes out speedily by the spring of the rod, or he dives into a snag or tangle for his freedom.

As the streams become larger the fisherman finds room for casting and for playing his fish once they're hooked. When the streams grow large, good casting, and sometimes long casting, is essential. The fish become larger, and considerable casting and playing skill become necessary. Wading, instead of being just a matter of wearing boots to keep one's feet dry, becomes an art requiring surefootedness and good judgment, lest a sudden dropoff or a little too much current give the angler a ducking and perhaps a bad scare.

Although trout may be taken in the lakes by flies and fly casting, especially when they are surface-feeding, they respond more readily to the larger flies and lures that are cast or trolled. They do most of their surface feeding in the spring and fall, seeking the deeper levels when summer warms the surface water. Then it may take considerable weight at the end of a trolling line to get a lure down to them. From the foregoing it is easy to see that trout are fish of widely varying waters and methods of capture.

One of the main drawbacks to trout fishing lies in the limited amount of suitable water or the great number of trout enthusiasts for the amount of trout water available. Fishing on the popular streams may be literally "elbow to elbow" because trout are primarily a stream fish and suitable streams are far too few.

In a lake where the number of fish per cubic foot is usually less anyway, there's no telling where the fish may be; in streams the fish are concentrated in the pools and are usually in less than four feet of water and, therefore, within easy casting reach of any angler who comes along.

In a lake it may be important only to get a lure or bait within reach of a fish. In a stream, putting a lure or bait within reach of a fish is a very simple matter, but to catch a stream fish the lure or bait must be the right one. In stream fishing the problem is one of knowing how to catch fish after they've been located rather than one of finding them. That is the basis for the preference of stream fishing and of trout fishing over other types by many of its devotees.

The study of stream insects and the seasons of their abundance is a part of the game for a seasoned trout angler. A few underwater insects are always present in the streams, others come in cycles. When the air suddenly fills with hatching insects and the trout start feeding like mad, the angler may not have too much time to match the insect with an artificial lure. If he has no suitable imitation in his fly boxes the chances are he'll go fishless, and if he fails to identify the insect and match it quickly, the feeding splurge of the trout may be over before he creels many fish.

There may be a dozen different insects showing on the stream surface, with the trout selecting only one of them for their food. The identification of that particular insect among the many on hand is another problem to tantalize the trout fisherman. Undoubtedly trout fishing is one of the more difficult forms of angling, save on rare occasions or in virgin waters, but it is this very difficulty and the variety of the problems encountered that make it top-flight angling.

Trout are essentially swift-water fish, and they are found in cold, clear rivers and streams and some of the colder, deeper lakes and ponds. Our trout are divided into four main species, the eastern brook, brown, rainbow, and cutthroat. Eastern brook trout are in reality a "charr," not a true trout, but they are essentially trout-like and are generally accepted in the trout classification. They are native to the streams of the Atlantic seaboard. The brown trout and the rainbow, or its sea-going phase, the steelhead, are native to the streams and lakes of the Pacific watershed. However, through widespread stocking any of these three species may be found in almost any section of the country where suitable conditions for trout survival are found. The cutthroat trout is native to the Rockies and the Pacific watershed and, having found less favor with anglers than the other three species, has been less widely stocked.

There has been and probably will continue to be considerable discussion on the question of whether or not the steelhead is a separate species, but the consensus among ichthyologists is that both rainbow and steelhead fit under the single classification of rainbow trout. Any species of trout when running to sea, whether it be brown, eastern brook, rainbow, cutthroat, or Arctic charr will become silvery when it strikes saltwater. That silvery coat is just nature's protective coloring to make the fish less conspicuous in their sea surroundings. When they return to their spawning runs, these silvery fish quickly revert to the usual stream coloration, protective for stream surroundings.

The range of trout fishing is wide. Anglers find these fish in the swiftest of waters, too fast or too cold for other game fish, or in lakes where the temperatures do not exceed their survival maximum, as well as in salt or brackish waters when they are on a sea migration. Trout will go to sea whenever the sea is accessible and offers more abundant feed than does freshwater. This is particularly true of the northern rivers where the summers are short and the insect life much less abundant than in warmer waters. Sea-running brown trout up to twenty pounds are taken from the salt or brackish waters near St. John's, Newfoundland. Sea-running eastern brook trout in the Canadian Atlantic streams range well over seven pounds. Steelheads on the Pacific slopes may reach more than twenty pounds.

Any of the trout species in favorable stream or lake conditions may reach an equal size, but the average trout taken by an angler is a small fish in the six- to eleven-inch range. The lure of fishing for him is not his size so much as his surroundings, shrewdness, and scrappiness. Trout are fish of the wilds, shy and easily frightened. They feed for the most part on small aquatic insects and are so selective that a close imitation of their particular food is essential to success. The trout, conditioned by bucking currents too swift for other gamesters, is a difficult battler on the light tackle required to hook him.

And speaking of hooks, the only one who knows what makes a good hook is the fellow who uses it. Hooks are made for a variety of purposes. The highest quality hooks in the regular runs are those to be used for dry flies. They must be very light so that they can be floated readily by the feathers and fibers of the fly. They must be strong in order to hold large fish. As a result, the steel must be of top quality and temper and the design so carried out that the weight of the steel is utilized to best advantage.

Such hooks usually have tapered eyes which are smaller and neater and use less metal. The bend is usually forged or flattened so that the resistance to unbending is greater than if they were left in their original round cross-section in that critical area. The points must be needle-sharp and the barb flared away from the wire for good gripping.

The temper of hooks is worth discussing. For dry-fly hooks and others, where the greatest strength is required, the temper of the steel should be such that the hook is at the critical point where it is as likely to break as to bend. It is at this point that maximum toughness will be found. Hooks that are harder will stay sharp longer but will be brittle and more easily subject to breakage. Hooks that are softer will bend more easily, lacking strength, and will not stay as sharp. Because they bend easily a soft hook may straighten out in a fish's jaw where a tougher one will hold.

Various types of bends have become associated with certain types of fishing. The round bend or "Model Perfect" is common among dry-fly hooks; the Limerick bend is favored for salmon wet flies and streamers. Long-shanked hooks were created for ease in unhooking fish, short-shanked hooks for light weight and inconspicuousness in floating crickets or grasshoppers over wary fish. Doubles, trebles, blued, bronzed or plated . . . they all have their place in the angler's coverage of fish and fishing. Most important for the angler is to get good ones and to keep them sharp.

CHAPTER 12

Fish Deep and Slow for Early Trout

THE VERY EARLY SEASON trout is almost as different from its mid-spring counterpart as if it were an entirely different species of fish. A trout in a murky, spring runoff at a temperature of around 40° may look much the same as he will two weeks later when the water warms and he's actively feeding. But the similarity doesn't go much further.

When the water is very cold, the trout are lethargic. They lose their urge to feed, and throughout the winter they tend to live on their stored-up energy. Even when food is maintained in normal quantities at all times, in a hatchery for example, the trout will feed less and less as the temperature falls. Trout that have come through a long, cold winter are wearied by the experience. They recuperate quickly, however, with the warming of the waters by the spring sun or rains and the increased food supply. What the opening day fishing is like will depend upon how far the change from winter to spring has progressed at that point.

If opening day arrives before the streams have had a chance to warm up, the fish will be moving around very little. If the streams are already warmed to around 60°, mid-spring conditions with a dry fly as well as a wet one will prevail. A trout under the latter conditions is a swift fish, eager but wary, that laughs at the heaviest flow of water and gathers in insects and other floating or swimming food with the unerring accuracy of a good first baseman.

When the streams are not very far above freezing, the angler probably will have a slim creel. Because he has no strength to waste in bucking the currents, the early trout tends to seek deep eddies. There is such a deep hole and whirling eddy in front of my former home on New York's Battenkill River. From my window I could keep a close tab on the movements of the trout. Both eastern brook and brown trout are present in the stream.

73

The former, better able to stand the cold than the latter, is the one that starts active spring feeding first. Above the deep hole and big eddy there is visible almost half a mile of smooth and steady flowing water without great depth. This beautiful run is barren of trout during the winter, but one day each spring I could see the flash of a feeding trout under the overhanging willow where the deep water ends and the shallower stretch starts.

A day or two later I could take trout partway up the long run, and within a week the better share of the trout that had wintered over or were stocked in the deep pool had worked their way out of the deep water, scattering throughout the length of the run into feeding spots under overhanging trees, behind occasional boulders on the gravelly stream bed, or beside the steep banks.

Before they move out of the eddies, trout won't pay any attention to a swiftly moving fly, and in some cases they're too cold and numb to be able to connect with it if they wanted to. It is under these conditions that many a normally smart trout fisherman gets skunked. Yet for those who know how to find the slowly eddying waters and understand the character of the trout, it may be the easiest time of all to catch fish.

Checking the water temperature is worthwhile, and it will often tell where the fish should be found, whether in the deep eddies or spread out through all the water; but temperature alone is far from reliable. The trouble with a thermometer is that it tells only what the temperature is at a given moment. If a full temperature record for the preceding week or two were available, the knowledge of the temperature at the moment would be more valuable.

For instance, suppose the trout in the stretch of the Battenkill previously mentioned had moved up into the long run because of an early warm spell, and then a sudden cold snap had sent the water temperature plummeting back to 42°. The fish already in the spring feeding positions, having a few good meals under their belts, would stay there and could be fished for. A similar reading of 42° on the stream thermometer, if there had been no warm spurt previously, would mean that there would be no fish in the run at all.

Temperature reading the same; fishing entirely different! The simplest way to find fish is to use the time-tested method of cut and try. Try the deep pools and eddies. Trout are there under almost all stream conditions. If there are no resulting strikes, try the slightly swifter water, and then the shallows, fishing each of them both slow and fast and both surface and deep. When you find the fish, concentrate on that type of water.

Early fishing is usually deep fishing. Trout normally lie deep during the early season for a very good reason. The irregularities of the stream bed are the cause of the eddies in the flow. If the stream bed were as smooth as a sluice there would be no eddies, no pools, and no rest for the fish in it. The top water is less affected by the roughness of the stream bed than the water at the bottom. Top water may eddy and boil and look like a good resting place for a fish, but no matter how good it looks the bottom looks better to a lazy or tired fish. It is at the low level that the comfort of motionless water can best be achieved.

Another reason for early fishing being better deep is that the spring runoff, which carries a lot of food with it, deposits it into the eddies along with the natural insect and minnow food already there. The early food is likely to be squirmy and crawly, slow-moving and sinking, in comparison with the later food in the form of fast-swimming nymphs or hatching and flying insects, which are found on or nearer the surface and which must be pursued by the trout if he is to catch them.

Deep fishing is easy and normal for the worm or bait fisherman and difficult for the fly fisherman. That is why the bait fisherman usually fares better than the fly caster in the first days of the season. Fly rods do not cast sinkers well and, as a result, a couple of light split shot are as much as a fly caster can handle. That may add a few inches of depth to his retrieve, but his fly will still pass well over the heads and out of the realm of interest of most fish. When the water passing over the top of bottom eddies that hold the fish is swift, it is practically impossible to get a fly down to within striking range.

That brings us to the second important factor in early fishing— the speed of the retrieve. A bait fisherman can let the sinker hold his bait in position on or near the bottom where the slowly cruising or drifting fish have plenty of time to look it over and take it. The fly caster rarely uses enough weight to hold his fly within inches of the bottom while he moves it slowly along.

Fly casting is a game of motion, of casting rhythms and of normal retrieves that are timed for mid-season fishing. Only by breaking the normal timing of the retrieve and slowing it down to a minimum can the fly caster hope to compete with the bottom-fishing bait angler. It can be done by using as much weight as the fly rod will handle, casting upstream at an angle and across the current so that the fly will drift and sink to the right spots. Then the actual fishing takes place when the angler moves his fly just fast enough to cover the water or to maintain a tension that will tell him when a fish hits.

Finally we come to the business end of the tackle, what to put on the hook. Will it be feathers or something natural? Worms are just about tops for very early fishing. Trout like them, but there are still better baits, especially where the fish are wary. They are the small, crawly, and squirmy things that live in the streams and become abundant just as the streams warm up.

Among them are the caddis creepers, or straw-men, that every trout fisherman knows, small, grublike insects that live and crawl around in a little house of tiny sticks or stones. Trout will take them, house and all, but to make your caddis creepers more tempting than the millions of others already available in the stream, take them out of their cases and hook them lightly through the back of the neck with a No. 14 hook. A 2X leader is usually fine enough and a single buckshot or a couple of BBs is usually enough to get it down to the fish.

Waterworms (crane fly larvae), which can be dug from rotting leaves in the eddies or from certain mossy places, are ugly-looking to the human eye, but to a trout they are beautiful and delicious. One of these on a No. 12 hook is unusually deadly. Either helgramites or stone fly nymphs from the gravelly riffles will catch fish where few other baits will. Both can be captured by holding an old wire window screen in the current below rocks that are being turned over. The current washes the nymphs against the screen and holds them there until they can be picked off by hand.

Fishing with feathers is more difficult. A trout takes a fly and spits it out quickly when he finds it's a fake. The strike must be fast and, since the retrieve must be very slow, a great many fish are missed through not striking quickly enough, and a lot of anglers do not feel the gentle strikes because there is no strong movement of the rod to indicate it.

Fishing with nymphs on small hooks and fine tippets is a delicate and sporting type of angling and an exceptionally effective one. A good live-nymph man can outfish a worm fisherman nine times out of ten. When an angler gets to the point where he can replace the real nymph with an artificial and still take nearly as many trout, he need stand aside for no one.

Fish Deep and Slow for Early Trout

Things to remember for very early trout fishing are (1) that you should fish slow and deep, (2) that trout like worms and live larvae or a good imitation of the same, as to both appearance and action in the water, and (3) that early trout are more likely to be in the deep eddies than anywhere else in the stream.

The problem of getting a fly down deep for early fishing is a serious one for most trout men. Any weight at the end of the leader makes fly casting difficult, as we have said. It means that timing for the casting must be absolutely perfect or else the whole rhythm of the action is disrupted and the caster loses control of direction or distance. Also, when the sinker reaches the end of the back cast, it does so with a jolt that is likely to flip the leader into a messy tangle. Weight concentrated in any one spot along the entire length of fly line and leader will have the same effect.

The secret of success is to use only a slight amount of weight commensurate with the skill of the caster . . . or to use a method of weighting that will distribute the lead over a fair length of the leader instead of concentrating it at one or two spots. When more than one split shot is used, it is wise to separate them, putting each one just above a leader knot (when using a knotted leader) so that it cannot slide along the filament toward the hook under the repeated shocks when the direction is reversed sharply at the end of each forward or back cast.

The best way I know for sinking a leader is to space a series of small weights along its entire length. This causes the leader to sink, a distinct advantage over trying to sink it at only one spot, since when only one point is sunk and the butt end of the leader is near the surface, any movement of the retrieve tends to lift the fly up and away from a low level instead of moving it ahead at the same depth. Bits of fuse wire or small lead strips can be twisted or cramped securely around the leader and will serve to take leaders down for uniformly deep retrieves.

How good is a weighted fly? Some weighted flies are good and some are bad. The good ones are those that are very lightly weighted. As soon as a fly is heavily weighted it loses all its action. It is far better, I believe, to put the weight ahead of the fly and to let the fly move freely under the influence of the currents and eddies, as a natural insect would do, with a sinker ahead of it to control the level than to try and combine lure and sinker in one unit. A heavily weighted fly does not ride level but rides sharply tail-down and with little life. Instead of looking like a deep-traveling minnow or insect, such a fly looks like what it really is, a feathered sinker.

The angler who dashes madly from pool to pool in an early-season trout stream hasn't learned the lesson that it takes plenty of time to study any bit of water being fished. A smart angler never hurries; he covers every pool thoroughly. Your arrival at the pool may have startled the fish and put them into hiding. They will get over their fright in the time you spend looking over the currents and pockets and deciding the most likely spot at which to begin your fishing.

It is particularly wise to go slowly if you are not well acquainted with the water you are about to fish. Don't wet a line until you have studied the direction of the currents where fish are likely to be lying in wait for food and the location of rocks and other obstructions where fish are likely to be gathered because they afford protection and cover.

CHAPTER 13

The Lost Art of Worm Fishing

LET'S HAVE A standing ovation for the worm, the lowly little critter who is all things to all fishermen. No other single bait is so adaptable, so much at home in all fishing circles—or so maligned. When a man takes his son fishing for the first time, what do they use for bait? A hundred to one, they use worms.

Or take the veteran fisherman who has spent two unsuccessful weeks fishing with dry flies for landlocked salmon. On the last day of his vacation when he's wondering how he'll explain an empty creel to the folks at home, what do his thoughts turn to? Worms, sure-fire, never-fail worms.

Yet, when that fisherman puts aside his fancy flies and tries for his landlock with a worm, he has a guilty feeling. Chances are, he did his very first fishing with a cane pole and a worm, but now, he feels, he has advanced beyond such crudities. Besides, he has been listening to the whispering campaign that is always going on against the worm; he has come to believe that worms are unsportsmanlike because fish can't resist them.

That's poppycock. It's true that almost everything that swims in freshwater, from sunfish to salmon, seems born with a taste for worms. But it doesn't necessarily follow that all you have to do is drape a worm on your hook, toss the rig into the water, and brace yourself for the inevitable strike.

Any fish can resist any worm if it's served up to him in a haphazard fashion that arouses his suspicions. Fishing with a worm can be a real art, requiring every bit as much skill and finesse as snaking down the driest dry fly. It's high time fishermen stopped looking down their noses at the worm as the fishing accomplice for children and beginners. The fact is, fishing with a worm can be just as simple or just as difficult as you care to make it. Why wait? Likely as not there's a supply of the new secret-weapon bait within a hundred feet of you at this moment. Dig them up and try them out.

The worms most often used in fishing come in two models, regular and king-size—the earthworm and the night crawler. Earthworms abound in almost any rich soil; you'll have no trouble finding them. Night crawlers take a bit more effort. They get their name from their fondness for leaving their burrows to crawl abroad on nights when the earth is wet with rain or dew. Hunting them is almost as much fun as fishing with them. Most experts go forth equipped with a dimmed flashlight and tennis shoes. You spot your quarry and advance quietly until you can grab it.

Now that you know how to get your bait, let's shift perspective for a moment and assume the fish's point of view. If we can better understand what appeals to a fish, we'll have a clearer idea of the worm fisherman's problems. As a fish, you have certain known characteristics: (1) you're mad for worms, (2) a good deal of the time you're hungry and even if you've just had a big dinner, you're not above grabbing a between-meals snack if it's attractive enough—or if you just want to make sure nobody else gets it. *But* (3) you're suspicious; you've got to be or you don't live long. You play everything safe—especially tidbits that don't look just right to you.

Maybe you're primarily a lake- or pond-dwelling fish, like a panfish or a largemouth bass or northern pike. If so, you rarely see worms except those washed into the water by the runoff of rains. They're either sinking to the bottom or already on the bottom when you spot them. And since worms can't swim, they're wriggling frantically, trying to get out of the unfamiliar aquatic atmosphere.

But what if you're a river fish? Then your worms will come twisting and turning downstream with the current. They may be bouncing along the bottom or they may be caught in the swifter upper currents. In each case, the situation and the circumstances may vary; still, a pattern does emerge, and it offers the secret of successful worm fishing: for best results, your worm must arrive in the fish's dining room as if he just happened along naturally. And, with very few exceptions, he should come on the scene full of pep and wiggle. Your task as a fisherman is obvious; now, how do you accomplish it? Let's get technical.

First, use small hooks. The exact size, to be determined by experimentation, will depend on the size of the worms you use and the kind of fish you're likely to catch. Your tackle box should hold hooks in a range of sizes. Start off with a very small hook, say a No. 12. If you get strikes but fail to hook your fish, shift to the next larger size and try again.

Your object in using a small hook is twofold. It's easier to conceal the hook—you don't need to thread so much of the worm onto it to hide it from the fish's suspicious eye. And you allow the worm more freedom of movement to cavort—and thus to advertise his presence. He'll live longer, too.

Next, use a long leader of the daintiest practical size. Again, experimentation will have to be your guide. Just don't try to land a ten-pound largemouth bass using a two-pound test leader—unless you are more skillful than most of us. Be dainty when you put the worm on the hook, too. Your aim is merely to disguise the hook and hold the worm on it. Don't bunch up the worm. On a small hook, it is only necessary to slip the point and barb under the worm's so-called collar, a ring of thickness about one third of the way back from his head. On larger hooks, when you have to put on more of the bait, loop the worm. But always leave both ends free to wiggle.

Above all, keep a lively worm on your hook. When a worm shows signs of tuckering out, replace him with a fresh stablemate from your bait can. You may have to bait up every five minutes or so, and you'll go through a lot of worms that way—but you'll catch fish and that's what you're there for.

So much for your terminal rig—the part of your equipment the fish sees. Now comes the all-important factor—technique. How can you best deliver your worms to the right spot?

The first consideration is what gear to use. Tom Sawyer's old cane-pole-and-bobber rig will still catch fish; it's been doing so for generations. But more advanced equipment is easier to work with and more efficient, and more fun. The exact type of rig to use depends largely on where you fish.

For simply paying out line and letting your worm drift downstream on the current of a cascading mountain stream, fly-fishing equipment is in a class by itself. The relative rigidity of the line and its ability to float make it ideal for navigating around rocks and rapids with a minimum of snagging. Plug or bait-casting equipment or a spinning rig can be used the same way, but aren't so well suited to the job. If, however, you move to a pond or lake, and casting is the order of the day, a fly-fishing rig is out of place.

Even when practiced by an expert, fly casting—with its whip-like snap—usually tears a worm off the hook. Tossing out a worm with a bait-casting outfit is even more impractical; the worm just doesn't have enough heft to go anywhere. Not so with spinning. You can take a single earthworm on the end of a spinning rig and send him across the water for a surprising distance.

If you've a fondness for trolling, you can't go wrong with any of the three types of equipment. You need be governed only by your personal tastes. And for so-called still-fishing, either on the bottom or with a float, both spinning equipment and bait-casting equipment are suitable.

Now you're ready for the payoff—the actual delivery of the worm. Success or failure hangs in the balance; all your preparations, however elaborate, will be wasted if you mis-cue now. Just remember that you'll get the best results if you always fish your worm as if he weren't on the end of a line. Make him look natural.

If you're casting, flick him out onto the water easily. Your technique should allow the worm to drop cozily into the water with the least possible fuss—as if he had lost his footing and fallen into the water accidentally.

If you're trolling, try a spinner ahead of the worm. Just ease along. Occasionally vary the speed of the boat—which will change the level at which your bait travels through the water.

If you're still-fishing, know your good spots and let the worm (a lively one, of course) rest on the bottom. If you're in weeds, use a bobber to hold the bait above the weeds and in sight of the fish. Lower your rig into the water gently and move it around occasionally to cover the most territory.

If you're fishing a stream, float your worm downstream. But don't hold him against the current; no fish ever saw a worm battling upstream. When you reach the end of your line, reel in and send your worm off on another downcurrent junket.

Patience is your guide in fishing with a worm. Go slow. Take it easy. The worm is a natural bait and should be fished in a natural manner. If you've rigged your tackle right, your worm will bear a lot of scrutiny before the fish wises up to the fact that you're on the other end of the line.

Now, if the action is slow, there are some added tricks that will increase your chances of a strike. Try these: Chum. Use the old saltwater technique of piquing the fish's appetite by tendering him bits of food before sneaking your worm in among them. Small chunks of worm will work fine—even crumbs of bread if you're short of bait.

Dump clods of dirt into the water in both streams and lakes. You'll at least attract the attention of the fish. You may fool them into thinking there's been a small landslide and they'll be looking for food to follow in the wake of the sod.

Stir up the bottom. If you're fishing in a stream in hip boots or waders, use your feet to overturn small rocks. That will serve much the same purpose as the clods—and you'll also kick up tiny marine life, thereby alerting the fish downstream that dinner's on the way.

In fishing with a worm, as in fishing with anything else, never forget: angling is the most unpredictable of sports. Fishing rules are made to be broken. There are times when a whole worm will be refused but half a worm or less will be gobbled up. There are times when you will excite the fish and stimulate them to strike if you cast your worm with a great commotion, instead of stealthily. But—before you break the rules, *know them!*

All right, you're in business. Have fun, and if anybody sniffs at you when you open your little pouch of worms, be quick to quote the words of the immortal Izaak Walton, perhaps the greatest fisherman of them all. In the *Compleat Angler*, published in 1653, recalling one good day's fishing, he comments with satisfaction: "The last trout I caught was with a worm. . . ."

CHAPTER 14

Streamers for Trout

THE STREAMER FLY is a minnow imitation, and minnows are one of the favored foods of all trout, the basic diet of the larger ones. The name "streamer" applies to long, slender flies which typify the fish shape in contrast to the usual wet fly which follows or represents the various insect shapes.

The first streamers were used in the early 1920's and my first recollection of them is in an Abbey and Imbrie catalog in 1922. That original streamer fly was called a "rooster's regret" and consisted of a hook of standard shank length with a normal wet-fly body, two pairs of long hackles matched and applied in the manner of wet-fly wings over the back and extending a long way behind the bend of the hook.

To complete the fly, two or three hackles were wound around the shank just behind the eye of the hook in time-honored fashion. They were, as I recall, size 6 and available in white and barred rock colorations only. Dyed patterns were to come later. So were all the modern refinements.

Once it received public notice, the streamer-fly idea spread rapidly. Although they were decried by the conventional trout fisherman as monstrosities, the few nonconformists who tried them soon found that they took big fish that had long resisted the insect-like patterns in common use. Within a few years the streamer fly had gained wide acceptance, and the whole fly-tying fraternity began refining the crude originals into the long, slender, minnow-like patterns of today. They were easy to fish with, and no extra tackle or change of method was necessary in order to use them. Seldom has a tackle innovation been so quickly and universally accepted.

For a long time there remained a cleavage between wet flies and streamers, denoted by size. Wet flies were small flies, streamers large ones, but in time the streamer idea showed up in small hook sizes and the void between them was filled with such a variety of patterns that it is difficult to draw the line between long-shanked wet flies and short-shanked streamers. For the purposes of this discussion we will be concerned with streamer flies as minnow imitations, regardless of size, and will consider fishing them on that basis.

The first streamers were treated like overgrown wet flies and fished just as wet flies had been fished for generations. They were cast down and across the current at an angle of approximately 45° with the line of flow and the rod was twitched as the current carried and swung them to a position directly below the fisherman. When they reached the point where the current no longer gave them any motion with regard to the stream bed, they were recast at the 45° angle. That was and still is the normal way of fishing a wet fly and is probably by far the best way to fish a streamer when the trout are hungry and active.

This standard method of fishing covers a maximum amount of water with a minimum of effort on the part of the angler. As the caster moves down through the pool, his fly sweeps across that part of the water in which the great bulk of the fish are lying. The pattern of the fly's travel is like the contour plow lines on a good farmer's hillside. All the fish under the pattern get a look at the fly, fleeting though that look may be. Slower, more concentrated presentation may be better for spot fishing for individual fish, but no other coverage is so effective for actively feeding fish.

The motion of the streamer under this standard method is good. Though it is questioned by many, I firmly believe the main reason a trout hits a fly is because it appears to have life, that motion is more important than pattern. There is a constant stream of both floating and submerged particles being carried along by flowing trout water. As long as they follow the movement of the water without variation, the trout would have to make a close inspection of most objects to determine whether they be insect or similarly shaped and colored pieces of bark. However, as soon as anything in the size range of his normal food moves across or at any divergence from the flow, the unsuspecting trout assumes that, having life, it must be good to eat. Unless satiated, he'll take it. The more wary fish, wiser to the ways of anglers, has developed caution and looks things over more carefully. He studies size and shape . . . and looks for a leader or any other attachment he might consider unnatural.

With the standard method of wet-fly fishing the fly moves rapidly, and the fish hasn't much time to make a decision. Many a fly has been taken in haste before it "escaped" which, if fished at a slower speed would have been recognized as a fraud and ignored. The standard method gives maximum apparent life to the fly and the greatest water coverage with the least effort.

In normal fishing, with both fly and leader unweighted, the fly travels within a few inches of the surface. For feeding fish this is the preferred depth. The fly is visible to more fish over a wider area at, or just under, the surface than at any greater depth. It is silhouetted against the light and, as a result, is most conspicuous. As it sinks to lower levels it is more likely to blend with the darkening background. With more wary fish, where a slower retrieve and a more perfect imitation are required, this loss in range of visibility is not important.

In the early season when the water is cold and the trout lethargic, another factor enters the picture. The fly must be brought to the fish for, though he may see it at a considerable distance, he'll only consider it worth chasing if the chase is short and not too strenuous. Since the current is swiftest and the water deepest in the early days of the season, it requires the greatest thought and skill to fish a streamer slow and deep at that time.

In the early season the streams are wildest, and in that first spring washing of the valleys they have accumulated the greatest quantity of food for the trout. Then the trout of the cold, high water are concentrated in the eddies for several reasons. They like the quieter water since it demands less strength of them, and they are at their weakest when winter ends.

The bulk of the trout food carried by the stream is slightly heavier than the water which carries it and so it tends to settle toward the bottom. It collects and comes to rest in the eddies. The food is on or near the bottom and so is the fish. The mere depth of water over him is a source of safety from birds and other predators, another factor tending to make the trout choose the deep eddies during winter and early spring when he realizes he is weaker and less alert than usual.

It would be very difficult to reach the lower levels of the streams wherever the water is swift, but to fish near bottom in the eddies is not hard. Sometimes it can be done without adding any weight to the streamer by casting it above the eddy and letting the current swirl it down within reach of the fish. It takes time for the current to carry the fly down, or for its own weight and that of the line to sink it.

Two or three casts could be made by the standard method while one is being made at an upstream angle and allowed to sink into an eddy. Proportionately less water is covered, proportionately fewer fish see the fly, but slow and deep fishing will take three fish for one against the surface-fished fly when the trout are deep.

It is worth remembering that most silk lines are higher in specific gravity than nylon fly lines and will sink more readily. High specific-gravity lines are better for almost all phases of wet-fly fishing.

It is difficult for the impatient angler to wait till his fly sinks far enough before starting his retrieve, but wait he must if his fishing is to be efficient. Then when the retrieve starts, it is important—and much more difficult—to impart an attractive or life-like motion to a streamer at slow speed than when moving swiftly.

I like to give harder twitches of the rod as the depth of the fly is increased. A slow retrieve is necessary if the low level is to be maintained. A swift pull on the fly lifts it toward the surface, and even though a fisherman lets his fly get well down toward the bottom, if he retrieves normally it will shoot rapidly to the surface. To keep it down, the retrieve must be slow and the twitches widely spaced.

To feel the strike on a slow-moving fly is more difficult, too. The angler's sensitiveness to any variation of normal rod or line pressure must be increased and his reactions must be faster. I like to keep the rod low and at an angle of about 30° from the direction in which the line approaches the rod. Occasionally fish will hook themselves, but a well-timed strike is a practical necessity. Many anglers fail miserably at fishing a fly deep by muffing the strikes they do get, and after a brief trial at deep-fly work, go back to fishing the surface where most fish, in striking a swiftly moving streamer on a tight line, automatically hook themselves.

Any weight on the fly or leader detracts from the pleasure of fly casting. The addition of a sinker demands almost perfect timing from the caster. The back cast must straighten out but not lag; the forward cast must begin just as the backward inertia of the weight dies out. Deep fishing with a weighted fly or leader is more troublesome and slower than fishing the surface. Most trout fishermen engage in it only when they must and often fish an unweighted fly even when they know a little lead would bring them a heavier creel.

The size of a streamer is far more important than the pattern used. Few anglers realize that the right size streamer one week is not the best size to fish a few weeks later. Most anglers think of minnows as being of uniform size year round. They pick a fly that looks like a good meal for a trout and fish it all season long. A little thought would bring them the realization that minnows have a maturity size and also that they are a crop which starts at the egg and advances through a steady growth to maturity, usually in a period of a few months.

When the new crop is coming along in the spring, these very small minnows greatly outnumber the mature minnows in the stream. They may be smaller but they're more succulent and, perhaps even more important, they're easier for the trout to catch. Ordinarily a fisherman may choose a streamer to match the size of the mature minnows or match in his mind the size of the minnow that would fit best into the maw of the trout he's trying to catch, but when the new spring crop is growing up, his best bet is to match it in size.

Starting out with a No. 10 streamer to match the baby minnows one weekend, you will probably find that a week later a No. 8 will match them better. The following week they'll approach a streamer on a hook of size 6, and another two or three weeks should see them at a maturity size of 4. I usually carry my streamers in that range of sizes with a few No. 2's for streams with larger minnows—or larger trout looking for oversize minnows.

The common hook for the streamer fly is a long-shank type which brings the bend back near the tail of the fly. The long hook catches tail-striking trout and "nippers" that come up behind with a short strike. The long-shanked hook is not as efficient as one with a normal shank in playing a fish. More fish will be lost because of the hook's working loose under the greater leverage of the extended shank than with a normal hook. For fish that tend to hit a fly solidly in the middle or toward the head, the extended shank is a hindrance rather than a help.

The trolling of streamer flies in lakes is commonest in the northeast for brook trout and landlocked salmon. The flies are of good size and the strike to a trolling fly is more likely to be from behind than it is with a fly fished across the current. Long-shanked hooks are important in this phase of streamer fly fishing and, generally, the longer they are the better. Double hooks, in tandem, are effective, especially the "Lee" tandem secured in plastic which prevents twisting and tangling and gives added strength.

A streamer as a tail fly and a regular wet fly as a dropper placed well up the leader is an infrequently used but very effective rig. It can be fished normally, just as one would fish a single tail fly, but the greatest number of strikes can be drawn by a simple variation.

This is to keep the rod high and the line far enough above the water to make the dropper fly skitter while the streamer at the tail rides just under the surface. Maybe the trout think the streamer (minnow) is chasing the dropper fly. At any rate, they're very likely to either take the dropper fly away from the minnow or strike the streamer in retaliation for its invasion of their favored feeding grounds.

Minnows poke around among the rocks, they swim the dead-waters and the shallows, school near brushy snags. Study them and study their movements. A good imitation of their size, general color, and swimming actions is the key to success in streamer fishing.

CHAPTER 15

How to Use
Wet Flies

IN SPRING THE WET FLY is the favorite on the trout streams of the nation—the same old wet fly that has always taken and still takes more trout than the dry flies do, over the continent as a whole. Wet flies work better because under normal conditions the trout takes much more of his insect food under the surface than on it.

Many an angler prefers dry-fly fishing and fishes the floating fly even though he knows he's cutting down his catch by doing so, and not a few members of the fraternity are what is known as "purists" who fish only with the floating fly, regardless of conditions. Yet we must all agree that the underwater fly is a better lure for trout, all in all. During the first month of the season it is near its peak of effectiveness.

In the early days of spring the whole array of insects due to hatch out during the spring and summer are still in the underwater stage. A trout will take a dry fly then if conditions are right, but he'll take a wet fly, properly presented, much more regularly.

What flies are best to use? The patterns you have faith in, of course. The ones you know are tried and true, especially during those first very cold days when fish rise infrequently and when for hours at a time the most beautiful water may seem completely empty of trout. Use what the old-timers are using, and if you haven't a better selection, use one of these: Royal Coachman, Leadwing Coachman, Dark Cahill, Quill Gordon, Black Gnat, Professor, Blue Quill, Brown Hackle, Hare's Ear.

Early-season trout tend to lie low in the water, so take it easy and let your fly get some depth as you draw it through the water. If you're fishing with a nylon line, cursing won't help sink it, but a rubdown with soap to take off all the remaining traces of grease will.

A line with a specific gravity greater than 1.000—heavier than water—is best for wet-fly fishing. Incidentally, it will cast better, too. Such a line will sink more readily and will carry your fly several inches or more beneath the surface, depending upon the speed of the retrieve and the length of the cast.

If a few inches isn't enough, you may have to resort to using some lead. A small split shot or two, located just above the leader knots to prevent slipping, will help greatly in sinking your fly and shouldn't interfere too much with your casting. It's never pleasant to cast with a weight at the end of your fly line, but if you wait the required time on your back casts, you'll have little or no trouble with tangling leaders and will find a casting rhythm that will be smooth and easy. If the lead jerks on your back cast, make your pause a little longer. Steady casting without attempting long "shooting" of the line will be smoother and cause less tangling of the weighted leader.

Small lengths of lead wire or small lead strips can be wound tightly around the leader strands. By having several such small weights distributed evenly throughout the leader's length, smoother casting is obtained than when the weight is all lumped in one or two spots. A weighted fly will travel lower in the water than the conventional fly, either when used alone or in conjunction with some other weight. A few such flies in your favorite patterns should be in your fly box for early fishing.

There's an art to wet-fly fishing, and a thousand things to remember. There isn't space here to go into all of them, but here are a few simple tips. First of all, be sure that your leader and fly tippet match. A No. 10 fly, for example, will work perfectly on a 2X leader. It will work almost as well on 1X. On anything larger in diameter, the knot will begin to get bulky and have an effect on the way the fly swims through the water, and the leader will be stiff enough to alter its natural swimming course, often turning it on its side or causing it to travel through the water at an unnatural angle.

You can go too far in the other direction. On finer gut, the No. 10 hook becomes heavy for the strength of the knot. Below 4X there's a good chance that the leader material will fray at the knot or that the pull required to set a hook of that size will be enough to break the tippet at the strike.

The error is usually on the side of gut that's too heavy rather than a tippet that's too light, but either one is bad. The tippet size should change with any wide variation in size of fly. When you change from an 8 to a 14, better add a finer tippet, and when you switch from a No. 12 to a big streamer, better increase the size of the gut.

Most wet-fly fishermen cast across and slightly down the stream and let the current swing their flies across the flow to a point almost directly below them without changing the positions of their rods to any degree. By holding the rod high and upstream at the beginning of the retrieve and gradually moving it lower and pointing it more nearly toward the fly as it makes its swing, the fly can be slowed down, which means that it will sink lower in the water and give the fish more time to see it and rise to it. By starting the retrieve with rod pointed downstream at a low angle and moving it upstream at an increasing angle as the fly makes its swing, the speed of the fly can be increased, a factor that should make it more attractive in slack water.

Wet flies and nymphs are exceptionally effective under certain conditions when fished directly upstream. If your fly is a sufficiently good imitation of the type of food the trout are seeking, you won't have to impart any motion to it by means of the rod. The current will do the job for you. Flies fished upstream sink more readily and follow the natural path of most of the trout's food. Upstream fishing requires quick reactions and an instant realization of the strike when it comes. The shorter the line the simpler it is to feel the almost imperceptible halting of the fly as the trout closes his jaws on it, often for only a fleeting instant.

It may be surprising to find out how short a line can be effective in this upstream fishing, especially in turbulent pocket water. Traveling slowly, the fly goes right down where the fish want it. They can take it without exposing themselves and with a minimum of effort. But don't crowd your luck. Move slowly and quietly. Cast with care.

You don't *have* to impart any motion to your fly by means of your rod to catch trout, but almost all top-notch wet-fly fishermen do try to give special action to their wet flies. That's something each man must learn for himself. The action should be one that isn't tiring and that attracts fish. A simple vibration of the rod by making the hand tremble is favored by some. Others, myself included, prefer to retrieve in fairly smooth jerks of a foot or two at a time, combining the pull of line and rod, or to alternate between moving the rod and stripping in line.

CHAPTER 16

Early Summer Trout

TROUT FISHING IN APRIL and trout fishing in June are two different things. It is unfortunate that so many beginners at trout fishing start in with the opening of the season and, discouraged by the cold and windy fishing conditions, fail to stick at it long enough to enjoy trout fishing when spring is in full bloom.

April trout fishing often means ice forming in the guides and snow flurries whistling over the hill. April fishing is for hardy souls who are too eager to wait for the pleasant days to come later.

June fishing for trout may not be as easy for the beginner using bait as it is on opening day when the freshly stocked streams are thrown open to fishing, but it is more truly representative of trout fishing as a sport. In the early season, trout are often concentrated in the deep pools, while the shallow runs and pockets are empty of fish. In June the fish have spread out all through the streams, wherever their food is to be found. Under these conditions, the fly fisherman will find it easier going than in April, but the bait fisherman will find his quarry much more difficult to fool. June is a better time for the beginner at fly casting to make his start.

In June the streams normally run clear and at a moderate level midway between the high water of the opening and the low, slow flow of August. The trout have had weeks of good feeding and are full-bodied and strong. Their activity, supported by their added strength, is at its peak. Their wariness, after a month or so of being fished for—new stockings excepted—has increased, too. But their feeding habits, rather than being limited to sunken or bottom food at opening day or to an exact match of the fly hatches in May, are very wide in scope and cover everything from the smallest of flies and nymphs to grasshoppers, June bugs, and bumblebees.

June days are long and there are extra hours of daylight fishing added to each weekend trip. The angler's shirt is open at the neck, and his sweaters and woolly underwear are carried only as spares for an exceptionally cold and windy day. The water is clear except for roil resulting from an unusual rainfall. Rivers are easier to wade and fish. The foliage is lush and green. These are the days to remember.

The bait fisherman will find that trout are generally on the move. In April they may be lethargically concentrated in the deep and quiet water and by August they may have settled again into similar concentrations where cool springs attract them or where the few remaining deep pools satisfy their need for safety. The June fisherman rarely fills his creel by sitting on the bank with a can of worms and fishing a single eddy. He will take some trout, but rarely will he take them in limit lots.

Worms are exceptionally effective right after a thundershower or heavy rain has raised and slightly roiled the streams. Trout feed avidly on a sudden rise of water at this season, and the fisherman who can be on the spot with a can of night crawlers when the streams start going up should do considerable business. Best results are usually to be had by using a light sinker or none at all and letting the night crawler drift with the current.

A single No. 8 or No. 10 hook holding the night crawler near the band is inconspicuous to the trout and gives the worm a chance to show life and action. A big trout will take such a free-drifting night crawler in a single gulp. Even a middle-size trout is likely to take the major part of the worm into his mouth enough to be hooked. Only a small nibbler will grab one end and yank at a time when great quantities of food from the flooded fields are being washed into the streams. The small hook on a fairly light leader will fool and hold a big trout.

For success in June, under normal conditions, the bait fisherman should endeavor to cover more water than in his early fishing and to use other baits besides worms. Sinkers should be lighter or should be eliminated entirely. The trout are active and alert, and they'll take a moving bait with a rush instead of working up to it gradually and slowly sucking it in. By casting to a point upstream from a good trout location, the bait can be allowed to drift down to the fish naturally as the current carries it, and more strikes will be secured.

Many top worm-fishermen use a long fly rod or a spinning rod and wade upstream just as the dry-fly angler does, fishing the likely water from behind the trout in their area of blindness. This is more work than sitting on the bank and letting the bait lie motionless on the bottom of the pool, but it is also more productive.

Small minnows are deadly in June. Minnows are more or less an annual crop, and the minnows spawned the previous fall should be about 2 or 2½ inches long by June. This is an attractive size for a trout and is just about as small as an angler can handle in fishing without an extreme amount of care and ultra-fine tackle.

Grasshoppers and crickets are plentiful in the fields and are welcomed by trout. Stone fly and other nymphs are full grown and often big enough to use as bait. Most of these other baits look more natural to a trout than a worm which, although common in high water, is not often found in the streams in the clear water of early summer.

The fly fisherman finds June trout actively feeding at all depths. When flies are hatching, the trout will be seen rising to them, but when there are no hatches of flies, the fish will still have one eye cocked toward the surface for some bumbling land insect that may stray out over the water but lack flying power to carry him safely back to shore. Even when there are no signs of rising fish the dry-fly man may fish the water with a certainty that his fly will not go unnoticed.

While the hatches are in progress, the fisherman's best bet is to match them as closely as possible and to use as fine a leader as he thinks he can handle the fish on. When there are no signs of rising fish, a fairly large fly of heavy body is best to use, in an effort to simulate a Mayfly or the occasional stray land insect. A larger fly will be more easily seen by the fish than one of standard size.

The skater or fluffy spider (eight to ten turns of large hackle on a No. 16 hook) which is skidded across the water in a series of sharp twitches is an exceptionally effective dry fly at this time of year. Its action is readily noticed by the trout, and these flies will draw rises when nothing else seems tempting. This is a tantalizing lure, and I like to concentrate its use on the most likely spots, making a dozen or more casts wherever I'm sure fish are lying, rather than covering the water in a more uniform manner.

The dry-fly hatches of June are more likely to come in the morning or in the late evening, while those of May tend to take place in the warmth of midday. Once the fisherman learns to know his stream, he can plan his day in order to be at certain preferred stretches when the fly hatches are due and to fish the intervening water during the remainder of the day. The angler accomplished in all phases of trout fishing may, on a June day, fish dry-fly for a few hours in the morning and then change over to wet flies, streamers, nymphs, or bait until he returns to the dry fly again for the evening rise.

The wet-fly fisherman needs finer leaders and often must use smaller flies than for early fishing. The current has slowed down, wet flies travel through the water at slower speeds, and the fish have a better chance to look them over before making up their minds whether to strike or let the darn thing go on out of range. Because the fish has a better opportunity to study the fly, it must be chosen with greater care and must more accurately represent the living underwater food for which he searches.

Nymphs, which are better aquatic insect imitations than ordinary wet flies, are better fish-getters, too. The slower a fly travels, the finer the leader should be. If weight is needed to sink the fly or nymph to a desired depth, it should be added in the form of very small twists of lead or a single small weight at a fair distance up the leader from the nymph.

Streamer flies, which are minnow imitations, are effective at this time of year. It is difficult to advise a particular time of day to fish streamers except to say that they are worth using during periods when there is no surface activity on the part of the trout. Being a large fly, they're more easily seen in rough and boiling water.

They'll often take trout which are actively engaged in feeding on a hatch, and they'll draw strikes in the flat calm of clear, still water at bright noon. Streamers tend to take fewer fish than the smaller wet flies or nymphs, but the fish they take run much larger.

The spinning angler should use his finest line and work his small lures slowly across the deep pools. He should also work small metal or combination metal or plastic and feather lures in the tumbling pockets and shallow riffles. This is a time when the spinning angler can cover the river. The fish are no longer concentrated in the pools and runs, and he will often take more and bigger fish from the riffles and pockets than he can by fishing only the deep water. I like the twisting, darting, all-metal lures as well as any for June.

Bait casting with light lines and long rods will be just about as effective as spinning on the trout streams. The lures are about the same size and the line need be little, if any, heavier. More and more bait casters are showing up on the trout waters and they're making good catches. A plug halfway between the fly-rod size and standard bass size is a deadly lure for trout. Old-timers who have always felt no self-respecting trout would take anything bigger than a No. 10 Royal Coachman are being surprised by the size and number of trout succumbing to plugs on streams where bait casting used to be unheard of.

Originally bait casting was touted as a method for taking the big trout out of the streams, which it did. Most anglers who believed in artificial lures rather than bait accepted the belief common to the confirmed fly fisherman that the use of a plug rod on a stream was a method to be employed only when there were too many big cannibal trout and too few fish in the range that delights the fly fisherman. Spinning changed all that. When spinning took hold, it was natural for the bait-casting rods to follow.

The preferred lure seems to be the Dardevle-type wobbling spoon or a similar lure with considerable weight for its size, a lot of flash, and a good action at very slow speeds. If plugs are used, they are usually small and heavy, but a veteran I know swears by a jointed Pikie and takes a lot of trout with it.

Actually, casting lures will take trout at any time during the open season. In the high-water time following opening day it may be necessary to cast the wobbling spoon upstream to a point above the place to be fished and let it drift and sink to a low level at the right spot before the retrieve is begun. When that big lure comes sashaying along at the level where the trout are feeding, they have a strong tendency to wallop it.

As the water drops, fishing with the short rod becomes easier. Retrieves can be slower and the path of the lure more easily controlled. In the warm, low water of the late season when the larger fish are concentrated almost entirely in the deep pools and spring holes, the caster can consistently put his lure within striking range of trout. It is at this time that night fishing comes into vogue.

Fishing at night on a trout stream is rarely easy. With a fly rod the pools must be known intimately and adequate allowances made for back cast, direction, and distance. It is sensible only in open water, where there's ample room behind, or for a few individual trout that may be lined up in a given direction by the skyline when standing on a certain spot and lengthening the cast until a certain mark on the fly line is felt at the angler's stripping hand.

The spinning outfit is not as accurate nor, I believe, as easy to control as the bait-casting outfit. At night on a stream it is the more awkward of the two. The rod is longer, requiring more space, and it is more difficult to judge the distance of the cast.

Sometimes trout, especially the big ones, will take a lure with a savage rush, but they often dart in at a spoon or lure and touch it lightly or miss it entirely. A great many times they'll follow a lure, making occasional passes at it but failing to touch it. An angler may see several such flashes on a single cast, yet never feel the fish strike. Trout are not always hooked in the mouth, especially the small ones which are frequently hooked outside it, as occasionally happens with the larger spinning lures. Surprisingly, a small trout, from seven to ten inches long, can be taken on plugs, and the proportion of small trout seems higher for nighttime than daytime casting.

It doesn't seem to be hunger alone that determines whether or not a trout will strike these lures. At night the casting is likely to be concentrated in a few pools. A fish or two may be taken right at the start, and then, after half an hour or more of casting over the same water, two or three more fish may suddenly decide to hit. The catches using this method of night fishing have been excellent during a time when fishing by all other methods was poor.

Plug casting is best on the larger streams but will work on narrow waters as well. The casts need not be long and they should be fished carefully right in to the shore or boatside. The best outfit is your favorite, but all other things being equal, a six- to nine-pound test line and fairly small lures will take more fish than heavier lines and lures. A six-foot length of three- to six-pound test nylon can be spliced to the casting line for daytime fishing. Bait casting is an effective way to take trout and one that I feel sure will increase in popularity.

As an old-timer, I'm saddened a little by the throng of spinners and bait casters that will grace our trout streams in the future. It takes a long time to become a well-rounded fly fisherman, and fly casting is a delicate and beautiful way to take a delicate and beautiful quarry. But the heavy lures do take fish, and they're destined to hold high favor on the trout streams.

Night fishing with flies is effective, too, and will bring in superb catches when conditions are right. After-dark fishing is just getting good about June. Large flies like 2's, 4's and 6's are better than the conventional 10's and 12's. Both light and dark patterns work well, and a good policy is to use two contrasting wet flies with a white or light-colored fly at the tail. Night fishing calls for greater caution in casting, and only a man who knows his stream thoroughly and is either very brave or very foolish should do much wading.

Night fishing with dry flies is more difficult. Few fish will be hooked on the floating fly unless it is dragging or unless the trout makes a good, noisy rise. To be successful, night fishing with a dry fly calls for considerable advance daytime thinking and planning. An almost exact knowledge of big-fish feeding stations is essential to success. Where the big ones are known to feed regularly in certain pools at night and where fly hatches tend to come out after darkness rather than during daylight hours, night fishing with the dry fly is the answer.

The foregoing has been written about stream fishing. Trout are present in the lakes and ponds . . . and early summer is as good in the still waters as in those that flow. The land bugs that drop to the water from the fringe of overhanging leafy limbs around a pond draw the trout to the shorelines for mornings and evenings. Dawn and dusk are the hours when the cruising fish tend to move into the flow of either outlet or inlet. All methods of casting will work on a pond. Fishing toward the shore from a boat or canoe is the best bet for the caster, whatever his method.

If the pond is open and generally weed-free, spinning is the best method. If there are snags and weeds to contend with, the bait caster's slightly heavier line has the advantage over the spin caster, and when the trout are feeding on small food, which can only be imitated and cast by a fly rod, that method is the one to use. When fishing from a boat or canoe, the fisherman can carry two types of casting outfits with him and use the one most suited to the occasion. In general, lake fish respond better to a larger lure than do the trout of the streams. Lakes and ponds are often windy, a further advantage for the bait-casting and spinning anglers in comparison with the fly-rod man.

Where trout streams empty into lakes or ponds, the largest trout may move down into the still water. Even though such lakes or ponds may be noted for bass, perch, or other fish, there may be enough trout roaming the waters near the inlet to make it worthwhile to spend a few evenings there each season using lures attractive to big trout.

Don't overlook June on the trout streams. The opening-day crowds have dwindled to a few seasoned anglers, the fishing is never better, and the surroundings are never more beautiful.

CHAPTER 17

Catching Big Trout

THE TAKING OF ONE big trout may well be an accident, but when an angler takes very large trout consistently, season after season, it is the result of specific skill and understanding. The average fisherman working a trout stream catches average-sized fish. The less skillful fisherman usually catches smaller than average trout because the younger, smaller fish are not as wise as the big ones and, being easier to fool, they fall prey to poor fishing tactics. The very skillful fisherman, however, does not usually catch larger than average fish. He simply catches more average-sized trout.

The reason for this is the basic difference between fishing for trout and fishing for big trout. The ordinary expert trout fisherman has all the skills for taking trout, an understanding of their habits and of trout water, yet the catching of big fish requires more than this. The big-trout fisherman must know the stream thoroughly, spending many hours unproductively in scouting for big fish and watching them in order to be at the right spot with a satisfactory lure when one of these lunkers is in the mood to strike. If there are a dozen pools, each of which is capable of supporting a very large trout, he must know which ones actually do harbor an oversized fish and, in general, he must work out a campaign for each trout.

August is a good time to locate these old sockdolagers, and during August there should be a few good chances to take them. The water goes low in midsummer and the holes capable of holding big fish are easy to identify. There must be plenty of water in them and a good hiding place under a cut bank, a submerged log, rocky ledge, or similar cover. Using this hiding place as a home base, a big trout may forage as much as several hundred yards away, always returning to rest and hide when his feeding forays are over.

The fisherman who scouts the stream quietly, walking the

banks, spending time on the bridges and high points of lookout during the bright hours when the sun lights up the pools to advantage, will see big trout. Having located one, he will come back time after time to watch and wait and thus gradually learn the fish's habits and routine. The angler who fishes a pool rarely gets close enough to see these big fish; and, if he does, it is a brief, fleeting glimpse as the trout darts away. The action of the line in the water, the movement of the rod, the splash of waders, or the crunch of gravel underfoot gives notice of the angler's approach.

Big fish like big water and they prefer the wide, deep pools which are unwadable during high water in spring and early summer, but which can often be waded in midsummer when the waters are at their lowest and most trout fishermen have given up for the season. Bright sun and low water leave the lunkers most conspicuous. A good method of spotting fish on the larger trout streams is to use a canoe and come slowly down the river.

By careful inspection of all likely hideouts on a bright day, it is possible to spot about three out of four of the very large trout in an average stream. Spotting big fish takes time and trouble, but without an exact knowledge of where such fish lie there's only a casual chance of hooking one.

Big trout tend to be minnow feeders and, as a consequence, they settle where there are plenty of minnows to prey upon. This usually means the long, deep pools or steady runs where there is a large section of good feeding available without crossing any riffles or shallows, in other words, without leaving the pool. In this respect a long pool of only moderate depth is better than a very deep one which is small in size.

The most important factor in taking big trout is the timing. There are times when all trout, big ones included, let down their guard and feed with little caution. At such times the confirmed big-fish angler will be working a pool that he knows holds a lunker, while the average angler is happy merely to take trout that are larger than his usual average from good-looking water where he feels big trout should be, though he has not actually seen one there.

With a big trout located, or preferably a number of big trout marked down, the angler will want to keep them constantly in mind. If he's a versatile angler with a liking for, and a good knowledge of, all the methods of trout fishing he'll fish for them fairly often. If the fisherman is a specialist in only one field, he'll find few times when there's much chance of hooking one of these prize fish.

The dry-fly man has the least chance of taking a very large trout, for the big fellows go overboard for floating flies only a few times a season and can rarely be cajoled into coming to the surface at other times. It is at the time of the first big hatches of the spring that the big ones usually indulge a special hunger for insects and join the smaller fish in surface feeding.

In low water, big trout occasionally take a floating fly, but they're unpredictable in their choice of lure. It is impossible to know in advance whether a No. 16 spider, a No. 10 Wulff, or a No. 2 fly-rod mouse will be to their liking. The rise to the dry fly after the time of the big hatches has passed is a casual thing, the taking of a few flies only as a slight change of diet and not as a regular method of feeding.

The reference above is for daytime feeding. It may be a different thing after dark. Many old lunkers will surface-feed at night with considerable regularity, since on many streams the best hatches of Mayflies and larger insects come during the hours of darkness. Taking a big trout on a dry fly at night is an exciting business. To do it, the feeding station of the fish should be known with considerable accuracy.

Feeding positions are regular enough to mark fish within a few feet of the same spot, night after night. The cast should be practiced in daylight so that when actually in the dark there will be a minimum of slack line and leader as the fly passes over the fish. The strike should be made at the sound of the fish as he rises, but when there is very little slack to be taken up, a big fish in a deliberate rise will often hook himself on the dry fly. From that point on, it's a tough, exciting problem to subdue a big trout in a darkened pool. Although there's no longer any need to work in total darkness, the flashlights or headlights give only minor assistance in playing a fish which must be felt rather than seen.

The dry flies for night fishing are usually fairly large, mostly oversize imitations of the type of insect likely to be hatching out. Any large dry fly may turn the trick, as the fish seem less selective at night than in the daytime. The main advantage in having a big fly lies in being able to play the fish on a bigger hook and the heavier leader tippet that normally goes with it.

The wet-fly man is free to fish the water wherever he wishes, since his moving fly is always ready to bite into the jaw of the trout that takes it. The strike need only be a gentle lifting of the rod when the first pressure of the fish is felt. The wet-fly man can wade and fish through a well-remembered pool in absolute darkness, covering it almost as well as he would in daytime fishing. If he's careless he'll get hung up on his back cast or perhaps cast far enough to entangle his fly on the farther bank. Nowhere near as much planning and judgment are needed to wet-fly fish at night. But fishing with either the floating fly or the sunken fly after dark is a very good way to take big trout.

The nymph or wet fly in the daytime is more effective than the floating fly. It travels closer to the cruising or resting trout and is more akin to the type of food he prefers. Mornings and evenings are best for big fish, and streamer flies or minnow imitations are favorites. Imitations of the larger nymphs, such as the stone fly or crane fly larvae, are particularly effective. To fish for these big fish with wet flies, the casts should be made to the best feeding spots in their pools, usually the point where the current begins to slow down but before it loses too much of its speed.

This will be about where the water breaks away to turn back into large eddies. Practically all the food the current is carrying reaches this point, and a big fish, when feeding, chooses such a point to look over the entire food layout and take his pick before the smaller trout have a chance to work on it. To move farther up into the current calls for using up too much energy, and to drop back farther would permit other trout to move up in front of him and get the choicest morsels. In fishing for big ones the casting should be concentrated right on the prime feeding spot. There's little chance of picking him up at any other point.

The worm, minnow, and other natural-bait fishermen take most of the big trout. Just after a summer thunderstorm the angler who has located a big fish can be pretty certain the fish will be in his best feeding spot near his hideout, and a wriggly night crawler, hooked once lightly through the band on a 1X leader, coming down the current to him, is almost certain to draw a strike. The time to fish is from the moment the water starts to rise as the run-off comes into the river with its load of food until the river steadies or until the fish have satisfied their hunger and cease to feed.

A lively minnow moving around near the preferred feeding spot is a good bet, and the minnow fisherman may well spend hours in the right spot. If his minnows stay lively, he can work the same pool for hours at a time with a better chance of taking a lunker than the fisherman using any other type of lure or bait. The minnow is natural to the stream and the big trout's favorite food. A big trout coming up to his feeding station considers it natural to find a living minnow there, whereas the worm—except at flood times—or the artificial lures will almost always be spotted as out of place.

Grasshoppers, crickets, June bugs, and other natural trout baits may draw strikes where worms—which may create suspicion because of the trout's past experience in being hooked on one— and artificial lures draw no response. Big trout are moody. They're big enough to command the best feeding spots and to have their choice of the stream's food supply.

They're swift and strong enough to catch their food in good-sized chunks and, while the smaller fish may take his meal in a hundred different particles, the big fish is likely to get his dinner in two or three gulps. After taking a few fat minnows, however, a grasshopper, a small dry fly, a helgramite or a bucktail mouse may be appealing as a dessert. Don't overlook the field mouse, especially when the banks are undercut. A mouse imitation is good for big trout . . . and so is a live mouse.

Spinning and bait casting are the easiest methods to use for the taking of really big trout. The heavier lures can be cast to waters beyond the reach of the fly. They may be made to travel deep where they are within easy striking distance from the big fish as they feed or cruise near the bottom. Many casting lures are excellent imitations of the minnows which make up the bulk of the diet of the bigger fish. Metal wobbling lures that have considerable flash work well at slow speeds and are favorites.

Most big trout, as we have said, are caught by fishermen who have spotted them previously and made it a point to try for them at least once each time the stream is visited. The attempt may take only five to ten minutes, but it is always with tackle that will hold a big fish and a lure that should tempt him.

There are times when steady pounding will catch big trout, but I think they are relatively rare. One of them occurred on the Battenkill River in the Vermont section. Mead Schaeffer and Walt Squires located a big brown at the head of a deep run. They fished, using flies only, all that afternoon and were back bright and early the next morning to continue. From a vantage point on the bank the fish was clearly visible as one or the other of them worked on him from a position in the stream. A little before noon the fish came up to take Walt's No. 14 dry fly and, after an exciting battle, was brought in and beached. That brownie weighed 7½ pounds.

The usual story behind the capture of a big trout is one of constant attempts on each trip to the river and a final catching of the old-timer off guard and hungry. Fishing for big fish is something like hunting big game. There is much patient stalking and study attached to it. Action is not continuous, but when it does come it is truly exciting and the resulting pictures or the mounted fish stand for years as a measure of achievement and a point of conversation.

CHAPTER 18

Where Are the Trout?

ONE THING IS CERTAIN. Trout lie where their thoughts and in-stincts dictate and not always where you think you'd be if you were a fish. And their reasons for the positions they choose under varying conditions are quite logical. That doesn't mean we can ex-pect all trout to seek identical positions under any given set of conditions, any more than we can expect all humans to select iden-tical breakfasts on any given morning. They do follow general trends, though, and when an individual trout varies from the rest, he probably has his own good reasons for doing so.

The first of the three prime considerations of a trout in choos-ing his stream position is *food*, and feeding fish are the easiest to catch. One feeding fish is worth a dozen that are well fed at the moment and interested only in their comfort and safety. There-fore, it is most important for an angler to be able to pick out the type of water most favored by feeding fish. And, incidentally, the best feeding positions are almost always taken by the biggest and hungriest fish.

The preferred feeding spots in any stream are those in which the full flow or the major share of it is concentrated in a narrow channel. If the flow of water is too fast at the narrowest point of such a channel, the fish will take up feeding positions above or below the sluiceway at a point where the water moves at a speed that doesn't demand too much exertion in keeping pace with the flow. When water pours into a pool through a narrow spout, the fish usually lie at the point where the surface water begins to smooth down, and at favorable positions from that point on down to the tail of the pool where it spills over.

Where there are eddies and slower cross-currents near the head of the pool, trout will utilize this quieter water. In it they have a position they can maintain with ease and from which they can get at practically all the food the current is carrying past them, but no matter how inviting such a resting place may be, the fish will seldom use it if with every dart into the current for a choice morsel of food they're carried downstream and have to swim back again. Instead, they'll drop back farther until the main flow isn't too tough for them to handle.

A small eddy existing only in the lower level of the stream and caused by a ledge, submerged rock, or tree stump that lies in the center of a good, concentrated flow is an ideal feeding spot. It's easy enough to pick out these eddy-creating obstructions when they protrude above the surface, but when they're well submerged, there may be only the slightest bulge or boil coming to the top to tell the fisherman where to drop his fly.

These concentrated flow positions are preferred hangouts most of the time because trout rely very largely on the food that is carried along by the current for their meals. There are times, however, when the trout will leave them to feed in other quarters. When the current itself may be carrying very little trout food there may be an abundance of nymphs crawling or swimming in little deadwater pockets formed in the gravelly section of a stream bed where the slope is steep enough and the water swift enough to keep sand or silt from filling them in. In riffles of this type a trout can often find a hearty meal when his old standby, the main current, is carrying very few blue-plate specials.

The big eddies or deadwater spots sometimes provide excellent trout cafeterias, too. Under some conditions, caddis creepers, waterworms, and many other choice but poor-swimming nymphs are deposited in these pockets of slowly whirling water, and when the food is there you can bet the trout will find it. During times of very high water, these eddies are the choice of the smart bait-fisherman who knows that some old lunkers will be cruising these quieter waters and will consider a worm or a wounded minnow the logical thing to find there, along with the crawlers and wigglers of the nymph clan.

Big trout often cruise widely in search of minnows, crawfish, helgramites, and other residents of the shallows, and may range anywhere within a hundred yards of their normal feeding posts. But these cruises or journeys into the swift and shallow waters form the lesser part of their activity, and each big trout will tend to rely mainly on a good feeding spot in a pool or run and will have a good hideout as close to it as he can find one.

We can turn now to *comfort*, the second big factor in a trout's choice of stream position. This factor affects the trout's position in a number of ways. For instance, in the very early season when the water is quite cold and the fish are inactive, they prefer to do their feeding in those parts of the stream in which the sun warms the water and the bottom below it, rather than in positions of equal food-producing value that lie in the shade.

Because of this, their feeding time is likely to come when the sun is at its highest and brightest. The reverse will be true when the dog days come along, and the same fish, slowed up by the lethargy of midsummer's tepid water, will prefer the cool shadows to the warmer sunlit spots and will choose early morning, late evening, and the dark of night for their feeding, rather than the sunlit hours.

This desire for comfort in hot weather will pull trout out of their deep pools and safe hiding places to lie in the cool spring waters of small feeders that enter the stream, or to any spot in the stream where there is an oozing of cool water. And a feeling of discomfort, either because the water is too warm or too cold, will cause trout to remain inactive and pass up even the most luscious of foods that come floating or swimming by.

The third major consideration of the trout in regard to his berth at any given moment is *safety*. Although he may occasionally throw caution to the winds, as he does when the heaviest hatches of spring develop, and he may start feeding within a few feet of a casting angler, caution is one of his watchwords and safety his constant concern.

This concern for his safety makes a trout seek a resting place where he is protected from his many enemies. He'll slide under overhanging branches or cut banks or ledges or shelving rocks where he is sure no fishhawk can reach him. He'll cling to deep water as much as possible, for it gives him three-dimensional space in which to outswim his amphibious or aquatic enemies, whether they be snakes, bigger fish, or swimming animals like the mink or otter.

The ideal hideout for a big trout is one that provides both deep water and a hiding place. Streamwise fishermen watch for an overhanging stump, a pile of sunken brush, or any projection in deep water and near a concentrated stream flow. The closer the hiding place to a prime feeding spot, the more certain it is they'll both be the private domains of an old lunker. Nature has never recognized any law but force, and the bigger, more formidable fish are uniformly found in the better locations.

So much for the ABCs of why trout lie here or there. We still haven't pinned them down to any particular stream positions in this strange but inviting new stream we're about to fish . . . so let's assemble our tackle and have at it.

The easy way to begin is to start at a likely pool or run and fish through a fairly long stretch of water. Whether you move fast or slow will depend largely upon how you feel about trout fishing, but unless you're looking for prize-winners and nothing else, the thing to do is to fish *all* the water.

There's a natural tendency, even at the beginning of such a new fishing campaign, to devote a little more time and thought to the more likely spots, and that's as it should be. But to overlook the less likely water entirely is a mistake. By fishing all the various types of water at first, you'll soon find which produces the greatest amount of action.

When the action comes predominantly from one type of water, the thing to do is concentrate on stream flow of that character. When things slow down again, widen the scope of your fishing once more to take in the whole layout and you should soon know whether another source of food has lured the trout into different feeding grounds in the meantime.

Of course, this is easier to do on a stream where the fishing is good and there's plenty of action than on one of those hard-fished rivers where a few rises a day are an angler's normal quota. When the rises come few and far between in any type of water, it's good policy to fish the water thoroughly and concentrate on the best flow-feeding sections, with secondary consideration to the good hideouts wherein the fish may be lying doggo.

Even on hard-fished waters the policy of at least a skeleton coverage of all types of water the stream offers is sound. There is no one type of water that is consistently best and little that may not at one time or another produce a good rise. Trout are as fickle as girls in their teens, and I know I'm a long way from alone in having been startled by hooking an occasional sockdolager in water that shouldn't have held anything better than an eight-inch trout.

Having made our preliminary coverage and having decided that a particular type of flow is producing at the moment, the real skill of reading the river's wrinkles begins. Two feeding places that offer almost identical food opportunities to an old brownie or native may not be at all similar on the surface and yet a skilled eye will read the varying signs correctly and infer that both should hold feeding trout when conditions are right.

Generally speaking, smooth surfaces lie over slow-flowing water or over swifter water that flows as a body with little confusion caused by irregularities of the stream bed. Rippled water usually moves at a medium speed over a uniformly rough bottom at a shallow depth. Boiling water has been deflected toward the surface by a stronger flow or by striking a bold surface that pushes it upward. Wrinkled water indicates a steady, deep flow over or through a few large obstacles that provide good hideouts and resting spots close to a concentration of the main food-carrying flow.

White water is water that is traveling too fast and is too turbulent to provide comfortable feeding places. Fish may feed easily underneath such white water, but in that position they are cut off from sight or reach of any surface food that may show up or come by, and that's a distinct disadvantage. Only careful study will give an angler a thorough understanding of stream flows. Small streams and clear ones offer the best opportunity for study. But in any flowing water the signs are there to be read, and the heavy-creel lads have usually learned how to read them.

It's much easier to locate fish in small streams than in large ones. In small streams, fish of any size are bound to gravitate to the deeper pools, pockets, or runs, and seldom leave them. In big rivers the trout are free to move around, and almost any part of the flow affords adequate depth for a big trout to feed in and still provides a fast avenue for escape to the safety of really deep water.

In the brooks the choice of lure and its very careful presentation are the biggest factors. On the rivers those things are still important, but the great danger for the inexpert angler is that he'll spend the bulk of his day fishing water that is empty of fish at the time. Big-water trout have freedom of action and they like to use it.

Anyway, if you've been fishing only those rivers you know thoroughly, why not break down this year and try some new waters? If a wider experience will advance your knowledge of where fish lie *in any stream*, you'll be a better trout fisherman for it. The small-stream angler who branches out to the bigger waters is due to find an interesting problem. He may find, too, that big river usually means bigger trout and sometimes bigger thrills.

There's always another trout season coming up and when it's

over none of us will ever see it again except by way of trophies, pictures, or in the rosy glow of memory. But it can add to your store of stream lore and make the seasons to come more and more interesting. Why not put some extra time on stream study this year?

CHAPTER 19

The Silver Fontinalis

GREAT TROUT-FISHING streams are rare. And those that continue to hold their greatness through the years are rarer still except where fishing can be man-regulated and guaranteed. It is some special condition that makes a trout stream great, sometimes a condition that escapes even a skilled observer and permits controversial opinions on the reasons for a real run of big fish in a river that differs little from neighboring streams which offer only ordinary fishing for that particular section.

First on my own list, at one time, was the Russian River of Kenai Peninsula, Alaska. When I first fished it, this stream saw less than a score of anglers yearly and produced an amazing number of heavy, active rainbows. For many years it remained the finest trout river of my memories and seemed due to hold that place until my fishing days should end.

Under those circumstances it was surprising for me to find that the Fox Island River, a stream I had fished before, should suddenly move into first place. To get a fair picture of the Fox Island River of Newfoundland, it is necessary to go back a number of years. With Plus Parsons I had made the fifteen-mile auto trip from the Newfoundland Railroad station at Stephenville Crossing to Port-au-Port and then continued seven miles by small boat to the mouth of the river, a procedure that required about two hours. Fox Island is also a salmon river, and it was for salmon pictures that that first trip was made. Naturally, in investigating the river's possibilities we had heard that it was a remarkable stream for trout. But we had also heard that of almost every stream along the coast in varying degree, and we remained unimpressed.

When we reached the river, we found the anticipated low-water conditions that had been delaying the salmon run on Newfoundland's entire west coast. Salmon had only come into the river in one's or two's so we settled down to a few days of waiting for rain and fishing for trout.

The trout of the northern rivers that have access to the sea for their feeding take advantage of it. Almost without exception the big fish of these rivers are sea-fed. This comes about, I believe, because the feeding season in freshwater is so short and, similarly, the short season during which the temperature is suitable for fish-food growth causes the available food in northern streams to be less than that of equally large streams farther south.

Food in the sea is plentiful. There are smelt and capelin and mudge herring, to mention only a few of the prevalent food forms. The sea is a year-round feeding ground. Consequently the northern rivers often carry a greater poundage of fish in their annual runs than a similar river which, although more productive of more abundant fish-food in its length, must rely solely upon that food stock for its trout growth.

Like our own West Coast steelheads, these northern members of the eastern brook trout tribe take on a silver coloration during their stay in the sea, the typical dark streak along the back and the silvery sides and bellies that mark nature's protection for all her sea rovers. The wormlike markings are still visible in the dark green back-strip of a fresh-run sea trout, but the spotted sides and the red of bellies and lower fins are entirely missing.

When spawning season rolls around, these silvery fish, which have entered the streams sometime between May and September, will have reverted to the normal spawning coloration of the brook trout, and it will be impossible to identify the sea-run fish from another coming from a lake or river that is barred off from the sea. I do not know at what age or size brook trout go to sea, but I have found trout of less than six inches bearing the telltale silver of a sea journey.

The first afternoon at Fox Island gave us a number of trout, and we brought in five that averaged four pounds. If we had not picked up a stray salmon at the tail-end of our day's fishing, we would have had trout for our evening meal. As it was, when we sat down to the table, we were served with the salmon, and the trout, as was customary whenever salmon were available, were fed to the dogs. To understand this more fully it is necessary to realize that, to the Newfoundlanders, Fox Island is, and always has been, considered a salmon river. In their minds, the trout is an inferior fish compared with the salmon.

The basis for this feeling is that, on the tackle normally used— a ten- to fourteen-foot rod with a heavy line and leader—the trout is unable to put up a spectacular show. Secondly, he doesn't leap and his runs are not as long nor as vicious as the salmon's, which has both superior weight and the full store of energy that is to carry him through almost a year of starvation available for his acrobatics. To us, on the five-ounce rods we habitually used for salmon, he was a grand battler, and his experience in the sea with its limitless space gave him an extra distance and power for his runs and an edge over the normal stream trout.

The second day at Fox Island gave us another good catch of trout, all of which were returned to the water except my largest, a 6½-pounder. The third day was equally good. Then the rains came, and we had a day or two with the salmon before we moved on to the Humber Falls to film sequences of that salmon spectacle.

Perhaps you are wondering why I didn't then consider the Fox Island the best trout stream of my experience. It was because I had caught equally large fish in greater quantity at Russian River, and they were rainbows which I rate a little farther up the ladder than the eastern brooks, because of their leaping. You may be wondering, too, what I found later to change my mind when, in mid-June of 1940, Ralph O'Brien and I returned to Fox Island.

Conditions were somewhat similar to those of my first trip. The water was fairly low and, as usual, when in normal or low flow, the river was gin-clear. We could spot the fish fairly readily in many of the pools, but because of the clear water the fish didn't fool very easily. We used either my own big bucktail-winged dry flies or largish streamers on ten-foot leaders tapered to 1X or 2X.

Fortunately for the trout of the Fox Island River, that stream is listed as a salmon river by the Fish and Game Department, and surface fly-fishing is the only permissible way to fish either for salmon or trout anywhere within its entire length. We were a little earlier than on my first visit, and no other nonresidents or vacationers had preceded us. The fish we took were bigger.

This time I had come purposely for sea trout. Some salmon were already in the river, but we devoted little time to salmon fishing. Recognizing the stream as one of the finest trout rivers on the continent, I wanted pictures of it. We left the house at the mouth of the river early in the morning and spent the long day working up through the tidal pools that lie beside the islands on the lower flat and on up the three miles of boulder-strewn stream bed. This brought us to a good many pools before we reached Cragen's Rock Pool, which is as far upstream as the big trout travel.

Parsons and Walter Hynes, who had been guides for the first trip, were with me again, and a few days after our arrival, we were joined by Jack Meehan of St. John's, Newfoundland's capital, 450 miles away. We had those three miles of stream with a run of old-timers in it all to ourselves. We made the most of it, and during the first full day we took advantage of the sunshine to run entirely through our small stock of movie film. That gave us pictures of three good fish of better than five pounds, the largest a little under seven. We filmed no sequences below the five-pound weight, and even when I took a salmon on the 2½-ounce rod I was using for the big trout, we let the movie cameras remain idle.

Then, with our film stock exhausted, we had to wait until the fourth day of the stay for the long-overdue new supply that had come via St. John's and had arrived with Jack. It was well that we had taken advantage of the good light for pictures, because except for that first day, we had less than an hour of sunlight for the remaining seven days of our stay. Cameras weren't taken into the field for the next few days because of the lack of film, and our time was devoted entirely to fishing.

Ralph used a two-piece five-ounce rod and mine was a seven-foot two-piece job that was supplied with the lightest of guides and reel seat in order to give the needed backbone. Fox Island is not a large river and forty- to fifty-foot casts will prove adequate for normal fishing even under clear-water conditions.

The water stayed normal during the first four days. We took four salmon that averaged twelve pounds and, oddly enough, took them on the streamers that we were using for trout. The usual fly choice for salmon is from a No. 6 down in size, and for trout from a No. 4 hook up. Although trout often take the smaller salmon flies, it is quite rare for the salmon to take a larger fly than a No. 6 and then only in heavy, dark water.

We took plenty of trout. Day by day our catch increased, and the size of the biggest fish moved up until, on the fourth day, we had a combined catch of fifteen fish that averaged close to five pounds, and we brought back only the day's largest. It was no small triumph to take Jack in tow when he arrived that evening and bring him over to where the big one was hanging and say, "Jack, what do you think of this sardine?"

Jack had arrived at the house only a few minutes before we returned, and he was there to watch the scales swing down to seven pounds three ounces, marking the biggest fish of our Fox Island stay.

That night it began to rain, and although we carried cameras next morning they never left their cases. The rain kept on, and the river began to rise and turn brownish. Wading it at the usual spots below the pools became more difficult. Jack caught his first salmon, a sixteen-pounder, and Ralph took his biggest trout, a fish that weighed one ounce over seven pounds. These catches were made before noon because by that time the river was in a real flood state with tree trunks, bark, and branches coming down from the mountain slopes above. After midday, fishing was impossible since the pools had lost their value and the stream itself was a solid sweeping flow.

For three days the rain continued, and we sat by the windows and looked out on the tidal waters. Only those who have been held in the grip of such conditions, helpless to fish the river before them until the endless winds blew out or the rain stopped, can realize the agony such a situation brings. We sat with the guides and asked every sort of question about the fishing, and again and again turned our thoughts to some way of uncovering a fishing spot that would produce under those seemingly impossible conditions.

During two days of questioning, a slight hope had developed within us. We could see the brown fresh water pouring out of the narrow gut that was its only exit to the sea. Parsons had expressed an opinion that the trout dropped down the river when a heavy flood occurred. He had also said that sometimes at low tides the trout could be taken at the gut when the flow was narrowest and fastest. But he maintained stoutly that to go out there and fish under those flood conditions was purely a waste of time.

It took three days to work ourselves up to a point where we dared to go out, to almost certain ridicule by the guides, on the slim chance that in some pocket of that rushing brown water we could find a hangout for fish. Because I wanted to cover a lot of water, I took a red-and-white plug and a casting rod to use when we reached the open beach where such fishing was legal.

We started in the flat water just below the house and followed the shore around for a quarter of a mile to the gut. Ralph kept casting his fly out into the silt-laden depths but had no strikes, and was ready to give up his efforts when I took over as we reached the gut. I sent the red-and-white plug sailing out at ten-foot intervals along the beach for two hundred yards and then worked back without a touch.

As we walked dejectedly back along the shore, I turned over the forlorn hope remaining in my mind and decided to act upon it. The tide was moving to the south at the river mouth, and we had been on the northern side of the gut. I reasoned that the most logical spot was outside the narrows on the south side where the current eddied around and then swept on down along the shore. It wasn't much trouble to get across in a dory, and I started casting.

The first ten casts hooked ten fish, all typical of the Fox Island run, and those that came in were better than the four-pound average I had come to depend on. Because some of them were injured by the gang hooks on the plug and had to be kept rather than released, I left Ralph and rushed back for my own fly rod.

That evening we enjoyed the most exciting trout fishing I have ever experienced. The wind whipped at us from off the land, and scattered showers beat a tattoo against our waterproof clothes. We stood hip-deep in the swirling water, and all we had to do to cast was to hold the rod high and give it a twitch. The wind did the rest.

We moved slowly back and forth along that southern shore from the mouth to a hundred yards below. We struck a few dead spots, but the number of fish was amazing. Parsons and Hynes, who had come back with me, had never seen anything like it. It had long been a thought of theirs that only a part of the run came into the river to follow the smelt, while the bulk of it was content to remain in the sea and feed on capelin and other food. Our catch that day seemed certain proof. We kept the three fish injured by the plug and released nearly fifty in the three hours of fishing.

Those were sea fish, with the green coloring of their backs still vivid and their sides and bellies a uniform bright silver. Fish under three pounds were rare, and our largest was a seven-pounder. They rolled up in the waves as we played them, sending spray splashing high or following the steadier water beneath the waves on their longer runs. We brought them in to our nets at the beginning, but soon turned to the simpler method of the surf fisherman and brought them onto the beach with the waves.

The next day, our last, was a repetition of those few hours. Over a hundred trout fell to our flies. A few of the largest we kept, and they shaded or crossed the seven-pound mark. They seemed to be traveling in schools of about the same size. In the better light of day, with somewhat smoother water, we could see them feeding on the surface now and then. They were feeding on capelin, a slim fish about six inches in length, as they came in to the sandy beaches to spawn.

That was a long day and an exciting one. This new knowledge

shows that Fox Island will produce fish under any conditions for the duration of its trout run if they are properly protected and the size of that run can be maintained. Simply stated, as it is now, the foregoing statements may challenge belief, but it was as simple as the words that tell it, and the telling is entirely true.

We left then, without having brought in a fish near the river record of twelve pounds, which Parsons seemed to be constantly expecting. Quite a few fish have been taken over the ten-pound mark in the years that he has been guiding on the river. But it is the average weight and not the individual weight that determines a river's value, and perhaps it is just as well that we can still return to Fox Island and hope for even finer fishing than before.

Before leaving the small settlement at the mouth of the river, I wrote out a petition which the residents have since signed and passed on to their government for action. It provided for a limit of two fish per day per angler and extended the fly-fishing-only limit to a point half a mile down the shore on either side of the river mouth. It is hoped that this petition will be made the basis for a law to insure this remarkable fishing for all time. As long as sufficient seed stock is guaranteed, the bounty of the ocean will provide similar annual runs for a long time to come.

An unusual situation exists at Fox Island in regard to these trout. They enter the river in early June and seem to follow up the run of smelt. The smelt are seldom found above Cragen's Rock Pool, and that pool also marks the limit of the journey of the big trout up the stream. By the end of July the smelt have finished their spawning and return to the sea. When they go, the trout follow their lead and depart, too.

Eighteen miles to the north of Fox Island, the Serpentine River pours into saltwater. The Serpentine is a larger stream, one of the most beautiful and finest of Newfoundland's salmon waters. It, too, has a run of magnificent sea trout, and to complete the picture, they enter the Serpentine during the early weeks of August and remain to spawn. Those two rivers have the largest average for their sea trout of any rivers of the island. It seems logical to assume that the Serpentine, with its good spawning grounds, is the cradle of the big trout of both rivers, that it offers them good early stream-feeding and that the adjacent sea waters furnish exceptional saltwater feeding.

Apparently the Fox Island fish are a part of the Serpentine run. The Serpentine has a smaller average run of fish than Fox Island because all of its fish come in there to spawn, whereas the trout that enter Fox Island in pursuit of easy feeding on the smelt are all fully matured fish, big enough to enjoy that feeding. Except for a few, small, native-spawned fish, these big trout make up the entire Fox Island run, and that would seem to account for its remarkable average.

In the Serpentine the trout work quickly through the spawning grounds, which are quite crowded. Because of this congestion the angler catches a dozen small fish for one of the old-timers. Let's hope that the Serpentine will be included in any measure to protect the Fox Island run and given a limit commensurate with its average size, in order to preserve this interesting setup. The Serpentine is a relatively inaccessible river, with no permanent settlers upon its banks from source to mouth. The guides, hotel men, and outfitters are in favor of such a move, and therein lies a hope that Fox Island will remain a standard by which other streams may be judged for years to come.*

---

* The conservation practices recommended by the author were unfortunately not enacted. Now a twelve-inch trout is a very good fish for the Fox Island River.

CHAPTER 20

September on the Serpentine

THERE ARE TWO THINGS that I will always remember about the Serpentine. One is the fishing, which is tops, and the other is the trail that leads in to it. When the Newfoundland government decided they needed some additional information on that isolated stream, Harold Smith and I were slated for the job of supplying it. My first reaction was one of sheer pleasure at the thought of seeing again what I consider to be the island's most beautiful river.

The long, steep-sided valley that holds Serpentine Lake and the twelve-mile run of water below it was entirely uninhabited. It lies hidden away between the railroad and the Gulf of St. Lawrence, and empties into the saltwater over a shifting gravel bar that provides no anchorage; the rugged coast contains no harbor within twenty miles of the river's mouth. A fringe of timber clings to the lower edges of the lake shore and behind this green fringe the mountains rise up, bare and bold, showing the red and gray of rock and gravel.

The river winds down through a broad and level, wooded intervale for six miles to its high falls, then plunges rapidly down the last six miles to sweep over slippery rocks into the sea. The Serpentine Trail begins at a lonely sign on the narrow-gauge, single-track railroad that spans the island. It twists off through the bogs and timber for seven miles to the upper end of the lake. I had slogged across it before in heavy spring floods, and hoped then that the next time I crossed it the ground would be dry.

In my mind I had looked forward to the day when airplanes would hop off from nearby Corner Brook and reduce the time between the comforts of civilization and the river to a few air-spent minutes. The day of available planes hadn't arrived then, and at the end of an exceptionally rainy summer I knew the trail was due to be an even more slippery ribbon of soft, sucking mud than ever before.

It's a short trail, as trails go, but it is either sharply up, sharply down, or bedded in mud when it's wet. Four of us went in—two guides, Jack and Francis, who had seen the river in all its seasonal variations, and Harold and myself. Between the grub, bedding, cameras, and the rest, we were pretty well laden, and the eventual sight of the lake with its cached canoes was more than welcome. On the trip in, there were sections where we could have put all the packs into a canoe and paddled down the normally dry trail, if we'd had a canoe.

As we paddled down the lake we bucked a stiff breeze that came sluicing up the valley, bringing a fog blanket in from the gulf, and we reached the cabin at the outlet pool well ahead of nightfall. The salmon that had already reached the lake still had two months of waiting before their time to spawn. They roved the lake, often leaping clear, and during the morning and evening hours many of them left the still waters to join the others that lay in the soothing flow of the Home Pool at the lake's outlet.

This pool is probably the most favored on the entire river. From the cabin porch you can watch the restless fish as they leap or see their noses break the smooth surface, followed immediately by their broad backs and wide tails as they "porpoise." This is a spot for the dry fly, and it was one of my favorite bucktail-winged floaters that went out for their inspection. The season was on the wane, but these were to be the first salmon of the year for both Hal and myself, and the closest I had come to completely missing a season in ten years.

There was still half an hour's light when we began casting, and we both took our "first" for the season, a pair of salmon that were over ten pounds apiece. They went slithering up into the lake and its deep water in long runs and came back only with the utmost persuasion. Give a salmon some open water to run in, and he's tough on tackle.

These fish have picked up a sense of space and distance in their ocean stay, where they have no hiding places, and their safety depends entirely upon their ability to travel fast and far. The hooking and playing of a salmon is a story in itself, but the real highlights of this trip were not just catching fish, but catching particular fish in particular places.

The first of these highlights came the following morning when Hal and I headed downstream with Jack in the canoe. Newfoundland is home to Hal, but his fishing had been done entirely on the

northern and eastern parts of the island, and he had an idea that
trout were big when they went over three pounds. Like most Newfoundlanders, he counted trout fishing a few rungs down the ladder from the place held by the silver thunderbolts of the salmon
run.

I had spent some time on the way in talking about the big
trout of the Fox Island River, the next stream to the south, and I
admitted that I was looking forward to the late-season sequel to
the superb June and July fishing I had struck there in previous
years.

I knew we were due to strike these trout as we worked downstream, finding them in the places that are particularly suited to
trout and scorned by the salmon. Salmon in the rivers are not feeders. They lie out in the open and hang to the main flow of the
water. Trout will lie in under the deep-cut banks with their
canopy of alders, behind the logs and snags that form a protective
screen between them and their prey, deep in the rocky depths of
the larger pools, and in the diffusing eddies where a feeder stream
merges with the main flow.

On our way down the river that first day we stopped at one
such pool. An uprooted tree had been left by the ice to guard the
head of a long run. Below it the flow was steady and deep, curling
against the soft earth and eating away from beneath the alders,
with slow deliberation, the very soil that fed them. Snags jutted
out from the bank and rose from the sand and silt of the stream
bed. Alders covered the flats as they stretched away from the river,
then the timber took their place, and finally the mountains rose
up, bare and brown, to look down at the valley.

Hal started casting at the head of the deep water where the
tree had settled. He had switched, at my suggestion, from the No.
8 low-water Silver Gray he had been using to a streamer fly I had
dug out of my kit, a long smelt-gray mixture of hair and feathers
that hid a No. 4 hook at its head. With a doubtful expression he
cast the fluttering lure out into the current. Streamer flies were
little known in Newfoundland and it was the first time he had
ever seen one. As the fly settled into the current and he started to
retrieve it, he let out a startled yelp that he had a salmon.

With a rush his "salmon" took him well down into the pool,
steadfastly refusing to waste his strength in jumping, and Hal began to wonder if his first guess had been right. At the end of five
minutes, when the stubborn fish began to ease in toward us under

the tackle's pressure, we could see the bright white stripes that mark the forward edges of a squaretail's lower fins and get the glow of vermilion above them.

The water was deep and tinged with brown by the rain's quick runoff from the bogs. The coloring of the trout as spawning time neared was likewise rich and dark. The red of the sides glowed deep and warm, the back was dark with a brownish cast over the typical wormlike markings. The light streak that runs along the belly was sharply white against the fading edge of black that separated it from the flaming brilliance of the lower sides. The coloring seemed particularly vivid as I compared it in my mind with the green-backed, silvery fish that had come in from the salt-water only a month before.

That fish of about five pounds was the first of fifteen we took in the two hours that followed. Only one or two were under two pounds and classified as "minnows," and several were of a size with the first one. When the time was up, Hal was ready to agree that trout could put up a beautiful scrap and that trout fishing on that river could give more action and thrills than salmon fishing in many other waters. All our trout were released, since we still had a good part of one of the salmon we had killed on the evening before.

When things slowed up, we moved on down the river. The low clouds coming in from the gulf hid the tops of the mountains. The river was like a strip of dull silver, the dark waters holding secrets that could easily have been read in the sunshine. We stopped at pools that looked as if they might hold salmon and cast a few times, sometimes successfully and sometimes without the sign of a fish.

Late in the season salmon develop the tendency of following a fly without taking it, or rising short at the last minute, lifting the water in a heavy boil as they turn away short of the fly. Many of our rises were like that. We took pictures, made notes on our rises and catches in each location, and studied the land for possible campsites in the future.

At two o'clock we slid our canoe over the rocky spout at Little Falls, six miles below the lake. By three we had made our camp at the big falls and walked on down the trail to the long, deep bend of the river that is called Grant's Pool. This pool is more than two hundred yards long and fifty yards wide. The flow is steady and the uneven rocks of the riverbed are reflected in the eddies on the surface. From the point where the water rattles in over a wide bed in a shallow flow to the spot where it pours out over the lower edge, any cast may raise a salmon, and a lot of ours did.

It was weeks since anyone had fished there. A few bright fish had just come in from the sea, but the bulk of the salmon in the pool had come in earlier and had begun to lose their polished brilliance through long contact with fresh water; they had gained a wariness about rising and a knowledge of the points in the pool from which their best efforts at freedom could be made.

The gray bucktail-winged floater was top fly in size 10, and in about three hours we had captured four mature salmon and ten grilse, the latter being salmon of one year's ocean feeding and from four to five pounds in weight.

We saved a bright grilse to grace the pan and sent the rest back to their important stocking job that lay ahead. A total of six mature salmon, sixteen grilse, and twenty-seven big trout went down on the books for two rods on a September day that had included a good deal of traveling, considerable photography, and a number of pages of notes.

That was a day to remember and a day that is a tribute to the Serpentine's qualities as a fishing stream. But it was on the way out that both of us had our moments of greatest excitement. At Jeffries Pool, two days later, I started fishing for salmon and Hal rigged up for trout. Sometimes their resting places overlap, but in general, when fishing one of the northern rivers, an angler fishes for one or the other. Two things determine what the species will be: the part of the pool fished and the size and type of the fly.

I had made up a pair of white marabou streamers with silver bodies and some yellow and scarlet to give them flash. They were four inches long but were still tied on No. 4 low-water salmon hooks which made them light and easy to cast. Hal started using one of them at the top of the pool.

As I was plunking my pet dry fly down on the water in a monotonous rhythm just over the nose of a salmon that had given away his position by rolling up to the surface, I saw Hal moving downstream in the wake of a fish. That trout took him over his boots a couple of times as he worked his way in and out of the snags and left him with a firm conviction that waist waders do have their points.

I brought my line in to let him pass and then followed along to watch him bring in a trout that had the depth, if not the length of a salmon. It was a male fish, darker in coloring than most, and his chunky length reached from Hal's chin to a point well below his waist.

I had slipped up on bringing the scales on this trip, so late that night in camp we rigged up a balance and replaced the fish's weight on the balance with a number of boxes of film and pebbles in a salt bag until his weight was matched. Then we tied up the salt bag and kept it separate to weigh later.

It didn't take me long to tie on the mate to Hal's fly, and we both put our hearts into some intensive trout fishing. Trout of the same size usually travel in groups as they move up or settle into a given section of water. We each snaked out a trout that could push the first one in size, and at the weigh-in that night they came within a pebble or two of equaling his weight. The rest of them were not in his class and went back uninjured.

It had rained again the night before, and on that protected pool the black flies seemed to think it was June instead of September and came to life with a vengeance. It was they, as much as the lowering of the sun, that drove us back to the canoe and to our journey on up the river. Darkness fell before we had paddled into the trout hole that lies a few hundred yards below the cabin at the lake, yet I couldn't pass it without stopping for a cast or two. That was all it took. Something snagged the big marabou and came sailing out of the dark water into the equally dark air and fell back with a splash.

A salmon had apparently been cruising up through the trout waters, just to prove the unpredictability of the species, and had risen to my monstrosity. I had hooked salmon in the fading light before and played them into the darkness, but I had never fished or hooked one after night had really set in, although I knew they had been taken on a fly in the middle of the night.

It is one thing to use a lighter than three-ounce fly rod on salmon in the daytime, when you can see where the snags lie and have light enough to pick your way quickly to the proper playing position. It is a lot different to rely on sensing the location of the fish in the blackness and wading blindly over treacherous bottom to try to keep your line clear of snags whose positions are but doubtful memories in your mind.

With fifty or sixty yards of line out, your rod may be pointing in one direction while the fish is jumping his head off almost at your back. It's often a tough job to figure out where your fish is when the sun is out. At night you can't tell whether the sound of a splash means that some salmon is jumping casually, just for the fun of it, or that your hooked fish is really where the sound came from. Sometimes two fish jump at once and you wonder whether either of them is yours—or which one. There's nothing to do but rely on the instinctive reactions that come automatically, without special thought.

In the end, the salmon came in, all fifteen pounds of him, and the tailer slid up behind him into position and then closed down on the narrow flesh in a grip from which there is no escape. He was a bright fish that had not lingered much on his way up from the river's mouth. His runs had been fast and his leaps high. Probably his short freshwater stay had not yet let him adjust himself to river life, and his policy of keeping to the deep or open water had saved me from a snagged line. When I had worked the fly free from his jaw, I loosened the cable around his tail and let him swim away in the blackness.

We went on up to the cabin at the lake then, ready for the strong tea that would be warm and welcome and the evening meal that had been long delayed. There was the easy talk in camp that follows an exciting day, and finally we slept on spruce-bough bunks, with well-chinked logs between us and the showers that came down before the morning sun burned the sky bare and blue.

Oh, yes, the salt bag with the film and pebbles in it that had replaced Hal's fish with perfect balance shaded the seven-pound mark on the scales when we got back to Spruce Brook.

CHAPTER 21

Nestucca Steelheads

IF YOU DRIVE WESTWARD over the mountains from Portland to the edge of the Pacific, you may find the town of Beaver, Oregon, and the river that flows through it, the Nestucca. If you're there in the winter and you locate a guide named Leroy Fletcher, you'll probably end up with some magnificent winter steelhead fishing. We did.

Ray Prescott and I had enjoyed a steelhead trip in one of the tributaries of the Snake the year before, catching fish some six hundred migrated miles up from the sea. It had been great sport. We fished with flies and learned the techniques required, comparing them with those needed for the big brook trout and Atlantic salmon we sought so often on the eastern Canadian streams. It had been early fall and the warm, lazy days were as soft as June.

There, fishing for fish that had climbed the Columbia, then the Snake, and finally entered the Ronde, in comparing the steelhead with the eastern fish, we learned that presenting the fly to a steelhead was much more difficult. In general, we found that the steelhead weren't much interested in a free-floating dry fly and that a wet fly or a skimmed fly, which did interest them, usually had to be presented from almost directly upstream. Our best results came when the fly would swing across the current to hang, at the end of the swing, almost directly above the place where we felt the fish were lying.

In contrast, when fishing eastern streams we had a vastly wider latitude. If we felt there was a fish in a certain lie, we could present a free-floating dry fly to him from any position within casting range. It wouldn't matter where we stood, whether above, below, or to the side as long as we could let our flies drift over the fish. Or, if we were fishing wet, there might be some little advantage in presenting the fly we found best for steelhead, casting at a close angle downstream and swinging it in front of his nose, but we could feel free to fish from well to the side if we wished, and still be quite effective. We could even cast upstream and have the fly work down toward us with a reasonable certainty of interesting those salmon or trout.

The study of how a particular species likes to see a fly come to him is one of the interesting facets of fishing. Strangely enough, tarpon, lying in a fast freshwater run a hundred miles from the sea, took on the characteristics of the steelhead rather than those of the Atlantic salmon. The tarpon wanted the same consistent, short, swift sweep across their noses to a hanging standstill not far from their lie in order to be tempted into a strike.

I discovered this in the cloudy waters of the St. John, a long river draining from Lake Nicaragua to the Atlantic where the tarpon averaged over sixty pounds. When I'd located a fish by seeing him roll, I found that by positioning the boat a cast's length above and a little to one side of his lie, I could make this type of presentation and had the best chance of getting him to rise.

With those warm-weather steelhead we found, too, that the skimming or hitched fly which had been developed at my camps on Portland Creek in northern Newfoundland had a particular effectiveness. We skimmed the standard patterns, we skimmed unconventional patterns like the surface stone fly and the muddler, we fished wet flies in the time-honored sunken manner—and we caught steelhead in all three fashions.

We relaxed on the banks of the stream when the sky was too bright or the sun too warm. We waded deep, and Ray even fell in, without our ever feeling the cold.

On the Nestucca, where we went to catch the bright, new winter steelhead that had just come back to the river from the sea, conditions were very different. On our first day out, it rained hard. The droplets were so close to solid that they were practically hail. They rattled hard on the hoods of our rain jackets and beat coldly on our wader-protected knees as we sat in the McKenzie-type boat in which "Loy" swept us down the river.

Instead of the semi-arid country of our earlier steelhead fishing, we found ourselves in a continually damp area. Moss hung from the trees, and lush, green growth was everywhere. There was a perennial feeling of rain and fog and dampness. Instead of fishing with a fly in water that was essentially clear, we fished with spinning or casting rods in cloudy water where the bright red lures we used were lost from sight a foot beneath the surface. We were taking movie sequences and the problem of keeping the cameras dry enough to operate was far greater than keeping our fingers and arms warm enough to fish.

We'd trailer the boat upstream to launch it and have someone drive the car and trailer back down to a spot on the river near the village to wait for our arrival at the end of the fishing day. The McKenzie boats are essentially double-ended, much like an eastern dory, but with a bit more flare. Loy stood or sat at the oars in the center.

When the current was swift, he rowed upstream to slow us down, and when it was slow he rowed us forward to move us along. He was a master at holding us at just the right speed in the current to work across above a foaming rock and then slide smoothly down in a raceway between it and its nearest neighbor. It wasn't always easy and Loy's muscles bulged from time to time with his exertions.

We used stick sinkers made of cylindrical "sticks" of lead in varying lengths. That type would be least likely to snag in the rocks on the bottom. Hanging below the sinkers on a foot and a half of leader we fished our lures. Loy, when he fished, used salmon eggs, while we, dedicated to artificials, used such things as a fluff of blaze orange fibers, a bright red plastic berry called an "Okie Drifter," or a miniature single-hooked plug called a "lil guy."

Loy dropped anchor in the pools and runs he'd learned to count on for fish. Under his tutelage we learned to cast across and upstream and have our sinkers and our lures come bobbing down along the bottom, hopefully letting the current bring them past the noses of the steelhead as they rested in the comfort of the low-level eddies. We varied the weight of our sinkers with the depth and speed of the flow. The strikes, when they came, were gentle. It was hard to tell whether the object that stopped the uncertain downstream movement of lure and sinker was a rock, a snag, or the mouth of a steelhead.

If we waited for the line to come solidly tight, we often found it suddenly slackening off and wondered whether it had simply caught momentarily on a rock or snag and then pulled free with the drag of the current on the line or whether a fish had moved a few inches from his position to clamp his jaws down on it but, finding it hard and unpalatable, had spit it out. Had we waited too long to strike? Because we were uncertain, we struck quite quickly and perhaps we missed some fish that way.

But we did hook things; we hooked rocks and logs and weeds and steelhead. Ray hooked the first one in that day's driving rain and it raced away with a great burst of speed. We heard the throaty whisper of the Ambassadeur's drag as the line piled off in pursuit, saw the bright flash of the silver fish framed in tortured water. It was a ten-pounder, a bigger fish than any we'd taken on flies in the Ronde, a heavier fish not yet both weakened and toughened by hundreds of miles of migration. It leaped with a wild abandon as if the fury of the sea waves and the surf, only ten miles behind it, were driving it still.

Loy nosed the boat ashore when the time was ripe, and Ray stepped out to bring his fish to the beach. He followed the fish upstream briefly, then moved down with him in the easy drift of the water and, to end it, drew the tired steelhead out of the water on his side. It twisted briefly on the wet sand while Ray's numb fingers bent the hook free. Gently he turned it downslope toward the pool, and with a sinuous movement of its body, it slid into the rain-pocketed water and disappeared, leaving just the briefest latent image where it had been.

That was the first of many. In the five days that followed, we rose in the dark, frosty mornings. We warmed our hands on a heater that Loy installed in the boat for us. We wore gloves in the early hours when it was barely light . . . or in the evening . . . or when we fished the "frost holes," the pools that lie hill-hidden from the sun and never, during any part of the winter day, receive a touch of sunshine.

We ran the river day after day. We saw still-fishermen huddled over bright flowers of flame, and smelled the things they cooked for lunch. We passed under overhanging branches where dozens of lures, cast too high by over-eager anglers, hooked on branches that were beyond their reach, and were left hanging there. They showed like bright-colored berries on brown bushes in the fall.

Over frosty, moss-covered rocks rivulets cascaded down to splash into the sweeping river. Seagulls flew overhead, calling raucously, or sat pensively on the gravel bars, sometimes pecking at the moldering carcass of a salmon, spent lavishly by that species in its great, once-in-a-lifetime survival trek.

We rarely passed other boats with fishermen, for we were few in number and all traveling in the same direction. Occasionally, when we shot down through a long stretch of rapid water that held few fish, we'd come around a bend to find another fisherman anchored in the pool. Then we'd slide on through, take the next fast run, and drop anchor at the first available fishing spot.

Pale and yellow though the winter sun was, its rays seemed to warm us and our blood seemed to flow a little faster when we were out of the shadow and in its glow. Our noses ran, our rainclothes leaked. We felt encased in chill and damp. But we caught steelhead and we were happy. We'd set our goals at fifteen-pounders which Loy said we'd catch and which we did. They both came on from the same pool on different days. A big, long pool not far above the tide.

The river, tumbling down over a broad and rocky bed, split into two main channels just above the entrance to the pool's deep water. These runs merged together, swirling around great, mossy rocks with deep and twisting currents. Then the waters swept to the left in a steep and rocky race that carried white water and foam in a tumbling flow for about sixty feet through a chute into the main body of the deep, still basin where the waters rested lazy for a while.

Loy had to catch the current just right as he came sliding down through fast water to the head of the pool in order to get his anchor where it would hold. Back arched and muscles tense, he'd strain at the oars until we could drop the hook in the right spot. Once set in position, we faced a deep run racing over a smooth bottom which Loy felt was the best steelhead lie in the river.

The first time Ray drifted his lure through that run he found the only rock in it that could snag a hook and lost his rig. The second time he hung up again—on a big, bright steelhead. These fish that have roamed the wide Pacific bring back to the streams of their birth a special measure of strength and speed and a sense of space that adds a new dimension to trout fishing. This is especially true when the sea with its vast adventure lies not far behind them. Cooped up suddenly in a narrow run, and hooked, they feel a wild fright they can't contain. They bore downward, seeking ever-deeper water. They jump and land on rocks. They skitter wildly through the shallows.

In the small upper section of the pool, they feel the urgent need to break out into the large and placid pool below and sometimes to the sea still farther down. Ray's fish hurdled two rocks and caught the line ever so briefly on a corner of rock. He swung in under the boat as Loy, grinning at the prospect of so large a fish, swept down through the chute with anchor lifted. His grin faded when the leader caught briefly on an oar and resumed again when it slid free.

Then we were out in the open pool with the reel singing and the fish leaping far off. He stayed in the pool and we closed in to follow closely and wear him down. In time he turned on his side and let me slide the net beneath him. This was Ray's trophy, just under sixteen pounds, as bright as a new dollar, a chunky, well-formed male, his biggest trout, and perhaps his best for all the years to come.

My best fish came out of the same pool less than half an hour later. It wasn't easy to work the boat up above the pool again, but Loy did it by wading it up along the shore while we waded and fished the lesser eddies at the poolhead. Once more in position, I swung wide the bail on the Mitchell and dropped my "drifter" in a short cast off the bow and let the current sweep it away.

It bounced a dozen times before it stopped and held briefly, then moved off. The first slow movement became a surging rush that swept line from the reel and carried the fish far down into the lower pool before we could get the anchor up and follow. We were far behind when he reached the lip of the greater pool where it pours over for its run down to the sea. It was too far to put on pressure or for my tackle to have any turning effect. I let the line slacken, waited and hoped.

The great fish turned, jumped his way back beside us, and finally led us into quiet water. There, at length, the net engulfed her. She was a mate to Ray's. We guessed she might be just a shade smaller, but we'll never know. If I'm lucky, I thought, I'll catch a still bigger one. And so I let her go.

PART TWO

General Fishing

CHAPTER 22

Bass on Live Bait

THE ESSENTIALS OF BAIT fishing are much the same whether the quarry is bass or any regularly feeding game fish. The still-fisherman puts a natural bait where the fish will find it. The troller or caster brings the bait to the spots where he expects to find fish feeding or resting, making his bait so tempting that even a well-fed fish will strike anyway. Since a bass must have food to live and the bait fisherman uses this urge to fool him, while artificial lures may appeal to a bass's pugnacity as well as his hunger, the bait fisherman depends upon hunger.

Although the basic considerations are uniform, actual fishing varies from lake to lake or river to river because of depths of water, types of water, types of bass (whether smallmouth or largemouth), amount and type of vegetation, forage fish, etc. And every factor affecting the fish affects the fishing. The best one can do is to give general rules and suggestions. Utilizing these, the less experienced fishermen should improve his catch.

Bass feed, mostly, in water less than twelve feet deep. They may seek the comfort of cooler temperatures at a lower level, but the very deep water rarely has much vegetation or bass food. Of course, very shallow water produces food, but bass rarely feed there by day except on lakes that are not disturbed much by boats or anglers. Instead, they work the shallows at night or move into shallow water that is readily accessible to either deep water or a good hiding place. This leaves the broad, shallow stretches alone. The best fishing is in the six- to twelve-foot range.

Smallmouths gather at the rocky ledges and largemouths love the weed beds. That's a good rule to follow, although it is not one hundred percent accurate. Both species tend to cruise and feed part of the day and loaf along lazily or hide out the rest of it. The angler, trolling with live bait, should follow the water of the right depth around the lake shores mainly. When there are bars or flat areas of the correct water depth, he'll do well to troll there since water away from shore may have fewer weeds and snags.

Patches of weeds and lily pads located well off shore are excellent spots for both the troller and still-fisherman. The still-fisherman's choice is generally in coves of moderate depth, where a ledge runs out into the deeper water on either side and at the edges or in the open centers of large areas of vegetation. A cove usually gives a larger area of good fishing depth than a straight shoreline.

Although the caster or troller may move about in the hope of picking up a bass here and there, the still-fisherman should try to select a spot where bass congregate so that he may take his catch from a single anchorage. It is important that he find a feeding ground or a bass swim-way. Otherwise, he will not take top catches. Bass congregate on ledges as well as in coves. The inlets and outlets of lakes or ponds normally offer good fishing, and offshore bars and clear patches of deep water between shallow or weedy areas are natural pathways for feeding fish. Electronic fish-finders now can actually pinpoint the fish and the proper depths.

Since insects and small minnows cling to the protection of weed beds, bass search for them there, and the angler's bait should be in open water near their natural food. In open water, bait is easily seen by the fish and it is a great help also in playing a fish.

The proper depth to fish in trolling is important. The angler controls the depth of his bait by the speed at which he travels, the weight he uses on his line, and the length of line he has out. The faster the boat travels, the nearer to the surface his bait is. The heavier the sinker, the farther down it will go. The longer the line, the deeper the bait will travel, and the troller must keep to relatively open water, avoiding snags and weeds since even a single weed caught on the hook will give away the fraud and prevent a strike.

The still-fisherman determines the level of his bait by using a float. With a float, the hook can be set at any level, but without it the bait tends to settle to the bottom where it usually becomes hidden in the weeds or rocks. Bass may cruise or feed at any level and there is no perfect depth for all conditions. A good rule is to put the bait two thirds of the way down from the top to the bottom. However, in shallow water the depth setting is not as important as in deep water. Where the depth is less than six feet, a bass can see everything from surface to bottom, but where it is around fifteen feet, a deep-swimming bass might overlook a bait near the surface and a surface-swimming bass might fail to see a bait near the bottom.

In very deep water the chances are the best with bait lying near the bottom. Fish in deep water are usually seeking the comfort of the greater depth and will utilize whatever depth there is in their search for cooler water within the feeding range. In open and very deep water, fish that swim in the upper levels tend to swim aimlessly and without any regular pattern.

The still-fisherman, seeking to find a natural bass cruise-way, will not find one there. He must be constantly thinking of the general contours of the bottom and fish according to them. When bass are cruising the upper water without regard to the bottom, trolling or casting will be more productive than still-fishing.

Tackle for still-fishing need not be fancy. Any type of rod will do if it has enough spring for proper playing of the fish. Any serviceable reel that will hold enough line to reach and play the fish is adequate. Bait-casting rods are commonly used and permit long casting of a bait from boat or shore. But because they are short, they give the angler little control over the hooked fish and little chance to guide him around instead of through the weeds.

Longer rods, either of the bait or fly type, give the still-fisherman ample casting range and much more control over the fish he plays. In casting with these longer rods, the line is stripped from the reel and coiled in the left hand as in fly casting. The cast is made with a single swing and the weight of the float, bait, and sinker pulls the line out. Long bamboo poles with the line tied directly to their tips are effective for still-fishing. With them a bait can be dropped into exactly the proper spot and withdrawn again without getting tangled up with the weeds as happens with a short-rod angler who must reel in each time.

Trolling tackle can consist of either a long or short rod and a suitable reel equipped with enough line to troll and take care of playing the fish after he strikes at trolling distance. Ordinary trolling speed is one to two miles per hour, and the length of line ranges from thirty to ninety feet. Ordinary bait-casting lines are excellent for trolling. Metal lines are rarely necessary for bass fishing, as extreme depths are seldom fished.

Too many bait fishermen minimize the value of using a leader. A short section of almost invisible nylon may spell the difference between success and failure, however. Where bass are wary, the angler using a two- or three-foot leader when still-fishing and a six-foot leader when trolling will do much better than those who think a snelled hook attached directly to the line should fool the fish.

One of the most successful and interesting methods of fishing with live bait is by casting. The still-fisherman sits and waits. The troller is limited to those areas into and out of which he can drag his bait without getting fouled up. He's limited mostly to open-water fishing.

The caster takes his bait to the bass, searching out the likely hideouts and making the most natural presentation possible. He drops his minnow into a little pocket of open water surrounded by lily pads; he snakes a frog jerkily across the weedy water, or he works a night crawler-and-spinner combination just above the bottom over rocky ledges. He drops fat, black crickets beside half-submerged logs.

Bait casting is excellent for heavier baits that will stand the shock of the sudden casting start or the hard landing on the water. Fly casting will drop a minnow or frog lightly to the water, but the quick changes of direction on the back cast or false casts make this method hard on natural baits, too.

Spinning is the answer to perfect casting of natural baits. The cast is gentle and easy; the baits land lightly. The weight of most natural baits is sufficient for casting without having to use sinkers or float. The spinning line is light and gives the bait freedom of action. The retrieve can be slow and the depth controlled by adding weight if necessary to take the bait deeper; a small amount of weight may be needed for casting very light baits.

One of the many things that make the bass such a great game fish is the wide range of food that attracts him. He's interested in just about everything alive in and around the water, whether it's just big enough to see or almost too big to swallow. That makes him both a difficult and a satisfying quarry. When you're tossing plugs at him he may be looking for Mayfly larvae, and when you're fishing with small bugs or dry flies, his dream dish may consist of a six-inch golden shiner.

Occasionally bass are extremely selective and this is particularly true of smallmouths when Mayflies or dragon flies are hatching out, but the average bass on an average day might take a cricket, a stone fly nymph, a small frog, and a shiner in that order as they appear.

Favorite bass baits vary with the locality and waters as well as the time of year. The best bait is usually the most natural one, the type of food the fish is actually searching for. Minnows are the most common bait and one of the best. Night crawlers are high on the list. Crawfish in the soft, new shell are excellent, as are frogs, helgramites, dragon fly larvae, grasshoppers, crickets, etc.

A good, active bait will draw strikes where a sickly or dead one will be spurned. The bass is a game fish, well able to capture his prey even when it is healthy and agile. He tends to be suspicious or disdainful of baits that are sickly or dead, so the problem of keeping baits lively is one worthy of study. A live-well in the fishing boat or an aerating minnow pail is good insurance for the minnow fisherman. Other baits should be kept cool and well ventilated.

Crowding is bad and plenty of clean, fresh air helps keep bait alive and lively. Worms should have moist, clean earth to burrow in; when they are placed in the can, they should be placed on top of the earth. In that way they burrow down, which will permit air to penetrate to them. Worms thrown into the bottom of the can and covered with dirt tend to be smothered and weakened. If the worms are left to dig into the dirt themselves, any weak ones that remain on top can be discarded. If buried under the earth with good worms, they soon die and contaminate the others.

Worms, insects, frogs, and crawfish should all be kept in the shade, and crawfish, frogs, and helgramites will keep better in damp moss than in water. Choose a bait can big enough to give grasshoppers and crickets plenty of room. When they're piled one on top of another in layers, the weak ones settle to the bottom and soon have the life squashed out of them.

What size hooks for bass? Almost any legal bass can get a pretty good-sized hook into his maw, but the size of the hook isn't determined primarily by the size of the fish or his mouth. It depends upon the size of the bait to be used. The hook should be big enough to hook through the bait into the fish; it should be small enough to be inconspicuous when baited.

For big minnows, crawfish, and frogs, sizes 2 to 1/0 are all right. For small minnows or small frogs, hooks of sizes 2 to 4 will do. Size 6 is about right for grasshoppers and other large insects, but if the hoppers are small and the fish wary, a No. 8 or even a No. 10 will bring more action. If the hook is a good one, even a No. 10 will not straighten out under the pull of a walloping bass . . . but when you go to the very small sizes, hooks of top quality are essential.

The flash of a spinner ahead of a trolled lure, or a few inches above a hook when still-fishing, is attractive to bass. They can see the flash farther away than the bait. The flash attracts them, they come to investigate, see the bait, and are caught. Without a flasher, some of the fish would pass by without noticing the bait at all.

When a bass takes a grasshopper or any of the smaller baits, he does so with a single gulp and the strike should be immediate. When a bass takes a frog, minnow, or any good-sized bait, he'll usually clamp down on it with his jaws and hold it there for a bit. He may shake the bait as a terrier would a rat or he may even make a short, swift run to get away from another bass that's looking at it longingly.

After a while he'll turn the bait into the best position for swallowing (minnows and frogs go headfirst, crawfish tailfirst) and gulp it down. The angler must give slack line until the bait is swallowed, for a premature strike will find the hook still outside the bass's mouth and will result in a clean miss.

When a bass takes a float down, the angler should get ready. Whether the float just dips under and stays motionless or whether it goes under with a zing for fifteen or twenty feet, the angler should give slack instead of striking. When the fish stops and the float hesitates, the bass is probably turning the bait preparatory to swallowing it. When he makes the second run or moves off strongly, the angler can assume the bait is well down and can then lift his rod in the strike.

The trolling strike should follow the same pattern. The reel should be set at a very light drag and slack given as quickly as possible after the strike is felt. Then, gradually tightening the line, the strike is made only after the bass pulls heavily. Most of my trolling for bass is done with a fly rod, so I developed a system of coiling some slack line on the bottom of the boat. I plant one foot firmly on the line ahead of the slack while I row to hold it solidly until the strike comes. When I see the rod bend and the line tighten, I lift my foot and let the coiled slack slide out through the guides. I back-water at the same time, tighten up a little, and wait for the surge after the bass has the bait down.

The casting strike is like the others. With very small baits it can be immediate, but with most bass baits, the fish should be given time to mouth the bait and take it down before the attempt is made to set the hook.

A hook hone and a little sharpening will do wonders for dull hooks; dull hooks have no place in a bass fisherman's kit, for bass have tough mouths. Once a hook penetrates, it will hold well enough, but many a bass is lost because the hook was dull and failed to bite into the bony jaw or penetrate the flesh beyond the barb. Unless well set, a hook will work free at the first sign of slack. Keep the hooks sharp and the bait fresh and lively, and the bass should do the rest.

CHAPTER 23

Choose Your Lake

IF ACCURATE catch figures per angler were available, it would be a fairly simple matter to choose bass water that is highly productive, but in the case of most lakes, especially the large ones, such information cannot be obtained. Normally, an angler must choose a lake by reports from other fishermen or accounts in newspapers or magazines—or by seeing the water and deciding that it looks promising. Assuming a fisherman is scouting around for a new spot, what should he look for . . . and what questions should he ask?

The kind of water a fisherman seeks depends to a certain extent upon what angling method he's going to use. Let's assume our angler is a bait caster. That means he'll want a fair amount of open water where he can work without having his lure and fish fouled up in weeds. He will want a lake where there is either a shoreline that offers protective hiding places or large shallow stretches in the five- to twelve-foot depth which is best for casting success. If a lake is deep and the fish are feeding near the bottom, casting will be spotty or difficult, and results for the average fisherman will be poor.

If a lake is deep but has a good shoreline, fringed with weeds and overhanging branches, the results from casting should be better. If a lake has a good shoreline with a lot of protective cover and is blessed with many bars and offshore shallows which provide additional casting area, it should rank as a top lake for bait casting. The area of offshore bars and flat sections in the right depth range is so much larger than that of a shoreline that a lake with good offshore water need not have the latter to be an excellent producer. However, such lakes usually have good shorelines as well.

It works out, too, that the lake with large offshore areas of good casting and feeding water, all other conditions being equal, will produce more bass than the other types. They usually produce other species in abundance—perch or other panfish if not walleyes, pike, or pickerel. If other conditions are similar, the number and size of bass in a lake will depend upon the food available for them. Most bass food is to be found in water that has a fair amount of vegetation but is not choked with it, and in water where the sun's rays can penetrate to make the plants healthy.

The number of people one sees fishing a lake may have little bearing on one's chances for a good catch. He may find better fishing on a lake that is dotted with fishing boats than one where fishermen are rare. If a lake is a good producer it will support a lot of fishermen; if it is a poor lake for fish the catches of the few who fish it may be below average. The important thing to estimate is the ratio of fish to fishermen and decide on that basis.

The shape of a lake has an effect on its productiveness. A lake that is perfectly round has a minimum amount of shoreline for a given surface area. A few islands, along with many coves and peninsulas, may give a lake five times as much shoreline as a round one of the same size. Naturally, the lake with the longer shoreline not only has more good fishing water but also has a greater potential for producing bass food when the offshore waters of both lakes are too deep for best fish production.

The depth and contours of a lake's bed may sometimes be judged by the slope of the ground around it, but that way of guessing is chancy at best. Crisscrossing a lake to take occasional soundings or to search for weeds that denote shallow water is much more certain. The time to spot submerged weed beds is late in the summer when the weeds have reached their full growth. An excellent bar of a good depth for fishing might have weeds at a depth invisible from the surface in the early season, but reaching or almost reaching the top in August.

These offshore bars and reefs, with deep water nearby, are favorite feeding grounds, and as the season progresses with the warming of the water, they get better. The bass will seek comfort in the cool depths but will work up onto these underwater hills for the nearest supply of food.

Summing up, the bait caster can best judge a lake's capacity to produce bass for him by its extent of shoreline and its total area of water at a depth of less than twelve feet. The producing area divided by the number of fishermen who fish it is a pretty good way of judging where the best fishing may be found.

The fly caster's needs are similar to those of the bait caster. His lures will not travel as deep, on the average, and his need for shore-line, shallow water, or surface-minded fish is even greater than that of the bait caster. Wind will bother him, too, and if he's strictly a fly-casting fisherman he'll like the smaller lakes or those with protected coves much better than the broad expanses. On the wide waters the fly caster may find a bait-casting rod a helpful adjunct when the wind comes up and his fly rod can be used only with difficulty.

A fly caster can fish pocket water among the lily pads better than the bait caster since he can drop a lure neatly into a pocket, move it a foot or two, then flick it up into the air and down into another such opening, while the bait caster must reel in completely after each cast. A weedy lake with small pockets of open water is made for fly casting, and such waters, protected from the waves by the weeds scattered through them, are rarely too rough to fish with a fly rod. The main drawback to such large expanses of vegetation reaching to the surface is that, once a fish is hooked, he must be played in the weeds, which means more fish are lost, especially if the tackle is light.

The troller can make his bait travel at any level and for him the shoreline and bars are most productive, too. He will be looking for lakes with good fish-producing qualities and large stretches of open water where he can troll without getting hung up. He will normally troll just outside the weeds, through lanes in the offshore vegetation or around offshore reefs.

The still-fisherman can handle almost any type of lake but will find the going best when a good lake has numerous bars and submerged knolls where he will find bass concentrated. Unlike the caster or troller, he doesn't cover much water and depends upon the fish to come to him rather than moving to them. His luck is best where fish congregate or in a spot where the pattern of their movements brings many of them to his baits.

Every lake and every river is different and needs special study that can only be made on the spot. Skillful stream fishermen learn to tell by the pattern of the surface swirls, ripples, and eddies where the water beneath them is most suitable for the feeding, comfort, or safety of the fish they seek. Armed with this knowledge, they can approach even an unknown stream with a fair confidence that they'll put their lure or bait through the best water.

But with lakes the problem becomes much more complex. Save for occasional weed beds, there is no surface indication of the depth of water. Anyone can follow the weeds and fish the shoreline and, as a result, those areas are the hardest fished.

Particularly, there is no easy way for earthbound man to map out the contours of the lake bed and find those offshore bars and gullies where fishing is best. Sounding with anchor and rope, trolling and remembering where the fish are caught are the time-honored methods. Yet, by flying, any angler can manage, in about fifteen minutes, to map out the main gullies, bars, channels, and reefs in a lake he's never seen before.

Ever wonder how an osprey could spot fish so easily from his lofty position on soaring wings? Looking down from a high bridge will give the answer. As one gains altitude he can see objects in and under the water much more readily. At 2,000 feet an angler in an airplane can see the bottom of most good fishing areas and tell by the changing tone of the film of water where it is shallow and where it is deep. He will see where there are rocky ledges and where the floor of the lake is green with vegetation. At three hundred feet he will sometimes see fish. Flying over wilderness lakes, it is often possible to spot fish at the inlets or outlets before deciding to land and rig up the tackle.

The best airplane for this purpose is the slowest one and the one that gives the greatest visibility. An airliner gives you a view of part of one engine, a bit of one wing, and a speck of sky through a small window. But most light planes give you the feeling of sitting in a comfortable airborne chair, and you're able to look down all around you. The slow airplane gives a better chance to study the water and earth beneath it.

Preparations for such an aerial survey are simple. If possible, obtain or draw a map of the lake before the flight. The map should be on a fairly large scale to permit the making of notes and locating prominent landmarks such as white houses at the shoreline, rocky cliffs, or bridges. If no map is available, take up a sheet of paper or a drawing board sufficiently large to draw a map. A reasonably accurate outline of the lake can be sketched quickly from the air. Then various bars and ledges can be marked in the right spots. Crossing lines from prominent markings on the shore can be drawn on the map to make location of the spots from a boat later a simple matter.

The best time to make such a survey is in the late spring or early summer. Then the sun is at its highest and brightest so that the eye can penetrate to greatest depth and see most clearly. The water is usually clear then, too, and the lakes have not yet started to "work" and become cloudy. It may have taken some of the old-timers years to find the bars they fish so successfully and hold so secret. You can find them from the sky in a matter of minutes.

CHAPTER 24

Taking 'Em on Plugs

THE BLACK BASS built the great American sport of bait casting. From the day the legendary bass struck at the empty matchbox a fishless angler tossed overboard, giving him the idea of putting hooks on one to make a bass lure, bait casting has been truly American, unlike fly fishing which we learned from England.

There are several ways to catch this popular game fish, but none is so effective and pleasant, all in all, as bait casting. The fly fisherman has the devil's own time of it when the winds whip hard across the waters. Casting with the long rod is difficult in the wind, and his lures are not very conspicuous in the wave-churned waters when compared with the greater visibility of the bait-casting plugs and spoons.

While the still-fisherman is waiting vainly for bass to move into the vicinity of his offering, the bait caster can be sending his lure out to find the bass, wherever they may be. Bait-casting lures can be made to travel the surface, in midwater or deep. The amount of water that can be covered by bait casting is greater than by any other fishing means. The trolling fisherman, though he moves his lure, covers far less water than the caster. The casting lure suits the bass's temperament. While there are times when other methods are supreme, by and large it is bait casting that brings in the bass.

But the simple process of buying a bait-casting outfit and learning to cast with it doesn't insure a big catch. Unless you use your tackle with skill and have a knowledge of the bass and his habits, your chief reward will be exercise. So for those who are puzzled about how to proceed, here's the basic picture as I see it.

The biggest problem is to know in which sections of a lake or river to fish. If the casting lure is kept moving and it is one of the more successful designs, it will take fish from the right areas at the right depths.

The choice of lure is important, but there are enough time-tested casting lures on the market to simplify your choice to several that will cover the field as, for example, a surface plug, a bass spoon (perhaps with a touch of bucktail on it), a floating plug that dives, and a diving plug that sinks. If the beginner will pick out a few good lures in standard color patterns, he should catch fish with them.

For the purpose of this discussion, bigmouth and smallmouth bass can be classed together and considered generally. The relatively minor differences in their actions and habits won't disturb us. In general, both early season and late, bass are found in fairly shallow water. In the heat of midsummer they'll drop down to depths of ten to twenty-five feet in order to find cool, comfortable water, especially during the daytime. Again, after the northern waters cool off for the winter they'll sink to the deeper levels again to become dormant or almost so.

Their habits around the clock tend to follow a pattern, too. In the spring and fall they'll come into shallower water or rise toward the surface when the sun shines and the upper layer of water becomes warmer and nearer to the temperature that gives them greatest comfort and promotes their greatest activity. With the cool nights of early spring this surface water will become cold again and they'll sink to a lower level.

When the air temperature ranges from 60 to 70°, they'll find a considerable depth of water in which to be comfortable and active. When the thermometer climbs and keeps on climbing, the surface water will become too hot for comfort while the sun is on it, and the bass will sink to lower, cooler depths. On cool nights, however, they may come into the shallows or up to the surface again. These are generalities, but they're important.

Temperature of the water determines the comfort of the fish, and their comfort is an important factor in the spots they'll choose to lie in or feed in. Water that's too cool—which means 50° or colder—numbs the bass and they stop feeding. Water that's too hot makes them lethargic.

Abundance of food is a second prime factor. Bass will feed where the feeding's best unless it's too uncomfortable.

Safety, the third important factor in the actions of fish, is the least critical of the three in the case of lake fish. They have plenty of water around them in which to escape, whereas stream fish do not. Still sticking to generalities, it seems safe to say that it is wisest to fish the surface for bass in the early season during the warmth of the day and drop to a depth of two to fifteen feet during the evenings and nights.

During hot weather the nights may find fish on the surface or within a few feet of it, but the days are likely to find them down deep, so that a lure should travel at least six feet under water and preferably more. Fall should be the same as spring as soon as the nights grow cold again. In the in-between seasons, morning and evening should produce the best surface fishing, while midday and nighttime will require deeper running lures.

To fish the surface or just under it is the easiest type of plug casting. Using a floating plug or a diving plug that will float when at rest but which will travel underwater when retrieved, you can hold the lure to the upper level and see how it is acting. You'll also see and hear many of your strikes and that adds greatly to the pleasure of fishing the surface. You can fish fast or slow without changing your bait level by choosing plugs that will not dive too deep even when retrieved swiftly. Most anglers tend to fish surface and near-surface lures very slowly. The slow retrieve is probably the most effective, but it's a good idea to vary them with an occasional swift, jumpy retrieve when the usual method isn't bringing any strikes.

To make a lure go down deeper in the water, choose a deep-diving floater or a sinking plug. The speed of the retrieve must be coupled with the design of the lure to achieve a given depth. A deep-diver reeled slowly may only go down a foot or so. Reeled swiftly, it may go down six feet. One of the old-style sinking plugs with spinners fore and aft sinks deepest when the retrieve is slowest, and with increased speed it runs nearer and nearer the surface.

In recent years we've been blessed with the real answer to deep-water plug casting—sinking plugs that are equipped with a diving device that sends them downward as they are pulled forward. When they're cast out, a good start toward the boat will send them down sharply. A stretch of slow-moving water will let them settle still farther of their own weight and give the line a chance to sink lower in the water. Then, by varying between swift and slow retrieves, you can make the sinking diver maintain any reasonable depth you want and, unlike the old-time sinking plugs, it will have an attractive motion even though it moves very slowly.

Once the lure sinks out of sight beneath the surface, the angler has to guess at the depth at which it is traveling. Most guesses probably are on the deep side. It takes slow and skillful retrieving to make any casting lure travel its course at an average depth of eight feet. Even the sinking-diving type if retrieved rapidly will seldom go down more than four feet. The fact that the line sinks more slowly than the lure means that the latter is continually being aimed upward and pulled toward the surface.

The higher the rod tip is held, the harder it is to make a plug run deep. When you want to go down deep, work slowly. A thin line will tend to pull a plug toward the surface much less than a bulky one with greater water resistance, another good reason for using fine diameter lines for bait casting.

Some plugs develop greater action at certain speeds, but whether you run them fast or slow they'll still wriggle, and if you can coast them along in the vicinity of enough bass you'll have action. A little experimenting to check on the actual depth while you're retrieving your lures is worthwhile. Cast near a friend on a pier or in another boat and he can tell you how deep your lure is traveling on the way back. The more you know, the less you have to guess as to the whereabouts of your plug at any given moment, and thus the better you'll be able to fish.

For the beginner, the floating-diving type of lure or the surface lure is best. Fewer of these lures will be lost by snapping lines in backlashes or catching deep weeds or snags when the lure goes down too far. One worthwhile trick in the case of backlashes when using a sinking lure is to reel right in on top of any backlash until the lure is safely in the boat. Then pull the line off your reel until the backlash is uncovered and you can untangle it at your leisure with suitable verbal accompaniment and without the added worry of an expensive lure that may never return from its watery grave.

A dispassionate observer might find very little difference between fishing for bass with a surface plug and fishing for them with lures that travel underwater. Except for the lure, the tackle is the same throughout. The casting, the general knowledge required, the playing and netting of the fish—all these things are identical. Yet there is a great and vital difference.

Long ago I had a good fishing friend who was a dry-fly purist. To him trout were the best fish to catch, and the idea of wasting his limited fishing time on a fish in a lower sporting category was, in his judgment, pure foolishness. I liked to be with him and we spent many pleasant days together on the trout streams, but when the streams got low and the bass season opened he still stuck to his trout, while I switched to bass. Once in a while I managed to get him away for an afternoon of plugging or fly fishing for bass. Although he seemed to enjoy the spurts of action the bass gave us, he never lost that faraway look in his eyes, and I know that his heart was back on the trout streams.

It happened that our efforts at bass had been on typical summer afternoons with the surface rippled by the normal diurnal breeze. We caught bass, but we caught them under the surface on plugs or streamer flies. Though he loved to see those smallmouths leap, they failed to impress him enough to pull him away from the trout waters where, as he explained, he found dynamite under every riffle. I had all but given up hope of ever converting him when, by a fluke, I got him to go bass fishing with me one night.

For the first time in all our trips the water was glassy smooth. He had declined to fish and was doing the rowing. I put on a surface plug, and the first time a bass walloped it my friend jumped six inches off the seat and lost an oar. After the second fish we changed places, and for the rest of that three-hour session I rowed and he fished.

The excitement of the surface strike had done something the dynamic leaps of the smallmouths and their hard underwater strikes had been unable to do. He went on to become an enthusiastic bass fisherman, and I am certain that had it not been for that surface plug and the exciting strikes it brought, he would have stuck to his trout streams entirely, low water or not.

The surface strike is the main difference between surface fishing and using lures that come in underwater. The advantage of seeing and hearing a fish smash at the lure is of basic importance to even the most matter-of-fact angler, and as we go on we'll find there are a few other special advantages to be gained by fishing on top whenever conditions warrant it.

Surface fishing tends to cover less water than casting with a diving or sinking lure, for the fishing is slower. Because of this, it is obvious that where one lure will draw as many strikes as another, the faster-traveling underwater lure covering the most water will take the most fish. There are few days and few places where those conditions exist, however, and the simple act of putting a lure near a bass is not enough. It has either to please or anger him to draw a strike.

Few surface lures work well when fished fast. Only those with fore and aft spinners have a really wide range of speed with effectiveness at all ranges, and they, like the others, have better action at less than maximum reeling speed. Special designs call for certain speed ranges. A Jitterbug, for example, has no appreciable action as it starts out, but at a certain point it will start to sway. As speed continues to increase, it will work into its special tantalizing action. Under ever-increasing speed it will reach a point where the wiggle is lost and the lure begins to skip and skid. The Jitterbug's range is good and its action excellent, but no one plug gives its best action at all speeds.

Take plunkers. A sudden pull noses them down and they send out a splash, spray, and a noisy "pop." It is the sudden start that gives them their best action. If, once started, the speed is maintained, they have little action and will catch far fewer fish than if they are retrieved on a stop-and-start basis. A retrieve by means of short, sudden yanks and complete stops will give best results. Each type of plug action calls for its own retrieve.

While most diving and underwater lures can be retrieved with a steady reeling speed for top effectiveness, the retrieve for almost all surface plugs is better when it is slow and varied, often with considerable periods when the plug lies motionless on the surface. In this respect surface fishing has an advantage over the underwater retrieve. Let a plug plop down into the water and lie still. The splash and commotion of its landing will attract a bass's attention even though it may not have been within the range of his vision at that moment.

He swims toward the commotion to investigate . . . and there it sits. He spots the lure easily because it is on the surface. If the plug had sunk and were more or less motionless under the water, it would not be as readily visible. Even if it were partly hidden by weeds, it would be on the surface and against the light, the conditions under which a lure is most easily spotted, except under rough-water conditions.

The surface lure has a terrific advantage whenever there are large weed beds which do not quite reach the surface. If a lure dives, it gets into the weeds, and even when weedless, will pick up an occasional strand of vegetation or will have its action subdued by countless stems. The fish cannot see very far through the stems at the lower elevation, but they can all see the top. If a sunken lure passes within their vision, well and good. If it is barely out of their sight it might as well be a mile away.

A surface lure is much more easily located under the same conditions if the water is reasonably smooth. It is conspicuous and easy to see. More important are the ripples spreading out around it. A fish may see the ripples, ten feet from the plug, and he immediately knows where to locate the center of the disturbance. He will often swim that ten feet through thick weeds to strike a surface lure he could not see from his original position.

The surface fisherman attracts fish with these ripples as well as with his actual lure, and it would be valuable for this reason alone, if for no other, to use the splashing, stop-and-start retrieve with surface lures in order to make the ripples spread wide in an uneven pattern.

It is important to give a fish the chance to come in from either side as the retrieve is made. The more heavily fished the waters and the more wary the bass, the more important this factor is. A long pause at several points on the way in is good fishing technique, in addition to the shorter pauses all along the line. I like to give a short twitch immediately after the lure strikes the water to show any watching bass that it is really alive, then a fairly long pause before the next jerk. Although the making of two consecutive casts to the same spot is not often effective, it is much more so with surface plugs than with underwater lures.

Fishing with the surface lure is slow and intensive. It doesn't cover as much water, but it does it thoroughly. All this might sound as if surface plugs were the answer to the fisherman's problem and the only lures he'd ever need. This might be true if conditions were always perfect but, unfortunately for those wedded to the surface, these lures lose much of their effectiveness when the water is rough.

A plug lying motionless on still water is easily seen. Even the slightest motion it makes sends out a noticeable ripple in an expanding circle, visible to both fisherman and fish from afar. The same plug, bouncing around in choppy waves is difficult to locate, its form and motion lost in the movement of the waves. Furthermore, fish seem to avoid the surface water when it is very rough and feed at lower levels where they seem to find more comfort. The surface plug is a lure for smooth water and light ripples. When the ripples become waves, it is time to change to lures that go down into the smoother waters.

Even when it is rough in the open water of a lake, there are lee shores and there should be areas, especially along the shoreline, where the action of the waves is nullified by a coating of lily pads or other vegetation. Spotted throughout this blanket of lily pads there are usually pockets of open water. The high waves of the open water will have been tamed before reaching them, and although some smooth swells may roll across them, the waves won't be breaking there and surface lures will still have their usual effectiveness.

A cast into one of these pockets should be worked very slowly, for once the plug reaches the edge of the surrounding weeds it will probably cause a bass-frightening instead of a bass-attracting commotion when it starts turning over or hooking into the pads.

Surface plugs are extra good in the very shallow waters. Largemouth bass often move close into shore on the shallow flats. They may be found in water barely deep enough to cover them, and where any diving lure is sure to get into trouble. Surface lures will cover these waters nicely without snagging. It is exciting to see a bass boil up out of deep water to smash a surface plug, but it is much, much more so to see one start out some thirty feet away and race through water just barely deep enough to float him, and end the rush in the same sort of smashing strike.

One thing to be remembered when fishing a surface lure is that the strike must be fast and adequate. When a fish hits a lure that is being reeled in, he is likely to be hooked by the normal forward speed of the steady retrieve. With the stop-and-start retrieve on the surface the bass is just as likely to hit when the line is slack and the lure motionless as when it is being pulled forward. If the strike isn't started at the sight or sound of the fish at the lure, there's little chance of the hook's sinking home.

Five of the noisiest largemouth bass I can ever remember struck the surface lure of a friend of mine who was new to bass fishing. He was shocked into immobility by each strike. All five had time to shake the lure and spit it out before he lifted his rod. We alternated turns at the rod and I ended up with four good bass while he was blanked. I never knew a madder man. Needless to say, his affliction was purely temporary, and the next day he started setting the hooks at the first sign of a bass near his lure and did all right.

The longer the line stretching between lure and angler, the harder the strike must be. There is more slack to be taken up in a long line than in a shorter one. When the lure is close to the boat the strike should be fast, but it need not be quite as hard.

In choosing surface plugs, worry more about the shape than the color, and be sure to have a variety of sizes. Big plugs make the most splash and sometimes that's an advantage. Small ones work best when the fish are scary. The only part of a surface plug a fish sees is its belly. Don't judge the plugs you buy by looking at their backs. The only way a bass can see the back of a surface plug is to jump up in the air alongside it, before deciding whether or not to strike. Look at the plugs from underneath when choosing them and it may surprise you to see how similar and how simple they are.

Another point to remember is that the sound of a plunker is for the angler and not the fish. Water, motion, and splash will affect the fish, but the air noise, the "pop," is strictly for the anglers and the birds. It makes no difference to the fish. While it does no good, it does no harm, either, and it's fun to hear.

Choose a variety of actions in the plugs. Have one to two that will have best action at very slow speeds for pocket water, and some that will have their best action at a good speed for covering the large areas of open water. Half a dozen different lures should give you a fair coverage, but if you ever get seriously involved in surface plugging, twice that number won't begin to cover your needs.

Surface plugs and night fishing go well together, because although most days are windy, most nights are not. The sound of the lure as it is retrieved gives the fisherman a pretty good idea of where it is at any instant, whereas the exact location of an underwater plug somewhere out there in the darkness is much less certain.

Often the underwater plug is right beside the boat before the fisherman realizes it. If you are going to give any variation of speed as the water shallows or deepens on the retrieves, the ability to determine the plug's location accurately is important. When fishing a drop-off that is about thirty feet from shore, I like to concentrate on the area with some slow twitches, and when fishing across a rocky reef, I let the plug dawdle as it passes over the shallowest points.

I think bass like to hit something on the surface as much as the angler likes to see and hear them hit. Their surface strike seems more vicious or more playful than their strike at a submerged lure. They, too, must take a special delight in seeing the spray fly. Whether that is really true or just imagination, it's more fun to fish on the surface.

CHAPTER 25

Bass
on the Long Rod

FLY FISHING FOR BASS is older than bait casting, but ever since the latter took the field by storm the long rod has taken second place to the short one on totals of bass taken by casting. The fly rod will not cast as far as the bait-casting rod. It will not cast as well in a wind and the fly-rod lure cannot be retrieved as swiftly, except for short spurts, nor can the fly be made to cover as much water as the plug in a given amount of time. In spite of these handicaps, fly-rod fishing for bass has been steadily increasing in popularity.

The reasons behind this increase are several. Among them are the sheer pleasure so many anglers get from playing a fish on a fly rod, the exciting surface strikes, and the particular effectiveness of small fly-rod lures, where fishermen are plentiful and the bass have grown wary of large artificial bait-casting lures.

There is something about a fly rod that makes many anglers forsake all other types for it. Just as some trout fishermen will stick to the dry fly through thick and thin, so will a certain segment of the angling population stick to the fly rod, even though they know that a bait-casting rod would frequently serve them better. Fishing with the long rod gives them a certain pleasure unequaled by any other form of fishing, and if they're skillful they'll land a lot of bass.

Small fly-rod surface lures are killer-dillers. They'll take bass at times when all other types fail. The fly-rod mouse made of bucktail and the cork-and-feather lures rode into fashion on the early manifestations of fly-rod popularity many years ago and they're still well up near the top in effectiveness, in spite of an ever-increasing number of new designs.

Added to this efficiency of small surface lures (an efficiency that lessens as the water gets rougher) is the electric effect the surface strike has on the fisherman. The sound and sight of a big bass engulfing a floating fly-rod lure on a quiet evening is something to remember through those long winter nights. No wonder so many bug fishermen eschew all other methods of fishing and sulk when bug fishing conditions are poor.

Fly-rod lures in general have their greatest ratio of effectiveness where the bass are hard-fished and wary. A fly-rod lure is light and it may drop to the water with anything from a light "plop" to the soft whisper of a drifting feather. A long and delicate leader may be used if it's necessary in order to fool the fish.

There's a wider range of action possible with the long rod than with the casting rod, although the latter will cover more water. The bass bug can be made to hop clear of the water or to skip across the surface for fifteen feet or more at a swift pace and yet always be under control with the fisherman ready to handle the strike.

The spinner-and-streamer combination, an especially deadly fly-rod lure, can be fished at any depth from an inch or two to ten feet. The standard bass wet fly has a similar range, and the myriad imitations of crawfish, helgramites, frogs, and crickets give the fly-rod fisherman an approach to bass under almost any set of fishing conditions.

Here are some of the factors to consider in fly-rod fishing for bass. In a high wind, casting becomes very difficult. It also becomes dangerous for someone else in the boat if the caster isn't on his toes all the time. To overcome this, the fly-rod angler who is not alone in the boat should arrange to sit at one end and keep his lure passing through the air on the side away from his companion. It pays dividends to stick to the quiet sections of a lake. There the casting should be easiest and control over the action of the lure the greatest, both important factors in angling success.

The fly-rod lure is fairly small and is difficult to see in rough water. It's much more conspicuous where the surface is smooth, and this is doubly true of the small floating lure. Here is another potent reason for avoiding whitecaps with your fly rod. If you must fish rough water with the long rod, select a lure that will travel at least two feet down and preferably three to make it more visible to the bass, for they'll be lying or swimming at even greater depths.

The fly rod will not cast as far as the bait-casting rod. To offset this, the fly caster must move with increased silence and caution. Few anglers realize how easily lake fish are frightened, especially when the lake surface is smooth. The oars should dip lightly and the boat or canoe should move along like a shadow. There's no substitute for the silent approach in this game, and the poorer your casting, the greater the need for caution in this respect.

So much for the disadvantages; now we'll look at the brighter side of using the fly rod for bass. The fly rod won't cast as far as the short rod, but the lure can be picked up when it's still about twenty feet or more from the boat and whisked out to the fifty- or sixty-foot point where the bass are undisturbed by the boat. That last twenty feet of the retrieve is usually barren, and with the fly rod it can be eliminated. While the bait caster must fish his lure right up to the side of the boat in order to cast again, the fly fisherman can keep his lure moving through the most productive water at all times.

He can do something else the bait caster cannot do. He can drop his surface lure into a small opening among the lily pads. After watching the ripples spread out and disappear among the surrounding pads, he can give the lure a couple of twitches and the bass enough time to take it before flipping it skyward to continue easily through a normal back cast and forward shoot to another such weed-surrounded patch of open water.

The plug fisherman who fishes the same spots must either use weedless—and sometimes slightly fishless—hooks or hang a few weeds and drag them into the boat. In this business of towing in half a ton of weeds, the plug fisherman may lose his lure through breakage or his temper through annoyance. Also, this dragging of a mass of spinach halfway across a lake is sometimes noted by the bass and results in putting them on their guard.

The fly rod for bass should be a stout one, needing strength and power not so much in order to play the fish as to be able to cast the bulky and sometimes weighty fly-rod lures. With a powerful rod, a heavy fly line is used to match or "balance" it. The heavier the fly line, the lighter, in proportion to the line, any fly-rod lure becomes. When casting is *perfectly timed,* even a heavy bass bug can be cast without difficulty on a fairly light rod. But let the timing stray a bit from perfection and the shocks (such as a lure still going out on the back cast after the majority of the line in the air has a good start on the forward cast) will make casting difficult in the extreme.

So let's use a nine-foot rod weighing from 6 to 7½ ounces, and a line with a weighted section of size 9 or 10. That will give power enough for long casts, weight enough in the line to absorb the minor mistakes in timing, and a good leverage for playing the bass, especially if they're boring down into weedy waters.

The reel for this fishing may well be an automatic, since its extra weight will be just about right to balance the rod described above, and its spring will have enough power to play a bass well. The big advantage of an automatic reel lies in being able to keep the bottom of the boat free of coils of loose line, always in danger of tangling if the fish makes a sudden rush at the strike. This is particularly valuable at night, when any loose line is a hazard.

Then, too, when fishing toward the shoreline from a boat, many a bass will make a swift run for the nearest deep water when the hook strikes home. This may bring him toward or even under the boat. He'll come so swiftly that no angler can either strip or reel in line fast enough to keep up with him, but an automatic will maintain a good tension and bring the line in without a tangle.

However, any single-action reel big enough to hold the necessary line is adequate for this fishing. About thirty yards of backing is advisable on the reel for those who may be inclined to troll or make very long casts. For those who limit themselves to sixty-foot casts, the backing will not be necessary. The spool of the reel should be fairly well filled with line, though not so full that it scrapes on the crossbars. A well-filled fly reel will retrieve line faster than one with only a small amount of line on the spool. If the spool needs a filler, any strong and heavy line can be added as backing in the right amount to fill the spool properly.

The fly line for bass should be a forward or torpedo taper, if you can afford one. The perfect line for bass bugs or fly-rod lures has a fairly short front taper (not over eight feet) to a fine end of size F. If the taper goes to G or H, it should be trimmed back to F size. The tapered bass leader for attachment at this point should have a butt end of about .028 inch diameter. For most bass fishing, neither a long nor a tapered leader is necessary, but there are times when length and fine diameter really count. A tapered leader will cast better and does a better job of fooling the fish than a level one of the same average diameter.

A good level line will do very well for most bass fishing, but when it comes time to lengthen the cast, the lighter "running line" behind the heavy "belly" of the torpedo type taper comes into play and adds extra distance to the casts. Since a lake that is smooth, clear, and hard-fished calls for long and careful casting—except at night—that extra distance is worth having.

Anglers having an interest in experimenting with different tapers may splice together various sections of line of different diameters to make lines ranging from something better than a level up to a perfect taper for a particular rod. A twenty-foot length of A line spliced to seventy feet of F line calls for only one splice and will do a fine casting job. The number of splices and lengths, for something near perfection, may run up to ten or more.

Although artificial lures are most commonly used with the fly rod for bass, the natural lures may be used with this tackle as well. The chief difficulty in using natural baits is to cast gently enough to keep from snapping the bait off the hook. A little practice in delaying the forward cast until the back cast is complete will usually do away with the jarring shock so likely to cause this sort of damage.

Live grasshoppers, crickets, helgramites, frogs, or shiners are better than any of the imitations, and with the fly rod the fisherman can drop them into exactly the right spot to draw an instantaneous strike. A weighted spinner-and-worm combination makes a good deep-traveling rig for working around rocky ledges for smallmouths, or at the edge of the lily pads for largemouths.

Generally speaking, fly-rod tackle for bass must be rugged. They're a rugged fish and they're usually found in tough situations for fly-rod tackle. If there isn't a log, stump, rock, or dock to get the line fouled up in, it's two to one there'll be a bunch of lily pads or weeds handy for tangling purposes. For the usual fishing, a ten- or twelve-pound test leader is a good choice. Since most bass lures are fairly heavy, this is at least equivalent to using a two-pound test leader with a No. 10 fly.

A bass fisherman rarely has to go as fine as a four-pound test tippet on the fine end. It is only an added hazard to use a fine leader with a heavy lure. The working of the heavy lure on the leader near the knot while casting will often cause it to break prematurely. The leader should be about six feet long for average fishing, twelve if the fish are wary.

How often have you seen a bass scoot away from a plug that drops to the water near him? Such a fish is edgy and nervous, not actively hungry. He's neither curious enough nor hungry enough to come back and tackle it. When bass are near the surface but finicky, the long, fine leader and small fly or natural bait may turn the trick. The fly-rod lure will drop gently to the water. The bass sees the lure or bait without shock or surprise and, even though not particularly hungry, he may decide to strike. The accurate placement of a delicate lure is the forte of the fly fisherman.

In bugging for bass, the line and leader should both float. They'll pick up easily off the water and make casting simpler. The floating line and leader are more visible to the fish, and if they are extremely wary it may be worthwhile to sink them or at least sink the leader. For fishing with a sunken fly, spinner-and-fly combination, or any underwater bait, the sinking line is best.

Fly casting is more work than bait casting, and requires a greater percentage of time for actual casting against the retrieving time (when the fish are caught), but there are some compensations to help even things up. The bait caster must retrieve his lure right up to the end of the rod before he can cast again. He must reel in a long cast in order to pop his lure into a tiny hole in the middle of a bed of lily pads for only a second or two.

Much of the bait caster's retrieve is wasted, as the chances of a bass strike very close to the boat is small. The fly fisherman can drop his bug into a pocket, work it carefully, then pick it up and flick it into one or two others while the bait caster is on his first retrieve. He can also fish the pockets in the pads without getting hung up, whereas any method of casting requiring a complete retrieve after each cast would mean bringing in a mess of weeds a long distance to the boat . . . or using a weedless lure, which may not give him equivalent action or hooking power.

Should an angler always sit down in the boat to cast? Does good form require it? I sit down to be more comfortable and to be less conspicuous to the fish, but for no other reasons. When the fishing is hot and I want to watch the fish strike a sunken lure, I stand up for a better view. Some fly casters can handle line better standing up and that's a good reason for standing, too.

One man standing up in the average boat at a time is enough. Two casters, both standing, are a boatful and may lap over into one another's territory, perhaps to wrap a leader around an un-suspecting neck. Fly casting, especially in the wind and with lures of any noticeable weight, is somewhat unpredictable and requires alert consideration of the caster's fishing partner. He'd best be on his guard on his own account also, lest he pop a hook into his own eye when a sudden gust sends it wavering off its course.

When fishing shallow, weed-free waters, long casts pay off and long retrieves are worthwhile. In normal fishing, few strikes are encountered within fifteen feet of the boatside. Therefore, a forty-foot cast gives only twenty-five feet of fishing, while a sixty-foot cast will give forty-five feet, or almost twice as much. Fish are caught while the lure is in the water, not while it is waving around in the air. The more water each cast covers, the more fishing time the angler spends for a given amount of casting time.

In fly casting there's usually a point beyond which picking up the line from the water for the back cast is easy, and within which it is difficult and calls for extra time and effort to extend the line beyond the guides to normal casting range again. The fly-rod fisherman's fishing should be done beyond that lower limit, and within the upper limit of his easy casting range.

The fly-rod retrieve should be slow. The fly-rod angler should really cover the water. He cannot hope to attract fish from quite as great a distance as they'll travel to reach a plug and its greater commotion. His fishing is finer with more subtle lures. By fishing slower, he gives the bass a better chance to notice his lure, look it over, and strike. Many a bass that won't rush in to grab a big lure before it passes out of range will move in slowly and take a smaller, more reasonable lure.

Surface bug fishermen like to see those big rings spread well out from their bug on smooth water before they give it the first little twitch of life. They like to fish smooth water, which means that any slight commotion their bug makes is much more apparent to the bass than it would be if it had to compete with rippled water or waves for their attention.

The slow, spasmodic retrieve is most productive of strikes. Many a bass-bug man likes the popping kind and draws a satisfaction in hearing the popping or plunking sound a concave surface makes when jerked along the topwater. After exhaustive tests, showing that fish are not frightened or affected much by sound waves, it seems reasonable to assume the popping sound to be more pleasant to the angler than alluring to the bass and that any lure making a similar commotion, but no sound, would be just as effective. That's the way I find it, and a good lure needn't pop to catch bass.

When a bass hits a sunken fly-rod lure, it is usually with a solid wallop that stops the lure instantly. Because bass have tough mouths, it's good policy to strike hard as well as fast. After watching a few lunkers come up to shake their heads and throw lures that hadn't driven in beyond the barb, the reason for the hard strike will be completely clear. A good, sharp hook and a stout leader allow a fly fisherman to really lean on his rod and make it bend at the strike.

The fly-rod lure is a light one, and a bass has considerable difficulty shaking it free. He can throw the heavier bait-casting plugs with much greater ease. A little slack line while playing a fish with a fly rod isn't too likely to mean a lost fish if the hook has been securely set in the first place.

The underwater strike is felt, but the surface strike is seen before it is felt. Only when he strikes does the angler feel his fish. This is true because the underwater lure is retrieved with tension on the line, and only in the rare case of a fish coming in from directly behind can there be a strike without the angler feeling it instantly. The surface lure, when fished under constant tension, is about the same, but with the customary stop-and-go working of the surface lure, most strikes come on a slack line. Then the fly-caster must strike quickly to set the hook as soon as he sees the fish boil up and engulf his bug or hears the splash or sucking sound that indicates a strike.

Bass have sharp teeth and they're hard on lures tied with thread. Flies and bass bugs made without thread or tying and having all the feathers or fibers embedded in indestructible plastic are preferable.

The long rod has greater resilience than the casting rod and exerts greater control over the fish while he's being played. These two factors weigh heavily in the fly-rod man's favor. He doesn't have the reeling leverage to horse a fish in that's granted by the bait caster's quadruple multiplying device, and he may have a little more difficulty in stopping a fish short when he breaks for a snag, but because of the extra, shock-absorbing spring of the fly rod, he has more chance of landing the fish he hooks than the short-rod fisherman does.

Where the bass are hard to take and bored with a constant passing parade of big lures, the fly fisherman has his innings. His careful, more delicate fishing will bring results, especially when the waters are smooth or only slightly rippled, day or night. Fly casting is an interesting way to fish. It is a pleasant and effective way of taking bass and is becoming increasingly popular wherever bass are found.

CHAPTER 26

Black of Night

MY IDEA HAD BEEN to lure the old postmaster into my small air-plane and fly him into one of the Adirondack lakes for an afternoon of bass bugging. Instead, I found myself at the oars only four miles from home, on the small lake where I kept the plane moored. We were passing it again on our third complete circuit of the shoreline. Al hopefully plopped a bug alongside one pontoon and worked it slowly back into deep water. Nothing happened. And nothing had happened all afternoon.

It was Al's idea. With the summer cottages empty and the normal buzz of outboards just a memory, he felt dead certain we could tie into some of the big bass that occasionally came from this little pocketful of water. "And besides," said Al, "nothing in the world would get me into that flyin' machine of yours."

The sun hung low in the sky and we had every reason to expect the sharp coolness of an Indian summer evening to descend. We might get halfway around the lake again before dark, and now, with October on the downhill half, night fishing didn't hold much promise. A few lily pads grow around the edges of the lake, but not enough to provide good cover. Tall elms and maples line its shores and beneath them the summer cottages crowd against the shore.

We fished the edge of deep water, sometimes tight against the overhanging bushes, sometimes at the edge of a bar that Al remembered. Al dropped the bug lightly beside the float again, gave it a rest period, then shuddered it a few inches to another pause. A largemouth about nine inches long tugged it under and hooked himself.

He came skittering across the water to the boatside under the influence of Al's good right arm. Reaching down, I shook him free with a flourish and said airily, "Bass! One of those lunkers you were telling me about, perhaps?"

He grunted and we moved along. A big crappie grabbed the bug and then shook free at the side of the boat. At least, the little ones were beginning to show some interest. Another undersized largemouth fastened himself to the bug and I set him free. Al's considerable figure doesn't bend quite so easily as mine, so I do most of the bending over.

Al was just saying for the fifteenth time, "There's always a good bass along this stretch of water," when the bug went under with a solid, sucking sound.

Nine feet of split bamboo arched and vibrated as the old postmaster and the fish measured strength. Then the fish came our way. He leaped twice coming in. He dived into the pads and brought a mess of them up to the top with him, but Al worked him free. I slipped the net under him and lifted him into the boat.

"He's a nice bass," said Al. "Not a big bass, but a nice one, Lee. He'll weigh nearly a pound and a half. And didn't he take it pretty?"

"Going to put him back?"

"Well," said Al thoughtfully, "maybe we ought to keep this one. It's late in the season and maybe we won't get too many between now and quitting time."

The sun coasted down behind the trees and the new moon started her short arc across the sky. We could hear the smaller fish—bluegills, crappies, punkinseeds—popping away at surface foods everywhere about us on the still water, but nowhere did we hear the heavy surge of a surface-feeding bass. We changed placed and I picked up the fly rod.

There's a pleasant rhythm to bug casting with the right gear. Give me a rod with plenty of power, a long rod without too much weight but with strength right out to the tip. Just plain casting, picturing a lazy old largemouth underneath that fluttering, struggling bug, watching it and then passing it up just before you pick it up on the back cast, or maybe grabbing it, can be richly satisfying when the air is warm and still around you. The insect pests of summer were gone. A couple of ducks dusked in. Still, I couldn't help thinking that we should have been coming in for a landing at that moment after an exciting afternoon of bass fishing in some far-off lake.

Al was saying, "I took two nice ones off that rock there, casting a Dardevle one day last summer. This is real good water and you'd better be ready when he takes it."

It seems to me that Al has taken a big one from every rock and stump, from under every overhanging tree all along the shore-line. His philosophy is one of optimism. If a fish doesn't strike on the first cast, one will surely hit on the second. If not on the second, at least on the third . . . and so on. The longer he fishes, the more certain he becomes that the *next* cast will turn the trick. So Al wasn't surprised when a bass whooshed up and engulfed the bug, but I was.

Realizing that I was a bit late in striking, I really leaned into it. The boat shifted and Al hung onto the oars to steady himself. The rod held its arc and then bent downward, down toward the water until the line began to hiss out through my fingers where I held it at the rod. The fish splashed up and shook, then headed out into the deep water. His leaps were silver flashes in the gathering dusk.

Al slid the net over the side and submerged it. When the fish had spent his strength I slid him above it, half on his side.

Al lifted him in. "Better than three pounds, maybe four," was his verdict. "This was *always* a good shore for bass. There're weeds on the bottom and they like it here."

The light had gone and the shore was only a dim outline. There was still no wind and the warmth felt like August, strange after the cold, frosty nights of the week before. It was like summer fishing but without the hum of insects or the peeping of frogs; a special night, and I began to have a feeling of gratitude to Al for having brought it about.

There'd be other days and nights to come with a wind to riffle the water and send a chill through your clothing; there'd be other evenings to fish if I liked, but none of them would contain this blending of the best of both fall and summer.

The bug dropped, danced its little act, and came back to the boat time after time. Places Al remembered as having yielded lunker fish in the past produced nothing to break the even tenor of the cast and its retrieve. Eventually, as if goaded by some inner force he could no longer contain, Al demanded that I change bugs.

"That dark thing you're throwing around is just black paint and brown bucktail. These bass want something lively and colorful. Let me pick out one for you that's got some color in it."

He spread my lures on the boat seat and eyed them from above the flashlight's beam. He pawed over with his big hands a dozen bugs that had taken fish in the years behind us, spinners nicked by the teeth of pike and walleyes, streamers worn thin and ragged by successful use. He touched them all and finally held up one of Barrett Cass's red-and-white specials. "Throw that thing out there and you'll drive them plumb crazy."

I like to think of night fishing as a mixture of slow, almost silent movement. The dip of oars and the liquid sound of water as they move the last cast a little bit astern, the "feel" of the boat beneath you and the slightest movement of your partner as he shifts for balance, the faintest rustling of leaves and the twinkle of cottage windows or the occasional sharp stab of a car's bright headlights. Tonight there was added the pungent smell of smoke drifting over from the dry marsh fire still burning under the sod. But all these things merge together and fade when you hear the sharp, wet sound a big bass makes when he takes a bug down under that placid surface.

I could feel Al's tenseness through the rigidity of the boat, then sense his relaxing even before I heard his breath go out. We could both hear the delicate whisper of the tight line cutting through the water and knew the fish had been hooked. We were prepared then for the leap that really shattered the silence of the night.

"Don't lose this one," said Al. "This is the one we came for."

Playing them at night, I picture their movements to myself as I read them through the bend of the rod and the pull of the line. A flashlight may tell you more accurately what a fish is doing, but they'll come in more quickly and won't be half as wild if you can take them in the dark. It's a matter of the sound of a leap and then the angle and arch of the rod.

The size of the line in your fingers is a measure of the distance, judged by the taper you've come to know so well. And at the very end the least faint ripple and its reflection of light or the faint glow of a silvery side or belly mark the fish for you. When using a bass bug there's little chance of a hook hanging up in the net twine, and if you do miss once, there's no harm done. The fish sank into the net on the first try.

I held him up for Al to shine the light. He whistled softly. "I always *said* there was a five-pounder layin' along this shore."

We'd worked all the way around again to the point where the plane was pulled up on the shore and our car was parked. I thought I could catch the faint reflection of light from the little yellow ship.

"Let's make a few more casts," said Al, "just for luck. Uncle Davy and I saw three of the doggon'dest, fattest bass that ever swam right along here last week. One of them sniffed Uncle Davy's baitfish but wouldn't touch it. I heaved a frog out and he swam right under it all the way to shore but never opened his mouth to take it in. He'd be bigger than the one we just got. He'd go six pounds or more."

We moved on slowly. Cars hummed faintly on the highway just over the hill. Now and then a horn honked or a cottage door slammed across the lake. Mechanically I kept on casting, but it wasn't the same. We had a real fish in the boat and that was our evening. If we stayed out the rest of the night we wouldn't improve on it. I was glad I'd come, thoroughly happy and at peace with the world, but ready to quit and far from ready for the sudden and noisy strike that disrupted the soft darkness that hung over the shoreline.

Instinctively I lifted the rod hard. Almost as a matter of routine, I matched the fish's runs with the right pressure, countered his leaps with slack. Neither of us spoke a word as the minutes went by. The fish sloshed up beside us and surged away into the black silence. He drew line from the reel and it whispered away through the guides. We heard him surface a long way out.

"Is he off?" Al whispered.

The bass answered by drawing off more line. Then his strength was spent and he came toward us, shaking his head, backing away and boring down. When he came alongside, raising a slight wake and shining in the faint light, I heard Al's intake of breath and then the drip of water as he lifted the fish aboard.

"That's old Uncle Davy's bass," said Al. "Let me see the two of 'em side by side."

The reflected light from the flashlight's beam showed me Al's smile of satisfaction. I could picture him through the seasons ahead saying to someone, "There's always a big bass along this shore. I remember the time Lee and I were fishing one fall night . . ."

I could look forward with pleasure to having him remind me of that pair of bass next season when we fished again. We'd both had something extra, a dividend on a season already full and finished, which from that instant on became a matter of memory. My satisfaction was at least as deep and lasting as Al's.

A few strokes of the oars set the canvas scraping on the sand beside the plane. I'd flown to some fine fishing, but it was right here at home, too, in full measure when conditions were right.

Especially in summer when the water is low and warm, night fishing really pays off. There's so much commotion and so many fishermen on some of our waters during the daylight hours that I believe a majority of the bass do the greater share of their feeding after darkness falls. The walleye is by nature a night feeder. Big trout follow the lead of the bass and walleyes and tend to become nocturnal feeders during warm weather. Only the pike family fail to join in the nocturnal activities, and that, I believe, is because they're blind at night, just as we humans are. I know of no authentic record of a muskie, northern pike, or pickerel being caught by angling when it was truly dark.

If you live only to fish and the bass is your favorite, it would probably be worth your while to reverse the usual procedure and fish through the nights, sleeping during the days. I've tried it and figure it more than doubled my catch in comparison with what I'd have taken fishing only the daylight hours.

I used to start out just about sunset, after a good meal, with a solid lunch aboard the boat, a plug rod and a fly rod beside me. I'd fish through until dawn. It upsets your social life but if you really want fishing it's worth a try. There's no way of knowing for certain at what hour on a given night the fishing will hit its peak, but, by and large, I found most action with bass just after dark, around midnight, and in the pre-dawn hours. Just one angler's experience, for what it's worth.

The fish seem to see just about as well after dark as during the bright sunlight. They'll strike a lure just as it hits the water. They'll connect as frequently with a fast-moving lure. An all-black lure is my favorite for bass at night. There's no question about their night vision and so it seems logical that they'd feed during those hours when the lakes and rivers are quietest and they're safest from their worst enemy, the angler. If the bulk of the anglers fished at night instead of in the daytime, I think it might be the other way around.

There's no special trick to night fishing. Anyone can do it. Although bait will be effective, the angler who uses artificial lures gains most with darkness. The increased effectiveness of artificial lures at night is greater than the increased effectiveness of natural baits. Fishing at night is just like fishing in the daytime except that you handle your tackle by touch alone and the fish move into different waters.

If you're going to cast, you'll want to avoid backlashes. A back-

lash in the daytime is nuisance enough without adding the extra
difficulty of trying to untangle a bird's nest by dim light or none
at all. An anti-backlash device is a necessity for most casters, and
casts should be easy and shorter than normal daytime casting. For
safety's sake, if for no other reason, casting should be by the overhead method and not by sideswiping.

On all but the blackest nights your eyes will find enough light
to make out the shoreline. You should be able to keep your boat
on its proper drift, although every once in a while you'll find
your lure landing up on the shore or catching in leafy branches.
It helps a lot to know the water you're fishing. A flashlight is a
necessity, but don't wave it around any more than you have to.

As far as I know, any lure that will work in the daytime will
work at night, but some seem to be more successful than others.
I like all-black plugs and white plugs with red heads. Pork-rind
lures or bucktail-and-spinner combinations are good, too. All of
the surface lures seem to work well at night, especially when the
water is smooth. Because of the inability to see them, it's better
to avoid fishing in heavy weeds unless you're using a weedless lure.

A good weedless lure will pay off in night fishing even more
than in the daytime if the waters you fish are weedy. Many night
fishermen settle on a single-hook, weedless lure that they can cast
into any water and which will hook and hold fish.

The fly-rod fisherman will probably concentrate on floating
lures. I doubt if any daytime thrill for the bass fisherman can
equal the silence-shattering strike of a big bass when he takes a
floating lure on a still, black night. When the water gets choppy,
I think it's smart to fish below the surface, using diving plugs,
spinners, and streamers, or any of the deep-traveling artificials.
Rough water seems to limit the effectiveness of all floating lures.

Luminous lures will sure take fish, but I'm not sold on their
being any more effective, night in and night out, than nonlumi-
nous lures. There are points that shouldn't be overlooked, though.
For one thing, the angler can see them better and if you're a
novice at casting and working your plug, a luminous one that you
can see will make your fishing easier and your casting more accurate by letting you know just where the lure is all the time.

You'll need a light for landing your fish. Bringing them in
after dark isn't as simple as it is in the daylight. Your net should
be in position before the light is turned on, and the light should
be aimed at the fish instead of the net. Shining the light on the

net makes it stand out like a beacon and the fish will do their level best to avoid it.

A dull light that is just bright enough to see by is better than a powerful beamed job. Then you will have just enough light for the purpose and anything extra helps you little but will frighten the fish a lot. Another point is that you won't have such a long period of adjustment to darkness again after the light is turned off.

Both bass and walleyes will move into very shallow water at night, and fishing grounds that are unproductive during daytime may become the best areas of all at night. Fish that are deep during the day will swim closer to the surface at night, too. Many a walleye will come to the surface for a floating plug or fly-rod lure that they'd ignore completely during the hours of daylight.

Worms, minnows, and insects work at night, but worms and minnows seem to work best when trolled behind a spinner or cast out and retrieved slowly at a fair depth. Trolling two lines, one with an artificial lure and the other with a natural bait, isn't a bad idea. Be sure to troll slowly. If you find that one method is drawing all the strikes, you can switch both lines to the same type of lure or bait.

CHAPTER 27

Fishing the Lakes

ASIDE FROM THE BASS CLAN, largemouth and smallmouth, lakes and ponds provide good fishing for several other popular sport fishes. Chief among these are the members of the pike family, which is made up of the chain pickerel, the great northern pike, and the muskellunge. These voracious, slender fish vary principally in size and in coloration, their shapes and general habits being almost identical.

All of them have large mouths, shaped much like a duck's bill, and filled with countless razor-sharp teeth. Their bodies are long, thin, and slimy, and they swim with a catlike grace. They resemble cats, too, in their ability to make a swift dash or lunge to take their prey. Like cats they are not given to sustained runs or to a long chase for their food, but to the tricks of ambush and sudden capture. They are confirmed minnow feeders, although no live and struggling thing can be considered entirely safe in their neighborhood.

The flies most attractive to these fish are either streamer flies, which imitate minnows, or a combination of fly and spinner. I like to use streamers that contain considerable white or light yellow so they are visible to the fisherman for quite a distance. Flies should be on No. 1 hooks or larger and the spinners should be No. 2 to No. 4 single or tandem. These are large flies and, when combined with spinners, are fairly heavy and hard to pull through the water. Therefore, a strong and fairly long fly rod should be used for this fishing.

A bass bug rod of nine-foot length with an overall weight of six to seven ounces should be about right. A stout nylon leader may prove satisfactory, but there are times when even the stoutest nylon can be cut like thread by the razor-sharp teeth of any of the pikes. A short casting trace or a six-inch length of metal wire at the end of a six-foot nylon leader of ten- to fifteen-pound test is a good working rig.

Fly fishing for the pike family is exceptionally good in the spring because the underwater weeds, killed by the previous winter's cold, have sunk to the lake beds and the new growth has not yet come up. This provides open water and unobstructed fishing in the favorite haunts of the pike over shallow bars and coves where weed growth will soon make fishing difficult. The fish hooked under these conditions have room to put up a good fight on a fly rod without getting all fouled up and soggy with weeds.

Flies for the pike family can be fished near the surface as a rule. Casts should be long, to cover as much water as possible, when fishing open bars or shallow coves. They should be made to the best spot for presentation when fishing the shore wherever an overhanging bush or half-submerged tree offers a pike an exceptionally good resting place. Retrieves should be made in a series of long pulls to imitate the movements of a minnow.

The pike family all hit hard, usually latching onto a fly at the end of a surge and holding that position until the setting of the hook drives them into action. In the clear water of early fishing, it is common to see the fish strike or at least see the flash of the gill covers or the white of the mouth as it opens at the strike. A predominance of white or light yellow in the streamer fly lets the caster keep his eyes on the lure as he fishes. And whether it be pickerel, northern pike, or muskie, the struggle they put up on a fly will be a worthy one for their size. Pike are able to stand cold water without losing their "kick," and a spring pike is a fighting pike.

Up in the Kempt Lake area of the Canadian bush, 150 miles northeast of Ottawa, there are no bass but a good supply of walleyes and red trout . . . and plenty of big northern pike. It was in mid-September when Neil Marvin and I flew in to let Charlie Nymisish, a knowing Cree, guide us in finding some pike big enough for pictures. In four days of fishing, we caught and released a lot of pike from five to more than twenty pounds. It was good sport, and a few comments on my notes from that trip and on pike fishing in general may be of interest.

The water of Kempt Lake drainage is controlled by dams, and at the time of our visit it was very low. The lake bed was generally sandy with very little vegetation and only a few rocky reefs or stretches of deep and rocky shoreline. Normally, pike are found where there are weeds and lily pads since such sub-surface vegetation gives them cover where they can merge into invisibility.

Because there was no such weed cover, we found them where one would normally fish for smallmouth bass, in among the rocks and reefs. In many cases when our lures would land beside an almost submerged boulder and start back toward the canoe on the retrieve, a big pike would explode under it before it had traveled a foot.

Pike are not generally rated very far up on the game-fish scale, yet in my experience I have found them equal in scrap, pound for pound, with muskies and many largemouths, particularly those from the warmer waters of the South. The pike's main asset is size, for they tend to run larger than most other game fish, and the problem posed and the skill required to land a fifteen-pound pike is undoubtedly greater than that demanded in the landing of a five-pound smallmouth. About half of our Kempt Lake fish made at least one leap. Some of them came clear of the water on the strike, and one twelve-pounder made five clean leaps, three of them consecutively on a straightaway run.

Pike are confirmed fish-eaters. While a hungry pike will take almost any lure, the most tempting are those best imitating a live fish. The prime artificial for pike is probably the wobbling spoon. Plugs are almost as effective with the underwater travelers, being superior to surface lures. I took a few on the Kempt Lake trip on a spinning outfit using four-pound test monofilament and they posed a good problem in tackle tactics because of the light line used.

The fight of the pike is a variable quantity. He may come in to the boatside with very little scrap, holding his energy and perhaps unaware of the danger. Many a pike that has come within reach quickly and been missed by gaff, net, or eye-grip has fought for a considerably longer period after being missed than it took to bring him to the boat in the first place. On light tackle where the fish seem to sense a greater chance for freedom, they put up a good battle, leaping more frequently and making longer runs. The angler who has only played them on lines of fifteen-pound test or better may be unaware of the type of battle they put up on lighter gear.

Although northern pike sometimes wallop a lure the moment it touches the waves in the manner of a smallmouth bass, they have a general trait of following the lure for a distance before striking, often following till it comes to the boat, then making a lunge for it. This trait lends excitement to pike fishing. When a fisherman is near the end of a cast, hurrying a little, perhaps, to reel the lure in to the rod tip so that he may speed the next cast out to a particularly inviting spot, the strike of a big pike, coming half out of water beside him in a flare of spray is something to remember.

I will never forget a day on New York's Saratoga Lake when the fishing had been dull for hours and I let a long cast with a Dardevle come in slow and deep. The retrieve brought the flashing metal up almost vertically at the end of the retrieve and when the lure was about a foot from the rod tip a six-pound pike drove up at it hard from below. He connected just as the spoon was coming out of water and with a flip of the rod I landed him in the lap of my friend at the oars who had no idea there was an interested fish within a mile of my lure.

More often than not, that trait of following a lure works out in favor of the pike. As they follow and see the boat or canoe, they become suspicious and shy away. The angler has a chance to see them then but, although he knows the fish's location, he cannot lure them to strike and be hooked. On the Kempt Lake trip, Neil hooked a thirteen-inch walleye only to have a big pike latch onto it almost immediately. The pike relinquished the walleye as he approached the shore.

He would follow a lure close enough for us to see him, but he always failed to strike. Half a dozen times he took the walleye in his mouth when it was cast out to him, but each time, although the treble hook was changed from lips to dorsal and to tail, he evaded its points and kept his freedom.

Trolling is an effective method of taking pike. They can follow a trolling bait for long periods without any danger of their being frightened away as they would be if following a cast lure to the boat. Then, when the spirit moves them, they'll make a pass at the lure and be hooked. Revolving spoons with feathered or bucktail trebles are excellent pike lures. When trolling with either spinning or wobbling spoons a small keel sinker and a swivel are good insurance against a twisted line.

Care must be taken in handling pike at the end of the fight. Their teeth slash through human flesh with surprising ease. Most big pike are too large for the average net and are awkward to hold on a gaff. The old-timers like to put a forefinger and thumb into the eye sockets in a paralyzing grip that is quite secure. Getting a lure out of a pike's mouth is sometimes as difficult as getting him to take it.

The walleye is not a member of the pike family but is a true perch with the normal characteristics of an overgrown yellow perch. The walleye is another popular fish that will bend a rod in the lakes and ponds. These fish are distinguished by the bright opacity of their eyeballs in the light, the characteristic from which they derive their name. Their coloration is bluish or greenish on the back, shading to yellowish cream or white on the belly. Unlike the pike family which has spineless fins, the walleye, like the bass, has spines on most of his fins. Walleyes range in size up to eighteen pounds and are generally big enough to put up a good battle.

Walleyes are largely nocturnal in their feeding but may be taken throughout the daylight hours. During the day they tend to range the lower levels near bottom, but at night they may feed well up toward the surface. For daytime fishing with a fly rod, the lure should be a streamer fly and spinner or a fly-rod plug, worked slowly and preferably at a depth of several feet.

To accomplish this, a buckshot or small sinker should be used on the leader a foot or so ahead of the fly, and a sufficient period of time should be given after the cast to let the fly sink well down before starting the retrieve. Neither line nor leader should be greased and the fly caster should work for greatest possible fishing depth.

Walleyes travel in schools and where one fish is caught or a strike recorded, the surrounding water should be fished with extra thoroughness before moving on to new territory. While the spinner-and-streamer fly is the best daytime combination, small floating fly-rod lures may be most effective at night. Best daytime fishing should be during the early morning hours and late evening. Walleyes are moody fish, and when the angler knows there are fish in the water he's covering but they won't strike his artificial lures, it's a good idea to resort to the worm. Worms dangling enticingly upon a hook preceded by a spinner are perhaps the walleye's greatest love.

The casting of worms requires care, and worms are a nuisance, maybe, but doggone it, they're a good bait to fall back on when artificials won't produce. The spinner-and-worm combination should also be fished slowly and near the bottom. The strike for this rig should be fast and hard, the same as for an artificial.

Look for walleyes in both rocky areas and in the weeds. The advantage of spring fishing for walleyes lies in the absence of weed beds and in the extra hunger all lake fish have after the winter period of cold water and reduced feeding. For walleyes, the fly rod is less effective than is the bait-casting or trolling rod. It is the old problem of covering water at considerable depth. Fly rods don't accomplish this easily. Except for night fishing, the walleye angler must get his lure down deep for best results, and sinking a fly-rod lure to such depths makes for slow and laborious fishing. The fly-rod angler should concentrate on the hours of twilight and darkness.

Walleyes, though predominantly minnow feeders, take the same general lure patterns that bass do. Because the walleye's mouth is small, the smaller plugs seem to be most effective. My favorite for walleyes is a small, deep-running plug with action, like the River Runt. Walleyes are generally found near bottom regardless of the depth of water they're traveling in. Northern pike are as likely to be found lying lazily in the sun just under the surface with fifteen feet of water beneath them as they are to be near bottom at the same depth. As a rule, the slower and deeper an artificial lure travels, the better it is for walleyes. For pike the upper half of the water's depth is most effective.

The greatest difference in fishing for the two species, pike and walleyes, lies in their feeding hours. Northern pike are entirely daytime feeders. As a longtime fishing editor, I've sought for many years to get authenticated records of pike striking an artificial lure when it was fished in total darkness and have always failed, rumors to the contrary. Twilight catches are often reported, but nowhere have I verified the striking of a plug by a northern pike in pitch darkness. Walleyes, on the other hand, strike best between the hours of ten P.M. and dawn. Northern pike will strike well at any time during the day but seem to hit most often when the sky is overcast or in the early morning.

The tendency of walleyes to strike at artificial lures seems to vary with the section of the country and from one lake to another. Most walleyes of the far north strike artificials readily. Below the Canadian border, plugs seem to lose some of their effectiveness and natural baits like a night crawler fished slowly and deep behind a spinner prove superior. As the water gets warmer, the walleyes seek the lower levels of the lakes for their feeding and travel, and the deeper they are, the smaller and slower the lure or bait must be to be effective. But walleyes that fail to take artificials during the daylight hours often take artificials after dark.

The type of artificial lures to be used for walleyes and northern pike depends, too, upon the anatomy of the fish. Northern pike have broad, flat snouts. The upper jaw is paper-thin in spots and offers little flesh for the hook to grip. A single hook striking into the fleshy lower jaw of a pike will hold securely, but if it hooks into the upper jaw it is almost certain to tear a large hole in the flesh when the strain of playing the fish is exerted. In a moment of slack a hook falls easily out of such a hole. Therefore, it is wise to use plugs or lures carrying at least one good-sized treble hook and preferably two when fishing for pike.

Walleyes offer a good hold in either jaw, and a single-hooked lure should bring in as many fish as one carrying two or three trebles. This is fortunate since the best walleye lures are the smaller ones, few of which can carry two or three standard trebles.

When a northern pike strikes a lure he does so with a smash, lancing in from the side to jar the hand that holds the rod. The walleye seems to strike from behind in most cases, appearing to bounce up and hit the lure and then stop dead for a moment. The angler should strike hard for either fish, hard enough to set the hooks well into the flesh. Naturally, it takes a harder strike when fishing a three-treble plug than when casting with a single hooked lure, but in any case the strike should be a substantial one.

A very important trait of the walleye is his tendency to travel in schools. Veteran walleye anglers, when they catch a walleye or see one flare at a lure, stop or circle to cover the area thoroughly. It is rare, indeed, for walleyes to travel alone, and when good catches are made it is usually with several fish coming aboard from a number of schools rather than widely separated single fish.

Walleyes usually start their resistance as soon as the angler tries to draw them toward the boat. The big ones will cut off to one side or the other and the smaller ones will twist and shake and make short darts to either side. When it first sights the boat the walleye is almost certain to break away on his best run of the fight, boring down as he streaks off. He's at his best in the final half of the fight, and more walleyes are lost at the net than at any other period of their playing.

Whether or not you rate the walleye at the top of the heap for power and fight, there's little question but that he rates at or close to the top when it comes to serving him up on the table. Walleye is flaky, tender, and delicious, and I'm sure I echo the sentiments of many when I say that if I were limited to only one freshwater fish to eat, I'd pick the walleye.

Fishermen will also find fast action on the lakes with panfish.

Included in this group are the perch, sunfish, bluegill, and crappie. They move toward the surface and the shores and into the range of fly fishermen whenever spring warms up the water. This occurs in May in most states above the Mason-Dixon line. When they conclude their winter period of semidormancy, these little fighters are hungry and eager to take a lure. They are not as selective nor as fussy as the hard-fished trout and consequently will give the angler much more action than he is likely to find on the trout streams.

Flies for panfish range from No. 6 down to No. 16 and the brighter patterns are better. Black Gnat, McGinty, Royal Coachman, Professor, Parmachene Belle, and Brown Hackle are among the best, but almost any of the accepted fly patterns will attract these fish and their hunger seems insatiable. Small streamer flies, very small spinners or flashing lures, or a combination of spinner and fly will lure panfish, too, and most of them are quite ambitious in the size of lure they are willing to take. Small floating bugs are also deadly for most panfish (yellow perch excepted) and give the angler the same thrill he enjoys when using a dry fly, the pleasure of the surface strike.

Nymphs or imitation insects are probably the most consistently effective artificial lures for panfish. Whether made of feathers, fur, rubber, or plastic, these specialized flies most closely imitate the natural food of the panfish. Imitation crickets, grasshoppers, and grubs all fall into this general category. No ardent panfisherman's flybox is complete without an assortment of them to round out his feathered lures.

Wet flies are fished in the conventional way for panfish, making the cast and bringing the fly back in a series of jerky underwater movements. The retrieve should not be too swift but should have a more or less continual movement. For best results the fisherman should fish from a boat, toward the shore, dropping his flies at the edges of lily pads, rocky ledges, half-submerged logs and brush heaps. Angling partners can take turns with the oars, but a lone fisherman can do well by taking the oars between short casting periods or by anchoring at the better spots and covering them thoroughly before moving on.

Dry flies will draw strikes when cast out and allowed to drift, unmoving, on the surface, but they will bring more strikes if they are twitched occasionally or pulled very slowly across the surface in a series of short, jerky motions. The best dry flies are those with a definite insect shape with upstanding wings and a full body. Flies that ride high on the surface can be given more action than the low floating flies without having them sink . . . but when a dry fly has become submerged, it may be fished in by a wet-fly retrieve with good success. Spiders, variants, or skaters which can be skidded lightly across the surface have the same deadliness on the lake for panfish as they do on the stream for trout. The small floating bugs should be made to swim and flutter along the surface with frequent pauses.

The nymphs and special insect imitations are fished best by allowing them to sink from one to five feet, then working them up toward the surface in short, swimming darts. The weight of the nymph itself will usually cause it to sink slowly. By greasing the line and leader up to a point at the required depth to be fished from the nymph, it can be allowed to sink until the greased portion of the leader is reached. Slow, jerky retrieving will cause the nymph to swim toward the surface, and whenever the retrieve is stopped, it will sink again to the proper level.

During this method of fishing, the angler must watch his leader closely since he will be able to see the strike's movement of the floating section of the leader long before he will be able to feel the strike through the movement of the line. The angler should strike as soon as he sees any movement of the floating section of the leader. The ungreased portion of the leader may be kept sinkable and free of grease by coating it with one of the leader-sinking compounds or by rubbing it down with toothpaste to remove the oily film which causes floating.

By using a split shot or wrapping a small amount of lead wire around the leader, and by keeping both line and leader free from grease, the nymph can be fished slowly at a considerable depth. The movement of the lure will then be gradually horizontal instead of toward the surface when retrieved, and the strike can be felt directly through the line to a much greater degree. However, the greased leader technique gives a much more varied retrieve and, though slower moving and without the same water coverage, should be much more effective.

Yellow perch and crappies are most often found in schools. The sunfish and bluegills are more likely to be found individually or in pairs. Yellow perch tend to cruise near the bottom and are best attracted by a slow-moving fly fished deep. If one perch is caught, there should be others nearby, and intensive casting in the area should bring more strikes. All panfish are to be found near shore, on the very shallow bars or around the weed beds. Panfish are plentiful; sport with them is rarely restricted by bag limits, and when crisped in butter, they may be small but they're sure delicious.

All panfish, of course, can be caught with worms and other natural baits and also with small fly-rod plugs and spinning lures, but in my estimation, taking them on flies is the acme of the sport.

Weeds affect the lake fisherman in a number of ways. First, they determine the minimum breaking strength of the line he can successfully use. Line breakage will normally come from one of two causes: either from trying to pull a lure free from weeds it has hooked onto or from having a fish wind the line around a group of stems and, with the line thus solidly held, pull hard enough to break away.

Lily pads and those types of water vegetation having strong and sturdy stems call for a fairly strong line, while weeds with weak or slender stems can be pulled out or broken off by a relatively light line. A ten-pound test line is adequate for most weedy fishing, but occasionally a fifteen-pound test line is advisable. Only for exceptionally large fish in water loaded with tough stems is a stronger line needed.

On the score of fish breaking away, the most important factor is the density of the weeds. Where there are only a few stems, widely separated, as in the case of sparse lily pads, a light line may still be used. Although the individual stems may be too strong for the line to break or pull out by the roots, the chances of a fish's making a complete circuit of a bunch of them are slim. The drag of the line sawing against a few stems is not great, either, and a light pressure until the angler can reach the spot and clear the line will usually take care of the situation.

But the drag of the bend of the line pulling against scores of stems mounts up, and the fine but thick weed stems do call for the heavier lines. I use heavier in a relative sense. A five- to seven-pound test line will handle most fish, even in a slight scattering of lily pads. A ten-pound test line will take care of fish in thick but fine-stemmed growth, and a fifteen-pound test line is all right for everything but big fish in large concentrations of strong-stemmed growth.

When the weeds are scattered or in thin bands around the shoreline, the angler will take the most fish and have the best sport by fishing the open water adjacent to the weeds. He should fish from the deep water toward the shallow, cast to the weeds and then draw his lure away from them. Most strikes will come close to the weeds, but the fish can be played in the open waters away from them.

Open spaces in the solid beds of vegetation can likewise be fished with any type of lure by keeping to the open water, but where the weed growth is wide in extent and the fish concentrated within it, the type of lure used must be suitable for weedy work.

A wide-swinging lure with an action that takes it very much to either side of a straight line between the point at which it lands and the boat will strike more weed stems than one that follows the more direct path. Lures with many hooks will catch more weeds than lures with a single hook. Consequently, for weedy water the lures must be chosen with these factors in mind.

In moderately open water, diving lures with a fairly wide action can still be used, but as the growth becomes denser it is more important to use lures that flutter rather than dart. The fluttering type of lure has a fast action but doesn't sway much from side to side. It won't strike as many weeds.

One nice thing about surface lures in water containing scattered weeds is that the angler can see everything. By dropping his lure into the pockets of open water and guiding it carefully through clear channels, he can fish some of the weedy water without getting hung up.

When the weeds are really thick, single-hooked, weedless lures are a practical must. Lures with a quick wiggle or an easy wobble are tops in this field. They'll work their way through the stems without striking them with enough pressure to force the weed guard back from the point.

Weed guards vary greatly in design. I like guards that will move back with light pressure. A guard that requires a hard strike to set the hook may be a little more weedless, but it is sure to be a little more fishless as well. There's a trick to bringing a lure through the tangled stems without getting fouled up. It depends upon a delicate sense of touch and a realization of the slightest weed pressure on line or lure. By slowing down the retrieve the lure will usually ease around the stem or, settling slowly on momentary slack, twist to a position in which the hook point is away from the stems.

A fisherman with good weed sense will rarely get hung up,

while one without it who can't sense that first slight pressure will be fouled up in weeds most of the time. However awkward a fisherman may be at first, a little thought and practice will enable him to fish the weeds fairly well.

Another trick that comes in handy in the very weedy places is the use of the high line retrieve. This is accomplished by holding the rod high and having the line go straight from the rod tip to the lure without touching the water. This is particularly true with wobbling spoons having weed guards . . . or even such lures without them. The high line turns this normally underwater lure into one that skims the surface, passing over rather than through the pads and stems. In effect, it becomes a surface lure and one that is more easily seen by the fish than if it traveled quietly under the surface. The surface retrieve is faster, though, and appeals to the fish only when they are in an active mood.

Fish can't see far through a maze of vegetation. The lures should be worked slowly in that type of water most of the time to give the fish a better chance to see them and catch up with them. The coverage should be so complete that the lure is brought within the vision of any feeding fish in the area. This calls for concentrated casting.

Playing a fish in or around weeds is quite a problem, too. Of course, where there is open water at hand the wise thing to do is to try to keep the fish in it and away from the weeds. A fish is more fun to play when he has full freedom of movement and the angler has the best possible control over the situation. Yet many a fish has been lost by holding him too hard in an effort to keep him out of the weeds. A light pressure that lets the fish go into the weeds often means saving the trophy in the end.

Allowing a big fish to get into the weeds after he's hooked is not always disastrous and is certainly preferable to holding so hard that the tackle breaks. It may not be as much fun as playing one in open water but big fish can be handled in the weeds without being lost. A light pressure will do it. Patience, too, to give a fish slack and time to go back to the open water through the same passage he entered the weeds will very probably solve the problem.

When a big fish runs to the weeds, he's seeking safety from this thing that has hold of him. If after reaching them he finds the same nagging pull keeps on . . . or is supplanted by a light twitching which is even more annoying, he's as likely to go back and seek freedom in the open water as he is to drive on deeper into the weeds. If, however, as soon as he enters the weeds he gets an ever harder pressure he'll respond naturally and twist and turn in a frenzied effort to escape. That rolling and twisting will tangle the line and give him just the resistance he needs to pull free.

Sometimes when a fish is hopelessly entangled in the weeds, a fisherman can reach down with the landing net and bring the fish in, weeds and all. Even when a fish has made a dive into the weeds and becomes hopelessly fouled up, it's worth taking time to pull gently from all angles and allow periods of complete slack before pulling drastically.

Before you start fishing in weedy water, it would be a good idea to see just how strong a pull you can put on the line without having it break. If you know your line is strong enough to pull out the weeds in a given lake, it will save a lot of time that could be lost in moving the boat back to the snagged lures to unhook them.

CHAPTER 28

Angling Surprises

LAKE TROUT HAVE BEEN on the edge of my fishing world. Now and then I cross their paths and sometimes match my skill with their weight and strength. I've been much too restless, much too much a caster to take time out to troll when there were fish near the top to take my plug or fly. Still, there have been times when they've surprised me and given me a battle to remember.

Long ago, in the early thirties, when landlocked salmon fishing in the lakes of northern Vermont was very exciting, I fished at Big Averill Lake. We were casting streamers for landlocks about ten days after ice-out. There were few outboards then, and "guide boats," half rowboat, half canoe, were cherished for their speed and ease of travel. Wherever we went in those days, we rowed, and it always seemed that the far end of the lake was the one that held the most fish and the biggest.

We didn't know the lake too well and that day Vic Coty and I found ourselves over a very shallow, long-sloping beach at the south end of the lake at lunchtime, so we went ashore. We fixed our lunch and watched the smooth water stretch away toward the northern hills. The sun was warm and the first flush of insects was in the air. Flying ants went by as they were carried out over the water by the gentlest of breezes from the south. A few Mayflies showed up above the alders and drifted outward. We munched our sandwiches and saw a swirl or two, fifty yards or more offshore.

Fishing had been slow that day and whereas we'd been bringing in three or four good landlocks every day, we hadn't had a rise as yet. Usually, the fish were breaking as they chased baitfish or often seemingly just with the joy of spring. But today there'd been no action throughout a foggy morning and now a quiet, clearing midday. Those small low swirls that sucked down the swamped insects began to intrigue us.

We'd brought our books of streamers which were all we

expected to fish with in those waters in early spring. I had no flies to match those flying ants, but I did have a couple of No. 10 Gray Wulffs stuck in my hatband, so I tried one of those. Vic agreed to row for the first try and I tied the dry fly tightly to the leader. It was of tapered gut, nine feet long and a little too heavy for that size dry fly, but I hoped it would neither sink the fly nor put down the fish.

The first swirls we saw as we reached the area where the ants were floating were little more than dimples and we felt sure they were small brook trout, perhaps too small to hook and keep. Each time I dropped the fly near one it lay untouched until I tired of watching its motionlessness and picked it up to false-cast. Then we saw a spreading boil beneath a disappearing ant. We moved within range quietly and I cast . . . but nothing happened.

A small rise showed not far from the boat and I cast and let the dry fly rest until my arms were fidgety to lift it off again. At patience's final straining the fly disappeared and I struck. Had I hooked an alligator I couldn't have been more surprised. The fish streaked northward for the lake's center at a speed I'd never before associated with a fish on a fly rod. A landlock, I exulted, a mammoth landlock that will soon leap but probably tear free of that little fly.

But the fish didn't leap. He plowed right on until, finally, the water deepened to five feet or more. Then he sat and waited. When we moved up abreast of him, he twisted and turned but ran no more. When I brought him to boatside we recognized him as a lake trout of about seven pounds. I thought he might have been foul-hooked and that the tail pull had made him run so far so fast, but he wasn't. He'd taken almost all of my two hundred yards of backing, which I'd recently extended just in case I hooked a landlock big enough to fill my wall. There he lay, a lake trout that had taken a dry fly and run like a demon . . . and not a very big lake trout at that.

We laughed and then realized we'd found a situation in which lake trout act as bonefish do, racing for long distances to reach deep water, but when they reach it having nowhere to go and running little farther. When bonefish are caught in deep water they, too, fight comparatively listlessly and seem to have nowhere to go.

Vic caught a second fish and experienced the same long, exciting rush and the same quiet finale. Those were our only rises. We longed for a fly that would better imitate those flying ants but had none and watched helplessly as those cruising lake trout continuously passed our flies by.

The lake stayed calm and evening came on. Eventually we started casting our way back along the shore. I caught a six-pound landlock, a good fish for a fly rod. Even though it leaped three times, the battle was tame compared with the long reel-screeching runs the shallow-water lake trout had given us.

It was raining and it had been raining since I'd gotten up out of a soggy bed in a soggy tent and put on my waders and rain jacket. This was Labrador in 1955 and the great flow sweeping in front of me came out of Lake Michikamau. I wanted a few brook trout for the pan and I knew there shouldn't be any trouble in getting them. I waded out far enough for a decent back cast, slipping a little on the mossy boulders of the stream bed as I reached a depth between my knees and my hips and steadied there.

Three casts, I thought to myself, will mean three fish and that will do it. I could count on brook trout that ran between two and three pounds, regularly. I made the first cast and, starting the retrieve, was fast to a fish.

All of us who fly-fished in the wild north country have harbored the hope that when and if we got far enough off into the back-of-beyond we'd find a brook trout bigger than the record that Nipigon fish has held so long. Here he is, I thought, when I saw the swirl, felt the power of the surge, and heard the reel click telling me that line was fading away at an alarming rate.

The sweep of the current was steady and deep, the shore was rocky, and the evergreens crowded in over the banks. The rain-swollen flow with a massive lake behind it hissed and whistled its way through its misty channel. I followed the shore, sometimes hanging from branches with one hand where the water was too deep to wade, sometimes slipping and moving on my knees to save the "record" fish that was on the end of my line. I'd never caught anything but brook trout in two days of fishing, though I'd seen one small pike close to shore in a shallow eddy. Even if there were pike in the flow, I wouldn't expect them in fast water or willing to take a small wet fly.

Ten minutes later, I rounded a downstream bend and pressured the fish into holding up in a great, swirling eddy. Rain pounded down on the water and drained noisily off my hooded jacket. Most of it, that is. A lot soaked through and, with a few shipments of water that I took in over the tops of my waders, I can recall few times when I've been wetter.

The water that goes from Michikamau into the Nascaupie has a dark clarity. Put it in a glass and it looks clear; look at the rocks on a stream bed through it and it has the look of smoky quartz. I looked down and saw the white leading edge of a broad pectoral fin and I smiled inwardly. God, but he's long, I thought. I lifted hard and worked him toward the ragged shore. He's dark, I thought, then—too dark! I saw spots on his back instead of the vermicular markings of a brook trout. Finally I knew.

I'd had one of the most thrilling angling bouts of a long angling career, with a lake trout, a fish that is supposed to come up like a cod from deep water and to shun the fast rivers where it has to work hard to hold a feeding place. Had it been a brook trout, it would have been a record, reaching almost fifteen pounds. I made only that single cast that morning and we all ate well of a great, game lake trout caught in the rain.

Carl Fellows is a quiet man. He works with details in his title searches and he carries a thousand pertinent facts in his mind when he's at his job. Whenever he can he goes fishing. He likes lake trout.

Carl doesn't use a depth-finder or a fish-finder. He fishes now as he always has, moving his boat slowly at just the right speed with just the right length of line out so that his lure will skim along barely above the rocks and weeds at the bottom of the Maine lake he's fishing.

He takes a line between two points and cross-checks his position with objects on the shore. He may use a Mooselook spoon or a streamer fly—he may even use a shiner—and he usually has two different lures out when he trolls two lines. He always seems to be listening and his mind is running along with his lure just above the bottom. If he scowls and says "Shucks" I know he's missed in his complicated calculation and has dragged his lure on a rock where he didn't think a rock should be.

The lake he fishes, Flying Pond, is not known as great lake-trout water, but Carl can remember some fine fish that came out of it years back. Anyone can troll or cast a near-surface lure around the lake and, if he keeps at it, he'll catch some bass. If he's lucky he might even hook up with a good brown or a middle-sized landlock.

But unless you learn to troll your lure down the sunken valleys at just the right speed with just the right amount of line out—and speed up or shorten up when you want to lift up over a ridge on the lake bed to reach another valley or troll across a level plateau at a shallower depth, you can troll your heart out for lake trout.

The last time I saw Carl, he'd just taken a 14½-pounder, the biggest of the season for his pond, and he was happy. He'd won another round in a difficult game, a complicated game remote from the surface splashings of the plug and fly casters, a game that takes a lot of patient learning and a quiet, enduring skill.

PART THREE

Saltwater Fishing

CHAPTER 29

Fly-Rod Bonanza

THOSE FEW FORTUNATE fishermen who have taken Atlantic salmon, steelhead, and large trout with a fly rod can be forgiven if they seem to feel that they have been everywhere and done everything. But they haven't—unless they have discovered an even more exciting kind of fly fishing. It is available in only a restricted area but the area is open to all.

Ten minutes after making my first cast over these waters, I knew that I'd never fish there again without at least 150 yards of stout backing on my fly reel and an extra reel on hand in case I got stripped of that! For these were the bonefish flats of the Florida Keys, and I was just about to become one of fewer than half a dozen anglers who had ever taken a bonefish on a fly rod.

The Florida Keys stretch out into the blue water between the Gulf of Mexico and the Atlantic for more than a hundred miles. Around this chain of tiny islands are millions of acres of flats and bars and banks over which the clear saltwater ebbs and flows in an ever-changing pattern of channels and slopes. The bottom of white coral sand makes for easy wading. The sun is bright, the air warm, and fishing conditions are far more comfortable than in the north, where the angler must fight black flies and be prepared for anything from moderate warmth to bitter cold during his best season.

Sneakers and a pair of old pants or shorts, the standard outfit for wading the Keys, are a far cry from the bulky and expensive waders or boots worn in the North. Fly fishing in the Keys is done primarily by wading but to a lesser degree from small boats. A guide is just as important in these waters as he is on a trout stream or a salmon river—a good investment but not a necessity.

You can park your car beside the main highway to Key West and fish fifty yards away. You can cruise down from Miami in a yacht or charter boat and live aboard it at one of the many yacht basins. You can fly down for a day of fishing in an amphibian that will first show you the fish from the air, then land you at the best spot, ready to wade or fish from the outboard-powered rubber boat that is part of the plane's equipment.

Freshwater anglers may spend several seasons with the fly rod before they take a two-pound trout or a four-pound bass. The various species of fly-rod fish you catch in the Florida Keys start at around five pounds and run up to more than a hundred! All of them are swift racers that have known the wild freedom of the limitless sea. They habitually try to out-distance danger instead of darting into the nearest hiding place as most freshwater fish do.

In mid-spring the biggest fish move into the shallow water to feed and spawn. Then you may find a tarpon of more than a hundred pounds lying in water so shallow his belly will rub the sand and his backfin will show above the water.

Ever hear of a permit? A shy fish, he is, built like an overgrown pompano and not too unlike a common sunfish in general shape. Permits are rare and not one angler in a hundred thousand has seen or hooked one. He's a tough fish on tackle and he likes flies, too, although until fairly recently he was only fished for with bait. You may find thirty-five pounds of him all in one lively piece, and if he latches onto your fly, he'll be as tough a proposition as angling has to offer. Or you may strike a barracuda, ladyfish, channel bass, snook, tarpon, or bonefish. But it is the bonefish that is most suited to the tackle and the bonefish is the real prize of the Florida Keys.

Because bonefish work across the shallow flats on the rising tides with their noses down and their tails occasionally waving above the surface, it has been generally believed that their only interest is in bottom food and that none of the free-swimming lures like flies and plugs would excite them. So strong was this conviction that for years no one thought of fishing for this silver dynamite except with bait. The lads with four-ounce rods and six-thread lines had so much trouble handling them that they couldn't conceive of bonefish being taken on the sort of tackle that was sometimes inadequate for trout—until recently, when a few adventurous souls went to work with conventional fly outfits and proved it could be done.

These pioneers used mostly a fly designed by Homer Rhode of Miami. It looks something like a shrimp, one of the best of bonefish baits. Two pairs of hackles swing back behind the hook shank and several hackles are wound around the shank just behind the eye of the hook. As it is pulled through the water, the feathers take on apparent life because of the "ballooning" effect of starting and stopping.

The fly rides just under the surface, a complete reversal from the previous bottom-fishing methods. Rhode, a top guide, believed that the larger bonefish give up bottom feeding almost entirely and seek their food in midwinter at or near the surface. All agree they're swift enough to capture any smaller fish they decide to chase. While some of the other species come into the shallows only in the spring, the bonefish will be on the flats all the year around.

Homer Rhode was busy with other work in Miami when I flew down in my little Cub, and he couldn't go to the Keys with me. I spent two days vainly searching for someone with a knowledge of fly fishing for bonefish who would fly down to the Keys and spend a day fishing. Finally, another pilot, Lee Pruyn, joined forces with me to see what we could discover. We took off just before noon and in an hour were flying over good bonefish water. We dropped down to three hundred feet and began to look things over.

Although I'd only seen two live bonefish before, they were easy to recognize when we flew over them. They have a silvery sheen that is almost mirrorlike in its reflecting qualities when they show their sides, and that, together with their distinctive shape, makes them unmistakable. As we flew southwest, we saw bonefish scattered here and there, as well as long barracuda lying like logs on the sandy bottom. When we reached Long Key, we saw several schools of bonefish that seemed larger than the others. We landed, beached the plane at the edge of one of the deep channels where it could be secured above the rising tide, and rigged up our rods.

The time-honored procedure of a bonefisherman is to search till he finds tailing fish. Bonefish move in over the flats as the floodtide covers them. As they nose along the bottom in this shallow water, their tails break the surface and betray their position. When the bonefish are spotted, they are stalked, and the bait, usually shrimp rigged up with a slight sinker, is cast about fifteen feet ahead of them.

Then if the angler is lucky and the bait still fresh, one of them will take it and at the first sting of the hook will scoot for deep water . . . but fast. Homer Rhode had suggested that we use the same system of spotting fish, then stalking and casting to them.

We watched the water where we had located the bonefish, but

we saw no tails. As time passed we realized that we had missed the best part of the tide and the water had become so deep that the tails of the bonefish didn't break the surface as they moved along. So we waded out and fished the water blindly just as we would have fished on a lake at home for bass. Lee Pruyn used his bait-casting rod with a Pal-O-Mine plug, and I used my nine-foot bass rod with a ten-pound test nylon leader and one of Homer Rhode's shrimplike flies.

Lee sang out when he saw a bonefish flash toward his plug but turn away just short of taking it. A few casts later he had a smashing strike. He let out another yip and I turned to see his short rod arched and the line whistling out as the fish moved toward deep water. The run was not a long one. The fish circled, then jumped. Instantly, we recognized it as a barracuda, evil of eye and sharp of tooth. Lee led the fish to shore and gingerly freed him.

At that moment something hit my fly and began slicing toward deep water. The reel handle blurred and the line sizzled out so fast I felt a hollow feeling at the pit of my stomach. Remembering that my leader was good for ten pounds strain, several times that of my fine salmon leaders, I increased the pressure only to find that the fish was spurred on to even greater speed. I quickly eased off again to let him run himself out.

My reactions, of course, were geared to the fight of an Atlantic salmon, generally considered top fish in freshwater. While I could let a salmon take line out between my fingers without having the braided nylon burn me, the speed of this fish was much greater. After burning my fingers on that first run, I let the click act as a brake and watched fly line and then backing melt off the reel arbor. Had that bonefish maintained his run just a little longer my fishing would have been over till I got a new refill for my reel. Although I'd come adequately supplied with light plug casting and trolling tackle, my only fly line was on that reel.

With his first run over, the fish let me stow some line back onto the reel, but at thirty feet he saw me and took off again. The fire had gone out of him, though, and his second run carried him less than fifty yards into the backing. Corked by the second run, the next time he came in he stayed there. After a few short darts and swings he let me reach down and pick him up—a five- to six-pounder.

I tried to release him, but the sturdy 2/0 hook, crunched between his powerful jaws, had been bent into a complete circle

Lee Wulff with a fresh-run salmon from the Ecum Secum River in Nova Scotia, 1933. Note: He wears the first fly fisherman's vest, which he invented and made himself. It has become almost a uniform for today's fly fisherman.

LEFT AND ABOVE: *A series showing the author landing salmon with a tailer he designed. This tool is as effective as a gaff and easier to use than a net; in addition, it is easy on any salmon that are to be released.*

The author with a 35-pound salmon from the Humber River in Newfoundland, 1946.

A fine dog salmon from the Serpentine. Note the lightness of the rod used to take this fish.

The happy results of a good day in 1947 on River of Ponds in Newfoundland.

The explosive, water-spraying leap of the Atlantic salmon is like that of no other fresh-water game fish; sometimes the angler literally "looks up to" this fish.

The author canoeing the upper Humber River (when it was reached only by a 60-mile upstream canoe trip).

Here a head-and-tail roll of a hooked salmon has made a one-in-a-million composition that the photographer caught in a series of beautiful arcs of salmon, rod, and man.

Bad weather brought good luck on a Fox Island River: a 7-pound-plus brookie from big water.

A good moment shared by father and son, like-father like-son, with an excellent catch of squaretails.

Good concentration and good form by Barry Wulff here promise a Western Brook squaretail safely in the net (a moment after this picture was snapped).

The author with a big brook trout in hand pickup. Lee Wulff began and publicized the hand pickup of trout and salmon in the days (1935) when a landing net was deemed essential for the well-equipped angler.

Brook trout sometimes feed in salt water, and when they do the bounty of the sea produces big, fat, deep-bodied fish like this pair of sea-run brook trout from the Fox Island River, 1940.

BELOW LEFT: *A high, Rocky Mountain lake affords proofs of the angler's statement that "trout fishing is so rewarding because trout live in such beautiful country."*

BELOW CENTER: *A squaretail from the upper Eagle River in Labrador.*

The Boulder River in Montana.

The Minipi River in Labrador makes one wonder why the angler did not take along a larger net.

Guide Sam Shinnicks looks over a White
Wulff when that fly pattern was first introduced to the salmon rivers. Few guides
seeing it for the first time thought it could
catch a salmon.

An underwater view of some of Lee Wulff's
dry flies, 1952: (TOP TO BOTTOM) Surface Stone
fly; Gray Wulff; Hackle-less dry Wulff.

The author and his wife, former casting champion Joan Salvato, demonstrate fly casting.

The fish (pickerel and perch), the lures (spinners and spoons), and the rod (a good old bamboo pole) mark the tackle and trophies of the angling beginner.

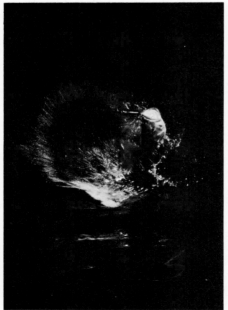

*Night-fishing for largemouth bass
can be very productive if you can see
your bug and maybe have a flashlight or two handy to find your fish.
But, day or night, the bass usually
shows himself with an explosive leap
or two to add to the sport.*

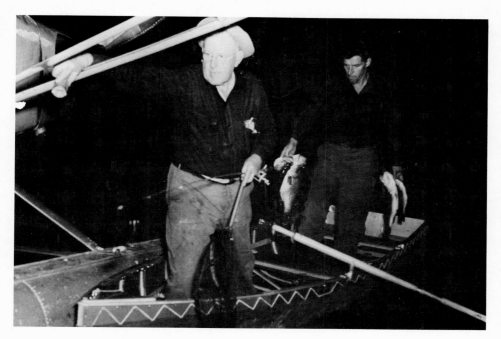

Al Prindle, postmaster at Shushan, New York, lights the way to the plane's pontoon for the author and a good catch of bass.

When the Great Northern pike come big they can make a good-sized boy look small.

The author helps rig bracing for his feet so he will be able to turn himself in the swivel chair (on a converted boat) to fish in Bonne Bay, Newfoundland, 1938. He trained a local crew, made his own baits . . .

With Tom Paugh, fishing the Virginia surf for "The American Sportsman" TV series.

The author and his wife with a 631-pound tuna she caught.

Tuna fishing, Wedgeport, Nova Scotia, 1936.

The author, who was one of the pioneers of the new sport of taking big fish from salt water with a fly rod, shows that it can be done with a 130-pound tarpon.

around the upper edge of his jaw! I had to get out my knife to spread the metal enough to free him. I watch him swim off with the satisfaction of having found some magnificent fly-rod fishing, the knowledge that he would be just the first of many fly-rod bonefish if Fate spared me the years to catch them.

Next day, Dave Meyer, an old hand at bonefishing, flew down with me. Again we left Miami late, and again we found fish in the same area. We landed, rigged up, waded out to our knees, and started fishing. Dave, using four-six gear, impaled a shrimp on his hook and cast out. He'd seen a bonefish move by while we were setting up our tackle.

The fish struck and Dave drove the hook home. Then followed the normal fight pattern of a long, sizzling run, two shorter ones, and some lusty infighting before Dave skillfully drew him to his waiting hand. He'd weigh about eight pounds, a beautiful blue-gray and silvery fish. Released, he swam off lazily and quickly blended with the pale blue water and white sandy bottom flecked with its grayish brown seagrass.

Twenty minutes after Dave's fish was released, something hit my fly and raced away toward Mexico. The double loops that lock my casting line to the backing clicked out swiftly through the guides. The backing kept running out in one long, sustained drive. My fingers edged in around the unseen spool of the reel and felt for the depth of the line remaining. The fish passed the mark where my thirty-pound salmon had stopped, hesitated briefly, then drove on with a new burst of speed that sent the whine of the tortured click to a new high.

The fish stopped just short of the end of my 150 yards of backing, stubbornly stayed beyond the length of my fly-casting line for five minutes. When he came in close, it was only to rush away again. The third time he came near I reached down over the back of his neck and, with all the strength I could find in my fingers, held him up just long enough to remove the hook.

Lady Luck rewarded me with one more strike and fortunately it was my third and not my first, because that fish in a single persistent rush cleaned me out of fly, leader, line, and backing. Before I had a chance to get back to the Keys again my plans were changed and I left Miami to return North. But I've had many more sessions with these great fish in the years that have followed.

I've been a party to some long discussions as to the relative merits of bonefish in comparison with such fish as Atlantic salmon.

The fact that bonefish supposedly couldn't be caught with artificial lures weighed heavily against them. My experience with salmon has been long and thorough. Now I have some firsthand knowledge of the bonefish on almost identical tackle. Having fly-caught some bonefish I'm not going to give up salmon fishing, but I do try to spend at least a week every winter or early spring fishing in the warm salt shallows.

The bonefish is a feeding fish and not to be compared with the unpredictable, nonfeeding salmon when it comes to the problem of bringing him to the feathered steel. Bonefish will take big flies on fairly heavy leaders, heavier gear than Atlantic salmon require. But bonefish are a more wary fish, harder to locate, and when they're hooked they have the whole Atlantic Ocean to run to. There's no doubt that they'll make longer, swifter runs than most salmon do. I believe bonefishing will be tougher on fly tackle and that reels for them will have to be precision-built with the best of materials to last very long.

Salmon utilize the running water in which they fight to make things difficult for the angler. Their sudden leaps catch many a fisherman off guard with too solid a pressure, and so they break the fine leader and go free. The bonefish doesn't leap. If he did, he would be just as spectacular and unquestionably more difficult to handle. As it is, there's little choice between the two. If you're looking for one of the supreme thrills in fly fishing, the bonefish will give it to you.

CHAPTER 30

A Fly Rod over the Deep Blue

THE STAR DRAG is neither a Hollywood society dance nor an automobile race. It is a little gadget that revolutionized big-game fishing. Before its advent, every time a fish took line from the reel, the handles spun around swiftly, often dusting the knuckles of the angler as they whirled in reverse, and the only brake the fisherman had was the pressure of his thumbs on the spinning spool.

Most of the old-time fishermen were men of enterprise and daring like Pete Boschen who took a five-hundred-pound swordfish with a "knuckle duster" and a rod held in a belt socket against his body, standing up in the boat. Angling outfits had to be tended in those days at the strike, to set the hook yet keep the reel from overrunning.

Then came the star drag, a brake that could stop a fish without requiring strength and pressure by the angler, and a clutch that stilled the bone-bruising handles and, finally, these new outfits with the do-it-all reels could be set in a socket at the stern to set the hook automatically and, in playing the fish, they could be set into a gimbal attached to a chair, in turn attached to a boat, which made them, in essence, a part of the boat itself. Thus they came under the control of the captain and were no longer the sole province of the angler.

The star drag made big-game fish easy to catch and, beginning in the early thirties, everyone got into the act. All you needed was a smart captain, a willing mate, and a little strength to take the biggest fish that swam. I say "little" advisedly because many of the big fish were caught by frail women who obviously were not as strong as the average man. Men may have worked hard in the swivel chair, but the women, with the captains running the show for them, did the job just as effectively. The star drag opened up the oceans to the anglers and we explored them, found the game fish, large and small, in all the oceans, and caught and catalogued them. No matter how big they were, we had the tackle and the captains had the skill and the know-how to find and conquer them.

Records were made and broken, step by step, until we now have reached a point where the top fish of any species is more likely to go twenty years unchallenged than not. Hence the size of the fish is less important than the tackle it was caught on, and the skill required by the angler draws a continually increasing interest. There's renewed interest in light tackle. There's interest in casting. It's part of an effort on the part of the fisherman to take the rod out of the swivel chair or trolling socket and hold it himself. We're moving toward angling recognitions that will have less to do either with being able to hire the smartest captain and spend long periods in untapped, out-of-the-way fishing areas or the luck of finding an outsize fish, and more to do with the proving of angling skill in handling fish of a size generally available.

Of all the fishing methods, standard fly fishing is the most personal and the most difficult. It takes more skill than spinning or bait casting, requiring the ability to coordinate the movements of both arms over a long period of time instead of the movement of only one arm for less than a second. A fly and a fly line are affected by the wind through which they slice and drift. The fly caster must learn the variables of air movement, just as a sailing skipper must know the wind and sea. The comparison between fly casting and sailing is apt, because they are the oldest forms, respectively, of casting with an angle and serious sea travel. Both have a long history and a great tradition and both, for modern man, are a continuing challenge.

Fly casting calls for projecting a lure, which has almost no weight, for a considerable distance. To do it one must have within the line itself practically the same minimum weight that a lure should have in order to throw it the same distance. The diameter changes and the distribution of the weight throughout the line follow complicated patterns. Fly rods and fly lines vary just as sails vary to match the purpose and loads of the ships that carry them. The fly caster must put a good deal of his physical being as well as his mind into the placing of his lure. If he fishes in the true tradition of the single-handed fly rod and the dragless reel, he will be as far from any connection with the boat and as much *on his own* as an angler can possibly be, which brings us to a rainy day in the Pacific off Piñas Bay, Panama, in April, 1965.

I was dog-tired and the words of my guide, Smitty, had a familiar ring: "You'll never land one on that tackle, sir." He knew, of course, that no one ever had.

Six months earlier, on my first try with this *standard* fly-fishing tackle, I had lost the only sailfish I had ever hooked, after two hours and twenty minutes, and Stu Apte, ace guide for saltwater fly fishing, had muttered almost identical words. That time the sail had been nearly whipped and his unexpected spurts of speed and his break-free after slowing almost to the point of exhaustion were due to a shark on his tail hitting the leader.

This time the fish had been played for two hours through drenching rain and whipping winds to the point of attempting to bring him alongside the boat. Smitty, my guide, accustomed to handling strong wire leaders, touched my very light monofilament, I thought (though he swore he didn't), and the twelve-pound test section of the leader had parted.

With knees and thighs bruised and sore from banging against the sides of the twenty-one-foot open boat, weariness had flooded through me once the tension was over and this second sailfish had broken free. The clamminess of the rain-soaked clothes added to my dejection. Weariness touched me, but not dismay. This was but the first day of seven, and I *knew* Smitty had to be wrong. All it would take was time. That first stormy day of my second attempt had resulted in two strikes where the line had tightened up to a solid pressure, only to have the hook fail to penetrate beyond the barb in the tough part of one fish's mouth or on his bill, as well as that solidly hooked fish I'd lost.

We were fishing out of the Club de Pesca de Panamá in the Pacific off Piñas Bay. The time was late April and the sailfish were plentiful. Boats with standard trolling tackle (star-drag reels, wire leaders, and baits the fish would swallow) were averaging four sails or more a day.

My goal was to reach a little farther into man's capability to take big fish on light tackle and take a sailfish on a 5½-ounce single-handed fly rod with no butt, detachable or otherwise, a fly reel with no clutch and no drag, just a light click to keep the reel from overrunning, a foot-long section of twelve-pound test monofilament less than a foot away from the 4/0 streamer fly. A rod like this cannot be held against the body for reeling and pumping, and every bit of pressure on the fish must be put on through the arms and elbows with the rod held away from the body.

Stu Apte had felt it could not be done because the single-action fly reel would not take up line fast enough, especially with a right-hander reeling left-handed. Smitty believed failure was inherent with a twelve-pound segment of leader located within scraping distance of the sailfish's rasplike bill. My notes for the next day read:

> Out at eight-thirty. Two fish up at about nine-thirty. One took teaser and swallowed it. Both struck at fly. First one pricked and shook free. Second bill-hooked and off after one long run and some headshaking. Half hour later two sails up behind camera boat. They reeled in teaser and stopped. Cast in behind their boat. Hooked one. Boat slippery . . . reel click broke. . . . Smitty's handling awkward . . . water very rough. . . . Landed after two hours (later weighing ninety-five pounds at club). Hooked second fish one P.M. after he swallowed teaser. Same playing problems. Finally tagged, billed, and released after two hours and five minutes.

What the notes don't tell is that we had found a new system of fishing for sails. When I had been at the Club de Pesca before with Stu Apte as guide, he ran the boat and he figured out the procedures, leaving it to me to cast when the opportunity presented itself. Stu is a master at guiding and few anglers would question his fishing patterns. Smitty, on the other hand, was a temporary charter-boat captain totally unfamiliar with a fly rod. It fell to me to do the overall planning.

We trolled a small baitfish called a ballyhoo on a line without a hook.

When the first sail showed up behind this teaser, Smitty was supposed to reel it in before the fish could strike it, while I cast my fly directly in front of the fish. When the first fish came up, Smitty was slow to reel in. The sailfish got the ballyhoo and swallowed it. Automatically I shouted, "Cut," and Smitty switched off the motor. I cast back about sixty feet, near where the ballyhoo had been taken, and started to retrieve the fly. The boat was motionless and the wake of our slow trolling had died away. The top of a sail poked up through the water and the fish closed in on the fly, bill slashing. After a second's hesitation I struck and felt the hard, answering pressure for just a moment. Then there was slack. The fly had pulled free!

At the same moment I glimpsed a dark purplish shadow in the water off to the starboard—a second sailfish. The fly landed just over his back and he whirled to the surface to take it, his whole head clearing the water. The strike sent him into a flurry of headshaking. Water foamed and his bill slashed back and forth in the air. Then he ran out the fly line and went deep into the backing. When he stopped I could feel him shaking and surging again. Suddenly the line went slack and I reeled in. The fly was still on, but the abrasion leader was roughened for about four inches above it, where it had wrapped and held for a while around his bill.

I learned to recognize this pattern of action as typical of a bill-hooked fish, for it happened afterward at least a dozen times. At the strike the fly wraps around or hooks into the bill without penetrating as far as the barb. The pressure on the bill causes the sail to try to shake the nuisance free, whereas a hook sinking into one of the soft, tender parts of his mouth will cause him to run or jump instantly. When he fails to shake free the fly on his bill, he finally runs, which increases the pressure and changes the angle of pull of the hook, and may loosen it. When he stops to shake again, or jump, there's slack and the hook falls free.

After drawing strikes from both those sailfish we decided to let any sailfish that came up behind the boat strike and eat our hookless ballyhoo, which was simply tied to the end of the leader with thread, instead of trying to pull it away from him, on the theory that a hungry fish is more likely to take a fly. Our new system was to encourage the sail to take the ballyhoo. Pleased with that small fish in his stomach, a sailfish proved to be much more eager to take a fly. And in this way, with the motor cut on the instant the fish got the ballyhoo, there was no question but that this was *fly casting* (from a drifting boat with a dead motor). It turned out that of the more than twenty times a sailfish struck and swallowed the teaser I had a strike on the fly within two or three casts *every single time*.

Just on the off chance that he might attract a sailfish, the mate on the camera boat had been dangling a hookless ballyhoo teaser in its wake, too. Half an hour later a pair of sailfish showed up behind them and one got the teaser. They stopped and pointed to the spot where the fish had been. Smitty raced the boat across the two hundred yards that separated us and, as we sloshed to a stop, I started casting. One of the sails must have been right underneath the fly when it lit, for it couldn't have traveled more than two yards before I felt the strike and saw him come into the air and start skittering in a semicircle around the boat with the reel's click screaming.

The wind was freshening and the sea was showing some anger. The open cockpit of our little boat was newly varnished and wet with sloshing water because the bilge pump was out of order, which made it as slippery as glass. I slid all over it, banging into the sides repeatedly as I changed sides to play the fish better or as Smitty, secure in a chair behind the wheel, slewed the boat around as if I, too, were comfortably established in a swivel chair. Accustomed to bigger boats and well-stationed anglers, he raced ahead or reversed like mad, then spun off on a new tack as he tried to follow the fish and gain line. We solved the problem of the slippery deck later by getting the pump fixed and spreading sand on the slick varnish, but that day it was murder and I still wore great bruises from the first two days of fishing when I left Panama a week later.

The ordinary single-action fly reel, with only a click to prevent overrunning, was not designed for such heavy fishing. The metals in it were not tough enough to do their job well. Halfway through the playing of this fish the vibrating dog of the click wore the head off the pin on which it rocked and it popped off, leaving me with an absolutely free-turning spool, a nightmare of the first order.

Without a drag the angler can only put tension on his fish through a finger grip on the line, which, if it isn't done perfectly, can burn like sin, or by finger pressure against the inside of the rotating spool, which can burn like hell, too. When using a single-handed rod, which cannot be rested against the body, it takes one strong arm to hold the rod and the other one to do the reeling. In the moments between reeling in and having the line rush out with the accompanying swift whirling of the handles, the click is a sort of third hand that gives a gentle pressure to prevent a tangling overrun. With neither a third hand nor a click, I was just plain lucky to avoid an un-untanglable tangle. Still, somehow, every backlash was straightened out before the tension reached the breaking point.

Halfway through the struggle the motor began to stall. The line would be going out, surge by surge, getting nearer and nearer to its end. The starter would be grinding away, wearily and ineffectually, to the accompaniment of a wheezy, one-cylinder hiccoughing of the motor until, finally, it would start and race into a roar with a great explosion of carbon dust spreading out on the sea behind us. Then I'd slowly work the lost line back on the reel.

Smitty, accustomed to a regular fishing cruiser, to a fine line that cuts through the water quickly, to strong leaders and, more often than not, to deep-hooked fish, was uncertain in his boat handling. He'd watch the line and, creeping up its path through the water, he'd end up on top of it. Then he'd have to back up and swing wide to avoid having the line catch on the hull. Every time he reversed the engine I had to give up my playing pressure, lose some line, and give the sailfish a bit of rest before I could put maximum pressure on him again.

However, that fish was destined to be caught. At the end of two hours he came alongside. Smitty gaffed him and we brought him aboard. He wasn't too big a fish. We kept him just for the record, to prove that the job had been done. At the clubhouse he weighed ninety-five pounds, about average weight for a Pacific sailfish. It was a breakthrough, a record that established the feat, but one that will not stand when others start bringing the larger fish in on the same tackle.

The fight with the second fish was almost a replica of the first. The reel had been switched over to the spare click and it lasted for over an hour before it gave out. The big problem this time, topping all the others, was the need to bring the fish in close enough for Smitty to grab his bill without having to put a hand on the leader. When at last it became easier to move the fish than the boat, when I could stop him in his runs and bring him back and make him circle the boat, I found a chance to guide him alongside. Smitty reached his bill and held him until we could tag him, take the fly out of his jaw, and let him go.

This second fish in one day, caught on the same streamer fly and the same tackle, established unquestionably the effectiveness of the method. The three others that were played until Smitty could bill them during the following five days were further proof and icing on the cake. I fought two others to a standstill; both were up on the surface beside us several times and Smitty could have taken their bills in his gloved hand except that the boat with the cameraman was on the wrong side of us each time and they couldn't have filmed the action.

I had to let each fish move off again several times and try to get him up alongside again on the side toward the movie cameras. In one case the fly finally pulled out and in the other the bill scraped over the twelve-pound test section of the leader just once too often and it parted.

Fly fishing, in the most demanding sense, has now moved forward another notch in the taking of big-game fish. Up until now any sailfish or marlin and most of the big tarpon that have been boated have been taken with what amounts to trolling reels on heavy two-handed fly rods. The second handle or "butt" of a fly rod, no matter how short it be, or how detachable, takes a fly rod out of the standard category and puts it into the heavy or unlimited class where there's no basic difference between it and the rods now being used for trolling.

With a single-handed rod (the reel must be even with or extend below the butt of the rod), all the pressure on the fish must come through the angler's arm and elbow, a far cry from resting a butt against one's chest or a belt socket, a manner in which almost anyone can land a sailfish. The essence of the sport in fishing is to take the available fish and, by the use of very sporting tackle, demonstrate an uncommon skill. If the skill required is not uncommon, neither is the angler.

Playing a fast fish in deep water with a fly-casting line poses a new problem. The fly line is, by nature, bulky. It will not cut through the water swiftly the way a trolling line will under any tension the angler can put on the fish. Instead, it acts like a rope attached to a dog running wildly around through high bushes. Wherever he goes, it goes, and then, when he passes around a bush, the line (rope) must follow him around it and around every other bush on his tortuous course. The fly line becomes, in a sense, a part of the fish that trails him. The angler must follow the line to a point where the fish *was* before he can turn the boat toward where he *is*.

When the fish goes deep, the line trails behind him at his own level and the angler's pull does not lift him toward the surface but merely adds its drag in the same direction as the fly line's friction, directly astern. A sailfish, down deep on a fly line, cannot be lifted. The line cannot be brought to the surface until the fish swims up with it. In this sense the angler is at the mercy of a sounding fish, and a deep fighter could well take an eternity to tire.

The single-action reel (without any multiplying device) tests the fisherman's speed and endurance in reeling. Braking his fish with only the pressure of finger against a moving spool or on the line itself is a tough test of his coordination in touch. The playing of a fish with this sort of tackle is something akin to fencing or four-wall handball. It requires swift movements combined with excellent judgment more than youth or strength or dazzling speed.

It is a glorious thing that a man whose hair has gone gray and whose muscular power is not what it once was can continue to improve his abilities to take on the top challenges of angling. Few sports or games offer such a lifetime of enduring activity and challenge.

Pacific sailfish are about on a par with the big tarpon in size. They leap as often and run farther and they have the added challenge of being fished for in deep, deep water which adds a new and difficult dimension. They are available over a great part of the Pacific and in considerable quantity throughout the entire year. Even in August, the poorest month off Piñas Bay, I have had five sails strike at a fly in one day. In the end they may take the play away from the tarpon as the biggest and most exciting fly-rod fish.

Recently there was an unofficial meeting of some representatives of the Salt Water Fly Rodders of America, the Federation of Fly Fishermen, and the International Women's Fishing Association to discuss fly-rod specifications. The consensus was that there should be three basic categories, standard, ultra-light, and heavy.

Standard would call for a twelve-inch section or more of not more than ten-pound test strength in the leader, a rod between six and nine feet long of not more than 5½ ounces total weight, and a single-action reel of not more than 4⅛-inch outside diameter with no clutch and only a click, with a maximum pull of half a pound to prevent overrun, and a reel that must reach or extend below the lower end of the rod at all times.

The ultra-light-tackle category would call for a segment twelve inches or longer of not more than five-pound test in the leader, a rod of not more than 2½ ounces total weight, between six and nine feet long, and a single-action reel as above. A five-pound bonefish or a ten-pound striper on this outfit would represent a considerable feat.

The heavy classification would allow multiplying reels, clutches, drags, butts of not more than eight inches, detachable or fixed, with a segment twelve inches or longer of twenty-pound test in the leader. This tackle is comparable to the lighter trolling rods now used.

To qualify for fly-fishing records the angler must be able to false-cast a reasonable distance repeatedly with his outfit. This automatically eliminates heavy lures and out-of-balance outfits. The classifying segments of the leader would have to be not more than six feet from the fly, a space which could be used for abrasion leader, if desired.

Up until now fly-rod specifications have permitted not more than twelve inches of abrasion leader (any strength to prevent damage from sharp teeth or rough bills . . . I used sixty-pound test nylon monofilament) next to the fly. Our experience with sailfish brought out a weakness in this ruling. As our skills progressed, Smitty was able to follow the fish well and keep the boat at a consistently good angle for playing, and we learned to work together as a team. The last four fish were brought close enough to the boat to have been gaffed within forty to fifty minutes of being hooked. Because I was determined to release them with no injury other than the implanting of a tag in their backs, I had to play them another full hour before they could be brought to the surface alongside the boat because of that twelve-pound test segment less than a foot from the fly.

With ordinary trolling tackle a ten- to fifteen-foot wire leader is used at the end of a stretch of doubled line. Thus, when the fish is close to the boat, he is held by very strong tackle. The mate can pull a hundred pounds or more once he grabs the wire leader . . . and if he simply grasps it near the line end, cuts it with a pair of pliers, and lets the fish swim off or float away, it counts as a legitimate release. To require that a fly fisherman, who has already done a good tackle job to this point, must play a fish another hour simply to be able to tag and release it doesn't make sense. Most skippers, under these conditions, will insist on gaffing their fish, so that they may be counted for the record, rather than run the risk of losing them through further playing. The end result would be the gaffing of many fish which would otherwise be released, a move against, rather than for, conservation. The suggested new allowance of six feet of abrasion leader does not in any way reduce the skill required to play the fish to gaffing position, but will mean that at that point the captain can grasp the abrasion leader and draw the fish into position to take his bill or tag him for releasing.

Many of us who are accustomed to fishing all kinds of water believe that the International Game Fish Association's big-game-fishing rules hamper the development of their segment of the sport. It is simple logic, when considering angling as a whole, to let it fall into classifications as to skill in which the size of the individual species is important only in relation to the tackle. Looking at it one way, angling is divided into the use of natural baits or artificial lures, with artificial lures calling for more skill and deception. Because of its ruling against the use of treble hooks, thereby preventing the effective use of plugs, catching a tarpon on a light casting rod with a plug or spoon which hooks into its *jaw* does not qualify for an I.G.F.A. record, but one taken on heavy tackle with a bait it has swallowed and a hook sunk deep in its stomach does.

Looking at it another way, all fishing can be divided into three basic types: still-fishing, trolling, and casting; with the greatest skill falling to casting and the least to still-fishing. Practically all big-game fishing (under I.G.F.A. rules) is done in the two lesser categories.

If the same fly-fishing outfit that is used to take a bass in a lake can reach out into the ocean and (simply with the addition of a little backing line) take a fish as big as a Pacific sailfish today (and tomorrow take a marlin), it should encourage all those with spinning and bait-casting outfits to cast for *their* fish in an effort to increase their angling participation in the taking of big-game fish. Big-game fishing is still a game in which the captains and mates develop great skills and, except for the light-tackle buffs, the anglers pay the charters and take up the slack from a swivel chair. They never really get deeply into this exciting game.

CHAPTER 31

Marlin
on a Fly Rod

OFF ECUADOR, in April, the Pacific is often oily smooth. Then, if you leave Salinas and run due west for fifteen miles, until the headland has all but disappeared in the haze on the horizon and the sky and the ocean are wide and empty, you'll begin to see marlin tails and fins breaking the surface. These striped marlin may be almost motionless, with the slow lift of the rollers washing over their partly exposed backs. More likely, they'll be cruising along at anywhere from half a mile up to seven miles an hour. Although marlin are solitary rovers, now and again as many as seven get together, tails and fins showing, as they ease along just under the surface of the ocean.

This Pacific area just off the mouth of the Gulf of Guayaquil probably has the world's finest marlin fishing. Scattered among the hundred or more striped marlin that an angler may see on an April day will be an occasional black marlin of five hundred pounds or over and, possibly, a big blue. A small fleet of local fishermen in picturesque lignum vitae-hulled sailboats have trolled handlines in the paths of the *picudas* for generations, but as yet the area has not been fished hard, either commercially or for sport.

Billfish fall into six main species. The Atlantic sailfish is the smallest and the white marlin next, both weighing normally under a hundred pounds. The Pacific sailfish averages near a hundred pounds and may run up to more than two hundred. All three are slender, willowy fish endowed with considerable speed and great propensities for leaping, but they are not comparable in long-range speed and endurance to the three larger billfish species; the striped, blue, and black marlin. These three are sturdier and heavier throughout their length. The striped marlin, smallest of the three (averaging around 150 pounds off Ecuador), goes up to a record 430. The Pacific blues go up to 555. The black marlin tops them all with a record weight of 1,561 pounds. They're all of the same general makeup, with little difference as to fighting quality.

To take one of these tough, durable marlin on true fly-fishing tackle, I realized, would be comparable to scaling Everest, an angling feat not yet achieved by any man. I'd taken a number of Pacific sailfish and knew how tough *they* could be. To take one of the top three, a swift and enduring striped, blue, or black marlin would make angling history and stimulate a greater interest in the taking of all the big-game fish of the sea not only by fly casting, but by the other, less difficult casting methods as well.

Marlin will hit feathered lures, and one striped marlin, a 145-pounder, had been taken on a fly by Dr. Webster Robinson, a much-admired angler of Key West. To take his fish, he had used a multiplying reel and a nonstandard fly rod with a butt. Even a very short butt changes the character of the tackle, and a reel handle that doesn't spin as line races out makes playing any fish much simpler. To qualify for the Federation of Fly Fishermen's standard classification, the rod must be single-handed with no butt, the reel must be simple single-action, and the fly must be cast, not trolled, to the fish.

I wanted to prove that ordinary fly-fishing tackle, the sort that is in normal use for bass-bugging the lakes, would (with some extra backing) take a striped marlin, and that drags, multiplying reels, and rod butts are not essential. I chose a glass fly rod made by Garcia, single-handed, weighing only five ounces and selling for about $12.

My reel, a Farlow "Python" (single-action without brake or drag, with only a slight click to prevent overrun), cost about $30. I'd have to brake it with my fingers against the reel spool. My fly line was No. 10 forward taper with three hundred yards of seventeen-pound test, braided-nylon squidding line for backing. It added another $20 to the cost. The leader, key link in the tackle chain, costs very little but is extremely important for record recognition. Mine had an eleven-inch shock section of eighty-pound test nylon next to the fly, then the section of more than twelve inches in length and maximum twelve-pound test that is required by practically all fly-rod groups for records.

Florida fly-rod groups and the Salt Water Fly Rodders of America insist on less than a foot of shock leader next to the fly (where teeth, mouth, and bill can chafe), while the Federation of Fly Fishermen, largest of the fly-fishing organizations, will allow up to two feet, a considerable advantage when fishing for billfish. I made sure that my tackle would qualify for all sets of specifications, even though such a small difference as the shorter shock leader could spell the difference between success and failure.

With me in the boat was Woody Sexton, who has a fine reputation as a guide, angler, and sportsman. Woody didn't normally guide for marlin and had never taken one, but he knows the field of fly fishing, and is a top fly-rodder in his own right. Guide and angler must have a close relationship and, when I had worked with Woody on a big fly-rod tarpon in the past, we'd had that. The boat was a fifteen-footer with a thirty-three-horsepower outboard. We were taking light fly-fishing gear in a very small boat out into the largest of oceans, and most of my friends and fellow anglers felt that the striped marlin would be just a little too tough for the tackle and for me.

With ABC's American Sportsman crew all set to film the attempt, failure would be very distasteful. Ninety-nine times out of a hundred, when an individual sets out to break a world record he fails. The odds against success are long and in this case mine were even longer. I had been counting on two weeks of shooting time, but other commitments had forced American Sportsman to cut the time to only one week. Seven days is a short period in which to break a record, and the realization of the cost of the expensive sound crew standing by would add to the pressure.

The previous April, I had caught Pacific sailfish with a fly off Piñas Bay, Panama. Then I'd used a trolled teaser, a ballyhoo without a hook, to draw the sailfish within fly-casting range. Off Ecuador we could do without the aid of trolled teasers, since marlin showed up plentifully on the surface. A month earlier off Ecuador I'd taken an eighteen-pounder, trolling on a twelve-pound test line, the first ever taken on twelve-pound line in that area.

I'd had the advantage of a trolling rod, a belt socket to hold its butt, a star-drag reel, and a twelve-foot, eighty-pound test leader. It had taken forty-five minutes. So I knew twelve-pound test would be strong enough to take a marlin, but the strength of arm required to tire him, the capacity to handle line at great lengths and speeds on a single-action reel, and the ability to bring the fish to gaff on fly tackle without the aid of a strong, long leader with which to pull him in those last yards were yet to be proved.

The first day out, we left Salinas an hour and a half after sunrise, and ninety minutes later we sighted marlin fins in still air over a smooth sea. Had we been fishing in conventional fashion we'd have been aboard a fishing cruiser more than twice as long and twenty times as bulky as our skiff. We'd have been trolling, and long outriggers would have projected to each side to increase the scope of the baits that followed in our wake.

There would have been a cabin to relax in for comfort and shade while waiting for fish to strike, rod sockets to hold the rods while the baits trolled, star-drag reels to set the hooks when outrigger slack was used up, and a swivel chair to sit in comfortably while playing a fish.

For fly fishing we needed a boat without a cabin or outriggers, a boat as free of encumbrances for the caster as a rowboat on a lake. Fly-fishing rules call for casting to the fish. They forbid trolling. Accordingly, when we spotted a fish we tried to place ourselves in his path, so that he would pass within casting range and, as he swam by, I'd cast from the drifting boat.

It wasn't easy to reach the right position. Marlin at the surface rarely set a purposeful course. They tend to meander as they travel. My fly was a big one, a 4/0 tandem made with long rooster feathers in a mixture of red, white, and yellow. Woody had dubbed it the Sea-Wulff—a bulky fly that cast about as easily as the average bass bug. With the first four fish, we were able to get into position for only one good fly presentation.

The wake of our approach to the first marlin (before Woody put the motor into neutral) was too great for the big fish and, as it hit him, he sank far enough under the surface to be invisible. His tail showed again beyond us when he was well out of casting range. Trying him again with a more careful approach, I placed the fly a dozen feet ahead of him. He showed not the slightest interest. After that, his course became increasingly erratic, and during the long and difficult maneuvering toward a third try we spotted a second marlin tail and decided to try for that one instead.

He came up to us as we lay quietly on the smooth water. He was headed almost directly toward us, and I cast when he was sixty feet away. He turned from his path a few feet to look at the fly and followed it until he saw the boat. Then he slid down out of sight, failing to reappear on the surface again.

The third fish was a wild one. He was cruising along swiftly, tail tip showing from time to time. We circled to put ourselves in his path but cut a little too short and the wake was high enough to put him down out of sight. Had we been trolling a fly, it might have passed near him and drawn a strike. Once a fish is out of sight there's not much point in casting, the ocean being as big as it is, but I tried a cast anyway, to where I thought he might pass, but without result.

We left that fish for a fourth we saw lying almost motionless on the surface. He looked big and lazy and unconcerned. We came in very slowly, making almost no wake, and coasted to a stop, motor in neutral and idling. The cast was a long one and the fly dropped beautifully, I thought, right in front of his nose. Instead of gulping the fly down, he took offense and vanished dramatically with a great splashing surge.

We saw marlin every few minutes, it seemed, throughout that day, but if they showed any interest it was merely to swim along-side or under the fly for a moment. I had the feeling the heavy shock leader was spooking them. Woody thought it was the sight of us, since they usually were headed right toward the boat when they moved in on the fly. Once two fish moved up swiftly on the fly at the same time and I felt sure the usual feeding jealousy be-tween fish would cause one or the other to show off by proving he could get the fly first. Neither cared that much.

Time went by. The afternoon breeze came up and the fish tended to cruise a little faster. Waves built up and the tails were hard to see. The only way we could get flies to the fish was to cruise parallel at the same speed and fifty or sixty feet away and cast the fly just ahead of them, giving the fish a quick look as it landed and the retrieve pulled it away. We found three fish curious enough to follow the fly toward the boat, but once they were in close and easily visible, they'd sink down and come up a few minutes later on another course. By three-thirty when we had to start our run back to Salinas, our total sighting for the day must have come close to seventy.

It was hard to believe that we could have seen so many marlin without drawing a strike. In my experience with Pacific sailfish I'd found them much more willing to take a fly. We were deeply dis-appointed; the cameras hadn't rolled seriously all day and the chances of hooking a marlin, let alone landing one, grew more remote.

The breeze came up earlier the next morning and for the first three hours we didn't see a fin. At eleven the breeze slackened. Suddenly, as if by magic, marlin tails were everywhere. We moved in on fish after fish without getting a good presentation.

We wondered why the fish were so wary. Woody and I had to swing wide as we passed them until we could draw far enough ahead to swing into their paths. If we moved in too far ahead, they meandered off and passed at too great a distance. If we cut in too close our wake sent them down. The sound of the outboard in close may have distressed them more than a normal marine motor does.

The first three fish we were able to cast to were headed toward us. They moved in behind the fly, turned away if I stopped the retrieve, or followed in too close to the boat and spooked if I didn't. The fourth fish was barely within casting range. Luckily, a long cast just reached him. He came up under it, slashed with his bill, and almost in the same motion turned back and took the fly. The time was just noon.

At first he was slow and gentle. He eased along, as if unaware that he was hooked. Once the hook was set, my pressure at the reel was as light as I could make it. I wanted to avoid the swift, raging surges and the long, coursing leaps that would break the leader if he undertook them at the peak of his strength. I hoped to take the edge off his wildness before he fully realized his danger. For a quarter of an hour his only indications of discomfort were a few vicious headshakes.

Little by little I built up the pressure. A school of pilot whales loomed behind us on the same course. As they reached us, the marlin moved off and I had to increase the pressure a little. So he moved faster and faster, until the click of the single-action reel was screaming and the handle was just a whirling blur. He jumped a dozen times in a run that took him far off, and I could only hope the trailing line and backing would not break the leader's twelve-pound strength, even though I was putting practically no finger-pressure on the line at the rapidly spinning reel.

The leader held. The marlin sounded. When he ended his dive, my reel was almost empty and the line was going straight down and out of sight. It is hard to know what direction to follow under these conditions. We drifted and waited for several minutes until we could detect a slight angle in the downward sweep of the line. Woody headed us in that direction.

The line was slowly coming back onto the spool. Less than a third of the backing had been reeled in when suddenly we saw our marlin leaping two hundred yards away. Knowing he had brought the far end of the line up to the surface, I could put more heart in my lifting to straighten out the belly. Eventually the tail of the fly line came onto the reel spool.

Twelve pounds is a considerable pressure, but an angler cannot begin to approach his tackle's limit unless both boat and fish are moving slowly and the situation is not likely to change suddenly. I thought I could sense that the fish now would hold a steady course. I increased pressure with my fingers on the reel spool, ready at any instant to lift the finger and release the spool. From this point on, I knew I had a chance to nag the fish with my tackle, telling him he wasn't free, making him struggle.

The difference between playing a big fish with a rod that has a butt and playing one with a single-handed fly rod becomes apparent after about ten minutes of the action. With a rod butt settled comfortably against the body and one or both arms on the grip there's good leverage, and with a little effort the angler can keep up a good strain for a long time. But when the pressure to gain line must be put on by holding the rod and lifting with only one arm while the other hand does the reeling, it takes a well-conditioned arm and considerable endurance. It is for this reason that I was using my strong right arm for the holding of the rod—where strength and delicacy are most needed—and using my weaker, less-trained left hand for the reeling.

Woody maneuvered the boat beautifully. Pressure built up on the fish and occasionally he made more jumps, but his earlier exertions were telling on him, and these leaps were not swift enough to snap the leader. Another long, searching dive took him down until I was again near the end of my backing, and this time he stayed down a quarter of an hour.

At the end of two hours he was back on the surface, really tired. So were we. He set off at a steady pace, about six feet under the surface. When we closed to within thirty feet of him we could see him plainly, but when he pulled as far ahead as sixty feet we lost sight of him. A pair of marlin appeared and joined him, swimming parallel courses about thirty feet to each side. We followed him. The idling motor gave a little help, but most of the boat's forward motion came from the tackle's pressure on the fish.

We skirted a big school of mackerel. We saw a solitary shark fin on the surface, but it never came close. The wind lightened and smooth patches of oily calm showed up between wind riffles. We could see our fish often, and occasionally we could see the fly itself. After one of the marlin's periodic gymnastic flurries that ended with particularly frenzied surface thrashings, we swung up close behind him and my heart came into my throat. The leader was wrapped around his bill and the fly was dangling free beside his head.

I felt like giving up right then. My arms had been aching for hours and sweat was pouring down my back under my shirt. We knew it was only a question of time before he'd shake his head or slide backward in full exhaustion, which would create slack and either free the leader or draw the twelve-pound test over the roughness of the bill and chafe it through.

If we'd had a typical trolling leader, we'd have had no problem but, tired as the fish was, I had to bring him within gaff reach on that twelve-pound leader . . . while it lasted. Time moved slowly and the fish kept working to the westward. The camera boat crowded up a little closer. The fish was now well aware of both boats and, seeing danger in them, stayed from ten to twenty feet deep. All the pressure I dared exert wouldn't bring him up. Finally, in sheer exhaustion, he stopped and started to slide backward, tailfirst. I felt slack for a horrible instant, then he thrashed forward and I had solid pressure again. When we could see the fly once more it was embedded near the corner of his mouth and holding.

It held that way until he came in. He surfaced to thrash a few minutes later, and when Woody closed in I held as hard as I could. He was on his way down again when Woody barely reached him with the gaff back near the tail. Spray flew as Woody held the gaff and rope. I got a glove on one hand and tried to reach the bill. It was too far away. He swung around, head under the boat and tail out flashing. When his head showed up beyond Woody, I raced around, got a grip on his pectoral fin, then his bill. Soon we had him on deck and lashed down.

It was already four-thirty and we were well to the westward, out of sight of land, with a twenty-five-mile run back to the bay at Salinas. We slid in as the sun was setting. The International Game Fish Association representative checked the tackle and the marlin's weight. The scales showed 148 pounds, making him the largest marlin ever taken on twelve-pound test leader and the first ever taken on the Federation's standard fly-fishing tackle.

As things stand now, most big-game fishing is a static ritual: the captain and crew prepare the baits, find the fish, present the baits, and set the hook in the fish before the angler takes over the relatively simple job of sitting in the chair and playing the fish with tackle that is usually much heavier than necessary. But angling is changing.

Better tackle and better boats are available. Ship-to-shore radios make today's venturesome fisherman safer in a small boat than he used to be in a cabin cruiser. The big-game fishing world, once limited to those with a very considerable amount of time and money, is opening up so that almost any dedicated angler can afford to fish for almost any kind of fish.

For the good of game fishing in the future we can hope that anglers will start being prouder of the quality of their fishing abilities than of the abundance of their catches. Light-tackle fishing seems due for a great surge in popularity, and fly fishing, as well as other types of casting, is about to spread out from the streams, lakes, and saltwater shorelines onto the deep blue seas.

Casting is a personal game. The rod stays in the angler's hands and he moves the bait in a manner he thinks will be attractive to the fish. He searches out, dreams up, and experiments with lures that will catch more fish for him. We have only begun to think of the lures we'll need when artificial lures become common for all ocean fish, and baits on the oceans become as unacceptable to most anglers as worms are on a trout stream. It is more of a challenge to fool fish with an artificial lure than it is with a morsel of food, and it is lots more fun to cast a lure right where the fish will take it than to watch the captain, through his skillful boat-handling, place it in the same spot.

Everything points to a new surge of interest in open-sea fishing. Freshwater fishing is limited and most of our freshwaters are heavily fished. Where fishing is private it's expensive. The best Atlantic salmon fishing, for example, can cost the angler as much as $5,000 per week. But the seas are free and open, and in a matter of hours a jet can get you to a spot where the fish are big and exciting. The sea off Ecuador is only one such spot, in a world that is three-fifths wet.

CHAPTER 32

Angling's Charmed Circle

IT IS ONLY WHEN all the winter's tourists have returned to the north and spring's warm breath enfolds the Florida Keys that the biggest tarpon of all come into the shallow flats and channels that surround them. They cruise with the tides, feeding on crustaceans and small fish. Sometimes they circle slowly, as a group, in a sort of mating dance. Sometimes they travel a steady course, "rolling" as they go, one fish after another bringing its mouth, then its head and finally the whole upper half of its body above the surface. Very often the largest fish, which approach or exceed the two-hundred-pound mark, meander slowly at a five-foot depth, singly or in two's or three's, working the tide changes. Anglers, seeing them, feel their pulses quicken. The hand that grips the rod grows tense, particularly when it is a fly rod with which an ambitious angler plans to tackle these magnificent fish.

Would you like to enter the charmed circle of anglers who can manage one of the sport's most difficult feats? Come, stand beside me on the stern of a sixteen-foot skiff as we approach Loggerhead Bank. Stu Apte, one of Florida's best, is guiding you for tarpon. Your tackle is a nine-foot fly rod with single-action fly reel (Beaudex) possessing no adjustable drag or brake, a reel designed for lesser fish. You are reeling left-handed and the single-grip fly rod will be held in your right hand all through the tension and struggle of playing a tarpon if you hook one. You are doing it the hard way and if you succeed in taking a tarpon of more than a hundred pounds you will have earned the respect of your guide and of all the anglers who know enough to know that this is one of the angling feats to separate the men from the boys.

The outboard that drove us out at a twenty-five-mile-an-hour clip has been tilted up out of the water and a canvas spread over it to keep the loose coils of fly line, which fall to the deck at your feet, from catching or tangling on any protuberance of the engine.

We have sighted a school of rolling tarpon and are trying to intercept them. Between the thumb and forefinger of your left hand
you hold a tarpon fly, an orange-and-yellow imitation of a shrimp,
tied on a 4/0 hook. Between it and the tip of the fly rod in your
right hand the leader and a twenty-foot loop of line hangs down
to drag on the water. (Line for fly casting must be off the reel and
free to cast out before the cast can be made.) Over the other three
fingers of your left hand hang long loops of line that rest on the
canvas at your feet. Nearly seventy feet of line are off the fly reel
and ready for casting. Somehow you must keep the long loops of
line from tangling in spite of the wind and your movements as
you watch for the fish. If, when a tarpon is sighted within casting
range, you have changed your position and a foot stands on the
loose line at your feet, as well it may, the cast will be abortive and
fall short.

Stu stands on the bow of the boat and from that point of vantage drives us ahead, stern first, by pushing with a fourteen-foot
spruce pole. It has a "foot" or broadened area which keeps the
butt of the pole from sinking into the soft bottom when the thrust
is made. He has gauged the speed of the tarpon and is poling, all
out, to intercept them. The morning sun is still low and there is
a fair breeze blowing which will make it difficult to see the fish
under the surface when, if we are lucky, we draw close to them.
Only the occasional surface roll gives away their position as we
stare across the hundreds of feet that separate us.

Suddenly Stu points and as he calls you see the tarpon underwater. The school has turned and is coming directly toward us.
You send the cast out without a tangle and drop the fly seventy
feet ahead of the boat just as the lead fish are approaching. You
start the retrieve with your left hand by giving a few short, swift
jerks to impart to the fly the semblance of life.

The wind is driving the boat toward the fish and they are coming fast. We close in too swiftly. One of the leaders spurts toward
the fly, but as he reaches it the looming boat frightens him. With
his mouth partway open to take the fly, he turns away short. A
great muddy boil comes to the surface where he and each of the
other tarpon of the school reverse their course and speed away in
retreat. Tarpon in the shallows are as easily frightened as trout
in a mountain brook. That opportunity to hook a tarpon has come
and gone.

Loggerhead Bank is a crescent-shaped area several miles long which is barely covered at low water and deep enough for tarpon to feed on it anywhere at the flood. Two narrow channels cut across it and the incoming tide pours through them as well as through the broad, deep areas around each end. We choose a position at one channel's mouth where we'll be in the path of any fish coming either through the channel or trimming the edge of the bank where the water slopes off gradually from a few feet to ten or more.

Stu drives the unshod end of his pole into the soft bottom and ties the bow rope to it. As the sun rises higher our eyes will be able to penetrate the water better and the slackening wind will make it possible to cast well in any direction. If the tarpon come by we will see them underwater as silvery-gray-green forms, slightly darker or slightly lighter than the bottom below them, depending upon the angle of the sun. Sometimes the most conspicuous thing about them will be their shadow on the places where the bottom is clean and hard and neither grass nor sponge nor soft marl can absorb it. They are hard to see and all too often an angler's first realization of their presence comes when they swirl and race away.

Half-a-dozen other boats are fishing the area, too. Most of them are using spinning tackle which lets them cast further and more easily than a fly fisherman in spite of any wind, and makes the playing of a fish much simpler. We watch them while we wait for tarpon, for if none of the other anglers show signs of seeing fish over a period of an hour or more, the chances are that tarpon are not in the immediate area in any numbers and fishing will be better at some other spot.

Stu sees the fish, a moose of a tarpon, coming toward us from downsun. He's traveling two or three miles an hour with a lazy movement of his silvery length and his course will take him within seventy-five feet as he passes between us and the bank.

It is time for a quick check of the coils of line in your left hand and the loops trailing to the deck. The fly must drop just ahead of the tarpon as he passes and, since this one is swimming near the bottom, it may take a few seconds to sink to a better sight level for him. A single, relatively short false cast should put you in posi- tion to extend the cast to the seventy-odd feet required. A second longer false cast or a third, flaring the fly over the water near him, will spook him and spoil the show. A fly touching the water over his back instead of ahead of him can put him to instant flight.

The moment arrives. You release the fly from finger and thumb. Your muscles move and the fly line follows the rod through sinuous contortions. Finally it straightens out and the fly falls ten feet ahead of the tarpon but a little short of intercepting his line of travel. It sinks slowly. He is almost abreast of it when you give it the first movement. The big fish shows no sign of interest and is passing it by when you give a second and harder pull, moving the fly about a yard. Slowly the tarpon turns and with a sudden rush opens his mouth to engulf the fly. You strike both with a lift of the rod and a hard pull on the line with the left hand.

There's solid pressure and the rod bends almost straight toward the fish. He shakes his head once, twice, three times, then launches himself halfway out of the water in a cloud of spray. He heads out past the boat to reach the deep water. There is slack and you strip line frantically to try to maintain some tension. He passes us at twenty-five feet and speeds on. The tension never comes again. The fly hit a hard part of his bony mouth and failed to penetrate beyond the barb of the hook. The slack and the continued headshaking let it work free. To hook solidly one tarpon out of five is all that one can expect.

Stu morosely reports, "That x#*# fish, #$%&xx*, could have won the tournament for you, xx$#%*$*, and would have made a magnificent mount."

Tarpon are right at the top of the game-fish list, along with the Atlantic salmon and the trout. To offer the sportsman the greatest challenge the gamest fish must be swift and strong. To be most dramatic they should leap when hooked and a leaping fish is more difficult to play. They should, preferably, be caught in moving water, which adds an extra hazard over the playing of a fish where the water is still. They should take an artificial lure, for the catching of a fish on a piece of the food it normally feeds on does not require the inventiveness involved in luring a fish to something inanimate that is contrived to look edible and alive. The lures these special fish prefer should be very small in proportion to their size, calling for small hooks on which it takes great skill to hold them. They should be caught by casting, for casting requires greater skill and effort than letting a line drag behind a boat or having a bait sit in a single spot to wait for a fish to come by. The trolling fisherman can set his line drag and let his mind go far away from the sport, knowing the fish will hook himself. The still-fisherman can drowse and dream while he waits for the tug of a fish on his line or the sight of his float being pulled under. The fish taking a natural bait will taste and swallow, often being hooked deep and badly hurt. The fish taking an artificial lure realizes the fraud immediately and, given a second or fraction of a second, will safely eject it. Casting requires constant attention. And fly casting requires a greater ability than either bait casting or spinning. The ability to overcome these difficult sporting problems with the top game fish lets an angler walk proudly among his peers.

The spinning fishermen have a distinct advantage over even the most expert fly fisherman since it is easy to cast farther and more accurately, even in a wind, by this method. Then, too, when a fish is hooked they have a good clutch-brake system on their spinning reels to keep the line's pressure automatically below the breaking point. Those who fish for tarpon with trolling rods, star-drag reels and lines of twenty-pound test or over have an even simpler job of landing their fish. The particular outfit you fish with now has a simple single-action fly reel without adjustable brake or drag. You will have to apply braking power by pressing a finger against the turning reel spool with one hand while holding the rod with the other. If you apply pressure too quickly blisters will form; too slowly and the reel will overrun, tangle the line and let the fish break free. Why do you use so demanding a reel? Simply to prove you have the skill to make it do the necessary work.

Your leader, in order to qualify for the Metropolitan Miami Tournament, must include a twelve-pound test segment more than twelve inches long. Leaders are usually made up with a less-than-twelve-inch section of eighty-pound test nylon monofilament next to the fly to absorb punishment given by the hard, rough jaws. The twelve-pound test monofilament comes next, to be followed by a section of twenty-pound test, then a forty-pound test section where the leader is knotted to the line. The fly-casting line is thirty-five yards long, bulky and strong, and attached to the casting line is two hundred yards of twenty-pound test braided-nylon backing.

A tarpon may take the fly and set off on a sizzling run. The motor may be started but before the boat can get full headway the fish can pull the line to its end and snap it.

Some tarpon seem just too tough to handle on light tackle. If not too fast at the strike-and-run they may be too determined as "travelers" and set so strong a pace over so long a period that it is the angler who is worn down and becomes weak and careless instead of the fish. To hold a fish of record weight (present fly record is 148½ pounds) takes plenty of skill and stamina. Still, that record should not stand too long. There are plenty of fish of more than two hundred pounds swimming the shallow waters in season and, with an increasing number of fishermen using the fly, some lucky angler should soon hook and land one. These thoughts run through our minds as we wait and watch for another tarpon to come within fly-rod range.

No tarpon comes by for the rest of the morning. We see one boated and several others hooked and lost by others fishing in the vicinity. Then the action stops and one by one the boats give up and go off to seek out those small, special places where tarpon may feed and which each guide has found and keeps secret. Stu's secret spots prove barren. Late afternoon sees us back at Loggerhead Bank hoping we will strike a few tarpon coming in on the early flood.

Stu shuts off the outboard a quarter of a mile from the bank and poles stealthily in. As we reach the bank's edge we see three tarpon cruising toward us, all in line. The biggest is at the tail where you can't present a fly to him without spooking the fish just ahead, which would most surely spook all three. Your best chance is the lead fish, the smallest of the three, weighing under a hundred.

You make the cast perfectly, just ahead of the leading fish. You twitch the fly. He spurns it, passing underneath, but the middle fish surges forward to take it. The line tightens and the tarpon leaps.

You are busy keeping the slack line from tangling as it whips out through the guides and then the reel is singing and your finger is pressed against the metal spool to brake him. Finally the motor starts and you gain back some line as we close up after the long run. You were lucky. When the tarpon leaped and caused some inescapable moments of slack, the hook did not shake free. On his sudden surges, as you follow, you are careful not to let the strain build up to more than twelve pounds. You remember through your trained muscles just how much pressure it took to break that twelve-pound monofilament when you pulled in practice tests against a fence at home and you stay three or four pounds under that pull. When his speed is gone and he resorts to bulldog fighting you finally make him tow the boat and then are able to keep up a steady pressure of nearly ten pounds. Your arm, never relenting its strong but sensitive pressure through the rod, grows weary but does not weaken. All goes well. In an hour and a half he is ready for the gaff. Normally the guide gaffs the tarpon, using a "killer" gaff with a long handle if the fish is to be kept and mounted, and a "release" gaff, small and easily held in one hand, if the fish is to be freed.

Every part of the play an angler can conduct completely on his own adds that much more to his interest and to his stature among other anglers. This fish is big, but not big enough to win the tournament or to mount. It is the release gaff you pick up as we work to the shallow water where the flow of tide is running as swiftly as a salmon river. You slide over the side, determined to bring the fish within your own reach with what, for most people, is ordinary freshwater-bass fly-fishing tackle, but in spite of the fish's size and the run of the tide you manage it. The gaff grips his chin and you hold him up momentarily for a picture before you shake the gaff free and let him swim away. Stu gives his estimate as a hundred and twenty pounds. Not a monster. Not within twenty pounds of the present record, but the *greatest sport* can lie not merely in maximum size but in taking the *available big fish* with *extra handicaps* as you have just done.

Stu Apte is probably the best or the luckiest tarpon guide in the Keys. Tarpon caught under his guidance have been at the top of one of the tournament's tarpon listings each year for the last three years and include the present world's record for the fly rod for both men and women. He has an exceptional ability to see tarpon, the energy and judgment to pole a boat swiftly and to make seemingly miraculous interceptions. He has an instinctive ability to know where tarpon will be cruising and particularly when and where tarpon will show up in some of his secret spots. He is as good a fisherman as any of his clients and knows how best to work the boat and give him every chance to hook and save his fish.

He can take a pretty poor angler and, by giving him a spinning outfit and the breaks of downwind casting and expert boat handling, probably help him catch a hundred-pounder, perhaps even the biggest tarpon of the season. Such an angler can talk of the monster tarpon he caught, but when Stu Apte and the other knowing guides who work the Keys talk about good anglers they have known, they talk of those who can do it the hard way, of the fly-rod anglers who can handle any big fish well and for whom, perhaps, the biggest tarpon that swims would be neither too big nor too tough.

So you have taken a big tarpon on a fly and it is a source of pride. How else can you set yourself apart in angling? Although there are many ways, most of them will be difficult to explain to your friends and best understood by the angler himself, who recognizes that his own feat was far above the normal effort required in a particular form of angling. Although great feats may come in any form of fishing, the easiest way to enter the charmed circle·is to fish for the most sporting fish with the right tackle and the qualifying method.

When a wise old brown trout is rising and small-selective, it takes a hell of a fisherman to take him. If the sun is bright and the water smooth even the finest leader seems to stand out as bluntly as a clothes rope. The successful small fly, a 16, an 18 or an even smaller No. 20, must have the magic endowment of looking alive, though it has not the power to move a single whisker as it drifts freely with the current. The leader, in attaining the fineness of near invisibility, dwindles in strength to less than a pound. The cast must be perfectly placed, preferably falling to the water in a downstream curve, in order to let the fly drift to the fish ahead of the leader and line. The rod must have great delicacy and the playing of the fish must be done with exceptional care. When a trout of four pounds has been fooled and played to a finish on a No. 20 fly, the angler will have recorded a feat that few others have managed and they, too, were master anglers.

The Atlantic salmon angler who fishes the tough, low-water conditions when salmon seem to resist all angling efforts and is able to take a fish of fifteen pounds or better on a leader of three pounds or less in tested strength, demonstrates that he, too, has learned to fish exceptionally well. I have taken a number of good fish on a No. 16 fly and on a 1¾-ounce fly rod (an outfit considered by most far too difficult to tackle run-of-the-mill trout with), but none of them weighed as much as twenty pounds.

A group of us have spent parts of the last two seasons trying to catch a salmon of more than twenty pounds on a No. 16 (single-hooked) trout fly. So far no one has succeeded, but eventually I am sure one of us will manage it. It is difficult enough to hook salmon that weigh twenty pounds in most rivers on *any* fly and when and if one of us does manage to hook and land one on a 16 he will be doing something in angling that never before has been achieved and recorded. The grip of so small a hook is so delicate only a master player of fish can hope to subdue a twenty-pounder. To tackle the job is something like climbing a great mountain . . .

because the challenge is there and a man wants to prove he can meet it. The fisherman who is lucky enough to hook the biggest salmon of the season and who lands it on a twenty-pound test leader and a 1/0 fly may brag of his catch and his luck but not of comparable angling skill.

In each of the above cases the greatest credit is due to the angler when he accomplishes the entire capture of the fish on his own. It takes more skill and provides more pride when the angler nets or lands his own fish without the aid of a guide. In that way the fish is captured by an individual instead of by a two-man team. Doing it alone is the hard way. In any case he must hook and play it on his own in order to call it *his* fish.

In big-game fishing it is next to impossible for the angler to do the entire job of capturing a fish. Big-game fishing is a *team sport*. The captain, who sets up the fishing, usually finds the fish, makes or checks the bait, plans the presentation and directs the playing of the fish. He has the most difficult job on the team and usually has most of the fun. The real thrill for an angler in big-game fishing is being an integral part of a smoothly working team. That requires not only a good knowledge of the whole operation but an intimate understanding of the fish and the moods and the abilities of the other members of the team. Unless an angler can distinguish himself by using light tackle his participation in the taking of any big-game fish is well submerged in the group effort. Because he has paid for the boat and the crew's time he may take the liberty of saying he "caught" the fish they bring in, but those who know the score realize the average big-game angler hires most of the brains and skill that accomplish the capture of "his" fish.

This is not to disparage big-game fishing. The capture of big-game fish is as thoroughly a sport as any other type of angling. It is to suggest that the big-game angler should say *we*, not *I*, when telling of his catches. The angler who takes a marlin on ten-pound test line most assuredly shows great tackle skill. But as with the matador, the tennis champ, the golfer, the fighter pilot, the greatest glory seems to fall to those who go farthest *alone*, either in the crucial moments or for the full game.

CHAPTER 33

Casting Techniques
Go to Sea

IN THE PRECEDING CHAPTER I mentioned angling's charmed circle
... that group of anglers who recognize and accept within it others
of their breed who have demonstrated unquestioned ability. Among
the feats that could bring an angler a place in this select group
were the taking of a tarpon of more than a hundred pounds by
fly casting, the capture of a four-pound brown trout on a No. 20
fly, or a sixteen-pound salmon on a No. 16. Now in addition to
these and other standbys, there are some newer ones which have
developed as angling in its finer forms moves out to cover the seas.
As with a stone falling into still waters, the circle widens.

The saltwaters have always held the bulk of the world's fish,
the greatest variety as well as the swiftest and biggest of all the
game fish. But the seas lacked the two things which did most,
originally, to charm and hold perceptive and devoted anglers.
They lacked the flow of stream waters with their problems of
eddies and currents, light and shade. They lacked the presence
and the sheer magic of the underwater insects which, inspired by
sun, temperature, and time, leave their subaqueous home and,
becoming airborne, fly away. From this natural insect activity came
the sport of fly casting and, as a natural sequence, all casting with
angling tackle.

Real underwater insects may not be native to the sea, but
anglers are casting artificial flies there more and more, intriguing
the fish to strike so that they may test their tackle and skill. This
is the wave of the future: the movement of the essential freshwater
methods, thoroughly refined, time-tested, and sporting, to the last
strongholds of the ocean. Not only have flies and fly casting reached
out for the swift, dramatic ocean fish but the whole field of casting
is at last moving to the sea.

The key to this new movement is one of the wonders of our modern living—nylon. Nylon in monofilament form has a strength up in the range of steel wire, with far greater flexibility and elasticity. Now instead of sitting idly (or tensely) by while the captain does the real fishing with a bait of *his* rigging on a rod safely set in a socket that makes it part of *his* boat, maneuvering his bait to a fish he's located, an angler can hold his own rod and make his own presentation to a sailfish, a marlin, or a tuna. Again, let me ask you to join me as we reach beyond the normal standards of angling into the area of its newest and perhaps its greatest challenges.

For big bluefin tuna, at the moment, there is no place like Newfoundland's Conception Bay. There are no commercial fishermen with heavy lines or harpoons to make the fish edgy or drive them off to other feeding grounds. On a typical warm summer day the air will be calm or the breeze light. In the morning there will be white patches of flashing foam where the tuna drive bait to the surface and feed until the small fish scatter. As the day wears on, the tuna will slow down and, if the water is smooth, cruise just under the surface. From the highest point on every tuna boat a lookout watches and when a surface-traveling school is spotted, the boats move in to present their baits.

Rippled water over the tuna's backs will mark the schools, and the occasional fins and tails that break out into the air are confirmation of their presence. By then the schools have finished feeding and move aimlessly and lazily under the surface sun. Under these conditions, when they are easiest to find, the tuna are least hungry and hardest to catch.

Conception Bay is fifteen miles wide at the mouth and extends fifty miles into the heart of the Avalon Peninsula. Its inner areas grow shallower, but near the entrance the shorelines are steep, the water dropping to ninety fathoms a few hundred yards offshore, deepening gradually after that to 135 fathoms and more. The lower waters are chilled by Arctic cold and most of the tuna never leave the upper fifty or sixty feet which, under the summer sun, have a low fifties average water temperature.

Although fly-fishing tackle is most challenging and difficult to use, it is not always the best way to fish or to demonstrate great skill in fishing. The fly line is a thing of the air and, when the air is rough, fly fishing becomes rough, too. In addition, when the waves build up, the fly, which must be light enough for casting, is often too small to attract attention. With the larger lures or baits that can be used with spinning, bait casting, or trolling, success is more certain and the tackle challenge may be comparative. The taking of big bluefin tuna in all probability is impossible on standard fly-fishing tackle.

The big bluefins that come into the Newfoundland waters in midsummer average close to six hundred pounds. They are the toughest of all fish on angling tackle. They don't waste their energy in surface leaps; they just dive and drive ahead, knowing that to stop swimming is to die. Tuna will strike a fly well and lesser tuna have been taken on fly-fishing tackle, but these monsters of the Atlantic would require the "pumping" that normal fly tackle doesn't allow, and their great weight calls for at least fifty pounds to hold them up, exhausted, in the water.

Back in 1938 I was fortunate enough to take Newfoundland's first rod-and-reel tuna in a makeshift boat with a local crew I had trained for the job. I knew the fish and the challenge they offer, but with well-developed tuna angling the thrill of 130-pound tackle had faded. More recently I had been trying something no one had yet done: take a big northern bluefin on the International Game Fish Association's regulation fifty-pound test tackle.

Not only was I up against holding so big a fish on so light a line, but the I.G.F.A. regulations, valuable as they have been for the sport, have several flaws. One of them lies in limiting anglers using fifty-pound test line to only half the doubled line and leader length that is allowed for the heavier line categories. The reason for any hard, strong leader is to prevent the fish's jaw, fins, sword, spear, skin, or tail from chafing or cutting the softer line. How anyone can feel that *any fish* should not be played on the *same leader,* regardless of the rest of the tackle, is hard to understand.

In 1938, when the regulations were formulated, I wrote articles questioning this phase of the rules—with no success. The result of the ruling is to give an overwhelming advantage to heavy-tackle men in the capture of big fish. The fifty-pound test angler must play his fish right to the boat on the line specified; the 130-pound test fisherman can clamp his drag down when his fish is *sixty feet away* and throughout the toughest part of the battle play his fish on *twice the specified strain.* Knowing these things, the tuna skippers of Conception Bay gave me little chance to score with a fifty-pound test line. That I had hooked four fish and lost every one during the 1966 season did nothing to change their minds.

In 1967 the losses continued. The first fish I hooked was in close and tired, turning on his side after two hours. We had readied the gaff just before he broke away. Ironically, the 250-pound test leader, not the fifty-pound test line, had broken. One after another, in as many days, twelve more tuna were hooked and eventually lost. One had surged, after six hours, into a mass of net ropes and buoys with what seemed like the last of his strength. One, played from three in the afternoon till past midnight, had escaped only after the captain had had his hand on the leader and had let go to wait for a better grip, a chance that never came. Moments later he was free and, again, it was the wire leader, not the fifty-pound test line that had broken. With this background of unlucky failures we went into our final day of fishing for the season.

We had been lucky with strikes. While the fleet of nearly thirty boats was averaging only two fish a day on the pier, we were averaging a strike a day. This we attributed to two things: the use of a big plastic squid with which I was able to *cast* to the schools when they showed on the surface, and a new bait I'd discovered. These tuna, all in their teens with one or more escapes from tackle to their credit, were so smart that, as one observer said, "They can tell the skipper's name by the hull of his boat and tell by looking at the bait whether the skipper or the mate prepared it."

Single baits underwater, single baits skipping the surface, and multiple skipping baits were being used in profusion. No one had used an underwater school, so I set one up and it worked. I called it the "bomb." It was made up of five mullet, all attached to the leader and swimming underwater, with a hook in the tail mullet. The drag of the bait was heavy and we had to slow our speed down to half normal to hold that flashing school of fish behind us on the heaviest drag I dared set. We didn't cover as much water, but we did attract a lot of tuna. Our strikes were almost equally divided between the artificial squid and the bomb.

August 17 was our last fishing day for the year and we were just going through the motions. The evening before, we had lost our thirteenth fish in as many days, lost him when he'd been too tired to do more than weakly waggle his tail. He'd fought long and hard and had twice made the unusual long, deep dive to the bottom in 125 fathoms of water. At the end he'd just been heading down and staying beyond our reach. With twilight upon us I had brought the strain on the line up to the maximum I dared.

Maybe I misjudged the safe strain. Maybe, after six hours of wear during the fight, the line had weakened a little. The doubled line had been partly out of water when the single line had parted. It was hard to imagine a better chance. This time we had no excuses, no broken rudders to contend with, no motor failure. We just hadn't been able to do our job. That failure had cost us our hopes.

Ralph Le Drew, the skipper of the *Ruby L,* sat at the wheel on the flying bridge and swept the water with his eyes as we cruised a quarter of a mile offshore in about a hundred fathoms of water, heading east from Portugal Cove. We had been out since seven, as usual, hoping to hook a fish early enough to have lots of daylight to play him in. We had seen a few schools splashing the surface as they slashed briefly through schools of billfish, but they weren't staying up to let us approach and present a bait to them. At nine-fifty we drew a blind strike.

He was a wild one. He hit with a foaming smash and raced away at high speed on a long run. The reel was almost in free spool and, since he'd gone deep and the line was going almost straight down into the water, it took us a minute or two to determine which way it angled in order to move in that direction and get back some line. At the strike, when a fish is strongest, even a little drag at the reel can add enough pressure to the heavy drag of the line itself—as the fish sweeps it through the water behind him—to make it break near the fish.

A fresh, wild fish with a lot of line out is a problem. I had learned not to put on much pressure when a tuna was far out—to wait and work up to him slowly with the boat. His first run had taken out half my line. It took us twenty minutes to get back in close where I could approach maximum line strain. I had put on a fresh two-hundred-yard segment to replace line worn by the lost fish of the day before, and when that knot came in through the guides and down onto the reel we could start to wear him down.

His first long run had taken him well away from the school, which was a good break. Hooked tuna often stay with their school, and the other fish, moving along in formation, may strike and cut the line; approximately a fourth of the tuna hooked are lost that way. Our tuna headed across the channel toward Bell Island and we followed. For the next half hour the best I could hope for was to hang on while he used up some of his energy. Unless he paused, I worked with a light pressure, keeping within 150 yards except when the tackle pull annoyed him enough to make a long run.

He stayed well away from the shores and nets and we were working as a well-trained team should. My wife Joan was swinging the chair to keep my rod square with the line's angle to the water. Ralph, at the wheel above, watched the line for his directions but depended more on my words or hand signals. The line was too fine for him to see it at any depth, but I could recognize, from the pressure at the rod, the slight changes of its angle, and the amount of line on the spool, about where the fish was, and thus could indicate the proper heading.

We would work up, at an angle, weaving toward the fish to gain line, then veering away to keep the line from coming too close to some part of the boat where even the briefest contact could catch one of the many fine threads braided into it and so let its strength evaporate.

Our tuna stayed in the three miles of channel between Portugal Cove and Bell Island for two hours, never getting within a half mile of either shore. Several times the skipper of the car-and-passenger ferry shifted its course to give us a little more playing room, since the fish seemed determined to stay in his normal path. By noon I was bearing down with a good pressure and the fish was feeling it. Things were going deceptively smoothly.

Twice the fish showed on the surface, a good sign. Then he headed toward a shallow beach on the island, free of nets and buoys, ideal for the final moments with a big fish where he loses the advantage of going deep in his time of tired desperation.

Reaching the shallow water, he rolled on his side, righted himself, rolled on his side again, turned back under the tackle's pressure. Ralph swung the boat around to close in. Dennis Morgan, the mate, took the gaff from its hooks and laid it ready on the deck. Then the boat angled away a little—and stopped. The motor coughed and died.

Ralph tumbled down from the bridge, shouting for tools. Dennis dived into the cabin to get them. The fish was forty feet away. He moved slowly off. Ralph and Dennis knelt beside me and pried up the boards to get at the rudder. We were rudderless—drifting dead in the water.

I got out of the chair and, holding the rod in my hands, worked around to the forward deck to keep the line clear. I couldn't see what was going on in the cockpit. I looked out on the smooth water. It was quiet except for the sound of a few gulls near the shore and the soft song of the drag of my reel as the fish drew line. It doesn't require much time for a tuna, even a tired one, to take out a thousand yards of line.

It must have been only a few minutes, but it seemed like hours as I watched the spool grow empty. It's always something, I thought, and waited helplessly for the "pop" that would come at the bitter end. The spool was almost empty when I heard the motor's roar and we surged ahead, just in time. They had rigged the rudder so that we could steer under headway but not when we were backing up.

Slowly I nursed the line back. Had the fish been wild or fast-moving then we couldn't have made it, but he slogged along on a steady course for the open sea. By one-thirty we were squared away again. We could stay within a hundred yards of him most of the time. It was the old exercise of following the twisting course of a deep-running, half-tired fish through the maneuvers natural to the last half hour of a normal tuna fight. The fish was slow but tough —and he didn't tire.

I've had this happen with fish before. They spend their first burst of strength in a wild fight to exhaustion. If they're not captured, then they pick up a "second wind." After that they fight with a hard, dogged resistance. No speed. No verve. Just a seemingless endless toughness that keeps them out of reach for a long, long time.

We settled down to the rugged routine of fighting that durable fish in an increasing sea. The thing I feared most, as the hours dragged by, was a moment of carelessness on the part of someone in the crew. If Ralph took more than two bites of a sandwich without checking me on the line's position, I'd call for a slight shift in direction. If Joan or Dennis, at the chair, was slow to swing me with the moving line, I exaggerated the need for a quick response. I fought the fish with the grim determination that this time we would not make a mistake, no matter how long it took, feeling in my heart that even then some quirk of fate would free the fish.

Working there in the chair, my mouth dry and my muscles tense, I recalled the remark of a non-fisherman that fifty-pound test line for these tuna was unsporting, that it just tortured the fish I played unnecessarily over a long period of time. I recalled the cross-country races of my youth and running many miles to such exhaustion that we sometimes fell near the finish line, unable to take another step, yet later that day, or the next, we'd race again.

I thought of the tuna I'd lost a few days earlier when, after $5\frac{1}{2}$ hours, the weary fish had blundered into a mess of net ropes and broken free, and I remembered that the following day we'd seen him trailing fifty feet of my line, my plastic squid in his jaw, swimming happily along with the rest of the school. We were engaged in a contest that would try us both but—unless he were vanquished —that would hurt neither of us beyond the need for a day of rest.

The fish took us outside the mouth of the bay into the open Atlantic. We took time for another sandwich and a swig of orange juice. I ate little and had no liquid, except for an occasional swallow, from early afternoon on. I had to stay with the rod or lose credit for the fish, so going to the head was out of the question.

Twilight came and darkness followed swiftly. We knew what to do. Five days earlier, in even rougher water, we'd played a fish eight hours until midnight before losing him, and all of us had learned a little about playing a fish after dark. We rigged our single small bulb on the back of the cabin. It spread a dim light on the cockpit that carried over, on one side, to the waves beside the boat. Through the last of the dusk we could see very little, but when darkness set in and our eyes grew accustomed to it, I could see the line at the tip of the rod and ten or fifteen feet beyond it.

At the wheel, Ralph or Dennis had to go entirely by my hand signals. Occasionally, after their eyes became accustomed to the blackness, they could make out the shape of the fish as he churned into phosphorescent flame the small sea life he came in contact with.

My watch touched nine-fifty—the twelve-hour mark—and moved on. About that time, as we gropingly fought to bring the fish in, the doubled line showed up close to the tip of the rod for the first time since the rudder failure. I sensed a renewal of hope in the crew. Dennis readied the gaff again. Joan was a little more tense at the chair. The darkness was a devastating problem. We had to work inefficiently with the greatest of caution lest, in our blindness, we let the line touch the boat.

It was three quarters of an hour before the doubled line came into the light again. Five times I had the doubled line up to the tip and each time had to let the fish go out. Unless I could get the doubled line well into the guides I dared not put on enough strain to hold him.

Then a thought struck me. The light! We'd been trying to bring the fish in on the side where the light was shining. It might be bothering him enough to make a difference. Ralph, who had come down to the lower wheel, to steer after the first showing of the doubled line, swung the boat sharply. The line swept out astern and then around to starboard into the blackness. Dennis, partway up the spotting tower, watched for the mass of phosphorescence to show up.

He gave us a warning just before the doubled line showed up. It came a foot into the guides and I held it there for the second or two Ralph needed to race across from the wheel and take the leader. Dennis moved in beside him to strike down into the inky water with the flying gaff. He struck far back, but the grip held, and in a flurry of spray and the heavy sounds of body against the boat the tuna was subdued and brought aboard.

I looked at my watch. Eleven-fifteen! Then I looked back at the tuna. He was just average for Conception Bay, but just average was good enough. Later I was to learn that he was a new world's record, 597 pounds, but at the moment all I could do was reach down to touch him to convince myself that he—and the crew and the night around us—were real.

It was after two when we completed the run back to the fishing pier. Out of the darkness came the honking of horns. Having followed the struggle through our ship-to-shore, a considerable crowd had gathered to give us a welcome. There was champagne and the warm grip of skippers and friends, and we were deeply touched. Finally it was all real and wonderful.

The knowledge that this big tuna was taken on fifty-pound test tackle will induce many to try it. They'll succeed, and even bigger fish will fall to that line strength. And each man who does it will walk with more pride as an angler than if he'd stuck with the 130-pound tackle presently used almost exclusively for these fish.

More important, from the point of view of sport was my success in *casting* successfully for these big bluefins. It was a great regret that the fish I landed was not one of those hooked on an artificial lure by casting. For artificial lures and casting open a new and better era for big-game fishing. When they become accepted methods for the big-game fish, then big-game fishing will have fully matured.

In our time-tested and tradition-seasoned freshwater fishing, there is a general recognition that artificial lures and casting are a mark of finer sport. Just as those who shoot their birds on the wing have a more lofty place in the hierarchy than those who shoot them on the ground, those who can fool their fish with something unreal and who hook them in the mouth instead of the stomach (which can take away the will to fight) receive greater acclaim. Casting for tuna and marlin, no matter how large they may be, is possible now; as tackle for this phase of fishing is developed, it will become easier and easier.

The nylon leader, strong and highly resistant to abrasion, makes casting possible. In the late thirties I tried to cast with a 12/0 reel and stainless steel cable leaders. It was just too difficult to have much hope of success. The lack of anything but steel leaders to do the job was one of the main reasons why big-game fishing stayed in the twin ruts of still-fishing and trolling. Now, with a soft yet strong nylon leader which can be reeled in through the guides and onto the reel, casting is not too difficult.

I used a thousand yards of fifty-pound test braided Dacron on a 9/0 Penn Senator reel and a Garcia fiberglass rod. The reel spool, loaded with line, builds up considerable inertia during the cast. There is no level wind and no anti-backlash device on this size reel, so good casting calls for the skills required in the twenties before these devices made bait casting easy.

The sheer weight of the 9/0 outfit calls for a bit more than average strength to handle it easily. Yet any healthy, well-coordinated individual can train his muscles and develop the skills. Then he will no longer have to rely completely on the captain and the mate to cut and make up baits. When fish surface or come to a teaser he can cast his lure to an individual fish and then personally control the retrieve speed and action of the lure. It will give him an advantage over all fishermen who must wait until the captain swings his boat into the path of a surface-cruising fish, showing him not only the bait but the wake of the boat, the wash of the prop, and the smell of its fuel at the same time.

It will give any angler a chance to be in on the development and popularization of the hundreds of artificial lures that will fool and catch tuna, like the Dardevles, Jitterbugs, Hawaiian Wigglers, Abu Reflexes, Rebels, and a thousand other lures that fool and catch freshwater bass. Judgment in choice of lure and the motion the angler gives it on the retrieve will have a lot to do with getting strikes. The angler will play a major part in both hooking and playing a big-game fish. The ocean stretches away. The circle widens toward the far horizon.

CHAPTER 34

Killers in the Rain

THE THIRTY-NINE FOOT MOTOR-SAILER *Miss Red Wing*, with five of us aboard, headed into Smith Sound, Newfoundland, on the afternoon of August 14, 1940. Forty-foot outriggers raked upward and dwarfed her stubby mast. Lines trailed back from her outrigger tips, and two two-pound mackerel baits skipped along attractively behind us, one on either side. A swivel chair with an incomplete circle of boards to serve as a foot brace for an angler graced her stern.

For the third straight season I was gathering information on giant tuna and broadbill swordfish in the water surrounding Newfoundland. That, in itself, was exciting enough, but even so it hadn't completely prepared me for the scenes we were soon to witness.

After taking two fish, one of 498 pounds and the other of 560, both smaller than average for those waters, when the tuna first struck in at Conception Bay in late July, we were stymied by storms that lashed in from the northeast and drove the tuna offshore. Thus we were moving northward to more sheltered waters after ten days of inactivity. At Petley, I met a man whose sixty-odd years had failed to lessen his interest in life and the creatures of his world. Since my first visit a year before, he had kept a daily record of the presence of tuna. Depending on him for word when the big concentration of tuna arrived, we had grown weary of waiting and come ahead of schedule.

"There's a few tuna been around since the middle of July, but they're not really showing good yet," was his greeting as I stepped out on the wharf. Then he added, "If you stick around, you're sure to see a few, and the big schools are due to be showing up any day now."

The water lay quiet beneath a leaden sky, and our eyes scanned it continually as we talked. Before a full minute had passed, the telltale wake of a school of tuna, lazily cruising the warm surface water, broke the even pattern of the reflection. Four or five fins and tails were showing and the undulation of the water over a wide area indicated that the school was made up of many fish. Almost before our mooring lines had been made fast they were untied, and we headed out on a course designed to bring us just ahead of the tuna school.

As we maneuvered for position to present the baits, bigger fins showed up farther out in the sound. They were neither tuna fins nor the fins of dolphins or pilot whales, so common to those inland waters. They rose high and sharp when the animals to whom they belonged came up for breath. After seeking them for a long time, I had found a pack of killer whales.

We headed for the whales and let the tuna go. Our small harpoon lines, equipped only with swordfish darts, were soon rigged up, and the still cameras came out of the wheelhouse onto the deck where they stayed in spite of the increasing sogginess of the mist. I knew what was coming and wanted to be ready.

Two years before, I had come to Newfoundland with the purpose, among others, of studying the big-game fishing possibilities of the island. Beginning in deep, landlocked Bonne Bay on the Gulf of St. Lawrence, a week of fishing had given me the island's first rod-and-reel tuna, but before the first day's fishing was over, the presence of killer whales in those waters was brought home to me.

The tuna were boat-shy and easily frightened. Presenting baits to them was very difficult, and the reason for their timidity was *Orcinus orca,* the killer whale. The Newfoundlanders had called them "swordfish" and described them as "great blowing fish with a high sword coming out of their backs and white patches over their eyes"—a crude description of the killer whale.

Later in that season, while fishing at the lower end of Trinity Bay, I had been wakened at five-thirty one morning by an excited knocking at my window. The boatman hired for the few days of my stay had arrived in the morning dark, only to hear the "puffing of some big fish out in the cove," and he thought it was "swordfish" driving the tuna. In the fading darkness we could hear the breathing as they left the cove to swing around a point.

Established in a fourteen-foot skiff, we headed out with our tackle. Tuna were showing all along the shore in small schools that hugged the rocks and sent waves up on the short shale beaches as they moved along. We waited, drifting quietly, about forty yards offshore.

When the first school of tuna approached us, I threw a squid bait weighing about a pound in their path. The water erupted around the tuna as they made frantic, explosive turns in the shallow water and fled from that tiny splash. Those great, voracious ocean travelers were as frightened as mice before a terrier. All that day and part of the next they never left the shores, trimming the beaches and rubbing their bellies on the seaweed-laden rocks.

Chasing the remnants of the school around the point in the breaking day, the killers had driven one eight-hundred-pound fish up on a shoal, where a young fisherman on the way to tend his trawl had harpooned and killed it. The killers vanished with the daylight, but the memory of the scare did not leave the tuna for a moment. They stuck to shallow water and, although they were too frightened to take a bait, several of them were harpooned.

One harpooning attempt resulted in a near-tragedy when the keg used as a buoy at the end of the harpoon line wasn't thrown overboard quickly enough when the tuna was struck. Rising up in a welter of spinning rope, it struck one man, breaking his arm and carrying him overboard with a blow on the head that knocked him unconscious.

Tales of the "swordfish" or "swordfish and thrashers" are common in Newfoundland. Many men have seen the tuna driven ashore. Others have watched the big, high-finned "fish" pen tuna up in little coves and come in to take their pick of them, one by one. One man vividly described the action when perhaps two hundred tuna had been penned in a tiny crescent of shallow water between two small wharfs. The fish were crowded into the space as if in a purse seine while two big killers patrolled the exit to the deep water and two or three smaller whales made repeated trips into the shallows to seize a tuna and drag it out to be devoured.

Though I was certain that this and other similar tales were true, it was difficult for me to believe that anything which swam could run down a tuna. Tuna are streamlined to an amazing degree. All but two small fins fit into grooves in the body and present a smooth exterior as the fish slides through the water under the power of a wide and swiftly vibrating tail. They are among the fastest fish in the sea, and I had wondered how any pursuer could ever catch them, especially if he had to take time out every now and then to come to the surface for air.

Even after having seen the terror that these big, comparatively awkward-looking creatures could create among the tuna, there was still a question in my mind. Here, before us, was a made-to-order situation to show how it was done. Three times I had seen killers as I traveled the shore waters, but never until the afternoon when this story begins had I seen them near tuna.

As we took our position behind that pack of killers we were just in time for the excitement. Later we found that there were only five animals in the group—three big males between twenty-five and thirty-five feet long and two smaller animals—but as they struck the tuna there seemed to be twice as many. In rising up for breath they exposed the distinctive white patches over their eyes and wishbone-shaped ivory markings just behind their dorsals. They were round and powerful and sinister as they slid along and took their breath in quickly with a sharp, whistling sound.

We could sense the change the moment they sighted the tuna. Where they had been cruising along at about five miles an hour, breathing regularly, they suddenly started off on the chase at what we estimated to be twenty-five miles an hour, and only one of them came up for air at a time. We followed as best we could at less than half their speed.

About half a mile from the starting point a big tuna cleared the water in a long, low leap. While he was still in the air one of the killers broke out into the open at the spot from which he had emerged, and they came down together in a smother of foam. Another patch of water flared into action and another. Then the chase was over as abruptly as it had begun.

We closed in a quarter-mile gap to reach the spot where the orcas were coming up to breathe and then going down again to feed on the tuna they had killed. The rain had been increasing steadily as we followed the killers until, at last, it came down in sheets that restricted our vision to a hundred yards or less. Our cameras, try as we might to shield them, became soaked and temporarily useless. I stood at the bow holding the fourteen-foot harpoon pole with its bronze swordfish dart on the steel shank—extremely light gear for the purpose, but with the aid of the .45-70 rifle in the wheelhouse we had used it successfully to harpoon and kill a number of pilot whales equally as large, though not as fast as these animals.

Tense and ready, we moved up slowly on the killers. Harpooning is a dangerous game, and because of our forward rigging and the lack of a pulpit, my throwing angle was limited to about 90° forward and to starboard. To strike an animal and have the line go out in any other direction would endanger other members of the crew.

A dark shadow rising near us from the depths materialized into a killer whale. He came up less than twenty feet away, but amidships on the port side, out of the throwing angle. We could only stand and watch him break the surface, and marvel at the ease with which he carried a seven-hundred-pound tuna crossways in his mouth, a burden that seemed to bother him no more than a minnow does a pickerel. His quick, explosive breath was still ringing in our ears when he swept far down into the clear green water.

That was the only killer to come up within fifty feet of the boat, and thirty-five feet is about the limit of hand-harpooning range. Even though they were busy with their feeding, a time when most fish and animals are most easily approached, the orcas were still wary. The most powerful and dreaded of all living animals was not one to approach heedlessly a moving object only slightly longer than himself.

It seemed logical to think that any animal so wary would flee before turning to attack something strange. I called for a volunteer, and one of the crew, Ned Wayburn, offered to join me in the small boat. We made an attempt to close in with the fourteen-foot skiff, outboard equipped, that we carried in tow. The whine of the outboard seemed to frighten them more than the big boat with its heavy-throbbing motor, and we had no opportunity to find out whether a killer, harpooned from a skiff, would really flee when struck and fail to associate us with the sting of the dart's penetration or the line's pull until we could get back to the *Miss Red Wing*.

Their feeding over, the pack headed inland through the narrow channel of the sound. Spreading out, they took the left side of the water, with one old whale going down the center, while the other two large animals, each with a smaller one near him, divided the left-hand side of the sound into more or less equal strips as they swam its length. Their speed was about six miles an hour, and we traveled along behind the two in the center of the pack, where we could keep an eye on the animals on either side, as well. Breathing at about five-minute intervals, they continued on their course.

The downpour lessened and eventually turned to a light mist with the approach of evening. The cloud-strained light turned the long finger of landlocked saltwater into an unbroken mirror of silver as it lay between high, spruce-clad hills that hemmed it in. For an hour we followed the pack as it worked inland, maintaining our position just behind the center pair.

From the lookout on the spar we spotted a school of tuna five or six hundred yards ahead. When gorged and free from their usual restlessness and sharp feeding urge, tuna tend to come to the top water and swim along easily, with fins and tails sometimes breaking the surface. This school was traveling slowly, not more than two miles an hour, and the chances are that the big tuna were lazy and almost asleep. Immediately we turned to locate the whales, but although we watched carefully we failed to see one break the surface for his "blow."

We were unable to explain the sudden disappearance of the killers. Since there seemed little likelihood that they could have already spotted the tuna, we acted on the theory that they might have turned back just previously and, putting over baits, we headed for the fish. Our approach was only a mile an hour, lest we surprise them into flight as we came close enough to let them see our baits. Their own course was erratic and aimless, and promised to make proper presentation of the baits very difficult.

Our entire complement of five was on deck, all eyes focused on the rippling water and tuna fins a hundred yards away. Save for our own slow drift, that was the only motion in the stillness of air and water. Without the slightest warning the killers burst up under the school like a bombshell. One of the tuna was carried high into the air amid an arc of blood and spray.

Under the bleeding fish, lifting him as he ripped him open, came one of the biggest of the killers. The force of his drive carried him vertically upward beyond his own thirty-foot length to allow ten feet of clear air to show beneath him before he fell back into the sound. As he reached the peak of his leap, I remembered to swing the camera up. Without time for sighting, I clicked the shutter in the hope that a miracle would place the action within the small angle of view of the long lens. As the first big killer struck upward others in the pack closed in from below at his side.

The flight of the remaining tuna was instantaneous. Like a summer squall driven vertically down to strike the water with the full force of its plummeting wind and then spreading out in a hundred speeding streaks, the tuna broke formation as sudden death came up like a thunderbolt from below. They spread, fanwise, dark blue wakes trailing behind them, as they shot along the surface at full speed. The school had been headed directly toward us, and giant tuna passed only a few yards on either side of the boat. They went like torpedoes, blue-backed and silver-sided, leaving only a swiftly vanishing ripple behind the water they had bulged up.

None of the killers made any effort to pursue the tuna, either because they had killed what they wanted in that first rush, or because they doubted their effectiveness on scattered fish. The feeding scene that followed was a repetition of the first one. The silence was broken by the noise of water parting as these sleek yet magnificent marauders came up for their whistling breaths.

Again, one of the killers brought a tuna up above the surface as he held it in his teeth while breathing. The others probably dropped their fish and let them settle in the water for the short time it took them to renew their air supply before returning to their slowly sinking food. Again, none of them came within harpooning distance.

How the orcas located the tuna, how they were able to get together for the kill and follow their leader up under the unsuspecting fish in an attack that was perfectly synchronized with his amazing rush, remains a mystery. I felt they must have been able to "talk." The entire action was so startling and so quickly executed that it hardly seemed real, but the bloody water with the killers milling around in it and the appearance of the tuna in the killer's mouth were testimony enough to the scene that five pairs of eyes had just witnessed.*

With their feeding finished, the pack turned back toward the open water of Trinity Bay and traveled out of the sound. They reversed the formation they had used on their entry; one big orca swam the center line, and the two pairs roughly trisected the water on the side opposite the one they had covered on their inward journey. Darkness was approaching as we tagged along in their wake. High fins rolled up above their broad backs as they lifted to the surface with their need for air.

We left them to angle across to our night's anchorage at Petley on the other shore. Looking back from half a mile away, we saw the white foam of water breaking. Binoculars gave a more complete picture of giant tuna being driven into the shallow water on a beach. They went skittering up into the shoal like shiners flying in a silvery shower before a largemouth bass. For a moment it

* This story was written just before the Scripps Marine Laboratory at La Jolla, California, first confirmed that whales do, indeed, "talk."

looked as if one or two might be stranded on the gravel, but they all worked off to safety—or the teeth of the orcas. We held to our course in the gathering night, bucking a rising wind.

It was with eagerness mixed with trepidation that I developed that film a few days later. We did have pictures of the fins and backs of the orcas, but the quick swing of the camera at that one moment of almost unbelievable action had netted me only a blank piece of hills and sky.

Killer whales are the scourge of the seas. No living thing, from the smallest seal to the hundred-foot-long blue whale, can stand against them. They hunt in packs of from two or three to thirty or forty, and to sight a lone killer is rare, except for the very old males that are marked by the unusual size to which their dorsal fins and flippers have grown in proportion to their bodies.

Roaming all the oceans, they are most common in the Arctic and Antarctic, where seals, walruses, seabirds, and the marine mammals from porpoises to whales furnish them food. Records show that a small orca of twenty-one feet had in its stomach the remains of thirteen porpoises and fourteen seals.

Uncanny intelligence has been attributed to them by many observers. They are credited with rising halfway out of the water to look over the ice floes, and then, having located a seal or any other animal, they rise up beneath it to break the ice and precipitate their quarry into the sea for an easy capture. Though the truth of some of the tales told about them may be questioned, one thing is certain: wherever they travel, all living things save man in his ships must flee before them.

PART FOUR

Rods, Tackle, and Technique

CHAPTER 35

Fishing Temperaments

VOLUMES HAVE BEEN WRITTEN about game fish and their moods. There can be no question that the moods of the fish, and the angler's ability to cope with them, is a prime factor in filling the creel. The lure or bait that may be deadly one day or one season may not necessarily draw a bit of interest the next. Smart fishermen allow for this display of temperament on the part of their quarry and are prepared to deviate from the accepted rules and practices when time-tested methods fail to bring results.

Yet, temperamental though fish may be, I believe anglers are even more like prima donnas. There are anglers who like to sit and watch a float riding the water placidly, but expectantly, and will fish in no other fashion. Others may be happy only when trolling behind an easygoing outboard.

Probably the most fanatic of all the temperamental anglers are the confirmed dry-fly-only anglers or "purists," fishermen who will only fish with a floating fly. The devoted single-plug or single-method fisherman, who lets his own temperament decide his fishing lures or method and puts his own whims and feelings above those of the fish he hopes to catch, rarely brings home large creels of fish.

There can be no question that certain people are more suited to fish in one way than another. After all, we are fishing for fun rather than solely for the purpose of catching fish, and it is natural for each fisherman to suit his angling to the method he likes best, and fish for the kinds of fish that give him the most sport. It must be equally obvious that the angler who insists on one method or type of lure makes the catching of fish, day in and day out, much more difficult than it is for the fisherman whose main idea is to fit his thinking and his fishing to the whims and moods of the fish he is seeking.

Many a fisherman will find the answer to his comparatively

small catches in his own temperamental insistence that the fish take his offering in the way he chooses to present it if they want the honor of getting into his fish box. The case of the dry-fly man is obvious. He insists that the fish come up and take a floating fly. He will neither sink it nor let it drag or skitter across the surface. He has made his fishing more difficult and he has to be good to be successful.

The wet fly, one may reason, travels underwater. Therefore, it comes well within the range of the fish which are also underwater. A reasonable conclusion, yet the wet-fly fisherman who fishes conventionally with normal cast and retrieve keeps his fly within a few inches of the surface. It is just about as much to ask of a fish that he come to within three inches of the surface as it is to bring the tip of his nose out into the air in order to get the fly.

The fishing of a wet fly in the normal manner, just under the surface, is easy and pleasant. To cast upstream and let it sink as the current carries it along, maintaining a tight enough line to strike, is difficult and sometimes tiring.

To cast with a split-shot or any other light weight on the leader is unpleasant unless the timing is perfect. In both cases, there is more stripping of line to be done, more false casting, more work. Not one wet-fly fisherman in fifty has the patience and energy to fish his fly deep, but there are times when only a deep-drifting fly will be successful.

In still-fishing, the nervous angler may lack the patience for steady fishing in the good spots, and by shifting hither and yon, never settle anywhere long enough to make a good catch. The lazy lad may sit too long, time after time, in unsuitable places.

The plug-caster who favors one lure, one depth, or one general pattern of fishing over the others may similarly handicap himself. Only the fisherman who is able to fish with any method and to sense the need to change and be willing to experiment when the usual methods fail can make consistently good catches. Such a man is a top fisherman, and they are far from common. Temperament will let few of us fish in such a way without inner revolt.

If we like to troll, then troll we will, making our adjustments within the range of trolling. If we are inventive enough, we find ourselves able to catch fish under almost all conditions, and have found the answer to fishing in our own preferred fashion while still getting enough action to maintain interest and bringing in enough fish to satisfy our pride of accomplishment.

The dry-fly man, becoming inventive when the going is hard, finds ways and means to create a surface interest by outsized flies, or by patiently creating the impression in the minds of the fish near the bottom that they're missing a bet if they don't come up and investigate all those insects floating by. Thus, the sport becomes a compromise between fishing the way we like to do it by forcing the fish to take an interest, or adapting ourselves to whatever sort of presentation will please the fish.

How many ardent anglers, when proclaiming their love of fishing to their friends, hear this reply, "I would never have the patience to be a fisherman. I can't sit still long enough!" To a great many people, fishing is simply a matter of sitting in a boat or on a bank watching a bobber and waiting interminably for a fish to come along. We all know such a conception of angling is quite inaccurate, for if it were a true picture of modern fishing, those who are wedded to casting would have none of it.

The man or woman who loves to follow a winding stream or buck a heavy current to wade a productive dry-fly river need be neither lazy nor particularly patient. The casters are usually the least patient of people, constantly on the move. They are not content to choose a good spot and let the fish come to them. Instead, they never cease searching for fish to present their lures to. Patience is a virtue and the caster needs it as much as any other human, but only in order to be sure his equipment is right and his fishing techniques accurate and effective. He need never sit or stand motionless for long periods in order to be an excellent fisherman.

No sport has a wider range of action or greater choice of tempo. Fishing can be hard work or no work at all, invigorating exercise or a thorough, relaxing rest period. The angler can catch almost any game fish by a wide variety of methods covering the whole range of requirements from rigorous physical activity to virtual loafing.

But the individual species vary, too, in the type of sport they offer. Fishing for bass, America's preferred game fish, is filled with excitement. No matter how casual the fisherman may be, when a good bass strikes there is bound to be some fireworks. With a bass on the hook, almost any angler has his hands full, and those whose hearts or muscles are very weak had best leave bass waters alone and concentrate their efforts where a quieter quarry, like the bullhead or perch, is all that will take the hook.

Some fish, like the lake trout, vary widely during the season. A laker on the surface in the cold water of spring or fall is a hard customer to handle, while the same fish taken on deep trolling tackle during the summer months will put up less struggle and pose less of a tackle problem.

The real thrill and skill requirement for lakers is in locating the fish. The angler is up against the problem of finding the fish in order to present his bait or trolling rig. He cannot tell by the look of the surface what lies beneath. Will the lakers be twenty feet down . . . thirty-five . . . fifty? Where are the spring holes where the big fellows gather to enjoy the cool waters that come easing up through a porous bottom? A thermometer will help. An electronic fish-finder will make it really simple. Experience on a given lake plus information gleaned from the old-timers will help in locating spring holes, or at least the best known of such places. The weight of the sinker, the amount of line used, and its type and weight as well as the speed of the bait must all be calculated correctly.

When the hunch or information on location is good, and the tackle execution perfect, then fish are caught. The thrill for the angler lies in the sense of achievement from a campaign well planned and properly executed, and though the summer fight of the laker may not be brilliant, it takes a wise fisherman to bring them to the boat. For many an angler, the capture of a lake trout is rightly the top thrill in angling.

The greatest angling thrill for most experienced fishermen is the rise or strike. The greatest satisfaction comes from the outwitting of the fish, fooling him into taking an imitation, or so presenting the natural bait that he is hooked in spite of his native cunning. Old-timers contend that anyone can learn to play a fish, but few indeed are ever able to understand fish and water conditions so well as to be able to know consistently where to find good fish and what to present to them. With knowing anglers, a real campaign to catch a certain fish and the final capture of that particular fish will be more rewarding than the run-of-the-mill capture of another fish twice as large.

Many a halfhearted angler has been changed into an enthusiast by the discovery of a new fishing technique. Spinning, for example, made casting possible for thousands who hadn't the patience to go through the long training period required to become a skillful fly-caster. Once they've mastered spinning, they find that both bait casting and fly casting have become much simpler for them to learn. And should they tire of spinning or want to extend the scope of their fishing, the other doors have opened a little wider.

A chance encounter has often introduced a now devoted fisherman to his favorite field of the sport. One of my friends just happened to be driving by a bridge where shad were being caught on the fly nearby. It was a Sunday afternoon, and he and his family stopped to watch. The fishing intrigued him and, although he had not fished at all since his early youth, he plunged into shad fishing with real enthusiasm. He now ties his own flies, works on his tackle in the off season, and has definitely joined the ranks of those who spend a major share of their leisure time fishing for pleasure.

Often a change of fishing method will give a new interest to the sport. After several weekends of trout fishing, in which I have been clad in waist waders and burdened down with all the equipment necessary for the sport loaded into a short vest to keep it above the water line, it is a pleasure to sit in a boat and cast for bass. After the hot, restrictive waders and the cumbersome clothing, an opportunity to fish in slacks, sneakers, and a sport shirt is welcome. The raincoat, tackle, and other items do not have to be carried on one's person, but can be lodged on a seat in the boat. There are so many varied and pleasant ways to fish, I'm sure the angler who limits himself to only one is missing a lot of fun.

And on the subject of temperaments, it's worth remembering that youngsters like action and results. Starting a boy or girl out on one of the advanced types of fishing like fly or bait casting requires them to remember too many things to be careful of, gives too many tangles and backlashes to work out. There's too little action and too few fish hooked, because a good caster is not made in a day. They take a good look at a well-snarled reel and, not having the patience to unsnarl it, they lose interest and look for something else to do that will provide more action. Kids go fishing to catch fish, and the best bet for them, as for all beginners, is panfish on a bobber rig with bait. Here there will be plenty of action and a chance to develop some of the basic fishing skills before they progress to a casting outfit.

We're all individuals, and to be good at this fishing game we should let our temperaments guide us in our methods. Being an active, restless individual by nature, I found the greatest fishing success in letting those instincts rule. So I've fished hard and long, covering a lot of water. Only with the mellowing influence of the years of fishing behind me can I now find the patience to do an extensive, long-range stalking job on a big fish, a job that would have irked me too much even to consider ten years ago. With this gradually changing temperament, my fishing practices will change to suit it.

I believe it's a mistake to take someone else's style and copy it unless it fits your nature. It is wise to have your eyes peeled for a successful angler who fishes as you'd like to fish and learn your tricks from him. Take your natural inclinations and build your fishing habits to fit them. A survey of top-flight anglers in any field would show a wide variety of approach. On my home stream I can think of half a dozen techniques among those fishermen whom I consider tops.

One man I know is always on the move, casting a long line and covering a lot of water. He's looking for feeding fish and he figures that the more water he covers, the more trout will see his fly. Even when fish are rising but don't like the fly he's using, he'll only try one or two changes and, if they fail, he'll sail right along, merrily looking for trout that like the same kind of flies he does rather than accept the challenge of matching their food—or mood.

Another friend usually takes a short stretch of stream and works it thoroughly. Both men catch about the same number of fish per day's fishing. I know anglers who will keep moving only until they locate rising fish, even though those particular fish may be small and logic tells them that trout usually start rising all over a stream at the same time and that bigger trout may be rising in the pools just above or below them. The problem of fooling those particular rising fish is more important than just trying to make a big catch. To leave a rising trout is an admission of an inability to catch him, so they stay on as long as he feeds. That's neither bad nor good. It's fishing! And fishing is a sport in which each partici- pant should perform in the way he most enjoys. If success in fishing were measured solely by the size of the catch, it would be a poor sport indeed.

Yet, the catch of an angler is a measure of his skill, though not of the pleasure it gives him or his contribution to the sport. Few dyed-in-the-wool fishermen are content to spend much time at fishing without developing a fair skill at the game, not just in casting or wading, but in terms of ability to catch fish. By follow- ing your temperament you can increase your catches.

That old question of fast or slow fishing on a stream is one of temperament. We can do best those things we like to do. Those who like to fish fast should fish that way as long as they can make it productive enough to satisfy them. They should slow down only when ready to subject their natural desires in the manner of their fishing to the more important necessity of catching some fish by another method.

If you're one of the let's-get-going fraternity that are fidgety and want to be on the move continually, making yourself settle down to conservative, deliberate presentations, absolutely perfect casts, and all the other things that go with slow, precise fishing will be something like making a naturally left-handed kid write right-handed.

It may give you minor complexes and make your outings less pleasant, even drive you to some other activity, which would be particularly unfortunate because fishing is broad enough to suit any temperament and no temperament is a limiting factor to success. A word of caution to those who are teaching someone else to fish: Don't figure your way is the best way or the only way. Give them only basic information and let them work out their own approach.

Don't assume that you can avoid fundamentals or be shiftless and still be successful in catching fish, though to some onlookers that may actually seem true. No matter how you fish, it's got to pay off with fish to some degree. If you can catch them with a minimum of trouble that doesn't mean you're lazy; it's often the result of efficiency and a particular mood. The fish are your problem. If you solve the riddle of catching them and enjoy yourself while doing it, you have your temperament working for you instead of against you and that's as it should be.

Let's go back to the fast or slow approach on stream fishing for trout. Here are a few tips that may be of some help on that score. Sometimes coverage of a lot of water is definitely more productive than giving a shorter stretch a thorough working-over. This is true when only a small proportion of the fish in the stream are on the feed and those few are just plain hungry and don't give a hoot what comes along in the way of food. Whatever it is, they're ready to take a whack at it. This condition is fairly common and the long-legged guys make the best of it.

In two miles of stream there may be only a dozen fish in such a feeding mood. The water-covering angler may raise them all, regardless of the lure he uses. Under such conditions it's smart to fish fast (and it's funny how even a ruffled temperament is soothed by a heavy creel). If you pick up such a bunch of fish on such a day don't give credit to the particular fly you used. You might well have used a different fly for each fish or have used the same fly for all with identical results.

Then there are days when the angler need not move out of his tracks to take a goodly string of fish. Yet, unless he solves the riddle of the very special food the fish are working on, he won't take any. And there are days when all of the trout can be coaxed into rising but none of them will come readily. For these two conditions, the slow-moving, thorough fisherman takes the honors and the dashing, slap-it-to-'em-and-move-on maestro has to change his style or come home blanked.

My advice is to start each day with a test period. Take your favorite method and try it out. If it works, keep it up until it ceases to work. Whenever that time comes, whether early or late, experiment. Cover a likely stretch of a stream, noting where your rises come and whether they're all coming from water of a similar nature (i.e., pockets or runs or deep pools), and if so, concentrate on that kind of water.

Being basically a "mover," I'll usually work down through a stretch of water that has a good variety—runs, riffles, deep water, pockets. If nothing much happens, I go back to the starting point and come through it again with a different fly, or if I fish down wet, I may go back dry. I reason that it's more sensible to give the fly of your choice a chance to draw fish from *every* type of water before you give it the gate. If you think it was good enough to make the first choice, it should be worthy of a good trial. If you work it down through the riffles but take it off just before you reach the pool, you may throw away the one chance of making a killing. I think it's better to come through a stretch several times, each time with a suitable presentation, than to switch around willy-nilly. This can't be a hard-and-fast rule, of course, because some lures just don't make sense in all types of water, and you may fish a stream where the water is all the same and flies can be changed at will.

If, for instance, you're fishing a small nymph on a fine leader and come to some fast heavy water where it can't be fished, I think the wise thing to do would be to fish that rough stretch through with a larger fly or streamer and then return to the same small nymph and fine leader to finish out your cross-section of the stream. On a later test you might fish the entire stretch through with the streamer or large fly.

I do believe that fishing a pattern of definite nature such as this cross-section of both lures and water when you start out is good fishing practice and that anglers must have some such routine if they hope to be consistently successful. There's little luck left in fishing where the trout are wary and the haphazard angler can count on nothing better than haphazard catches.

I like to take that representative stretch of stream and work it over a few times until I find out what's what. I reason that there are bound to be fish in any such stretch, and moving on and on endlessly doesn't help a bit. If I find that there are a few eager fish and that all of them rose on the first or second time through, I fig- ure that the fish are either lined up for that particular type of fly or that there are only a few feeding fish and they'll take the first thing that comes along. I work further on that theory and drop down to another stretch and proceed to use the same flies. If that works I move along steadily, using the best of the flies or covering the water once with each of the best two.

CHAPTER 36

Tips on Spinning

THE SPINNING OUTFIT has a definite place in American freshwater fishing. It is better than either a bait-casting or a fly-casting rig for certain conditions. In my view, it will never do away with either of them, but it makes an excellent supplement to any angler's tackle.

The fly rod will cast anything from a knot at the end of a 10X leader up to a bass bug or a spinner and streamer. A bait-casting rod will cast anything from a lure the size (not necessarily the same weight) of a bass bug or spinner-and-streamer combination up to a five-course meal. The spinning outfit hits the middle ground between the two since it requires a little weight in the lures it uses but can't use too much of it. It has the advantage of having a fairly long rod in playing the fish and of not requiring a back cast. The spinning outfit will do very little that either a fly rod or a bait-casting rod cannot do, but in its field it is exceptionally good.

The key to catching fish by casting is the lure and its motion. It matters not in the least to the fish just how the lure reaches its destination or what gyrations the angler must go through with whatever tackle he uses to make it travel. All the fish care about is where the lure is, what it looks like, and how it acts. It's up to the angler to decide how he'll do his casting and what type of lure he'll use.

Another consideration is that the fish see the bulk of the lure and not its weight. Certain lures, easily used on a bait-casting outfit, appear to the fish to be almost identical with a spinner and streamer that can easily be cast on a fly rod and has very little weight. The fly rod will cast lures big enough to take any freshwater game fish (I've used them with double spinners and long double-hooked streamers for muskies) and small enough to imitate the tiniest midge.

The bait-casting outfit, using a fairly long rod and a very light line, will cast lures as light as $\frac{1}{4}$ ounce. Such a lure will take trout, panfish, bass, and all the rest of the game-fish group. The fly rod offers a maximum of delicacy in playing a fish, and the bait-casting rod offers a minimum of space requirement for its casting. Where, then, is the advantage of the spinning outfit? Let's take a look.

Comparing it first with the bait-casting outfit, we find that one advantage is psychological. A confirmed bait caster who shies away from any line lighter than a fifteen-pound test will buy a spinning outfit and use a three-pound test line on it without a qualm. The light line is the key to casting light lures just as much as the longer rod is, probably more so. Anyway, the psychology is all with the spinning outfit because it can't operate so well with a heavy line and no one tries it. If it can convert more anglers to lighter lines I'm all for it.

Another factor favoring the spinning outfit is that it takes less skill to handle the weight range of spinning lures than it does on a pepped-up bait-casting layout. The spinning reel operates simply and with a minimum of inertia to be overcome by the lure when it is cast. The spindle doesn't turn when the cast is made; the line just peels easily from the cone-shaped arbor.

Lures in the spinning range are deadly on many fish. They're good for bass, the larger trout, and practically any fish that can be caught by casting. The tougher the fishing, the more valuable the spinning outfit, since it means smaller, deadlier lures and enables the angler to reach the deeper waters of the big stream pools, inaccessible to the fly caster.

A third advantage is that the spinning rod's greater length gives it better control over the lure as it is retrieved and greater control and delicacy in playing the fish. This can be very important, as many fish are lost because of the limited shock-absorbing power of the shorter bait rod.

Unlike fly casting, the spinning outfit doesn't require a lot of space for a back cast. That opens up those waters whose banks are wooded and which are too deep to wade. When the fly fisherman can't get far enough into the stream to have room for his back cast and has to resort to roll casting, he's limited in the length of leader he can cast and the weight of the lure, as well as being handicapped by the disturbance roll casting makes on the water. In roll casting, the first cast is most important. Surface disturbance caused by this type of casting quickly puts wary fish down. The spinning lure is easily cast and is of a size to interest all but the smallest of trout.

The fine line used in spinning doesn't frighten fish when it passes over their heads as much as the bulky line required for fly casting. The angler with a spinning rod will disturb a pool far less than the fly caster, another important advantage. He is less frightening to the fish for these reasons: his line is lighter and hence less frightening; in angling, the pickup with which the fly caster rips his line off the surface and into the air for the back cast is eliminated; the angler moves along the banks, unlike the fly caster who wades well out in the stream, disturbing the fish.

On the other hand, the spinning outfit will not cast well in a high wind, while a bait-casting outfit with a small, heavy lure will function in a gale. The spinning lure has one disadvantage in common with the bait-casting rod—it cannot present a featherweight lure such as an imitation of the natural insect food of the trout. The spinning angler on the trout streams is out of luck when the fish start taking flies selectively and the fly fisherman is having a field day, unless he adds a weighted "bubble" near his fly.

His trout fishing is largely for fish of twelve inches or more, and in taking such trout, he'll have an advantage over the fly-rod fisherman perhaps half the time. The spinning angler on the lakes must watch out for a high wind which will cut down his water coverage drastically and the consequent rough water will make his smaller lures less attractive than the bait caster's larger ones.

The spinning rod is used very effectively in Europe for Atlantic salmon but, unfortunately for its New World devotees, the use of anything but a standard type of salmon fly is forbidden by law on this side of the Atlantic. Lures heavy enough to sink down and permit unscrupulous anglers to foul-hook the salmon as they lie in full view in the pools is barred on our streams as a conservation measure. European fishing, controlled and restricted, does not need such a safeguard.

The small lure, the real basis for spinning, which comes in between the almost weightless artificial fly and the standard bait-casting lure, is extremely effective. The wariest bass will often hit a small lure where a big one will fail to draw a strike.

It is the same with pike and walleyes. They, too, have seen a good many treble-hooked creations of standard casting size. Many of them bear scars from the sharp hooks of plugs from which they have torn free. Their hunger becomes renewed, but their caution has been built up to a high point. Spinning lures will take them.

Although Atlantic salmon waters are generally restricted to fly fishing only, landlocked salmon waters are open to spinning, and these fish, like the trout, come to the upper waters for their feeding in spring and fall. They are especially active when played on the light spinning line without any of the weight required for deep fishing.

The fine line, incidentally, adds greatly to the effectiveness of spinning. Just as the wariness of fish makes the smaller lures more deadly, lures attached to heavy and visible lines will be refused while those attached to fine, almost invisible spinning lines will draw strikes.

Because backlashes are eliminated, and casting with the spinning outfit is easy, it is especially adapted to night fishing. Small floating lures are extremely deadly after dark and many big bass and walleyes can be taken this way . . . even by the beginner.

The problem of playing a fish is simplified by the clutch-type drag which is built into the spinning reel. If the tension is properly set, even a sudden rush by the fish will not break the line. Whether the handle is held solidly or even, when it is being reeled in, the previous set tension cannot be exceeded. At night, when the sudden rush of a fish is harder than ever to anticipate, this advantage is especially valuable.

Rivers flowing into and out of many of the best trout lakes are quite large and a cast with a spinning outfit will give adequate coverage of these spots where fly casting will not reach the best waters. In addition, the roving trout that have come to feel the current's flow often cruise at a considerable distance from shore. Here again, spinning casts will reach many fish which are out of the range of the fly caster.

Typical of this kind of fishing at its best are some of the north country rivers of Quebec. In September the big trout nose into the shallows and work into the flowing water that leads into and out of the lakes in which they have spent the summer. Their color is rich and dark and their strength is at a peak for the year. Spawning time is a month and a half away and they're feeling the urge to have the flowing currents pass soothingly over their sleek sides.

Thus the concentration of big squaretail trout begins. Fish that have been scattered throughout deeper waters of the lakes during the summer, hard to find and catchable for the most part only by trolling, now gather in tight little groups in the pools of the inlet or outlet. A single cast over these pools in September will show a lure to more fish than an hour of casting will reach when summer finds them widely scattered. It is the time for good catches of big trout.

In choosing lures for trout and landlocked salmon "flash" is usually important. They are minnow feeders as a rule, and metal lures and wobbling spoons are highly effective. Special plugs have a place in the scheme of things, and many of the very active plugs like the Flatfish are top-notch lures. Local favorites are well worth trying, and the local fisherman is always more likely to know what is effective and what isn't than the stranger fishing the waters for the first time.

Metal lures have the advantage of flash which makes them visible for a greater distance than painted lures. Because of their high weight for a given size they have little wind-resistance and cast easily. This is particularly important where wind is a factor. Metal lures, it must be remembered, sink and are more easily lost on snags or on the bottom.

Weight of line is another factor to be considered. A six-pound test line, either braided or monofilament, should be adequate for the largest trout or landlocked salmon. A four-pound test line will give slightly greater casting distance or permit the use of a smaller lure. If distance is a factor, the four-pound test line is in order, and with a little more care in the playing of a hooked fish, it will also handle any trout or landlocked salmon you are likely to hook.

It is always more fun to see a fish strike a lure that travels near the surface where the swirl or wave of the strike is readily visible. A lure that travels within a few inches of the surface should show every strike. It is worthwhile to start fishing at that level. If fishing at the high level fails to provide strikes, then it is time to fish a little deeper. Wobbling spoons reeled rapidly stay near the surface, but if they're slowed down they'll come in at progressively deeper levels until, in the end, a very slow retrieve will work them down near the bottom.

If you begin scraping the bottom with your lures you're going to lose some. Go prepared with a fair number, for the loss of a few lures is relatively unimportant when one considers the total cost of a fishing trip . . . and getting a lure down to the fish may mean the difference between a good catch and none at all.

For trout and landlocked salmon a 6½- or 7-foot light action rod is best, but a fairly stiff 7½-foot spinning rod is better for the heavier type lures that should be used for northern pike, lake trout, or walleyes. For these fish in the Canadian waters, a regular-sized Dardevle or a ⅝-ounce plug is normal, and such standard bait-casting lures require a fairly sturdy rod. Don't overlook the spinner-and-streamer combinations for big fish on a light outfit. It is a light lure but looks big to the fish. Fast or slow, it has an attractive action.

For the same fish and for bass in our harder-fished American waters, lures of $\frac{1}{4}$ to $\frac{1}{2}$ ounce in weight will produce best results, and these can be handled on $6\frac{1}{2}$- to 7-foot light action rods, using lines of three- to six-pound test.

The line to choose will depend upon two main factors. First consideration is how open the water is. If there are no snags or weed growth, the angler can decide line strength upon the basis of his own sporting desires. The use of a lighter line represents a greater sporting achievement, requiring as it does more skill than a heavy one. A three-pound test line will do the job on any laker, bass, walleye, or northern pike if the water is open and the hook holds. It may take some doing, but it can be done. A four-pound test line is much safer and a six-pound test line makes it relatively easy to handle even a very large fish.

If, however, there are snags, banks of weeds, or beds of lily pads to consider, six-pound test line is definitely in order. Using lighter line where three out of five fish will wind it around the tough pads just doesn't make sense. A very light line, such as three-pound test, isn't reasonable if heavy lures are to be used, as there will be too much wear on the line at the tip and too much likelihood of its breaking when a fish strikes. A six-pound test line is light enough to cast any of the lures in the $\frac{1}{2}$ ounce or over classification.

Spinning at night with small floating plugs weighing from $\frac{1}{4}$ to $\frac{3}{8}$ ounce is extremely effective on bass and walleyes. They call for open water and good knowledge of the waters to be fished. The best time is when the night is black and, of course, fishing in pitch blackness is more difficult than when the moon or stars give their help. The actual playing of the fish is made much easier by correct adjustment of the drag.

Nightfall usually brings a dropping of the wind, a favorable circumstance for the spin fisherman, since high winds always complicate his sport. The range of spinning lures is favorable for the night fisherman, too. A bait caster, limited to large lures that hit with a splash, may often wish he had a fly rod along to drop something of smaller size to the water with a light "spat" instead. The fly fisherman often wishes he had a larger lure when the waters are rippled and the sound of his bug striking is lost in the chop of the waves. The spin caster can cover both ranges.

A weighted bass bug is just as effective when cast with a spinning rod as if it had been cast on a fly rod. Then, when the waves build up, the spinning rig will also cast a metal, wooden, or plastic lure big enough or deep-running enough to attract fish even in turbulent water.

The handling of a boat at night may require even greater caution than in the daytime. Although not as visible to the fish, it may more easily frighten them because much of the daytime noise is lost in the bustle of daylight activity and the motion of the waves. If the night is still, any movement of the water sends a ripple a long way and any solid sound within the boat will carry far.

Even in spin fishing, night fishing is not for the rank beginner. A little knowledge of casting and playing a fish is essential. To cast well in the darkness demands that a caster must have the "feel" of his tackle. His actions in casting and in retrieving must be more or less automatic. He must be able to judge by the speed of the handle how fast a lure is traveling on the retrieve. He must be able to judge by the feel of his rod how much it is bending. He must guess the whereabouts of the fish he has hooked at all times while it is being played, especially when it is near or likely to get under the boat. Without this basic familiarity with his tackle, the spin fisherman at night may have lots of excitement, but will probably take few fish.

CHAPTER 37

Fly Casting
Made Easy

THE PURPOSE of this chapter is to introduce something different in fishing—the constant-pressure method of fly casting which I originated and developed to make it possible for novice anglers to go fly fishing *and catch fish* after only an hour or two of instruction and practice.

Anglers have been taking salmon and trout with artificial flies since before Columbus discovered America. Fly tackle has changed, but the method of casting has remained much the same. The fisherman plucks his fly out of the water with an upward sweep of his rod, which tosses the line into the air behind him. He waits while the line straightens in the air, then casts with a forward and downward sweep of the rod.

Fly fishermen have been casting that way for five hundred years and more. They're still doing it. And for five hundred years and more they've been spoiling many of their casts by mis-timing their back casts and so starting their forward casts too soon or too late. They're still doing that, too.

My way of casting is a radical break from the traditional method. It shortcuts the beginning angler to fly-casting proficiency and enjoyment by keeping his line under constant pressure all the time it's in the air. Thus the forward cast may be started, without need of split-second timing, at any moment the caster chooses. With the constant-pressure system it actually is more difficult to make a poor cast than a good one.

Fly-casting technique is difficult to describe clearly in words. Years ago a woman asked me to describe it to her. I thought for a moment and asked, "Can you describe for me the taste of an apple?"

As with tasting apples, fly casting is largely something that you must actually do to get the right idea. You have to get the "feel" of it. Yet I'm sure that any person who reads this chapter carefully will be able to understand constant-pressure casting. Tests with several persons who knew nothing about fly casting have shown that this system can be quickly learned by following printed instructions. Just get out your rod and line when you reach that point and go through the prescribed motions step by step. The instructions work.

I originated the constant-pressure method of fly casting while I was operating a fishing camp at Portland Creek, north of Corner Brook in western Newfoundland. The guests who flew in to us had their hearts set on catching Atlantic salmon. Most of them were seasoned fishermen who only needed a guide to show them where fish were lying. But there were others who had no idea of how to cast a fly. A few of the novices were businessmen who'd been too busy piling up fortunes to learn fly casting—which may or may not be as important, depending on how you look at it. The wives and children of veteran salmon fishermen often came to me for casting lessons, too, because experienced anglers become too engrossed in fishing for family casting lessons.

If our guests had been seeking trout or bass I could have handed them spinning outfits, given them a few minutes' instruction, and sent them out with confidence that they'd catch something. But ours were salmon waters, and the law of Newfoundland, like the laws of all other eastern provinces of Canada, says that Atlantic salmon may be fished for in one way only—by casting with unweighted artificial flies. That rules out spinning and the other more easily learned forms of fishing. Of course a guide can hook a fish and then hand the rod to a guest, but the rule in our camp was that fishermen must hook their own salmon.

To give our unskilled guests a chance to catch a salmon we had to teach them the rudiments of fly casting in a hurry. The constant-pressure method of casting is the end result of my efforts, and those of my guides, to quickly train novices to make salmon-hooking casts.

One of my early pupils was a ten-year-old named Alice, the daughter of a prominent doctor who is an ardent salmon fisherman. She was a first-timer in Newfoundland, and never had fished anywhere, but she confided to me that she wanted to "catch a salmon all by myself."

Next morning I taught her casting by the constant-pressure method, and by noon she was making smooth casts of more than thirty feet—long enough for boat fishing. That afternoon I coached her in some other shortcuts in salmon fishing. The fish were rising to dry flies. I told her to cast and let her fly drift past her boat on the current. If she saw or felt a fish take it, she was to give her rod one quick jerk, and then hold it straight up-and-down as long as she could.

I warned her that when the fish made a run she wouldn't be able to keep the rod vertical, and told her when that happened she must take her hand away from the reel until the fish stopped. Then she'd raise the rod back to vertical and reel in all the slack she could get. With that advice I put her in a boat, pointed out the spot where she should anchor it, and went off about some camp business. At suppertime Alice came in with a twelve-pound salmon. Of course she was both precocious and lucky, but her performance demonstrates what a beginner can do with constant-pressure casting.

I have already said that constant-pressure casting is a radical departure from the time-honored conventional method. But for the benefit of readers unfamiliar with the old system, let's see what it is we're breaking away from. Let's strip fly casting down to essentials.

Flies, which are almost weightless, are propelled through the air by the motion of the fly line. Other casting systems rely on the weight of the lure, bait, or a heavy sinker to pull out line for distance, but a fly is powered only by the weight and speed of the fly line as it's swung through the air by the action of the rod.

The conventional fly cast is made up of two basic motions. The first is the back cast—an upward sweep from a horizontal position to vertical, which plucks the fly off the water and throws the line into the air behind you. Second is the forward cast—a forward and downward sweep of the rod that whips the line out over the water in such a way as to allow the fly to settle to the surface.

Those two rod motions are easily learned. The grief is in the timing, allowing precisely the right interval between the back cast and the start of the forward cast. I've never seen a novice who quickly learned to time that pause just right, and I know many fly casters who have worked for years without mastering it.

To be sure it's a clear picture we get, let's take a slow-motion look at what happens during that pause between back cast and forward cast. The upward sweep of your rod plucks your fly out of the water and throws your line into the air behind you—high above the level of your head if you have stopped the rod when you should have, in a position a few inches beyond vertical.

At this moment the rod is motionless, but the line is unrolling out of a partial loop to form a straight line behind you and more or less parallel with the ground. The instant in which the line finally straightens out and tugs back on the rod tip is the instant in which you must start your forward cast. The timing must be exact. A fly line, like an airplane, can't stand still in the air; the moment it stops moving it starts to fall.

The forward cast must start during the split second in which the line is straight behind you and pulling backward against the rod tip. If you start it a fraction too soon or too late the result will be about the same—a short, crippled cast that will dump a snaky line on the water. If you start it *much* too soon, you may snap off the fly or tangle the line. If you start it much too late, the line will have lost its tension so that it will collapse on the ground behind you or tangle into an unholy mess as it wobbles forward over your head.

You can tell a novice fly caster how to recognize this instant which arrives without warning and passes in the winking of an eye, but the beginner can't do it properly without long trial and error. The timing changes, you see, depending on the length of line that's out, the power of the back cast, the direction and force of the wind. Perhaps the best way to absorb timing is to watch your line throughout the back cast, and so learn where it goes and how long it takes to get there, but man isn't made with the sort of neck that allows him to look comfortably at back casts during normal overhead fly casting. You must eventually learn to do it by the feel of the rod and the line, and that's the most difficult thing to learn in conventional casting. Some fly casters never learn it.

The constant-pressure method of casting was evolved, in a roundabout way, from my efforts to overcome the mis-timing that hobbles beginners in casting. Constant-pressure casting doesn't require split-second timing because line is always stretched out behind the rod under pressure. Whenever the final cast is made, it's bound to be properly timed.

If you think back a few years, you'll likely remember the school pennants you waved at football games—how the felt pennant stayed straightened out in the air behind its staff while you kept the staff moving, and how the banner collapsed and drooped life-lessly the instant you stopped.

Perhaps the best way to start learning the few simple fundamentals of constant-pressure casting is for you to make the movements I am going to describe with an adaptation of the old school pennant. You can improvise one by taking any light stick about thirty inches long—a section of fishing rod is perfect—and attaching to one end of it a narrow streamer of cloth, ribbon, or roll bandage about two feet long. Wave this pennant back and forth a couple of dozen times to get the feel of its pull against the stick.

Now, instead of wig-wagging the pennant back and forth, try to swing it in a circle without turning your body. You'll find that to do so you'll have to raise your arm above your head.

From now on in, I'm assuming that you're right-handed. If you're a southpaw you'll know how to make the necessary reversals in direction. Imagine that you're standing on the center of a clock face painted on the floor. Swing your pennant *clockwise*—in the direction the hands of your imaginary clock would move. A clockwise swing seems rather awkward to most of my pupils, but the very backwardness of the motion is an advantage because it forces the student into a slow and even swing.

Keep on swinging your pennant clockwise until that direction of movement has become habitual with you—until it becomes fixed in what that ace sportswriter, the late Grantland Rice, called muscle memory. Later on I'll tell you another reason why that clockwise circling is important.

With that fundamental circling movement fixed firmly in your memory you are ready to progress to rod and line. Move outdoors where you have at least forty feet of open space around you and set up a fly rod. Any length will do, but one not more than eight feet long will be handiest. You can use a level, tapered, or torpedo-head fly line, but I recommend the torpedo-head. It casts easiest and farthest, and you are pretty certain to want one, eventually, for fishing.

Some beginners like to tie on an old fly with a broken-off hook or a bit of folded paper. That isn't necessary—you cast the line, not the fly—but it doesn't do any harm, and against some backgrounds it helps you to see what your line is doing.

Again imagine that you're standing on the center of a clock so you're facing twelve o'clock. Six o'clock is directly behind you; three o'clock to your right; nine o'clock left. Mark these hours with small stones, placing each one about fifteen feet out from the center of your crude clock face.

Pull enough line off the reel to stretch about twenty feet of it on the ground in front of you. Both rod and line should be extended toward the twelve o'clock marker. Now raise your arm above your head and, with the rod held parallel or almost parallel with the ground, start swinging it around in clockwise circles, the rod moving from twelve to three, and so on.

Keeping the rod parallel with the ground while you swing it in circles above your head may sound difficult, but you'll find that your shoulder socket, elbow, wrist, and fingers all are highly flexible joints. The line will follow the rod tip in a clockwise circle which will widen as you gradually apply more power. Try to swing the rod very steadily and smoothly. As long as you swing at even speed, the line will stream out behind the rod tip like a waved pennant. Practice until you're able to keep the line constantly in the air, and the rod continually bent under its "load" of line.

Now, with your rod loaded by the constant pressure of the line it's pulling behind it, you can make a forward cast at any instant you choose. Simply face in the direction you want to cast and then, while the line is curving behind you, sweep the rod forward and down. The line will stretch out and fall in the direction you point the rod during this final sweep. Try several of these casts.

Now you have learned to trail a fly line behind a smoothly swinging rod and to straighten it out in a short cast. Next step is to change the circle to an oval. To do that, while keeping constant pressure on the line, you must vary the intensity of that pressure by moving the rod swiftly along the almost straight sides of the oval, and less swiftly around its curved ends—as in driving a car on an oval track you might speed up on the straightaways and slow down to round the curved ends.

The ultimate object is to have the line drive forward and back with just enough width to the oval to keep a light but constant pressure on the rod tip as it curves around at the ends of its almost-straight forward and backward swings. If you keep the rod moving at just the right speed the line always will be dragging behind it, with its tip bent a little backward. You will feel this constant pull of the line. If you have any difficulty in maintaining a smooth rhythm and constant pressure of the rod on the line, revert to a slower swing around a wider oval for a few minutes, then work back to a narrow oval.

This change from circle to oval will give improved direction to your casts. To lengthen them, pull about ten feet more line off the reel and through the guides and put more power into your forward and backward drives. You are now approaching the form of conventional fly casting—but with revolutionary departures.

In conventional casting you move the line backward and forward over approximately the same air track with a switching motion of the rod, and there are moments when the line is not under pressure. In constant-pressure casting you swing the line around an elongated oval, and the line always is under pressure. In conventional casting your wrist does nearly all the work. In constant-pressure casting you rotate the line around its oval air track with a true swinging action of the rod, and your whole arm is working.

When you can keep twenty feet of line circling smoothly in the air, and you can drive that length of line out straight in front of you by giving a little flip to the rod, you have learned the fundamentals of constant-pressure fly casting. Most students can do this after thirty minutes of practice.

So far, you have been using only your right hand. But fly casting, constant-pressure as much as conventional, is a two-handed operation in which the right hand powers the rod, and the left hand controls the "shoot" of the line out through the guides, a trick that allows you to cast more line than you can conveniently keep in the air.

I suggest that in learning to use your left hand, you take the reel off your rod and place it, with plenty of slack pulled off it, on the ground at your feet. Hold a few loops of this slack line in your left hand. Make a cast. Just at the end of it, while the line still is moving forward in the air, release your hold on the slack and allow it to "shoot" through the guides—actually to be pulled through them by the momentum of the line tossed forward by the rod.

Those are the fundamentals of constant-pressure fly casting. Now let's adjust them to real fishing. You've been working your line in a horizontal plane a few feet above the level of your head. Swinging it first in a circle, then in a wide oval, finally in a long, narrow oval, you have been keeping it at a more or less uniform height above the ground.

The next—and final—step is much more difficult to describe clearly than it is to perform in actual practice. This step is to work from the overhead oval into a roughly vertical oval that is made at your right side. In other words, you gradually tilt the overhead swing, which has the line circling overhead like an elongated halo, until the oval is in the position of a rolling hoop at your right side.

At this point you'll see why I've been stressing this somewhat awkward clockwise swinging of rod and arm. It's an unnatural motion for most pupils while the line is overhead, but it smooths out as the rod arm is tilted to the right for the vertical ovals. It's the natural and necessary motion in this final step.

Practice until you have your oval swing working smoothly at your right side. The arm movement and the oval line travel are the same as they were overhead, and the constant pressure of the line on the rod's tip is maintained. You can easily see your line in this new position. Keep an eye on it.

Narrow your oval as much as you can. Now, gradually, tip it downward in front and upward in back. This will lift your back cast above most obstructions behind you. It will also lengthen your casts by making it possible for you to drive your line downward when you start your final cast from the top of the oval. A fly line has enough weight to make it travel easier and faster downhill than up.

Be careful to keep your oval as uniform as you can. Swing your rod underhand—below wrist level—at the low end of the oval. If the line isn't very low at that point in its circuit you won't be able to lift it high enough at the back of the oval. Don't fret too much about the line or fly touching the ground or water—a flick of that kind won't scare the fish you'll cast the fly to. Later on you can be perfect!

When you've got your long oval moving smoothly—snaking out low in front, lifting high behind you, moving with a steady pull on the rod—you're ready to deliver a fly. This is easy. When your line is at the height of its curve behind you, drive the rod forward and down with extra power. As the line shoots out in front of you, aim the rod *at the point* you wish to hit while fly and line settle to the water.

You can't show off among expert fly fishermen with a cast like that, but you can catch fish. And the constant-pressure caster can pick up the tricks of conventional fly casting without a lot of fishless outings and discouraging line tangles. The system's a boon for beginners.

CHAPTER 38

Spare the Rod
and Prove a Point

WHAT I WANTED TO GET was absolute proof as to how essential the rod is in playing a fish, especially a fish on a fly. I've sat in on sessions with other anglers before the fire in fishing camps and doodled on angling banquet tables while the subject of how light a rod should be or should not be has come up for the full round of discussions. Like most other factors in angling, this one is a thoroughly debatable issue and one that gets its share of attention. And, as is usually the case, there is much more debating than actual research. So I've gone a distance in making up for that lack, leading me to an interesting experiment and some final conclusions.

Fishing for bass, muskie, trout, and the rest of the American freshwater game fish has contributed to the experience on which I base my conclusions in regard to the use of light rods; the use of light tackle for the big fish of the sea has given me an understanding of the playing of all fish that I could never have attained without it. For this chapter, however, I'm going to use the Atlantic salmon to illustrate.

The Atlantic salmon, when fresh-run from the sea, is not surpassed by any other fish in freshwater as a tester of tackle and angling skill. The length of their runs, due to their life in the sea, is attested by the amount of line required on the reels of anglers who seek them, beginning around 150 yards and going upward. They are fish of the open water that depend upon their speed and strength for freedom. Weeds and snags are seldom encountered, and the battle is one of space and constant motion. The final factor is their stored-up energy, sufficient strength to see them through almost a year of starvation.

In playing a fish, the rod acts as a cushion to soften the shocks of the fish's movement on the weakest part of the tackle, which is usually the delicate leader or the grip of the hook in the fish's jaw. In a secondary measure, it acts as a lever with which to guide the fish or move him in a given direction. In considering the length of the rod in comparison with the hundreds of yards of line out when playing a marlin, for example, the length of the rod becomes insignificant.

Long ago, when I began fishing for Atlantic salmon, I used a nine-foot five-ounce fly rod. All around me were two-handed weapons, wielded almost exclusively by men who firmly believed that salmon couldn't be played successfully on rods like mine. My experience with the five-ounce rod led to the eventual use of my lightest trout rod for salmon—a two-piece 7-foot, 2½-ounce rod. In those firelight and banquet-table discussions many experienced salmon fishermen still held that the 2½-ounce rod, even more than the five-ounce rod, was incapable of handling a determined salmon and that a good "sulker" would leave me helpless.

But in 1940, the first year I used the 2½-ounce rod, none of my fish gave me special trouble, and they came in at about the same speed as on the five-ounce rod. An eighteen-pounder was my largest fish of that season, which still left room for the doubters to say, "You're just catching small ones. A thirty-pounder will show up your small rod."

Then, in 1942, a thirty-pounder clamped down on my fly and was landed in twenty-six minutes without difficulty. More than a dozen salmon of over twenty-three pounds came in on the light fly rod without trouble in that season and the season that followed. I still felt that anglers placed too much emphasis on the rod's importance in the playing of a fish and that the use of a light rod depends more on the angler's skill than the fish's toughness. So I determined to make a test that would prove my point beyond the shadow of a doubt, that year, in 1943.

I decided to land a salmon with standard fly-fishing tackle except that I would use no rod at all. To do this I might have trolled a fly behind a canoe, which would have made the hooking of a salmon a relatively simple thing. But I wanted to do it by fly casting, and to do that I needed a certain type of pool to work in. Finally, I found one that suited me.

A tall man with a good, long casting arm can cast a fly for some distance without a rod. When you stand on a smooth floor, it's simple enough to cast a standard fly line thirty feet or more by hand. The pickup is easy from a polished floor, but not nearly so easy from the water. What I needed was a salmon pool with a rock at its head on which I could stand to cast with salmon lying near that rock. In addition, I needed a steady flow to straighten the line out quickly and hold it near the surface for an easy pickup. Those conditions were all met by the Seal Pool on Newfoundland's Southwest River.

The water bends in close to a big rock at the head of the pool and grows deeper as the stream bed hollows out with the slowing down of the flow. There, in the deepening water, the salmon lie. My tackle consisted of a No. 8 low-water type Dark Cahill, a six-foot leader of about 2½-pound breaking strain, an HCH nylon fly line, and 120 yards of braided nylon backing on my 3⅜-inch fly reel. That was all. The short leader was a concession to the need for keeping the fly near the surface; a longer leader is more difficult to cast. The pool had not been fished earlier that season and I hoped the fish wouldn't be too wary.

I took a long time in getting out to my position on the rock. My movements were slow and deliberate, and I remained motionless on the rock for a little while before I made my first cast. Then, holding the reel in my left hand and using my right arm for a rod, I began to cast while Pfc. Carl Lowe of a U.S. Army Search and Rescue Unit manned my camera and Charlie Bennett, guide extraordinary, looked on.

My first cast took the fly out about twenty-five feet, and it swung in a good arc on the retrieve. On about the third cast a fish swirled behind the fly and took a good look at it. He must have seen me in my exposed position on the rock, too, because he failed to rise again, and eventually I lengthened line and fished the water below his position. After a dozen more casts another salmon rose, taking the fly in his mouth just far enough to be pricked but not hooked solidly as the line tightened.

Reeling in, I slid down from the rock to wade ashore and give the water a rest before trying again. Near the shore, I slipped and went to my knees on a jagged rock, tearing my waders at the knee.

By the time I had taken off my waders and hung them up to dry, it was time to try again so I waded out to the rock, this time without benefit of waders, to make a second try. The rise was not long in coming, and I found myself fast to a flashing, leaping salmon that was off on a good run down the pool to the deep, slow water. My reel went over to my right hand and I let the fish take line freely. He wound up the run that carried him well into the backing with a couple of tumbling leaps as a final flourish and swung into the current again to work upstream toward me.

Then my left hand moved up to where my right hand was held high in imitation of a fly rod, and the fingers picked up the reel handle. I took in line. It was almost as if I'd been using a light rod as far as the effect on the fish was concerned. I moved my arm forward and back to help take up slack or give line speedily. The nylon line, resilient and springy, helped my arm and body movements in absorbing the sudden shocks at the salmon's end of our connection. Slowly the backing came back onto the reel, and the fly-casting line began to pile up on top of it. The salmon's first wild run and his sudden rushes had been safely met, and from there on his movements would be more predictable.

I took in line when I could, gave it when I had to, and dropped my playing arm when the salmon broke water in his spray-scattering leaps. There was, as I had anticipated, little difference in playing a fish in this manner and playing one with my light fly rod. From long experience I sensed when his runs would start and when they'd end and when he'd roll and go into a sort of underwater dance with its attendant head-shaking. Each time I was ready with the move to neutralize his action. In seven minutes he had unwound his bag of tricks and found none that worked. He was in close and groggy.

In this sport of catching fish I like to do the entire job myself. A fish is often tricked into coming within reach of another individual who snags him with a gaff, which does not give a true picture of the ability of one man to take one fish on certain tackle in a certain amount of time. I wanted to leave no loopholes; so I decided to land this one the hard way—by myself and by hand-tailing without the benefit of gaff, tailer, or sandy beach.

Charlie had been making grunts of satisfaction on the bank. Carl, who had alternated between taking pictures of me on the rock and trying to get the fish in the air on one of his leaps, moved in closer as the range of action narrowed down.

The salmon was visibly weary. He had run and leaped himself out, just as any other fish does when properly played, tiring himself with his own efforts, not being killed by the leverage of the rod. He headed in under the rock, and I leaned far out over the edge to put on the pressure required to make him angle off into the open water again. The current picked him up and swung him sideways, the long, silvery line of his belly flashing in the dull light of approaching evening. He came in again, and I held his head higher so that he slid against the rock on a slant that led him to the surface. The solid rock jarred him when he struck it and he whirled away, half leaping. When he stopped, I put the pressure on and led him in again.

All the line and part of the leader had passed in through the line guard of the reel when I shifted it from my right hand to my left and went down on one knee. With my right hand I reached out to let my fingers get into position to close on the narrow point at the base of his tail. At the right moment I clamped down in a hard grip and held.

Some anglers claim that this tail grip has a paralyzing effect on the fish's spine. Whether that's true or not, I know that most fish properly hand-tailed offer little resistance and don't begin to kick up much fuss until the grip is released and they drop to the earth or to the bottom of the canoe. This fish was like that, quiet until I dropped him on the sandy shore.

He weighed almost ten pounds, and the time it took to bring him in was just shy of ten minutes. This was, I believe, the first time this feat has ever been performed, and it leads to inescapable conclusions. The first of them is that a rod is not essential to the proper playing of a fish. Instead, the rod is more nearly essential in casting the fly within reach of the fish.

Few of the thousands of salmon I've seen could have been hooked without the aid of a rod, but the big majority of them could have been landed, as that one was, without a rod. Therefore, in choosing the rod the skilled angler should make his choice on the basis of the casting distance required rather than the size of the fish that must be handled on it.

As for a fair evaluation of the rod's position in fly fishing, it depends upon the stream to be fished and the individual who is doing the fishing. The rod must be capable of getting the fly out to the water in which fish are lying. One man may need a much longer rod than another who is a better caster. A tall man has the advantage over a short one in the use of short, light rods.

The rod is of great aid in taking up slack quickly when playing a fish and in absorbing the shock of the fish's sudden starts or in giving adequate slack for his leaps. The less capable the angler is in sensing these maneuvers of the fish in advance and the poorer are his powers of coordination in making the necessary adjustments, the longer the rod he will need to make up for that lack.

To be able to fish with a very light rod or no rod at all is an achievement, but it doesn't prove that the use of the very lightest possible rod or no rod at all is a sensible way to fish. The rod to choose is one that balances the individual's skill, his need for long casts, and the amount of fatigue he wants to put up with in his fishing day. If he casts hour after hour through the long days of June, a light rod with line to balance it is a blessing. He can wind up at twilight with his arm as fresh as when he started. His sacrifice will have been in passing up the chance of reaching fish that the extra distance of a longer rod would have reached, or the slight advantage he'd have gained in leverage to guide a fish or keep the line free from obstructions while the fish was being played.

The ability to get around in a stream to the proper playing position determines to a large extent what sort of tackle the angler needs. Those tough sulkers become just ordinary fish when the fisherman stays downstream of them and keeps the pressure on them to a point where they're using up energy rapidly, whether they stay in one spot or move off. For the angler whose canoeman doesn't want to bother to move him to the right position or to the man whose legs and wading ability won't get him around the stream in good shape, a rod of fair length and tackle of fair strength is a necessity if many fish are to be saved.

It all boils down to individual ability, and even in the case of the most gifted angler, there is a limit to the lightness of the rod which is dictated by casting distance required and wind that must be bucked or other casting difficulties. If an angler insists on fishing with a rod that is too weak to give him an opportunity to reach a number of fish roughly equal to that reached by his neighbors, he's handicapping himself, with his only possible gain lying in being able to cast for a longer time.

If he wants to prove he can perform a certain light-rod feat, the thing to do is to accomplish that feat enough times to satisfy himself as to his ability and then settle back to use the tackle that will give him the greatest pleasure yet won't cut his chances of hooking fish. And these conclusions, I believe, hold for all types of angling.

CHAPTER 39

Tips on Bait Casting

THE BEGINNER at bait casting is likely to be amazed and confused by the apparent complexity of the sport. Shop windows are loaded with lures. Their racks are lined with rods in varying lengths and strengths. The showcases sparkle with a wide variety of reels, lines, and kindred items. But bait casting need be no more complex than any individual wishes to make it.

Here are some suggestions which should help the novice start out on a sound, fish-producing basis. Later, when he has mastered the elements of this style of fishing, he may well branch out into a second and a third rod—spare lines and reels—and a multitude of casting lures, but in his first season he needs only a simple outfit and a desire to learn to use it well.

The choice of a rod should depend upon the waters to be fished and on the fish for which it will be used. Hard-fished waters call for a little more finesse and that means smaller and lighter lures, and the obvious choice is for a longer, lighter rod. A 5½-footer will do well for civilized fishing. Little-fished waters yield excellent catches to large and heavy lures, and an angler going into the wilds will gain from the extra splash and commotion the big lures make.

A 4½- or 5-foot rod will cast heavy lures easily and is somewhat easier to pack and carry. The species of fish to be caught is a qualifying factor. Northern pike or muskies respond to larger lures than do smallmouth bass, pickerel, and walleyes. The lighter the lures, the longer the rod and vice versa. A five-foot rod is a good choice for general fishing or for those who are not certain where they'll fish.

The strength of the line is dictated by the weight of the lure. A fifteen-pound test line should be adequate for any bait casting. The knowledge that there's a fifteen-pound upper limit on his tackle pressure should make the novice a bit more careful and thereby cause him to play his fish out completely instead of horsing them in, with the end result that he will land a very large percent-age of the fish he hooks. For the lighter lures, a line of ten-pound test or less will give better distance in the casts. This does not mean that fewer fish will be landed. Actually, the reverse is true. It figures out this way.

The number of times a fish is lost through line breakage is not great. At least five fish break the hook hold for every line that is broken. By using a light line and playing the fish carefully, many lightly hooked fish are saved instead of lost; and even if the lines were broken twice as often while playing fish (which is not prob-able), the net catch will be greater. More than that, since the lighter line permits longer and more accurate casts, more fish should be hooked, another factor favoring a larger catch.

The reel should be as good as one can afford. It should be level winding and, especially for the beginner, it should have a backlash-reducing feature. Any good reel of reputable manufacture will turn in a creditable performance, a factor that holds true right down the tackle line. It's wise to remember that the difference in efficiency between an average rod and the very best one is not likely to be more than a few percentage points, although the dif-ference in satisfaction and pleasure derived from its use may be very great. The beginner only needs tackle of good design and quality which will send his lures out to the fish and let him play them when they're hooked. The rest can come later. His chief concern should not be acquiring special or extra tackle, but having a good, dependable outfit and learning how to use it.

He needs only a minimal number of lures; I believe he will gain more by having only a few lures of the right type and then learning when to use them and why each is effective under certain conditions. To walk into a tackle store with hundreds of shining lures on display and pick out a dozen doesn't sound easy, but it is. Here's the system.

Lures fall into basic categories. There are floaters, divers, and sinking lures . . . and there are lures that work best slowly and others that need a swift retrieve for best action. Two floaters should be enough. Pick a small one with a lot of action when retrieved slowly, and a normal-sized one with good action but so designed that it will have good action when used under a burst of speed as well as slowly. We have ten left to choose.

For the novice the diving plug is a good one. If he does suffer a backlash (and even the experts backlash more often than they admit), these lures will float patiently where they land until the bird's nest has been untangled. When they are retrieved they dive under the surface with varying actions but rise again to the surface whenever the retrieve is stopped. Half a dozen diving lures should do the trick.

Two small ones, two of medium size, and two full-sized plugs make a balanced group. Two of them should be backward traveling plugs that will run deep. One of the larger ones should be of the long, narrow or pikie shape. Two should travel just under the surface or at slight depth and have a lot of action at slow speed. There should be one with a wide and flashy action which is excellent for open water but poor near any weeds.

Of the four sinking lures that round out the selection, two should be plugs and two made of metal. The sinking plugs should be designed to go deep and stay there. Both should have good action at slow speeds and be on the small side, varying more in shape and color than in action. Of the metal lures, make one a wobbling spoon and the other a weedless, flashy lure with a rubber skirt or pork rind or bucktail trailing behind it. If the waters to be fished are very weedy, add one or two weedless metal lures to the list and cut down on the diving plugs.

When it comes to colors, red and white, black and white, a variety of natural scale finishes, and the shine of metal will be enough to take fish. Any tackle salesman can help to fit a choice of lures to this description. With this assortment, if one does not catch fish, it is either a temporary thing that will pass with the varying moods of the fish or else the right choice is not being made from this limited group of lures.

Surface lures are best when the waters are calm and especially when fish are seen feeding near the surface. The usual pattern of surface fishing is to let the lure lie motionless for a second or two after it strikes the water, then move it toward the boat in a series of short twitches. Shallow-traveling lures should be retrieved at the speed which gives them the greatest amount of action. Deep-traveling divers must be reeled swiftly to get the maximum depth, but sinking lures should be given a pause after they land to let them settle down to the desired depth and then should be retrieved slowly enough to maintain that depth.

The preferred casting method is the overhead cast, but if you like to use a sideswing and your partner (if you have one) doesn't object, you may be sure it will make no difference to the fish. Distance is not essential in casting unless the fisherman is noisy. Short casts from a boat that moves quietly without splash of water or thump of oarlocks are effective. Except under low and very clear water conditions, long casts are essential only for the noisy angler.

Accuracy in casting is important where there are submerged logs, lily pads, rocky ledges, overhanging trees, and similar good fish-resting places. In the open waters, accuracy is unimportant, and in many lakes where fishing is done over a bottom of more or less uniform depth and character, success is simply a matter of covering as much water as possible with a lure the fish will take. For this reason, a lake with wide areas of water under twelve feet deep where plugs will be effective is a good one for a beginner to choose.

The choice of a lure is a major decision. It may be made by picking the one you like best to start with, then whenever fifteen minutes elapse without a strike, change to one of the remaining eleven until they've all been tried. If the strike comes on deep traveling lures, stick to that type, and if they come to lures on or near the surface, keep working that level. It's a good idea to set up a particular speed or manner of retrieve for each lure so that as they are changed, the speed and action of the retrieve are changed as well.

This is a much better system than that of changing lures but maintaining the same speed and style of retrieve for all of them. Later on, when new lures are added to the list, they can be retrieved according to the category in which they fall, whether slow and deep, fast and deep, slow on top or whatever.

Fishing from a boat is better than fishing from the shore, except on the smaller rivers. Fishing from a boat is easier when there is one to row and one to fish. Three in a boat is dangerous and not as productive of fish for each individual angler. A companion who will row quietly, slowly, and endlessly without complaining or asking for a chance to fish is a bait caster's dream. Fishing half the time and rowing the other half, the usual procedure, will usually give each of two casters more fish and more fun than if they fished alone either from a boat or from shore.

Under certain conditions, a lone fisherman in a boat can catch more fish than if he shared the oars and fishing time with a partner. When fishing the open water with a light wind blowing, a solitary angler can row or motor upwind and then cast continually as he drifts across the likely water. In this way he can fish about ninety percent of the time instead of fifty. If he has a wide and stable boat and an outboard motor which will move it very slowly, he can cruise along at the right speed and maintain the proper casting distance from shore with only an occasional touch of the controls by his left hand. A flick of the finger stops the motor or throws it into neutral when a fish is hooked.

When a game fish strikes an artificial lure, the angler should lift the rod sharply in a strike while at the same time holding the line solidly. The spring of the rod and the stretch of the line must be overcome with sufficient force to sink the hooks in beyond the barbs. The strike must be hard enough to set the hooks but not hard enough to break the line.

The strike is purely for the purpose of setting the hook and is a sudden, sharp movement of very short duration. It is rare that a line is broken at this point unless its hard pressure is maintained too long. When sufficient pressure to set the hooks has been delivered, the fisherman must be prepared to relax quickly and let the fish run more or less freely on his first surge. To hold back hard at the strike is to court disaster. Strike swiftly, and immediately relax the pressure to a normal playing strain.

In playing a fish, a light pressure should be maintained. The angler's reel permits him to give line freely whenever the fish pulls hard. If a fish breaks an angler's line it is almost always because the angler held on instead of giving line. It is better to give line too quickly than too late, better to play a fish ten minutes and land him than to lose him by trying to bring him in in five. Normally time is on the angler's side and a few extra minutes of playing will land more fish than they will lose. However, there is such a thing as playing a fish too long. Only time and practice will bring top judgment in this department.

A fish hooked on a bait-casting lure will frequently try to shake it free. Because these lures are weighty, the effort is often successful. The angler's best bet is to tighten up to the limit of his tackle's strength when a fish leaps or starts headshaking. This is the one time when the angler should hold as hard as he dares.

More fish are lost at the net than at any other time of the struggle. That's when the angler should be most careful and never rush things. The fish should be brought to the net, not the net to the fish; and until he's tired enough to bring to the net, no attempt should be made to land him. The safest course is to lead the tired fish over the net. If the pressure on the rod is then relaxed, nine times out of ten he'll sink right down into it. If he doesn't sink down but darts away, he should simply be worked in for another try. Sweeping a net toward a fish frightens him. He's naturally uneasy about any large object near him in the water but less likely to be afraid of something that's motionless.

The bait caster must remember that where multiple hooks are used there may be some points protruding around the fish's mouth which can catch in the meshes of the net. If it isn't certain the fish will be secured in the net, no attempt should be made, because if a hook does catch in the mesh and the fish remains outside the net, he's almost certain to tear free.

Nets are not always essential in landing fish. Pike, muskies, or large pickerel may be picked up by a grip of thumb and finger in the eye sockets. Bass can be lifted into the boat by putting the thumb inside the open mouth and gripping with the bent index finger under the lower jaw. In using either of these methods great care should be taken if the lure has more than one hook point. One hook in the hand and another hook on the same plug fast to a still-active bass spells real trouble. Walleyes are harder to handle. They have longer teeth than bass and are not easily handled by either mouth or eye grip.

There are fish in most of the waters we fish that are too big for our landing nets. Although such monsters are few and consequently are rarely hooked, when one of them does give the angler a real thrill (and the chance of a lifetime to catch one he needn't lie about), a knowledge of what to do can mean the difference between disaster and success. The playing of such a trophy to near exhaustion and particularly the final step of landing him present a most difficult problem.

To miss a fish on your first try with the net is to court disaster. If the whopper takes a multiple-hooked lure, one of the open points may catch in the net and give him the chance at the solid pull he's been hoping for to break free. The slightest pressure of the net against a tightly drawn leader may be just the extra force required to tear the hook out.

A fish brought to the net without having been played to complete exhaustion can summon up strength for a sudden surge that will carry him under the boat or down into the weeds or snags. This last wild dart is probably the moment when more fish are lost than at any other point in the conflict.

When the anxious moments of playing a big fish seem almost over it's natural for an angler to begin to press his luck a little.

When, after half an hour or longer, an old lunker is almost within your reach, each second that he remains uncaptured seems like an hour, and the temptation to rush him a little bit to get the agony over with becomes practically overwhelming. But when your trophy of a lifetime looms up at close range, there's extra need for cool-headedness and caution. The final moments are the most dangerous of all and that's when your timing and skill should be perfect.

If the fish is too big for your net, you'll have to handle him in a special way and in all probability using a method with which you've had little experience. Assume that you're in a boat and you hook a fifteen-pound walleye. He's fast to a Pikie Minnow and when he looms up beside the boat, long and greenish with that white tail-tip gleaming, you notice that only the middle hook is caught in the corner of his mouth and that the fore and aft trebles are swinging free.

You might be able to get his head and the forepart of his body into your small landing net and swing him up into the boat before he has a chance to flop free . . . and again you might not. You might try to sweep him into the net tailfirst and count on the extra lift you could give with the arch of the rod to get him into the boat . . . but this method fails more times than it succeeds. You might reach down and put your thumb into his open mouth, but if you did you'd run the risk of having one of the hooks sink into your hand and you'd be certain to be cut by the fish's teeth. Even in spite of the hooks and the teeth, you'd run a good chance of losing the fish by having him slip or twist from your grip.

There are better ways to do it. The simplest one is to go ashore and slide him up on the beach or out onto the rocks if the shore isn't too distant. In this beaching process the line or leader is seldom strong enough to drag the fish up onto dry ground. If the shore is sloping this can be accomplished by a steady pressure within the tackle's safe limits. By his flopping and twisting the fish will help a lot in getting ashore. He's headed shoreward and struggles tend to drive him forward rather than to the rear.

Often it's necessary to use one hand to help slide him out. A grip around the tail will push him forward in conjunction with the pull of the line. A good grip on his gill cover will serve to drag him high and dry. A well-placed kick may not be very sporting but it has been known to hoist a hefty fish from his native element well up the bank.

I know of one very large fish that was boated by the simple

expedient of playing him to exhaustion, bringing him to the side of the boat and then tipping the boat partway under water so that the big fish and about a third of a boatload of water came pouring over the side. It took a lot of bailing to reorganize things but it was worth it.

A grip of forefinger and thumb in the eye sockets of a big pike or muskie is common practice with many guides. A grip into the gills by thumb and forefinger from above will work on many large fish. A grip in the gills from beneath while the fish is in the water is tricky and more difficult. None of these methods is worth a darn unless the fisherman is skillful with his tackle and has played the fish to a point where he's helpless.

A method of safeguarding your catch is available if you have another rod rigged up in the boat or even if you have a spare reel handy and can fasten a plug or any kind of hook to the end of the line. When the fish is played out and can be held close to the boat, it's possible to set another hook into his jaw or body by hand or by the use of the rod. Then, with two lines fast to your fish, you'll be reasonably sure to maintain contact with him. If one of the two lines comes free, it can be reset into his jaw quickly, and the chance of both lines coming loose simultaneously is slim. With two lines fast to a fish, he can be held beside the boat and towed to shore or slid in over the gunwale with the aid of even a small net or a hand under a gill cover.

The stream fisherman fast to such a big fish may have to travel a long way downriver to find a quiet eddy where the bank is sloping or where the water is still enough to permit gripping the fish by hand or using the net to push him out onto dry land. In all these maneuvers the possibility of their failure must be borne in mind. The first attempt may be foiled by a sudden movement of the fish, but if the angler has used good judgment, nothing will strike the line or the lure. The fish will still be on the line and a second try will be coming up. Each try should be made with a possible retreat in mind that will permit another try and still another until the quarry is finally secured.

These suggestions assume that there's no gaff available. A sturdy gaff, even though small, can be used to bring in even the biggest of freshwater fish that have been played to exhaustion. Tailers, especially designed for Atlantic salmon, are more certain and more humane than a gaff but will only work on fish with a stiff tail. The best gaffing spot on a fish depends upon several factors. If the gaff is small, it's best to sink it into the lower jaw from underneath or into the back of the head from above and to the side.

If the gaff is normal for the size of the fish, it is best to gaff at the center of the body from across the back with the point down. There's a trick to gaffing, too. The same motion that sinks the steel into the flesh should lift him into the boat. The movement should be steady and smooth. It is easy enough for a fish to tear free from the gaff's grip if that instrument is held too rigidly or moved too swiftly. It's a strike that's well directed and hard enough to sink the gaff to its full depth, followed by a smooth carry-through, that is required to bring in the fish.

Although these mammoth fish rarely come the way of the average angler, it is of such stuff that dreams are made. It's nice to feel that you're equipped to handle the biggest fish that swims the waters you fish. A spare 10/0 hook on a short length of heavy line will do for a gaff in a pinch. The line can serve to lash the big hook to an oar or a net handle and even if there's no handle handy the big hook can be set by hand and the heavy line given a turn around the wrist to haul the fish in. If you're in waters that provide big fish frequently, an extra-sized net or a spare gaff is worth the trouble it takes to have it available. Don't forget, though, that if you're resourceful you've an excellent chance of landing your super-lunker on your ordinary fishing gear.

CHAPTER 40

How to Play a Fish
on a Fly Rod

To PLAY EVERY FISH he hooks without a single error is a fisherman's dream quite unattainable by mortal man, but to play a fish reasonably well is within the scope of anyone who can drive a car, sail a boat, or fly a plane. The angler's chances of landing his larger fish may depend a little on luck but a whole lot more on what he knows.

The fisherman's fly is a small steel hook camouflaged to look like something a game fish will take into his mouth. The fly rod is a delicately tapered length of split bamboo, metal, or fiberglass capable of driving out the almost weightless fly by means of the weight of the line. The smooth-running fly reel must hold without tangle that portion of the line not in active use. The line, soft and comparatively heavy, is the main connection between fish and angler. The leader, usually nylon monofilament, divorces the fly from the bulky, easily visible line and is the nearest thing to strong and supple nothingness many generations of anglers and scientists have been able to produce. These are the fly caster's tools. With them he must play the swift and powerful fish he hooks, parrying every run and leap, until at last they can no longer resist the delicate pull of the tackle and are captured.

The leader is the most fragile link in the tackle chain. An understanding of the exact rod pull required to break a leader of given size can be achieved much better by practicing with the fly hooked into the back fence than by learning the hard way with the fly hooked into the jaw of the biggest fish in the river in a game that's for keeps. Having learned the maximum safe pull, the angler should plan to maintain that much pressure whenever his fish isn't running or leaping. A freshly hooked fish can move like lightning and when he does there must be no drag to hold the line back. For perfection the angler's reaction must be fast enough to release all pressure for the runs and leaps, hold to the maximum safe strain when the fish is static, and so vary the pressure in between that the strain on the leader is always just under the safe limit.

The hold of the hook cannot be used as a gauge for proper pressure because the angler has no way of knowing how well a fish is hooked until that fish finally is either landed or lost. Normally, the hook's hold is stronger than the accompanying leader and the angler must work on that basis. If the hook pulls out and the fish escapes that's tough luck but not a playing error. On the other hand, when a leader breaks during the battle, either the angler exceeded his known limitations or permitted the fish to do it, and deserves a mark in the error column.

At the strike when the fish speeds away on a long run, the angler's first problem is to absorb the jarring shock of this sudden change from inactivity to high speed, a jolt great enough to break the leader before the fight has really started if there is even a momentary solid resistance for the fish to work against. Such a shock must be parried by the rod, and as the sudden pressure mounts, the rod bends with a cushioning effect until the inertia of the line and reel has been overcome. Once the line has started to follow the fish and the spool is turning, the strain on the leader relaxes and the main danger comes from the possibility of jamming the line at a guide or a tangle on the reel.

There's a common belief that the one important rule in playing a fish is to "keep the rod up." That's like driving a car in second gear. It may be necessary part of the time, but it's a slow way to travel and no way to win a race. The rod will absorb sudden shocks and should be held high when shocks are to be expected. When the fish is running swiftly, the rod should point toward him, the only hitch being that an angler whose reflexes aren't fast enough to get it back up again the moment the fish stops or turns can't get away with lowering his rod at all. Fish will run farther, tire more quickly, and leap with less chance of escaping if the rod is held low at the time. The extra drag of a high rod against a swift-running fish may be just enough to part an already stretched leader.

Any fish capable of making swift runs of more than twenty feet should be played directly from the reel. The fisherman's first reactions at the strike should be to see that his tip is up and make sure that any line coiled in his left hand for casting can flow out through the guides freely in case the fish decides upon an instantaneous run. If the expected run fails to materialize, the loose line should be wound back onto the reel. After the line leads directly from the reel to the first guide, there still remains the danger of a backlash if the tension is faulty and the reel overruns.

When a fish leaps, he poses another problem. The spurt to the surface just preceding the jump must be absorbed by the rod like the start of a long run, but the leap itself calls for the rod to be lowered quickly and extended toward the fish in order to gain every possible inch of slack. Flies and fly-rod lures are normally light in weight and give the fish little chance of shaking them free. Slack line under these conditions is not as dangerous as the possibility of having an aviating fish come tight against a stationary spool and line.

Most of the swift, erratic underwater movements of a hooked fish call for a delicate touch and a rod so lifted that its arc may increase or flatten under the varying pressures and maintain a continuous but always moderate tension. A fish that goes berserk to the extent of a series of sub-surface somersaults and barrel rolls can only be handled by prayer and as much slack line as is possible without lowering the rod more than halfway down to the fish. An old lunker that resorts to continuous vicious headshaking is the most difficult of all fish to play. He wastes little effort, tires slowly, and no other maneuver will loosen a hook or cut through its fleshy hold more swiftly than this rapid alternating of heavy pressure and complete slack. Most heavy headshakers escape. The angler's best bet is to scare them into making a few tiring runs or leaps by wading close, pulling hard from downstream, or even throwing stones as a last resort.

The danger of fouling the line on the rocks or snags can be minimized by staying as close to the fish as possible. The shorter the distance from fish to fisherman, the greater is the angler's control over both line and fish. The danger of fouling the leader in a snag occurs when the fish definitely heads for a bed of weeds, a sunken log, or something similar. That is the time to bring the leader strain right up to within an ace of the breaking point with the rod held high. If that fails to work, there is nothing to do but let the fish drive ahead without increasing that pressure.

The most important single factor in the playing of a fish in moving water may be the angler's ability to wade or the guide's ability to handle the canoe. The angler's position has a constant importance and tends to become the deciding factor between success and failure. Fish should always be played from a downstream angle within which the current aids the fisherman and not the fish. The fish must fight not only the full pull of the tackle but buck the current as well when he is played from below. If the fish gets down-current from the angler he can turn his body sideways to the flow and, with almost no effort, put a terrific strain on the tackle. To play a fish at a downstream angle is to give him a chance to rest and recuperate . . . and perhaps escape.

Fish are exhausted only by their own efforts. No amount of towing them around will tire them in the least, unless they resist. The wild runs and leaps encouraged by the variable pressure of light tackle take more energy than dogged resistance to a steady, heavy-tackle pull. The angler's job is to keep the game fish constantly on the move. A solid pressure often leads a fish to settle down and seek a truce while he figures out his next move; a light, constantly changing tension can drive him to distraction and early exhaustion.

There's a psychological side to playing fish, too. Like a human, if a fish can be convinced of the futility of resistance, he'll quit. When first hooked and at the peak of his power, a big fish cannot be stopped or even slowed down without danger of breaking the tackle. After the first run or two has been made and the extreme wildness is out of the fish's system, a knowing angler can sometimes figure out just how far a hooked fish can run before exhaustion will make him pause. If the fisherman can bear down on the fish heavily as he reaches that point for two or three runs in a row, it will convince the fish that whatever has hold of him can stop him at will, no matter how hard he tries to escape. But if the angler misjudges and has to let the fish break through his tackle pressure, it will give his quarry encouragement and keep him fighting.

Time is an important factor in the playing of a fish. Every minute a fish remains in the water is a minute in which escape is possible. The longer an angler must take to tire out a fish on a given leader, the less he has to be proud of. Long fights are usually filled with dull periods of stalling during which the angler is either afraid to use his tackle up to proper strength or fails to reach the right playing position. When a big-game fish is played out swiftly by a capable angler, every second is filled with excitement and action.

The word "never" may rarely be used in reference to as inexact a science as fishing, yet it is safe to say that a fly rod is never broken while playing a fish unless it is defective or unless the angler is at fault. One cause of rod breakage is failure to give slack when the fish demands it. The fisherman has a reel with plenty of line on it in order to let a fish run freely when he's too hot to hold. If the angler freezes the line too long and a rod break results, the fault lies with the angler for failure to release the pressure and gives him another mark in the error column.

The major cause of broken rods is the failure to keep the angle of the rod within 90° of a line from the reel to the fish. It is a practical impossibility to break a rod within this quadrant; beyond it, rods will snap easily. The greatest tendency to use an obtuse angle comes when the fish is in close, because so many anglers hold their rod butts against the body instead of at arm's length away from the fish. Then if a seemingly beaten fish makes a sudden surge, the rod snaps.

A right-handed angler should use his strong hand for the rod, a job requiring the greatest strength and control, and give the lesser task of reeling to his weaker left hand. Right-handers who have never tried left-hand reeling will find it simple enough after a few days' practice. Under this system, the rod never leaves the right hand whether casting or playing a fish. Gripped by the strong hand, there is greater freedom of movement than if the rod is held against the body for normal right-hand reeling.

The final moments of any fight with a fish are usually the toughest. There is a tendency to become tired and overanxious and to count the fish a little closer to complete exhaustion than he really is. Every fish should be played right through until he's safely ashore or in the boat; a fish being brought to the net, tailer, or gaff should always be played as if he still has another run or leap left in him.

Any fish slated for the frying pan or living room wall may well be played to complete surrender, but anglers who have come to realize the truth of the saying, "A game fish is too valuable to be caught only once," should remember that the longer a fish is played, the smaller his chance of survival when released.

CHAPTER 41

Using Featherweight Rods

FLY FISHERMEN have long believed that very light rods are not only hard to handle but won't make long casts. That used to be true, but modern techniques have made the featherweight fly rod much easier to use and have increased its range greatly. Important in these techniques is full use of the arm in casting.

Some years ago, in writing my *Handbook of Freshwater Fishing,* I described fly casting much as everyone else did, emphasizing movement of the wrist rather than of the arm, and warning against bringing the rod back much past the vertical on the back cast. At that time I had only limited experience with featherweight fly rods of 2 to 2½ ounces (scale weight of the complete rod). But since then, consistent, season-long fishing with such rods has convinced me that light rods are not only practical but that best results will be obtained with them when full use is made of the casting arm. Limiting the rod to the vertical point on the back cast, I've found, hinders rather than helps the cast.

In the traditional method, length and stiffness of the rod provide the casting power. And since the combined weight of the longer rod and the line-filled reel is great enough to make full-arm movement fatiguing, casting is achieved by wrist motion. (Almost every fly fisherman has been told that the perfect caster can hold a book against his body with the elbow of his casting arm while he's in action.) But with short rods the limited power of the wrist simply isn't great enough to throw a light line.

A second factor favoring the use of lighter gear is the improvement of rod materials in the past quarter-century. The impregnation of bamboo with bakelite, and the development of fine rods of glass fiber have given us lightness *and* durability. Glass fiber has the greatest strength for its weight, but there is a certain delicacy that's combined with power in split bamboo. Glass rods are more uniform, more durable.

In light rods it is the continuous casting, rather than the playing of fish, that causes deterioration and breakage. I enjoy casting and always work my rods relatively hard. And I cast them to the limit of my strength whenever there's a particularly distant spot I want to reach. In the past I could count on only about one month of life for a very light rod. Now they stand up, season after season, with practically no breakage.

A third factor lengthening the casts of short fly rods is the forward-taper fly line. Its advantage over the old double-taper comes only when the line really begins to stretch out and thirty-five feet or more are off the reel. Then the lighter line gets extra distance with the same amount of effort. Extra distance over a normal cast isn't so important with the usual 8½- or 9-foot rod, but the long "shoot" permitted by the forward-taper line makes it possible to reach out to all normal fishing distances with a rod of seven feet or less.

Obviously, the casting power of any fly rod is mainly limited by the weight of line it will handle in the air. And weight for weight, you get more line out with the featherweight outfit. However, there is a weight limit for any outfit. But supposing it's reached at fifty-five feet, say, you can still add length to the casts, and yet not overstrain the rod by using a long leader and learning how to snap it out.

Long leaders (mine range from ten to twenty-five feet) will extend the line's maximum casting distance by about eighty percent of their length. Under the old elbow-at-side casting motion, it was difficult to straighten out a leader, but with the full-arm motion—aided when necessary by a sharp pull-back of rod arm, line, or both—a very long leader can be straightened out completely.

Often there is an obstruction on the bank which limits the back cast and thereby limits the forward cast as well. But by bringing the line in low, and lifting it upward as it completes the back cast, you get good clearance above the ground or water at a point where you need it most. Thus you can get a full back cast at practically all times. When, under the same circumstances, the tail end of the back cast is lower—as it must be in the orthodox cast, when the line stays on a fairly level plane throughout—it seriously affects the length of the back cast and, consequently, that of the forward cast as well.

Another advantage of a high back cast is that it makes the forward cast easier. The force of gravity is always with us and it is easier to throw a line down than up. The forward cast from a high back cast is downhill, therefore easier and longer, pulling out many more feet of line.

Still another advantage of the high back cast is that it makes the forward cast low. A low forward cast leads to better fishing. It is more accurate, since the point of aim of the cast is closer to the water it is to land on. There is no gentle drifting down of the fly to the surface from a point six or eight feet above it. (When such a drop is desirable it can always be managed.) And casting a fly to within a few inches of its point of contact with the water is helpful when the wind is blowing. A strong breeze will blow any light fly and leader away from where you want it to land if there's much space between it and the water.

The low cast, essential for accuracy in a wind, is good at any time and worth using as a matter of normal form instead of only on special occasions. I've observed friends who were having difficulty casting in strong winds. They could shoot a very limited amount of line into the wind, and of course that's all that's necessary when wind-roughened water prevents the fish from seeing an angler at a distance.

Almost invariably they'd put their false cast to within inches of the point they wanted to reach. But then they'd let habit take over on their final cast, ending it several feet above the water, and the wind would blow it anywhere from five to fifteen feet away. I showed them how to make their final cast exactly like a false cast, down to the water, and drop the rod forward the instant the fly reached the aiming spot, just over the water. Doing that, they could cast accurately into the wind, and they took fish.

To save effort, the pickup of the forward cast should be made with a typical roll-cast motion, pulling the fly to the surface, then picking it up immediately for the start of the back cast. This is a good labor-saving trick used by many fly casters. The angler with a featherweight rod will often have need of it.

Short rods will not pick up as much line as longer ones of the same proportionate power. This means more line must be retrieved before the successful pickup can be made. Overloading the rod on a pickup usually spoils the chance of a good cast and in the long run is more work than the extra left-arm movement required to bring another yard or two of line inside the guides.

The angler's grip on the rod is, I believe, important. With the conventional wrist movement a grip in which the thumb rests on the top of the cork works very well. With small rods I lay my forefinger out full length on top of the rod for best results. This affords greater and more delicate control. It puts my hand at an angle where its overall grip on the rod is stronger and my wrist becomes a continuation of my arm rather than a loose joint.

Conventional casting calls for smooth, easy movement. Fly casters have long been judged by smoothness of line flow and easy grace of movement, even where changes of direction are involved. But all this goes by the board when you're using a featherweight rod. I drive out my casts with every ounce of power I can muster, seeking maximum speed. I depend upon perfect timing to let me use my strength and speed for the necessary fraction of a second when the direction of line travel is changed. Here, as in the case of a baseball player, one uses maximum strength and speed to move a light object. The need for snap and speed in getting the ultimate out of featherweight tackle cannot be overemphasized. Conventional casting with a light outfit will get moderate distance, but only coordinated speed and power will make it compete with standard outfits in covering the water.

Few anglers realize how fast a line can travel. Once I made stopwatch tests of the time required to straighten out back casts and forward casts. I ran the tests on my own 6½-foot two-ounce rod and my nine-foot five-ounce rod. The amount of line off the reel in each case was the same, fifty-five feet, and each leader was ten feet long. I made several runs of ten complete forward casts and back casts, during which the fly traveled 260 feet ten times, or a total of 2,600 feet of movement.

The average time for the featherweight outfit was 18.4 seconds, which was a rate of ninety-six miles per hour. Peak speed is much higher, since the fly has to come to a stop and change direction at the end of each forward and back cast. The average time for the nine-foot fly rod was 23.1 seconds, or a rate of travel of seventy-six miles per hour.

Most fly casters are convinced that it takes a heavy line to force their cast into the wind. That's malarkey! The solution is simple: send the line out with much more speed than the wind it faces. The featherweight rod with its higher speed can actually do a better job than a more powerful but slower outfit.

The featherweight rod should have a good deal of stiffness in the butt and be light in the tip. Here the so-called parabolic actions are not useful, since they have a pendulumlike swing. In the old casting method this swing reduces the problem of timing, because the parabolic rod tends to settle into a rhythm easily felt by the angler and easily followed by him. However, such a rod action hasn't the "life" to deliver the drive necessary for a maximum cast with a light rod. Its virtues are smoothness and ease. I like a fly rod that takes the maximum amount of change of pace and delivers its full power in the shortest possible time.

Let's consider the tapers of lines and leaders, prime factors in casting. For my two-ounce and 2⅜-ounce two-piece fly rods I use an H-D-F taper. Admittedly the H-D-G taper would add length to my casts, since the lighter-running G line, with its smaller diameter, would permit a slightly longer shoot. Were I casting in a gymnasium or only on windless days, the G would be satisfactory, but under actual fishing conditions—which often include strong and gusty winds—the G is likely to tangle.

Wind will whip the hand-held coils of light line around the reel or hand during the retrieve, causing an occasional jam at the first guide after a sudden strike and run by a big fish. The F line is large enough in diameter to resist this tangling and I find the sacrifice in casting distance worthwhile in saving more fish.

Most leaders have too small a butt diameter. A perfectly smooth continuation of the taper from the belly of the line right down to the fly calls for the butt of the leader to match the forward end of the line in weight per foot. Inasmuch as the specific gravities of most lines are similar to that of nylon monofilament, the diameters should be approximately equal at the juncture. Such heavy nylon rarely breaks and is slow to wear out. A long leader must frequently be drawn into the guides and I recommend splicing a section of heavy nylon or a twelve-foot monofilament (knotless), tapering from .028 to .010 directly to the line. Lengths of finer nylon can be added as needed as tippets.

In these high-speed casts with featherweight rods, the leader tends to straighten out well at the end of the cast. But if there is any doubt about it, a quick pull-back from the outstretched-arm position at the end of the cast will flip the leader out straight. A pulling-in of the line through the guides at the same time adds even more snap, and although both actions reduce the length of line out beyond the guides, the difference between a curled-back leader and a straight one more than makes up for the loss.

To illustrate this, try casting with a twenty-foot length of ordinary clothesline. You will see how easily the pull-back at the end of the cast whips the line out straight. While you have the clothesline handy, straighten it out on the floor, holding one end in your hand with your arm upraised. Lower your arm, then give a short, quick yank. You'll notice how the sharp movement carries all the way through the slack line and makes the far end move. Therein lies the secret of the dry-fly strike with the featherweight rod. If, by contrast, you lift your arm to full height again in a slower movement, the far end of the line will not move at all.

A line movement of only a fraction of an inch will set a small dry-fly hook. Once set, it will not fall out, so a moment of slack means nothing one way or another. With sixty feet of line and leader drifting slackly downstream, a quick movement of the rod butt toward the angler will set the hook, regardless of whether the rod is lifted or left pointing directly toward the fish. In any case, once the hook is set, the rod should be raised to cushion the shock of the fish's run, which will quickly take up the slack.

Striking by rod lift is bound to be slower than the "yank" strike. The spring of the rod, which is so useful in absorbing the sudden surges of a fish, now absorbs the sudden power the angler puts into his strike. It slows down all action and in many cases none of the movement of the strike ever reaches the fly or fish. A little line movement is worth a lot of rod lifting.

Because the casting of the ultra-light fly rods depends upon the movement of arm rather than wrist, a number of variations are possible. When faced with a solid wall of foliage behind him an angler standing on a six-foot beach or slab of rock can coil forty feet of line and leader at his feet (working backward from the fly) and straighten it out in front of him with a quick snap of the roll-cast type.

The line can be cast in a big vertical oval with its center well in front of the rod by varying the speed of the rolling arm motion. This keeps the line almost entirely in front of the caster, and as long as he has the feel of the weight of the line in the air, he can pick the right time on any circuit to shoot the fly out thirty feet or more. Many of the ideas proposed here contradict existing opinions. They are practical, however, and the proof of their efficiency is something I demonstrate every time I fly-fish.

Featherweight rods really do feel like a feather in your casting hand. They require a minimum of casting effort, and with one you can fish all day. When you become accustomed to such a rod, the standard outfits feel stiff and clumsy. The light rods do call for better coordination, but once you understand the need for the high back cast and perfect timing, proficiency comes quickly. And with it comes a pride no heavier tackle can ever give.

CHAPTER 42

How to Wade
a Stream

SOME ANGLERS WADE only to gain the best possible coverage of flowing waters, while others seem to get as much fun out of wading as a youngster does from playing in a mud puddle. Whatever the reason behind it, wading is most pleasant when the right equipment is used and when the opportunities and dangers are clearly understood.

Wading equipment varies with the need. When the water is warm or the wader hardy, no sacrifice need be made to keeping dry. In the sandy flats of the Florida Keys or in northern brooks during midsummer, the wader needs waterproofing only to keep things in his pockets dry, providing he intends to go into water of that depth. Where the waters are comfortable enough for lengthy periods of swimming, boots or waders only cause overheating and perspiration as well as restriction of movement . . . generally making the angler less comfortable than if he waded wet.

To wade the warm waters over a smooth bottom, a pair of old slacks and low sneakers are adequate. When the bottom area to be waded over becomes rocky or uneven, it is advisable to wear canvas shoes that cover the ankle for greater protection. I believe canvas shoes are preferable to the old-style leather brogans which are more durable but are heavy and require frequent treatment with special oils to keep them soft and pliable. The canvas shoes are comparatively inexpensive, lighter, more comfortable, and last almost as long.

From the irregular bottom we graduate to the stream bed composed of slippery rocks. Then, security of footing becomes a major problem. Rubber soles slip easily on wet stones if they are either smooth-surfaced or covered with moss and slime. Ridged rubber soles are better than the smooth ones, but in order to wade securely over slippery bottoms either hobnails or a rough-surfaced sole, like felt, is required. Wading shoes are made up in rubber, felt, and hobnailed leather or rubber. In addition there are slip-over chains and felt sandals made to fit over smooth soles which will increase their grip.

The general preference is for felt as the best sole for all sorts of wading. It grips well on the hardest of stone, is light and comfortable to walk on and, when dry and clean, can be worn on the finest hardwood floor or over the most delicate rug without any damaging effects. A fly fisherman in handling loose coils of line often finds them falling around his feet. Stepping on a line with felt soles will not damage it, while treading on a line with a hard rubber sole or hobnails may weaken or break it, leading to the disaster of a lost fish or the need for a new and expensive line.

The felt sole has two disadvantages. First, it is expensive and wears out rapidly. Second, it is not effective for gripping slime-coated rocks. Silt or slime fills in the crevices in the felt and away you slide. However, no surface has been discovered to cover all situations perfectly and felt is the best all-around sole.

Hobnails will grip where felt fails. The protruding metal knobs will dig through the coatings of slime, silt, or moss to find a hold on the rock beneath. If an angler wades mainly on slimy rocks, hobnails are his best bet, even though he can't wear them in the house, and though he will damage a fly line if he steps on it.

Rubber soles with corrugated bottoms will grip fairly well on rough stones, pebbles, and sand, but the sharp edge soon becomes blunted and, like the ordinary smooth rubber sole, will then slip at any opportunity. To wade with rubber bottoms, the foot must be pressed squarely against the surface it rests on. If the pressure is at even a small angle the foot may slip.

Anglers who find ordinary rubber soles adequate for most of their wading, but require occasional additional gripping power on special waters, may equip themselves with chains or felt-soled sandals. The chains operate much like tire chains and are held in place by a leather harness and heel strap. Several cross chains are held in position under the ball of the foot and give excellent gripping.

The felt sandal is large enough to fit over the regular shoe or boot foot. It is held in place by straps and is easily put on or removed. The big advantage in these accessories lies in the saving they permit. Through their use the more expensive felt or chain is worn only when necessary, and the cheap and durable rubber is worn when the wading is easy.

Where the water is cold or where long immersion proves uncomfortable, boots or waders solve the problem. Boots are more comfortable than waist waders because they allow more air to circulate in from the tops. Since they prevent the free circulation of air as well as water, boots and waders are very warm when worn away from the cooling influence of the stream. Waist waders are higher and hotter, but they let you move, dry-clad, to a considerable depth. Most confirmed stream fishermen prefer them.

In recent years plastic waders have appeared on the market. Beginning with plain tubes for legs, they have now reached the stage of being foot-formed. Waders come in two types, stocking foot and boot foot. Stocking-foot waders are worn over pants and socks but require a pair of socks and a pair of wading shoes on the outside. Boot-foot waders are simplest to use and are adequate for most occasions.

However, it is worthy of mention that waders are no aid to wading, merely to comfort. I had learned most of what I know about wading before I ever saw a pair by wading wet in sneakers— the hard, cold way. The heavier and stiffer the waders are, the more they deter swift, sure action; but waders keep you dry.

Strength is a factor in wading. Strength is wasted when a man can't use it with speed, but quick strength is desirable up to the greatest point at which it can be controlled. If a wader can jump six feet from a one-footed stand in eighteen inches of fast water, he has an advantage over the man who can't. When it comes to bucking a stiff flow of water, there is no substitute for strength, and the man who lacks it isn't as good as the man who has it, all other abilities being equal.

Daring is essential in a top-notch wader. The stream fisherman who will only dare what he has seen done before will never be really good. In the back of an expert wader's mind are a thousand imagined situations, each tentatively answered by his own mental solution. When one of these situations develops with the speed of a winking eyelash, his subconscious reflex must be relied on to carry him through, and if his thinking has been straight it is almost certain to do just that.

The hardest essential to acquire is wading knowledge. Can you read the contours of a riverbed by the surface water? Can you utilize the lower currents and eddies when you toil upstream against a difficult flow? Can you wade confidently in dark brown or muddy water through which you can't see bottom? Can you move quietly in difficult water without raising a ripple, traveling slowly but surely, with no quick movements to frighten fish? If you can't, there's much for you to learn that nothing but experience can teach you.

The angler who wades to get the most out of his fishing days will know his favorite stream bed like a book. By wading the deep pools under low-water conditions, he will discover the bars and ledges that can lead him through many of the same pools in normal flow and allow him to reach fish beyond the range of other equally able waders who haven't had a chance to learn the stream's best wading paths.

One of the most important principles of wading was discovered by Archimedes in a Roman bathtub. The weight of a body under water is equal to its above-the-surface weight less the weight of the water it displaces. The human body is very nearly equal to the weight of the water it displaces.

When a man stands on dry land his feet must support his entire weight. When he wades out into a stream until half his body is submerged, the weight supported by his feet is halved. When two-thirds of his body are under the water level, only one third of his weight remains to press against the stream bed beneath him.

The deeper he wades, the harder it becomes to hold his footing. A swift current around his ankles has little effect, but even the slowest flow is hard to counteract when a fisherman wades at arm-pit depth. Water as a medium is hard to resist or push around. In deep water it is easiest to move with the flow and practically impossible to move against it.

To wade with the current simplifies stream fishing, and many a mile may be covered in downstream travel with less effort than it takes to wade a single mile against it. Fishing a streamer or wet fly downstream ahead of you is much less tiring than casting a dry fly upstream and bucking the flow for every foot of progress. This difficulty in wading against the current leads to wading's biggest pitfalls.

To get into a position where the force of the flow is too great to go back up against and the water ahead is too deep to wade, is to end up by going downstream and taking a dunking. The upstream wader has the advantage of being able to back through any water he has traveled. The downstream traveler must always keep a weather eye open for water ahead through which he can't wade. When such a spot is sighted he must work toward shore, for it is still possible to work sideways to shore when one cannot move directly upstream, and to move obliquely toward shore at a downstream angle with the current even when motion to the side is impossible.

The force of the flow against you is dependent upon the silhouette presented to it. It may be impossible to hold a position when facing directly upstream, yet easy to work upstream against the flow when the body is turned to face the side of the stream. In the latter position only one leg obstructs the flow, the other is held in the protected lee of the upstream leg. The area of pressure is cut almost in half. The best way to make progress against a swift flow is to turn sideways, moving the upstream leg a little way into the current and then drawing the downstream leg up beside it. This method will get you out of some very tight places.

It is easy to fall while wading and hard to catch your balance once it is lost. Still, many a seemingly certain ducking has been avoided by the use of the surrounding water as a cushion. Because the body is almost weightless under water it sinks slowly. If there's a margin of six inches or a foot between the water level and the wader tops, there may be time to draw the legs up under your body and replace them in a new footing before you get that icy feeling as the water pours in over the top.

There is a great misunderstanding about the dangers of wading. For years I listened to stories of fishermen who drowned because they wore waist waders, whereas if they had worn boots or waded wet they could have saved themselves. From California to Newfoundland I encountered stories that pictured the air trapped in the waders holding up a fisherman's feet which, in turn, forced his head under water. A particularly graphic description was given to me by a self-styled eyewitness, in which the feet were sticking out of the water while all else was submerged, and they went around and around in a deep eddy out of reach of those who watched. It was awe-inspiring . . . but it was all bunk.

In order to trap the maximum amount of air in my waders I dived headfirst into a deep pool of the Battenkill River from the middle of a bridge many feet above a deep hole. To prove it, I had a friend photograph me headed down in mid-leap. The water was a little cold and the current rather swift, but swimming ashore was easy. It is the legs of a man that need buoyance, and with air trapped in the waders I found swimming easier than usual. Even without any air in them, waders have little or no weight underwater. They may not hold you up, but they will not drag you down appreciably, either. My investigation of several such drownings led me to believe that the real reason was panic or alcohol or a combination of both.

Most fishermen, whether good swimmers or not, can manage to get a breath or two while crossing even a long, deep stretch, and in almost all wadable streams there's shallow water not far below you. The real danger in wading is in getting a foot caught under a stone or snag where the current is deep enough and strong enough to force your body under. (Mister, that's really rugged water.) Such situations are extremely rare and easily avoidable. A greater hazard is to fall and knock yourself unconscious by striking your head against a rock. That, too, is most unlikely. The greatest dangers when wading are losing tackle and getting wet.

Waders and boots should be kept dry between periods of use. Sunlight and heat will cause them to deteriorate. Hanging them up by the feet is a good way to dry them. Turning them inside out as far as possible is a quicker way, though it is impossible to turn boots or boot-foot waders completely inside out. They should be thoroughly dry before being packed away even for a day or two when the weather is warm. Mold and rot set in quickly under these conditions. This does not apply to plastic waders which dry quickly and, having no fabric in them, do not rot.

Waders and boots tear easily. Everything from barbed-wire fences to jagged rocks claw at them constantly, and a patching outfit is a necessity. Rubber surfaces may be patched like a tire tube and with the same materials. Fabric over rubber takes more care. Plastic surfaces are easily patched, either with the kit that comes with the waders or with special tapes now available on the market.

The finding of a small leak may pose a problem. The sure way is to fill the boots or waders with water to see where it runs out. This is troublesome and the leak can usually be found by a quick visual inspection of the area suspected. If such a search doesn't reveal the hole, take the boots or waders into a dark room and insert a lighted flashlight inside them. Move it around in the neighborhood of the leak and look for a pinpoint of light which will usually show up at the hole.

All waders tend to become wet or damp on the inside when worn. The cold water chills the waders and causes condensation of moisture on the inside. This is especially true when the fisherman perspires freely or the weather is warm and the water cold. When there is an all-over dampness inside the waders but no particular spots that are soaking wet, the cause may be condensation rather than actual leaks.

Waders should fit well to be comfortable and should be high enough in the in-seam to give complete freedom of motion. A wader needs all the freedom he can get when out battling the flow, and a pair of waders or boots that restrict his movements will certainly cut down his sport.

Suit your soles to the bottom to be covered. Choose wading gear that gives adequate protection to the ankles, lets you cover the stream to the necessary depth, and gives plenty of freedom of action.

CHAPTER 43

What Frightens Fish?

SOMETIMES WE SEE BIG FISH only after we've frightened them into motion, and it's important for every angler to know what frightens fish and how long their fright will last. There is a pond near my home that harbors some sizable largemouth bass. In it there are wide stretches of shallow water covered with lily pads, and it is deep in these pads that most of the big fish seem to lie.

We catch a few, but we scare away a great many more when our plugs land close to them. The sudden appearance of the plug and its splash nearby seems to frighten them badly, and we find that our strikes rarely come at the instant when the plug lands but almost always after the fish have had a chance to look the lure over and decide to take it at a point some distance away.

When you have located a big fish by scaring him, the problem of how to hook that particular fish presents itself. At least you know where he was when you came along, and often you know the direction in which he was heading. It's worth the trouble to spend a little time trying to catch him.

The first requirement is patience. The fish has seen your lure and been frightened. He won't strike that lure or any other till he feels at ease again. How long it will take him to regain his composure and how far he'll travel during that time depend upon the individual fish and how badly he was frightened.

Unless the water is shallow, the fish should not move more than forty or fifty feet, which leaves him still within easy casting range. The first thing to do is to sit quietly for about ten minutes by your watch. A change of lures is a good idea, and a smaller plug that will strike the water with less commotion is more likely to produce results with these timid fish. Then when you send that lure to the spot where you judge the fish should be, watch out. If the first cast isn't productive, cover the area thoroughly before moving on. This system won't always work, but it does snag a big one often enough to make it worth your time.

Fish, like humans, have the greatest fear of things that startle them and which they do not recognize or cannot understand. A speeding motor car appears potentially dangerous to a pedestrian, just as any big, cannibalistic fish is a dread spectacle to a smaller one. And the reaction of fish and humans is much the same. Pedestrians keep a wary eye upon oncoming motor cars, but they don't run wildly out into the fields as each car approaches. Only when they feel that a car may strike them do they jump.

A small fish won't race madly away at the sight of a large fish. He'll watch him and be ready to scoot, but he won't start in flight unless the big fish comes too close to him or starts after him with a definite rush. I've watched small trout let big ones swim right up beside them and then get away when the leviathans did finally make a rush at them.

Game fish take the common dangers as a matter of course. They've lived with them and escaped from them ever since birth. A big turtle, a water snake, a larger fish are almost always at hand, so that the fish take them casually as long as they keep their distance. The unusual enemies that strike swiftly put them in a panic, though.

The shadow of a fish hawk will send them all scurrying for cover because there is seldom enough time lapse between the falling of the shadow and the striking of the talons to allow the intended victim to escape. To a fish, the hawk is a terror somewhat like lightning to humans. An otter or a merganser is also able to panic fish, for both can swim swiftly beneath the surface and follow and catch them. Fish will scatter when they see such a predator but will resume feeding shortly after he passes on.

The mere presence of a large animal or a person doesn't necessarily scare a fish. In dairy country fish become quite accustomed to cows, and where fishermen are plentiful, fish soon learn that humans in themselves are harmless. Accepting this fact, they concentrate upon avoiding the hooks or food imitations which prove to be the danger. If they tie in an angler's presence with the approach of a lure, they're naturally suspicious. Anything unusual is a cause for fright. A fish—or a man, too, for that matter—is usually frightened by any living thing he's never seen before, particularly if it is large enough to be dangerous. However, he must accept it as harmless if, after a reasonable period, it makes no hostile move. Otherwise, he would spend practically all his life in abject fear and it wouldn't be worth living.

If you can reach a position near a fish without frightening him and can maintain that position for a long time he'll accept you as part of the scenery and go about his business as usual. The big blue heron has only its immobility to save it from detection. It stands out in the shallows with no camouflage or disguise. But because of its immobility, the fish ceases to think of the heron as a source of danger.

It is motion that gives the fish his first warning of danger, and it is motion that you must avoid. If you want to gain a position near a fish, you must move very slowly or stand motionless in a spot where he will come to you. If you know a fish lies in a certain spot, you can scare him away with a stone or something he won't connect with you and take up a position nearby to await his return.

Bright or conspicuous clothing warns a fish of your presence more readily than a garb that will fade into the background. Movement, when silhouetted against the sky, is particularly visible. Shadows falling on the water frighten fish badly, perhaps because of their great fear of death from the sky in the form of a kingfisher, osprey, or eagle. Rapid motion of any sort is a sign of alarm for all wild things, and the slower and more deliberate the angler's movements, whether in a boat or on foot, the less he will frighten the fish.

One of my greatest achievements in approaching a fish without frightening it occurred on an Atlantic salmon river. I was making moving pictures and wanted to get shots of a salmon rising to a dry fly. My cameraman and I climbed on a rock from which I could cover much of the pool and where the camera would have an excellent vantage point. We'd no sooner reached our position when I noticed a large salmon lying six feet away. I realized that a real opportunity was at hand if I could put that fish at ease.

We stood perfectly still for a few minutes. Then I began to cast, not to the nearby fish but to those lying forty to sixty feet away. I made my casts with as little movement of my arm and body as possible in order not to alarm that salmon. I reasoned that if we stayed there without much motion and did nothing to frighten him, eventually he would accept us as some strange part of forest life which had not yet come to his notice.

For a full half-hour I cast to the distant fish and attempted to correlate the camera with the few rises I had to the dry fly. At the end of that time I hoped that the fish would accept us and also would accept the slight waving of my right arm and the small rod as a part of the picture, like a tree with a single live branch waving in the wind.

I figured that when my dry fly finally dropped on the water just ahead of him he wouldn't connect it with us, for if we had been intent on putting a dry fly there why had we waited so long? He, too, must have thought that the fly had no connection with us, for he came up three times to poke his nose at it curiously and a fourth time to take it squarely into his mouth, all within six feet of the movie camera.

I mentioned earlier that bright colors warn a fish of the angler's presence, which brings us to the subject of colors which attract or repel fish. Scientists have long since agreed that fish are not color-blind. They seem to like some colors and dislike others, but deciding which color or combinations they prefer is not so simple. My guess is that fish are like people and while they may follow certain general rules, they're not going to be consistent. A few of them are probably a little eccentric, anyway, and delight in color combinations to which other fish would give a wide berth.

It is generally conceded that wild, unfished-for trout like bright and gaudy flies, while those under heavy fishing pressure favor drab and dull-colored creations. That is an oversimplification. The truth is more likely to be that wild trout will take almost any fly and the educated trout will take only those that imitate in color and action their natural food as they see it.

To back this up, let's remember that a Black Gnat, for example, is a good wilderness fly but is very subdued in tone. A Dark Cahill or a Quill Gordon, killers of the smartest of our trout, are also very effective for their dumb brethren back in the bush, and a bright green fly, as vivid as a St. Patrick's Day parade, may be more effective than any other when the leaf rollers are dropping into our ultra-civilized streams.

One day on a trout stream where the fishing had been intensive for weeks and low water made the fish relatively easy to see but practically impossible to catch, a novice cast out a weird arrangement of purple, bright yellow, and strong green, tied on a No. 4 hook. The darn thing took two of the largest trout in the pool. The sentence that comes to mind in describing such a fly is: *No self-respecting trout would look at it.*

The trouble is, we as anglers tend to judge flies on the basis of our own likes and dislikes and, because we become conventional and settle into a rut, we think any fly is unnatural if it is bright or made up of certain colors. Knowing that most bright-colored flies do not work well, we get a feeling that all such flies are useless. We decide there's no fish appeal in bright green or yellow or red or wild mixtures of color. Who ever heard of an insect so garish?

Well, we all have if we'll stop to think a minute. Ever see a katydid, or a luna moth, or a monarch butterfly, or a ladybug? The list could fill pages and each one would be as bright as a Red Ibis or a Yellow Sally—or a Royal Coachman, which is a good fish-getter in almost all trout waters.

Fishing has been a more or less masculine sport until now. It shows it. Men are conservative as to color. They wear clothes that look like Gray Hackles, Hendricksons, Adams, or Blue Quills. A little teeny red stripe in a plain gray suit makes a man shake his head and mutter, "Too loud." But his wife will buy and wear a suit of electric blue, wild cerise, or vibrant chartreuse without a pang. It would seem that even the staid trout might like more color, that we've swung too far on the conservative side. Smart trout still fall for Silver Doctors, Mickey Finns, and the like. Next time the fishing goes sour, why not try to liven it up with a little gaiety and use your bright flies?

It is trout that are held to be interested mainly in drab shades and trout fishermen who are ultraconservative as to color. The rest of our game fish like vivid colors and their admirers readily admit it. Red and white usually tops the list for bass, and the flash of metal is deadly for pike and for lake trout. No collection of women's hats is more colorful than a window display of plugs and casting lures. Once we get away from the trout angle, fishermen accept bright colors as pleasant to use and effective on the fish. Here the reverse situation exists, and a wise suggestion would be to use more dull colors and be different.

One of my long-standing habits has been to repaint my plugs when their coats become chipped or cracked. The original coats were masterpieces created by inspired minds and skillful hands. They had to be good fish-getters in order to see enough usage to be all chipped and in need of repair. The original paint jobs were complicated and precise. My repainting technique could hardly be simpler. It consists of painting them black. Not black and white or black with yellow spots or black with blue zebra stripes . . . just plain black all over. And when they get scarred and chewed to the point where they need another refinishing, I paint them again— all black.

Night or day, early season or late, the plain black plug will pull in fish right along with and sometimes ahead of the gaudy new-comers in my tackle box when I run even-stephen tests of so many minutes to a plug. If I had used gray or dull green or cream, the results might have been just the same. It happened that at the time I started repainting plugs my car was a black one and the can of touch-up enamel I bought to brush over a scratched fender painted a lot of lures. I've gone through several cans of black enamel and I'm probably in a rut. Chances are black isn't the best color for plugs—just one of many good ones.

Most fishermen will find when they start checking up that they catch most of their fish on the lures they fish with most of the time. And it would be strange, indeed, if it were otherwise. We change over to our second and third choices only after our first choice in color or action has failed to produce. That puts two strikes against the others right off the bat. They see action only on bum days. Usually, too, because we're disgusted with our luck by that time, we keep switching fairly frequently, failing to give them half the opportunities we give our favorites.

Fish with the colors you think a fish should like. If they don't react, keep changing until you find color schemes that will take fish. Don't worry too much about imitating a fish's food. A bright red and chalk white is like nothing living in nature. When you find color schemes both you and the fish can agree on, they'll be your favorites and you'll work them hard. However, be sure the colors you and the fish both like are part of the lure that the fish can see. The tricky designs on the tops of floating bugs or plugs are wasted on the fish, no matter how effective they may be on the angler who buys them.

CHAPTER 44

Your Guide Is a Friend

MANY ANGLERS HIRE a guide with the sole idea in mind of increasing their catch of fish. Others see him as a guarantee of safety in an unknown and dangerous country, insurance that a trip, long saved-for, will be safe as well as successful. While one angler may regard his guide as a companion and friend, another will consider him a mere servant.

Some eager fishermen try to buy their guide's friendship (and with it his fishing secrets) by tips or extra presents, others seek the same end by being friendly and thoughtful. The lengths to which anglers go to get on the good side of their guides indicates how important that individual may be in the success or failure of their entire trip.

In this chapter we are concerned with deciding when a guide is needed, what to expect from him, and how to make both his time and yours pleasant and productive.

This is not always easy since guides, as well as anglers, are individuals, most of them on the rugged side. They tend to be unpredictable, independent, and to many a sportsman, exasperating. As a former fishing camp operator with a large staff of guides employed during the season, I've been in a position to analyze both sides of the picture, to know and understand both guides and anglers. It has been my responsibility to size up each incoming sportsman and give him a guide well suited to his temperament or needs.

The first question is whether or not a guide is needed, and if so, how many guides for a party. Sometimes this question is decided by local regulations, as it is in Newfoundland. In that province nonresident salmon anglers must have a guide, though one guide may serve two anglers, provided they "fish in company." More often it depends upon the fishermen themselves and is decided by the need for a guide's special knowledge, the need for a boat or canoe and someone to row or paddle it, or the establishment of wilderness camps and the cooking of meals.

However, on a wilderness trip most people need guides. A good guide is at home in the wilderness, and any sportsman who is not should certainly have one. Storms and disasters may strike suddenly, and only the physically well and mentally able should tempt fortune by barging into the bush without a good knowledge of the country and of wilderness ways.

The type of fish to be sought enters into the picture, too. If you're familiar with the fish you're seeking, a guide is less important than if they're new to you. The habits of bass and stream trout tend to follow a similar pattern wherever you find them. Unless conditions are extraordinary an accomplished fisherman will learn enough in a day or two about a given river or lake to get his proportion of the fish being taken during the remainder of his vacation.

But in fishing for lake trout, where submerged ledges and underwater springs are the key to success, the stranger without a guide will only catch fish by the greatest of luck. Atlantic salmon, unusual in their stream habits, vary so much from river to river that a guide on a new river is a good bet, even for an experienced angler.

Any angler with a trained eye can spot the good water. On a bass lake it is the shoreline or around the weed beds, rocky reefs, or shallow bars. In a trout stream it will be the pools, runs, and riffles, rather than the shallow dead-waters.

The guide's main value for the experienced fisherman in this type of fishing lies in handling the boat, helping with camp or cooking, and with the matter of special tackle and its use. He'll know the lures to use, the presentations to make, and how a fish should be hooked, played, and landed.

Knowing your own capabilities, it is up to you to decide whether or not a guide is in order. One thing is certain, however. No matter how good you are at fishing, the local guide knows more about his own waters than you do, and the chances are that you'll take more fish with than without him, at least during the first few days of your fishing.

When it comes to deep-water fishing around spring-holes and in submerged gullies on the lake beds, or for locating salmon (and in some cases migratory trout), having a guide pays off. Not until you know the waters as well as he does, and that means under all weather and water conditions that may develop, will you do as well without him. Accepting this and deciding, perhaps, that you do need a guide, the next problem is how to get along with him.

Your guide is an individual like yourself. Usually he lives on the fringes of civilization. There is food to be taken from the woods and sea and streams. There is lumber to be had for the taking from the nearby forests. His wife puts up berries, cans meat and fish. Give him flour, tea or coffee, a few other staples and he can survive. His home is simple, but he owns it. If he decides to stop working, his overhead is almost nothing. He can quit his job with impunity (and frequently does), whereas if you leave yours for any reason and don't take up another, within a few months you find yourself sinking into debt. He has at his fingertips, year-round, what you can afford to enjoy only a few weeks of the year.

So you cannot deal with him as you would an employee in your shop or store. He's independent and proud and wants to feel he's needed. He isn't just an extra expense. Although there is a little featherbedding in the guiding setup, it is quite limited. Most of the guides are in the profession because they love it, just as you love to fish.

They have a deep interest in the country they work in, and are usually old-time fishermen who find guiding, with its wider scope of interest and an outdoor setting, preferable to labor in a mill or on a farm, even though a guide's hours are longer and the work often harder. They've reached a point in the game where they fish through you. They guide your fly or direct your plug. They feel the pressure on your line at the strike just as much as you do and they take as much pride in the fish you bring back to camp as you take yourself.

It is natural for any angler to want the best guide available. Many ask for a foreman or one of the head guides, assuming that these are the men who can get them the greatest number of fish. Occasionally this reasoning is sound, but not as a general rule. The key men are picked as the best for the jobs they undertake, but being in charge of a party or a camp takes more than fishing or guiding ability. The top men must be responsible for the comfort and safety of their charges, and these qualities are more important than particular brilliance as a fisherman or a fishing guide.

The best guide from the visitor's point of view may be the one who is least dependable but who loves to fish and will have no other worries on his mind. He's the kind of fellow who, if left in charge of a party, would suddenly find himself out of grub or of certain necessities because of poor planning, but who knows where each salmon in the river is lying.

Barring unusual circumstances, an angler is wise to accept the guide chosen for him and make the best of it, whatever the outcome. The visiting fisherman who takes a look at his guide or spends an hour with him and then screams for another one is rarely furthering his own cause. Guides are human and generally equal in courtesy to the sportsmen they guide. They'll usually work their hearts out for an angler who appreciates their efforts, but they can turn bitter and resentful when their dignity or ability is questioned. It is plain good sense to try to get on with your guide. Camp operators choose the best men available. They vary more in disposition than in the necessary ability.

Some sportsmen become experts too quickly. They listen to their guides only until they catch a few fish. Then they decide they know the ropes and take over. The guide will usually let them have their way, putting the boat where the angler tells them to, even if it be right on top of the fish instead of in a good fishing position. They will let him pass his fly below a "taking" fish instead of just ahead of him as they did when their advice was being taken.

Guides *can* be wrong and often are, but the chances are any angler can learn more about fishing on local waters from the guides than he can hope to teach them. A little patience and a sincere effort to draw your guide out to his best ability should produce a good vacation companion.

No matter how smart you are, it is rarely a good idea to show your guide up. There are things you can learn from him, and this is your opportunity to get his special slant on the fishing. Try his methods before you trot out your own. Let him select the lures before you say, "This is the only lure that will take fish today." There's time enough to work out your own ideas after his have failed or else have been so successful that a little experimenting is in order.

The result of contrary behavior by the angler is usually unfortunate. If you insist on doing things your way rather than his, you had better be right. If you fail, having made it plain you know all about the fishing, he can hardly be expected to humbly offer you the fullest extent of his hard-won knowledge. He will justifiably decide to save those few special spots and the big fish they hold for the next charge he gets, who will probably be more appreciative of his efforts. His pride wounded, his feelings hurt by your early indication that his skills are superfluous, his natural reaction is to think, if not to say, "You know how to do it . . . keep right on . . . I'll let you find out about my river for yourself . . . the hard way." Under such circumstances he'll do just what his job demands, no more.

These are his responsibilities and he'll fulfill them. His first thought must be for your safety. This may take many forms. On a canoe trip in deep or rapid water, or on a windy lake, his judgment must keep you safe and dry. In case of accident or sudden storm it is he who takes the responsibility to get you safely back to camp and to keep you as comfortable as possible in the meantime. It is he who lays out your path through the woods and keeps you out of trouble.

Your guide has a duty to uphold the law and to see that you do the same. In many states and provinces he is a sort of deputy warden, sworn to guarantee your own conduct as well as his. The fish and game are the basis of his livelihood and he is charged with maintaining them. He must be on the lookout for fire hazards and must keep your campfires small and safe, though adequate.

Your guide selects your fishing activity for you. He must not suggest too tiring a trip for you if your hair is gray, yet must put himself through many an arduous journey in order to let a young and capable hiker reach the best fishing to which his legs can carry him. He paddles while you sit and he packs the load while you walk the trail empty-handed.

He makes camp when camp is to be made. He cuts the wood and tends the fire. He cooks to the best of his ability and is charged with having enough food to feed you well. He skins out the big fish you decide to have mounted (although this is an "extra" in the eyes of many). Often he reaches into his own small store of lures or flies to let you use—and possibly lose—one of his cherished favorites.

When the fishing is poor, he racks his brain to try to find some interest in the local scene for you, whether it be his knowledge of birds, plants, or animals . . . or the doings of himself and his neighbors.

No two guides are alike. One may be the best fisherman in the area, but so wrapped up in his sport that he forgets to bring the lunch, can't cook, and doesn't care about the way his food is fixed, anyway. His brother may not be quite so good a fisherman but may be an able manager who remembers the things that make for creature comfort. The sportsman whose main interest is in the catch he makes should have the first type, whereas the fisherman to whom comfort is more important might fail to realize the value of this guide's special fish-finding talent and see only his lack of interest in neatness, order, and knowledge of the art of good living.

The camp operator usually knows his guides well; it is you who are the unknown factor. Misjudging your needs, he may give you a guide who may have a fine record of pleasing patrons in the past but does not fit the pattern you expect. There are two conflicting personalities to contend with and a little give and take on both sides becomes necessary.

At my camp all guides were under instructions to refer to and address their sportsmen as "Mr." or "Mrs." First names were used only in the case of young people or where specially requested by the sportsmen themselves. This was in no way an indication of inferiority but a simple recognition of the fact that one man is hired to serve, the other paying to be served.

Guide and sportsman, together season after season, suffer no lack of dignity or friendship under this system, whereas the easy intimacy that goes with quick first-naming sometimes blinds a guide to his own responsibilities and suggests to him that he is hired for his charm rather than his abilities.

From long experience I know it to be wisest to make every effort to get along with your guide. That doesn't mean you must tip him heavily or follow his instructions blindly. It means that you utilize his knowledge of the local scene. Treat him with respect, while demanding that he fulfill his basic duties as a guide.

If you do get a guide who is lazy, incompetent, or poor company, see the camp operator before you antagonize the guide. Perhaps he has misjudged the type of guide you needed, and only he can make the change so tactfully that no one's feelings will be hurt. This doesn't hold, of course, if you've done the selecting yourself.

While at any camp you're in the hands of your operator and your guide. Both usually have had their fair share of experience at their jobs and will look after you in capable fashion, though neither will be willing to let you upset the normal schedule of activity without cause. If the camp is no good, it will soon fail financially. If the guide is incompetent, you will not have been alone in finding it out, and poor guides don't last long.

If others at the camp are catching fish and you are not, be sure it isn't your lack of fishing ability or willingness to follow instructions before you place the blame for it on the guide. And don't overlook luck, that fickle filler of one creel while another stays empty.

CHAPTER 45

Talk About Tackle

THE FISHING TACKLE in its various forms, which we accept so casually today, has had a long and slow development, and a quick look backward may give us a better understanding of its use.

We use tackle for a number of reasons. First among them is the fact that we wish to make fishing a sport rather than a business. The end attained in pounds of fish is less important to us than the combination of fish, exercise, development of skills, and the pleasure of matching our wits in a difficult game. It is simple enough to catch fish if we place no limitations upon our methods. It is to make what was once purely a method of obtaining food into a method of obtaining pleasure and relaxation that we have established open and closed seasons and written into our laws that essential phrase "with rod and reel only."

To begin with, tackle is divided into three main classifications according to its suitability for still-fishing, for casting a very light lure (fly casting), or for casting a lure by means of its weight (bait casting or spinning). Still-fishing varies with the needs of the particular fisherman. If he is content to have his bait only a short distance from where he sits, his tackle is easily acquired and can consist of a cane or cut pole, a length of string, a hook, a small sinker, and a float. As he reaches out in distance he needs a longer line and pole or some method of casting the lure to a greater distance than can be reached with the line attached directly to the end of the pole.

This brings us to the development of casting whereby line is permitted to pass out through guides spaced along the length of the pole (which thereby becomes a *rod*) under the pull of the rod-impelled bait. As a small boy, I used to coil a handline carefully on the shore and, swinging the hook and sinker around my head on a short hold of line, let it go at a propitious moment to send it sailing out to deep water.

The method lacked accuracy. A short rod with guides, still coiling the line on the beach, did it better. That was bait casting. The addition of a reel to hold the line, so constructed that it can be used directly in the casting, brings us to modern bait casting. Controlling devices to prevent backlashes are a relatively recent improvement and one that is still going forward toward perfection.

Spinning is another form of bait casting in which a different type of reel, almost perfectly antibacklash in action, is used. That is a brief glimpse of the basic picture. The actual development, with its step-by-step improvements and variations moving forward with the magic of increased skills and modern knowledge of materials, mechanics, and fabrication, is an amazing story that would take books, not a paragraph or two, to tell.

When you cast with a long rod using a heavy line, there's a pull at the end of the cast that has the power to take out line. This pull is in proportion to the working length of the rod, the weight of the line, and the amount of line out beyond the tip of the rod. The placing of guides on the rod and the permitting of free but controlled movement of line through them makes fly casting the means by which a very light lure can be cast.

It is the weight of the line and not the weight of the lure that pulls more line through the guides. And the lighter the lure, the easier it can be cast by this method, in contrast to bait casting where the heavier the lure (up to a point) and the lighter the line, the easier casting becomes.

A very little thought will keep us on a straight course in selecting tackle and give us a sound basis of reasoning for each choice we make. The fly-casting reel is essentially a carrier for the line. It is not used in every cast to take up slack or bring in the lure, but is used only when more line is pulled off for a series of longer casts, more line wound in for a series of shorter casts, or when a fish is played directly from the reel.

Since the weight of the reel must be borne in the caster's hand, the lighter the weight of the reel, the less the strain of holding it. And, over a period of hours, a fraction of an ounce can have a cumulative effect in greater weariness. Single-action reels are simplest and lightest, and so most fly reels are single-acting. That is, they make one turn of the handle for each turn of the spool. In order to have each turn of the handle take in the greatest possible length of line, fly reels are designed with narrow spools of large diameter.

Bait-casting reels are in constant use during fishing. They are of three styles. Some are single-acting and are made in a large web with an antibacklash device on the axle around which the web revolves. In this type the amount of line retrieved at each turn is considerable and the task of reeling a lure over the miles of travel it takes in a normal day's fishing is not too great.

But the bulk of the bait-casting reels are small and compact, and in order to make reeling easy, they are quadruple-multiplying. That means that one turn of the handle turns the spool four times and thus the line is brought in four times as fast as if the reel were single-acting. The fact that the handle turns only once to every four revolutions of the spool puts less inertia against the starting of the reel in motion for the cast and, similarly, less inertia to maintain its speed and cause a backlash when the lure starts slowing down.

The extra weight of the gears and level winder, the shallow spool of the normal bait-casting reel, and the tight loops in which it must coil the stiffer, bulkier fly-casting line make it a poor tool for fly casting. Spinning, although often considered as a separate phase of the sport, is essentially a form of bait casting since it depends upon the weight of the lure and the lightness of the line for its casting ability. In spinning, the line is wound on a fixed staff by a moving winder and it comes off the end of the staff instead of the side of the spool as in conventional bait-casting and fly-casting reels.

We consider that light tackle and heavy tackle are a general measure of the skill of the anglers who use them and that the lighter the tackle, the more skillful the angler must be. That's only a half-truth. Fishing skills basically can be divided into two parts. One is the ability to know where fish will be found and what baits they'll take, to realize the proper depth for fishing and the speed and type of movement of the lure. The other skill, essentially separate, is the ability to use tackle to do the job for which it was created, to cast efficiently, to play a fish skillfully.

Light tackle was developed, not as many anglers claim, to give the fish a greater chance to elude us but, instead, to enable the fisherman to catch more fish and to catch them under conditions when heavier tackle simply won't produce. If a fine leader will fool a fish better than a heavy one, it's a more effective weapon and not a poorer one, provided it is possible to land a fair share of the fish hooked.

If a light rod will enable an angler to fish for eight hours a day, whereas a heavy rod tires him out in six hours, the light rod is a more potent tool than the heavier one. One thing is certain, though. The lighter and more delicate the tackle, the greater the physical skill required to handle it. And angling, as well as being a game of wits, is a game of skill with equipment, the same as golf, and we derive a great satisfaction from our ability to play it to perfection, entirely separate from the hooking and landing of fish.

There is such a thing as perfect balance between the component parts of a fishing outfit. Perfect, that is, for a given individual or group of individuals. I don't believe there's an outfit put together that would be balanced perfectly for everyone. Each of us has his own particular way of handling and using his fishing gear. Each of us must decide what fits us or to what tackle we can easily adapt ourselves.

There are two ways of approaching the selection of an outfit. One is to search for the component parts which, when assembled, will cast perfectly with our normal hand grip and in our accustomed manner of fishing. The other is to look for tackle that fits within a certain reasonable range of perfection as we now see it, and to which we can adapt ourselves; then try to select each item within that range for its own perfection.

What we call normal or average is just that; it's the average man's selection. It is undoubtedly workable, undoubtedly good, but it need not be the very best for you. If you've been fishing with a fly reel that's too heavy for the rod, according to usual standards, you've probably let the hand that holds the rod grip it a shade nearer the reel to compensate for the extra weight at the butt— and having learned to cast well in this fashion you compensate to a great degree for this lack of perfect balance. If you fish that way for a few months or a few years, you'll find it strange to use a reel of the normal weight.

The personal element is very strong, and that element is subject to change through the years, months, or even weeks. It takes a lot of trying and a little time to become accustomed to each different outfit before you can be sure you've covered the field in your search for the perfect tackle for you. Too hasty a dismissal of a piece of tackle you might grow to like if given the chance may rob you of hours of fishing pleasure.

One of the outfits I like best is, according to normal viewpoint, hopelessly out of balance. It's a 2⅜-ounce fly rod coupled with a reel and line that weigh 8½ ounces (in order to hold a fly-casting line and 150 yards of backing). To compensate for the extreme weight of the reel, I grip the rod well down so that my little finger is usually just touching the reel seat. Having become accustomed to this low grip, I find that I much prefer it to holding a rod in the center of the cork and I tend to grip my other outfits in the same way when I first take them in hand. Then, gradually, my hand works up till it's nearer the center of balance.

Individual methods of holding a rod, hand shape, or similar factors will have an effect upon the choice of tackle. For example, in holding a fly rod, I put my index finger along the top of the rod, grip it on one side with my thumb and on the other with the remaining three fingers to press it tightly against the heel of my palm. Since I use an unusual grip, the tapered cork which is comfortable for another fisherman may not be at all comfortable for me.

The problem for the average angler is to find a way to try out the different methods of holding and using tackle—and the various types of tackle—some of which may take a good bit of using before you can get the "feel" of the outfit. If you fish in company with a group of kindred souls using various types of tackle, you may have an opportunity to put the outfits you're interested in to work under actual fishing conditions. Such practice opportunities are perfect but rarely available.

Winter is the time of year to try out rods, lines, and reels. It's true most of the country's fishing water is frozen over, but the statement still holds. If you've been casting with a five-foot rod and wonder if a six-foot stick and very light lures might add to your enjoyment, hie yourself over to the nearest casting club. There you'll probably find someone with just such an outfit that you can try out.

Chances are you'd have the devil's own time borrowing an angler's pet rod during the fishing season long enough to look the trimmings over carefully. But at a casting club the same angler will almost beg you to try a few casts with it. And, brother, if you just say, "I sort of like this outfit of yours, but I'm not sure I have the knack of handling it properly," you can have some free lessons right then and there.

Whether it's fly rod, spinning outfit, or bait-casting rig you're interested in, you'll find a good cross-section at the casting clubs, and you'll find assembled there the lads and lassies who know how to use them, how to get the most out of each type of outfit. I know a lot of fishermen who've changed and improved their choice of outfits through association with a club, and I know of no other way that an angler can try and become familiar with so many types of tackle.

Few anglers can afford to buy the whole range to try out. In a tackle store you can handle rods and flex them, spin reel handles, feel lines, but you're still guessing as to what a given piece of equipment will do until you've worked with it for an hour or so. A lot of tackle looks good in the stores but fails to work into your particular style when the cards are down. Look up a club, and you should not only learn a lot about casting but save money by knowing more thoroughly the type of tackle you ought to buy before you enter the store.

CHAPTER 46

Line-Rod Balance

THE FLY LINE is probably the most important part of the fly caster's equipment. With a good line even a poor rod will make accurate casting possible; with a poor line the best rod and reel will still leave casting quite a problem.

The fly line must be soft and flexible, having a certain appreciable weight for each foot of length. It must have a hard surface capable of long wear in passing in and out of the guides. It must be pliable enough to be reeled up and left for many hours or days without any tendency to maintain itself in coils. Having these qualities, a fly line may be the same diameter from end to end, called a level line, or it may be tapered, changing its diameter throughout its length.

Level lines are easiest to manufacture and are cheapest to buy. They do a satisfactory job of casting and are adequate for most fly fishing. The tapered line is a refinement of the level line, being finer at the end nearest the fly. This permits the line to land with greater delicacy at the point where it is fastened to the leader while still having enough body and weight in the rest of its length to do the required job of casting. Single-tapered lines taper only at one end and must always go onto the reel in such a way that the tapered end is nearest the fly.

Double-tapered lines may be reversed end for end, and in each case the line becomes finer as it approaches the point where the leader is attached. Torpedo or multiple tapers are fine at the point of attaching the leader, taper up to the greatest diameter, maintain that diameter for a given distance, and then taper back to a lighter line to decrease the load on long casts and the space required to hold a given length of line on the reel. The tapers from forward point to belly and back again to running line may be straight tapers or developed in two or more steps.

These special tapers are a comparatively recent development in fly lines. They are of a special nature, but few of them are perfect for all types of fly casting. However, the multiple taper, properly designed and balanced to the fly rod, is more efficient and has more delicacy than the level line and is the equal of any single or double taper.

A short front taper is all right with a short leader, but is a very poor choice for the angler who wants to fish a long, fine leader. A long front taper lets a fly land lightly, but a short, heavy section of line near the forward end of the line, though it casts like a bullet, lands like a ton of bricks.

Many anglers prefer to buy sections of fly lines and cut up their others of conventional taper to make up a line to suit their individual tastes. To do this, it is necessary to know how to splice a fly line and to join the sections together so well that they'll slip through the guides (or the angler's fingers) so smoothly that it's difficult to notice the joints. Lines for special purposes or to suit a particular rod can be worked out in this way by each angler.

To do a good job of splicing, the lines to be joined should be roughened for the distance of the splice, approximately half an inch, then frayed out for half that distance, and the frayed sections split into three parts. Then they are joined and the frayed ends wound tightly against the roughened surface of the other line with a single winding of fine thread. Three coats of rod varnish will finish the job, rolling the splices between two hard surfaces for smoothness as soon as each coat is reasonably dry.

One common fault in using a new line is the failure to trim off the fine level end accompanying many tapered lines. These level ends may be up to eight or ten feet long, and unless trimmed back to a point close to the actual taper, they'll make proper casting almost impossible. By passing the line back alongside itself, it's possible to judge with the naked eye the point where it ceases to change diameter, and any excess on the light end should be cut off to within a foot of the end of the taper. When an angler with a new line complains that it doesn't balance, I find there's better than a fifty-fifty chance that the fault lies in one of those untrimmed sections of fine level line.

When testing a fly line at the store before buying, it is good practice to take the loose end, lay about an inch of it back against itself, and twist the doubled line back and forth tightly between thumb and forefinger. When released, the line should show no signs of cracking or peeling and should straighten out smoothly again.

The color of a fly line is not usually of prime importance. If a very long leader is used, it is of no importance at all. My personal choice of color for fooling fish would be something similar to that preferred for leaders, either translucent or dark and non-light-reflecting. Yet in order to have my lines show up well in photography, I normally use one of light cream color or pale yellow.

Many anglers are stymied when trying to select a fly-casting line to suit a particular purpose or to balance a certain rod. But a few basic fundamentals can straighten out this problem.

Fly lines are heavy since it is only through the weight of the line itself that a featherweight fly can be cast at all. A fly line is much like the rawhide of that whip the mule team drivers crack lustily over their teams. It must be heavy enough to straighten out, stiff enough and bulky enough not to tangle into knots, and flexible enough to bend easily as it moves through the figure-eights of the forward and back casts.

Early fly lines were made of twisted linen treated with wax or an impregnation of oil to make them slide through the guides more readily. Later they were braided to avoid the kinking and tangling common to twisted lines. The oil finish or impregnation with a linseed oil type base and the use of braided silk brought fly-casting lines up to modern efficiency, in all but design.

The first fly lines were level because that type was the simplest to make. However, as finer leaders and more delicate casting were required to catch ever more wary fish, it was found that if fly lines tapered to a fine point at the forward end, the fly and leader could drop more lightly to the water and the bulky section of the line, which frightened fish, moved farther away from the fly.

There was a small sacrifice in the distance of a maximum cast, but that loss was more than made up by increased delicacy of presentation and greater catches. The tapered sections at the front were subject to the greatest amount of wear and tear and, being reduced in size, they wore out much more quickly than a level line would. In order to increase their utility, they were tapered at both ends, and when one taper wore out, the line could be reversed on the reel.

Finally, the "forward taper" in fly lines came along. The first one to reach the market, as far as we know, was the Hardy "Filip" line in England in the 1920's. This line, strangely enough, was a near-perfect fishing taper and, although all sorts of variations have been made since, few can approach or better its superb fishing characteristics. Hardy Bros. simply used the first thirty-five feet or thereabouts of their normal double-tapered line which included about fifteen feet of front taper and about twenty feet of the heavy level center section, then reduced the diameter to a smaller "running" or "shooting" line, which was still heavy enough to handle without tangling.

In fishing with this line the angler found it exactly like a double-tapered line up to the point where thirty-five feet was extended beyond the guides. Beyond that point the lighter line made casting easier, since it is the weight at the forward part of the line that makes the casting possible, and any line weight near the rod tip or still within the guides is a hindrance rather than a help.

A greater "shooting" distance was thus possible, since the line to be "shot" weighed less for any given distance. There was a certain length of line which, when it was back-cast, would give the maximum distance on the cast. False casting with a greater length of line would overload the rod, and using less line beyond the guides would not develop its full power. The result in either case was a loss in distance. These forward tapers were not reversible, and when the forward section wore out, a new line was in order.

In this country in the 1930's, with the advent of greater interest in tournament casting, the forward taper, essential to distance-casting competition, was popularized here for fishing as the "bug taper" or "torpedo-head" line. These early American forward tapers were designed by distance casters for distance casting, and they added length to the purchaser's casts. Yet as fishing lines they had serious faults.

In their efforts to make a line that would give the average fishing fly caster the maximum distance, the manufacturers had detracted from the essential fishing requirements of a fly line. They made the front tapers too short, and the back section of shooting line too light and too fine. Some of the forward tapers were less than four feet long, bringing the heavy section of the line within that distance of the leader.

Since the heavy section of the line was heavier than that of a double taper for the same rod, it resulted in a considerable loss of casting delicacy. That fabled fly caster who always let his fly touch the water before the line did certainly was not casting with a short forward taper torpedo-head line. The short front taper also made it very difficult to straighten out a long leader at the end of a cast. It was okay for fishing bass bugs and streamers where line thickness and commotion were not too important, but for delicate fishing and all-around use, the first American forward tapers were not as good as the double tapers.

The short, heavy section of belly line which supplied the necessary weight for casting was too short and too thick. The weight was concentrated far out near the front end of the line, and when a cast was imperfect, due to a gust of wind or a slight inaccuracy on the part of the caster at the start, anglers found it impossible to correct such casts, although they could manage it with a level or standard double-tapered line.

The shooting line was so light that even though the caster flipped his rod to one side or the other, a maneuver which would ordinarily throw a cast a foot or so either way, with the bug taper nothing happened. The forward end of the line kept right on going where it was originally headed, and accuracy under stream conditions was sacrificed.

A third fault with the early bug tapers lay with the small diameter of the running line. It was often size F or smaller, so fine that it would tangle easily. Although tournament casters working on smooth platforms and making occasional casts would have no difficulty with such a line, the wading angler with the stuff swirling around his knees in the current, soon found that size F was too small and that size E was about the minimum size in a fly line that will take the twisting of wind and current when held in the angler's left hand while casting, without developing into a tangle that could mean a jam at the first guide in case of a sudden strike.

A few of these bug tapers are still around, so watch out for them. The best design in fly *fishing* lines today has a sufficiently long forward taper to give delicacy, a fairly long, well-balanced weight section to give distance, and a running line just thick enough to prevent tangling between casts or on the retrieves when the fisherman must coil it in loops.

A factor to puzzle the prospective line buyer is the specific gravity angle. The higher the specific gravity of a line, the more it will weigh in a given diameter. A high specific gravity (heavy) line casts better than a low one. It has more weight for the same wind resistance. But a high specific gravity line will sink more readily than one with a specific gravity nearer to that of water. Nylon fly lines are much lighter than silk ones. All this has added to the confusion on this subject and is something every purchaser should take into consideration.

The higher its specific gravity (ratio of its weight over the weight of the same volume of water) the better a line will cast and the easier it will sink. The lower the line's specific gravity, the better it will float and the larger the diameter needed to balance a given rod. Since the specific gravity of a line is rarely listed on the package, the inexpert buyer must depend upon the dealer or someone else who should know. Remember that nylon lines tend to be lighter than silk lines (usually less long-lasting) which, however, tend to cast farther and sink more readily than nylon.

To sum up further, I recommend (A) the very heavy forward taper lines with short front tapers only for fishing where maximum distance and little delicacy is required and where leaders of less than six feet will be used, (B) for fishing where slightly less than maximum distance is acceptable and maximum delicacy is needed, the forward taper with at least ten feet of front taper and at least twenty-five feet of belly, (C) for moderate casts and maximum delicacy the same line as B, or the standard double-tapered one which is cheaper and will give twice the wear since it can be reversed, and (D) for maximum economy, the level line. By using an extra-long leader great delicacy can be achieved with a level line, and by using a reasonably stout rod long casts can be made. In the very light rods the level line and the tapered lines are more nearly alike and the use of any taper becomes less important.

Balancing a fly line to a rod is a matter of securing in the line the proper amount of weight in that part of its length which is to be extended in false casting to give a maximum use of the rod's power without subjecting it to undue strain. This statement is made on the assumption that the rod is right for the angler. If an angler is using too powerful a rod for his casting arm, he may have to compromise on a lighter line than perfect for the rod in order to get his maximum casting utility and fish with a rod and line that do not balance.

A line cannot be selected for a rod on a basis of its weight alone, its length alone, or the combination of both. It is the power of the rod rather than its length to which the line must be coordinated. A husky 7½-foot rod and a soft-action nine-foot rod might balance out with identical lines.

One of the best methods of fastening lines to leaders is by means of interlocking loops. Such loops are easily made by fraying out the end of the line, wrapping it with fine silk with a whip finish into a loop turned back upon itself and coated with thin rod varnish.

CHAPTER 47

Leaders Make a Difference

A LEADER is a length of a special type of material used to connect the lure (or hook) with the line. It differs in makeup from the line for two main reasons. Either it is less visible, or it is more durable.

An example of the latter type of leader is the use of a short piece of wire for pike or other sharp-toothed fish. A length of wire, either braided, twisted, or monofilament, used between lure and line, will prevent the cutting of the line by the teeth of the fish, an occurrence quite frequent when lures are connected directly to the line. A pike, pickerel, or muskie can slice through a line so swiftly and with such ease that sometimes an angler fails to realize he's had a strike until he reels in and suddenly finds the end of his line is lureless.

The choice of such a leader, usually not more than a foot and a half long, is not difficult to make. Braided or twisted bronze is the favored material, although other types of wire also work well. Length depends upon whether it is to be used in still-fishing or trolling or in casting with a bait-casting or spinning outfit. In the latter cases it is customary to reel the lure to within a few inches of the tip for the cast. A six-inch trace or leader will give protection without interfering with the cast.

The leaders most commonly used in freshwater fishing are those designed to be less visible to the fish than the line. They were first made of horsehair, the strongest and finest material available at the time. In the beginning, they were braided and of uniform strength. Later they were tapered, being heavier and stronger at the end attached to the line, reducing gradually to a single strand where the fly was attached.

It was the small size of the fly, scarcely larger than a gnat, that demanded so fine a strand. Of course, fish had to be played with extreme care if they were to be landed, but with tiny flies essential to raising the fish, anything heavier than a single strand of horsehair attached to them would cause the fish to take alarm.

There was then, as now, a continuing effort by fly fishermen to find new and better tackle materials. Silkworm gut was discovered, and horsehair became obsolete for leaders. Gut was much stronger, nearly transparent, and very durable. At the time it must have seemed like the perfect leader material. But the years showed up its three bad faults.

Gut was not uniform in strength or in cross-section. The length of each strand was limited to eight to sixteen inches, depending upon the diameter, each strand being made by drawing from the silkworm the fluid it would otherwise use in spinning its cocoon. Since only short lengths were available, leaders had to be knotted, and any material when knotted together is weaker at the knots than in the unknotted state.

Finally, silkworm gut is very brittle when dry and must be maintained in a moist condition for fishing use. This meant carrying leaders in dampened pouches, or enduring an occasional agonizing wait for a leader to "soak up" before it could be used on a big trout that was disporting itself in front of an impatient fisherman.

Then, in time, nylon monofilament came along to replace gut as the prime leader material. Nylon requires no soaking, therefore it can be permanently attached to the line or carried in any lengths or tapers, ready for immediate use at all times. The nuisance of carrying a damp leader pouch was eliminated.

Nylon monofilament is uniform in cross-section and in strength. There is no practical limit to the length of the strands of any given size. Even tapered leaders are now available in nylon in knotless form.

Nylon is good. It is semitransparent and subject to coloring or tinting as desired. Its strength, originally on a par with gut, has been increased to a point where it is now definitely the stronger material. Nylon is good, but anglers are certain to continue to look for something better, a material that will be as fine as a spider's web and as strong as a hawser.

We can accept nylon monofilament as the best leader material on the market today. Now, let us consider how best to use it. What tapers? How many knots? How long a leader and how fine a point?

For still-fishing and trolling there is no need to taper a leader.

A chain is no stronger than its weakest link, a leader no stronger than the weakest nylon in its makeup. A leader is tapered only to give the fly caster better control of his fly. For still-fishing, trolling, even for casting heavy flies or bass bugs, a level leader is the proper one to use. It should be fine enough and long enough to fool the fish, yet strong enough to land them.

For very big fish in waters where there are snags or weeds or where it is impossible for a fisherman to follow his fish, heavy leaders up to, let us say, fifteen-pound test are needed. From there on down to one-pound test for trout or two- or three-pound test for Atlantic salmon, it is the choice of the angler, the inevitable dilemma of angling. Fine leaders will fool more fish and bring them to the hook. More skill is required to land fish on fine leaders and a higher percentage will be lost. The extra sport of hooking more fish, even though there's more chance of losing them, is the case for fine leaders.

The fly-casting line is bulky, and if the leader is short the line tends to frighten the fish. Consequently, length of leader as well as fineness is important. A twelve-foot leader of six-pound test monofilament is about on a par with a six-foot leader of four-pound test in this respect. Obviously, it is much easier to land a fish on a six-pound test minimum than on a four. That is the case for the long leader.

Now to some of the finer points of leader selections. Theoretically, the leader should continue the tapering of the forward end of the fly-casting line. That means the butt end of the leader should be as heavy (in weight per inch or in stiffness) as the forward end of the line. Most leaders are not, and they are more difficult to cast because of it.

The heavy end of a leader to be attached to an HCH taper should be .028 inches, assuming the specific gravity of line and leader to be nearly equal, provided the leader is to be tapered and knotless. If the leader is to be knotted and drop down in steps, the first drop should come at the line end, making the first section of the leader about .025 in diameter.

In order to taper perfectly, the diameter at the halfway point should be the total of the finest diameter (terminal end) and half the difference between the ends. In practice, since the requirement of the leader is to fool the fish, it is best to taper the leader quickly to a small diameter and have the small end of the leader relatively uniform and fine.

If a twelve-foot leader is to be made up of six different diameters, they might work out this way: .028—1.5 feet; .025—1.5 feet; .018—1.5 feet; .012—1.5 feet; .008—2 feet;[1] and .007—4 feet. Such a leader might not cast quite as perfectly as a uniform taper, but that last six feet of fine stuff will fool a lot of fish that the uniform taper would not.

Leaders are used up and wear out. Fine ends break off and must be renewed. It is my habit to break off flies rather than untie them in order to be certain of strong material in the next knot tied. After a dozen flies have been changed, the leader may be six inches shorter, and after two dozen the fine end may need renewing. The angler should be prepared for this by carrying a coil or two of suitable diameters for this work. Nylon of the necessary length can be cut from the coil and added to the leader as needed, using the common leader or blood knot.

Nylon can be bought in coils in many diameters. Anglers who are deft with their fingers and either wish to experiment with tapers or save a little money can buy leader material by the coil and make up their own.

One of the factors affecting the choice of leader strength and length is the length of the cast to be made. Leaders lighter and finer than the fly-casting line are more difficult to cast. In order to cast a long leader, considerable line must be in action beyond the tip of the rod. Where short casts are to be made, as in narrow streams, short leaders should be used. Otherwise there won't be enough weight of line in action to permit easy casting.

Large, still pools call for the longest leaders and longest casts. When the wind puts a ripple on the waters, the leaders become less conspicuous and shorter leaders of heavier weight can be used with the same fishing effectiveness. This is fortunate since the casting of a long leader in the wind with any degree of accuracy is one of the most difficult feats in fly fishing.

Straightening out a long leader when it is windy can be accomplished by fast, snappy casts which are kept low to the water. A cast that terminates a few feet above the water (as in normal fishing to allow the fly to settle gently to the water) gives the wind a chance to blow it a long way from the intended spot. The cast should terminate only an inch or two above the place chosen for it to touch the water.

When a fair amount of line is being cast, a sharp backward yank with the left hand will tend to snap the line straight and force the leader out to the proper position. It can't correct all bad casts or counteract all bad gusts of wind but that particular trick can double a fly caster's efficiency on a windy day.

Wind is moving air. The cast that goes through it must either be moving at a greater velocity or depend on a heavy line to carry it through. A heavy line and a long rod will enable an angler to cast slowly and by sheer power, but with today's light rods and lines speed is the only solution for casting into the wind.

Although a leisurely cast works on calm days, the windy-day cast must be one of snap and speed. Casting into a good wind with a light rod and twelve-foot leader may seem impossible at first trial, but I can assure you that practice and skill will accomplish it.

One of the most important factors to consider when selecting the leader point is the size of the fly. Suppose you are fishing for an outsize brown trout in rippled water where the leader isn't too conspicuous. You choose an .009 point for the leader end and fish with a No. 10 fly. Failing to raise the fish, you decide to try a sparse No. 16 spider.

The .009 leader is too heavy to match the very small spider which will not float freely when attached to the stiff nylon. The leader diameter is too great in proportion to the fine wire hook and few wisps of feathers of the small fly. In order to fish that particular fly well, a section of .007 should be added. If, then, you switch to a No. 4 streamer fly, the .007 would be too light. The shock of the heavy hook bringing up tight on the false casts would put a severe strain on the nylon at the knot with the likelihood that continued casting would snap the fly off or weaken the nylon.

Leaders are chosen for their invisibility. One great consideration in this regard is the position of the leader relative to the surface of the water. A floating leader is very conspicuous. When the sun shines on it, a heavy and dark shadow shows up on the stream bed beneath it. This is caused by the bending of the surface where the leader lies upon it. The same leader passing through the water under the surface casts practically no shadow and is much less easily noticed by the fish.

Leaders float because they are about the same density as water, and if oily or very dry do not break the surface tension. There are various solutions on the market designed to cut the surface tension and make a leader sink. If none is available, toothpaste or soap will soften and clean them. Dry grass or fine sand rubbed on the leader will often remove the oil. Long casts, snapping fine leaders completely dry of moisture, are a cause of many a leader's floating, even though no oil or grease is present.

The surest way to sink a leader is to use a sinking line. The line, as it sinks, will pull the leader under. In the case of a long leader and a dry fly the cast is made, then there is a pause to allow the line to sink a bit. A twitch of the rod, carefully calculated, will move the line just far enough to pull the leader under right up to the fly. Then the fly is allowed to float over the fish, after which it comes in underwater in a normal wet-fly retrieve. This method may seem like a little more trouble and it is, but it pays off in fooling finicky fish and, surprisingly, adds many strikes from trout as the dry fly comes in underwater.

In fly fishing, the right leader is likely to be the key to success. It is the weakest link in the tackle chain and, therefore, deserving of special attention. Check the leaders for frayed spots and tangles or cast-knots. Test them repeatedly for strength. Use the longest and finest leader you can handle in each situation and you'll be rewarded with more and bigger fish.

CHAPTER 48

Choosing the Dry Fly

IN SELECTING DRY FLIES for trout fishing, there are several factors to consider. First comes the choice of patterns and sizes, which in turn is dependent upon the water to be fished and the insect life it produces. To learn this entomology thoroughly would require a great deal of time and study, time that might otherwise be employed in fishing, so it is simpler and just about as effective to get this information regarding suitable insect imitations through an old-timer or a reliable tackle dealer.

An experienced dry-fly man is the best source and one of the best ways of locating such a veteran is to join your local fish and game club. Your dues, usually nominal, will help out the cause of conservation and they'll put you in contact with the finest fishermen in the area.

It is in the early season that the dry fly must be most accurate in its imitation of the natural insect. It is then that the hatches are greatest and the variety most limited. Later on, when grasshoppers, beetles, and the other land bugs blunder to the stream's surface and provide food, the trout are more likely to take a strange creation that fails to match their known food.

Size of fly is important and a good dry-fly assortment should contain everything from No. 18 to No. 8. The 16's are usually spiders or variants—excellent fish-getters at almost any season—or patterns which simulate the actual insects to be found, although the artificial versions are usually larger. The 18's or smaller are for midges or tiny terrestrials.

Probably the No. 12 fly is most commonly used and the most effective. Some anglers who hold to the "big lure, big fish" theory use 10's and 8's consistently, feeling that a trout, feeding on a mass of uniformly matched insects which come floating down over him, will go out of his way to get one that is similar to all the others but just a bit larger and perhaps, they feel, a bit more tempting.

A fair general assortment of dry flies would include:

Pattern	Sizes
Assorted spiders and skaters	16
Midges, terrestrials	16
Quill Gordon	12, 14, 16
Light Cahill	12, 14, 16
Dark Cahill	12, 14, 16
Dark Hendrickson	12, 14, 16
Red Fox	12, 14, 16
Gray Wulff, White Wulff, etc.	8, 10, 12
Bivisibles	10, 12
Surface stone fly	10

This selection of flies gives a wide variety of sizes as well as shapes and colors. The spiders have a minimum of visible bulk to float small hooks. The skater has a great deal of feathery bulk and will skim beautifully, even over choppy water. It is the only dry fly designed for surface movement. The Cahill, Hendrickson, Quill Gordon, and Red Fox are variations of conventional body shapes and floating material. The Gray Wulff is a heavy-bodied, durable floater that matches some Mayflies and simulates some of the blundering land bugs. The bivisibles are high-riding flies which, I believe, give the fish the impression of fluttering insect wings in action. The surface stone fly barely floats, long and low in the water.

It is my belief that, although fish see and recognize color, they see dry flies *against* the light and make their decisions more on the silhouette than on the color. Therefore, having a variety of shapes of flies is equally or even more important than having a wide range of colors. It is important to have a number of *types* of flies, such as the filmy spider, the bulky-bodied Wulff, the low-floating stone fly, the fluffy bivisible, and the run-of-the-mill insect shape of most standard flies.

The above list is basic and general but not complete. Each area and sometimes each river to be fished will call for the addition of certain patterns and sizes. Late-season anglers are particularly likely to need fine leader tippets and very small flies—18's and 20's in your fly box may turn the trick when nothing else will.

Once the patterns and sizes have been decided, it becomes

important to look for other qualifications in the dry flies you buy. Look the hooks over carefully. Best quality hooks are either turned up or turned down at the eye and the metal is thinner at the eye than at the bend in order to cut down overall weight without loss of strength. The points must be needle sharp and the metal hard. It takes the best of steel to hold your dream fish and the hook should be more likely to break than to bend under excessive strain.

Volumes have been written pro and con regarding the use of dyed as against natural feathers for fly tying. In long and thorough experience I've come to the conclusion that fish can't differentiate between a dyed and natural feather as well as a fisherman and that most of them don't give a darn one way or the other. Anglers are more fussy in this regard than the fish.

One point is certain, though, regarding hackles. Hackles should *never* be clipped on the ends. Hackle fibers in their natural state taper to a flexible, delicate tip which bends where it rests on the surface of the water. This bending out or spreading accounts for the superb floating quality of feathers, the basic floatant for almost all dry flies.

Hackles should be stiff and springy, never soft and lifeless. To clip the ends of the hackle is to ruin the fly and means that the tyer didn't have the right size hackle for the job and cut down a larger one to make a sale. Clipped ends are a mark of inferiority. Avoid them at all costs in your dry flies.

Check the dry fly for balance. A certain amount of floating power is used to hold up the weight of the hook. The fly is usually floated by the hackle and tail. Unless the tail is sturdy, the bulk of the job of floating falls on the hackle which is near the head of the fly—yet the sinking power is concentrated at the center of gravity of the hook, a point that is pretty well astern. Avoid flies with heavy hooks but weak tails. Look for dry flies in which the hackles are set a little back from the eye of the hook so that the floating power is a little nearer the center of gravity of the hook.

The wrapping of the fly should be neat and finished off with a durable coat of varnish or head lacquer. Look over the heads of the flies to make sure that the loop is complete and there's no gap through which a fine leader tippet might escape at a crucial moment. Color is not a good way of judging hook quality. The best of the dry-fly hooks, those made with returned shank eye loops for Atlantic salmon, are usually black, as are the cheapest of panfish hooks. Some hooks made especially for the tying of spiders and variants are plated silver or gold. Most good dry-fly hooks are bronzed.

Dry flies for Atlantic salmon must be of top quality, as the fish are very large in proportion to the hooks that must hold them. Patterns for salmon are not as varied as those for trout since the salmon is not searching for food and the angler need not match a hatch of flies. For Atlantic salmon the sizes required may range from 14 to 4 with 8's and 6's being most commonly used. The patterns listed for trout are also effective for salmon.

PART FIVE

Armstrong Creek

CHAPTER 49

Armstrong Creek

THE WEEK I SPENT with Dan Bailey in Montana in August of 1941
just had to be the best trout-fishing week of a long career. Dan,
with whom I'd been fishing quite regularly on the streams accessible to New York City—the Beaver Kill, the Esopus, New York's
Ausable—had moved to Montana in 1938 to set up his fly business and I was returning from the making of a marlin movie off
Guaymas.

In those days before spinning, before fast airplanes (the DC3
was new), before campers, minibikes and nylon, the trout fishing,
especially the fly fishing, was fabulous. Dan took me to his favorite
places for a general coverage of the Livingston area. We fished the
Yellowstone where it sparkled over bars and lazed through deep
pools, fished it in sun and passing storm, mostly with wet flies
because it was a little high and cloudy.

We fished the Firehole in Yellowstone Park where we could
see and hear Old Faithful. We fished the Boulder both above the
underground flow, where the fast water was filled with rainbows
and cutthroats, and down below the upsurging subterranean flow
where the river moved slowly and there were big browns resting
under the overhanging branches of the cutbanks or feeding out in
the prime positions where the faster flow into the pools first slowed
down.

We climbed on horses and with the "63" Ranch as a base, we
rode up to the lakes above the timberline with Paul Christensen.
We camped, and caught trout till dark . . . and again at break of
day. We saw very few other fly fishermen and it seemed as if the
whole trout-fishing world was ours.

But the jewel of all the streams we fished was Armstrong Spring
Creek. It bubbled up out of the ground, a full-blown trout stream,
clear as a stream can be, lined with watercress, streaked and flecked
with mossy patches in its slow, deep flow. From the swirling pool

of its beginning, it flowed in meadow swings for two miles to empty into the massive Yellowstone.

Like the historic English chalk streams that cradled the art of angling, it flows spring cool in summer. In winter the earth's deeper warmth keeps it warmer than a similar surface flow would be and more suitable both for trout and insects. In its moss and cress beds, myriad insects found a haven. Under the overhanging branches of its banks or under the shading patches of moss great trout lay and rested, moving out into the steady flow when the insects found their time to hatch and tried to fly away.

There were stretches in its runs too deep for wading and sometimes it was difficult to reach a spot where there was sufficient back-cast room behind and ample forward space for a long and delicate cast to a wary fish that was rising just off the edge of a submerged log or under an overhanging branch. The stream bed was alternately hard gravel and soft, silty mud that made wading slow and sometimes awkward.

The small size of the flies required amazed me. Although I caught quite a few fish on a No. 10 Gray Wulff, a fly I had designed and Dan named for me a dozen years earlier, I found the actively feeding fish, particularly the larger ones, would insist on a pretty accurate imitation, especially as to size, and the sizes ran down to 16's and 18's most of the time.

In those days we were among the pioneering anglers to fish for fun and put fish back. Otherwise, our daily takes would have been tremendous. I recall that on one day Dan decided to have a fish fry, and that day we saved a dozen cutthroats averaging about three pounds apiece to serve a host of friends. Other than that and the breakfast trout of the mountain lakes, we put them all back.

The hatches were massive at times and the air would fill with tiny insects. Several species would come off the water at once, complicating the selection of a successful fly. The flies on the water were so thick it seemed an impossibility to add just one more with a hook in it and still have any chance of a trout's taking it. My stock of small flies was slowly dwindling. Those were the days before soft nylon came along to replace gut leaders, and I, dissatisfied with gut because of its stiffness, had gone to fishing with fine braided thread.

This thread was fine and soft and had a tensile strength comparable to 4X gut in an equivalent diameter. Its great advantage was that it was limp and a fly attached to it, arriving at an eddy, would swing around the eddy once or twice as if floating free instead of being dragged across it by the stiffness of the gut in an unnatural way. Its great disadvantage lay in its tendency to tangle and form knots and with them, weak spots. It was soft black and practically invisible. It gave me trouble, but it fooled a lot of difficult fish.

I well remember the last afternoon of that visit. In the lower mile of the creek where the big trout from the cloudy Yellowstone used to run up into its clearer flow to slurp up insects and lie more comfortably in its cooler waters, there was a wide, long, and deep pool that was shadowed by some tall cottonwoods. Big trout were rising to a sparse hatch which I decided could best be matched by a No. 16 Yellow May. The fish were wise and took considerable casting. The first one, a big rainbow, rose after perhaps a hundred careful casts. He took a long run, leaping, down toward the lower section of the deep pool where I couldn't follow and, bending around a patch of moss, he broke the hook hold and was free.

Dan commiserated with me when he came down from the pool above where he had released a fine pair of browns. Then I tried the little Yellow May again in the same swift run of curling water. The second big fish of the pair I'd worked on rose and took the fly. Again, the run was down through the length of the pool toward the Yellowstone, but this time I was able to get into shallow water and follow fairly well. As I came down, the fish came back and spent his strength in leaps near where I'd hooked him. In time I drew him to shallow water at my knees and picked him up with a firm grip over his back just behind his pectorals. I held him up for Dan to see.

"Well over four," said Dan. "Maybe closer to five."

He was a male rainbow, richly dark with a sloping head and a long, low underjaw. The fly came out with a slight pull of the thread and I slid him gently into the pool again and watched him swim away. He was lucky Dan hadn't yet inaugurated the trophy walls in his shop, for if he had, I'd have kept that rainbow to weigh and outline on the wall for all to see. That was my last afternoon on that wonderful pool and the last time I was ever to see it.

Soon afterward, the owner of that lower section of the spring flow that bubbles up on the Armstrong Ranch blocked it off from the Yellowstone and converted the flow into a series of pools for private fishing. Dan wrote, saddened, to tell the news. Over the years, however, he reaffirmed that the upper section, on the Armstrong Ranch, was still flowing its normal flow and was open to the public for fishing.

It was 1964 before I returned to Armstrong's Creek, to make a trout fishing film for the CBS Sports Spectacular. No other stream called me with such insistence as the perfect place to capture trout fishing with a camera. It had fish in a clear and a beautiful setting. Its open water, moving easy in the sun through cattle-dotted meadows, had the ragged and magnificent Absaroka Range of Rocky Mountain peaks as a backdrop against the sky.

There were more fishermen for diminished water then, and though Les Colby and I fished hard, nothing we hooked or saw came close to being worthy of a place on Dan Bailey's trophy wall. America was changing. There were no more far-off streams just beyond the horizon that were better than the streams that lay close at hand. Spinning, with its easily learned proficiency and its capability to fish a lure far and deep to cover all of the water all of the time, took away the sanctuary fly fishing used to leave the trout. The remaining fish became fewer and smaller and the fishing pressure steadily increased.

"Good trout fishing here will go the way of the chalk streams in England," I said to Dan. "It will have to be private if it is to exist. You're lucky that at least it will exist, though in private hands, for if the public owns and controls it, they will take too many fish and destroy the breeding stock, replacing them with fish from hatcheries and it will never be the same."

I had our eastern streams in mind, the Battenkill that I had loved so much and fished for years, and had seen despoiled by a Fish and Game Department that wanted to be democratic and give all the available fine trout fishing to everyone. They gave too much and before I moved away from its banks, a survey showed *no carry-over* in a stream that was still essentially the same as it had been when Dan and I had caught three-pound brookies and bigger browns that had been spawned and grown there.

Love knows no law, and when the inferior hatchery strains mated with the tough old stock of the 'Kill, the resulting cross could barely make it. With the next crossing of these fish and the hatchery weaklings, the ability to survive and reproduce was lost. Here, as elsewhere, the angling management didn't simply "crop" the stream, it plundered a stock of fish it could not replace. In the 'Kill, as elsewhere, we lost the great reproductive capacity of the nation's trout streams.

From time to time I'd hear from Dan with appeals to help keep Armstrong's open by a force of public pressure. The pressure failed. How do you tell the owner of a stream like this that he owes it to the public to keep his fishing open just because a great many good sportsmen kept picking up the litter of the bad?

In 1970 when the owners of the stream were offered a reputed $12,000 per year for the fishing rights of this stream and their Yellowstone frontage, it was a time of decision. Anglers everywhere may be grateful that the owners had that rare thing, a sense of public responsibility. For $6,000 annually, on a five-year lease with first renewal rights, Armstrong's Spring Creek becomes public fishing.

Fly fishing only with two fish per rod is the rule. The fee for the first year has been paid by equal contributions of $1,000 each from Trout Unlimited, Scientific Anglers, Inc., Sevenstrand Tackle Manufacturing Company, Shakespeare Pfleuger Corp., Dan Bailey's Fly Shop, plus individual contributions.

So Armstrong's Spring Creek becomes a very special trout stream, a stream where companies and individuals have gone further than simply putting fish back for other anglers to catch. Here they are buying fishing to *give* to other anglers, the kind of fishing most anglers dream about and few will ever have.

When the Montana Fish and Game Department conducted an electrical shocking project on Spring Creek in the late summer of 1970, the apparatus turned up the incredible count of 5,700 catchable trout per mile and I guarantee that count had to be way down from what it was when Dan and I fished there in 1941. The highest previous count per mile was 3,750 for the famous Madison at Norris, a stream more than three times as deep and wide. The trout of Spring Creek are all wild fish, as it has not been stocked for ten years, and then only lightly.

This is a new paragraph on a new page of angling in America and it is filled with questions. Can tackle companies and generous anglers raise enough money and secure enough streams to hold good fishing for the general public? Will a great stream like Armstrong's become so crowded in a few years that the fishing will become less attractive? Will the fish that remain, caught and released many times under the heavy angling pressure, become so smart that only the most educated anglers will be able to take them and the dub will fish in vain? What management will be necessary and is it possible at all to keep sufficient fish in Armstrong's and sufficient room for pleasant angling for everyone who wants it?

Whatever the answers, the angling world owes a debt of gratitude to Armstrong's owners and to the generous contributors who have made so fine a gift to public angling.

A Note on the Type

The text of this book was set on the Linotype in a type face called Baskerville. The face is a facsimile reproduction of types cast from molds made for John Baskerville (1706–75) from his designs. The punches for the revived Linotype Baskerville were cut under the supervision of the English printer George W. Jones.

John Baskerville's original face was one of the forerunners of the type style known as "modern face" to printers—a "modern" of the period A.D. 1800.

Composed, printed, and bound by
The Haddon Craftsmen, Inc., Scranton, Pa.

Typography and binding design by
Virginia Tan